T0312133

Profit and Prejudice

Avoiding prejudice will be critical to economic success in the fourth industrial revolution. It is not the new and innovative technology that will matter in the next decade, but what we do with it. Using technology properly, with diverse decision making, is the difference between success and failure in a changing world. This will require putting the right person in the right job at the right time. Prejudice stops that happening.

Profit and Prejudice takes us through the relationship between economic success and prejudice in labour markets. It starts with the major changes that occur in periods of economic upheaval. These changes tend to be unpopular and complex – and complexity encourages people to turn to the simplistic arguments of 'scapegoat economics' and prejudice. Some of the changes of the fourth industrial revolution will help fight prejudice, but some will make it far worse. The more prejudice there is, the harder it will be for companies and countries to profit from the changes ahead. Profit is not the *main* argument against prejudice, but can certainly help fight it.

This book tells a story of the damage that prejudice can do. Using economics without jargon, students, investors and the public will be able to follow the narrative and see how prejudice can be opposed. Prejudice is bad for business and the economy. *Profit and Prejudice* explains why.

Paul Donovan joined UBS in 1992 as an intern. He is a managing director, and Chief Economist for UBS Global Wealth Management. Paul is responsible for formulating and presenting views on economics and policy.

Profit and Prejudice

The Luddites of the Fourth Industrial Revolution

Paul Donovan

Routledge
Taylor & Francis Group

LONDON AND NEW YORK

First published 2021
by Routledge
2 Park Square, Milton Park, Abingdon, Oxon OX14 4RN

and by Routledge
52 Vanderbilt Avenue, New York, NY 10017

Routledge is an imprint of the Taylor & Francis Group, an informa business

British Library Cataloguing-in-Publication Data
A catalogue record for this book is available from the British Library

Library of Congress Cataloging-in-Publication Data
Names: Donovan, Paul, 1972– author.
Title: Profit and prejudice: the luddites of the
fourth industrial revolution / Paul Donovan.
Description: 1 Edition. | New York: Routledge, 2020. |
Includes bibliographical references and index.
Identifiers: LCCN 2020032292 (print) | LCCN 2020032293 (ebook)
Subjects: LCSH: Economic policy—21st century. |
Sex discrimination in employment. | Discrimination in employment. |
Manpower planning. | Organizational change.
Classification: LCC HD87 .D66 2020 (print) |
LCC HD87 (ebook) | DDC 331.13/3—dc23
LC record available at https://lccn.loc.gov/2020032292
LC ebook record available at https://lccn.loc.gov/2020032293

ISBN: 978-0-367-56677-7 (hbk)
ISBN: 978-1-003-09889-8 (ebk)

Typeset in Sabon
by codeMantra

Disclaimer
The opinions and statements expressed in this book are those of
the author and are not necessarily the opinions of any other person,
including UBS AG. UBS AG and its affiliates accept no liability
whatsoever for any statements or opinions contained in this book,
or for the consequences which may result from any person relying
on such opinions or statements.

To the many friends, colleagues and clients who offered me support, encouragement and advice as I was writing this book. Thank you all for your help.

I promise not to write another one for a while.*

*Terms and conditions apply.

Contents

Acknowledgements

Back in 2013, I was sitting at home one Saturday lunchtime, listening to the *Money Box* programme on BBC Radio 4.[1] Economists never rest. There was a discussion on the problems with the economic treatment of people in same-sex marriages, ahead of the UK parliamentary vote to legalise marriage equality. The discussion had me choking on my cup of tea, for I am nothing if not a British stereotype.

I had written on the economics of prejudice a couple of years earlier. The obvious inequality persisting in the economics of marriage equality prompted me to sit down and write an article. It was hardly the standard topic of economic research for a financial-market economist at the time. Despite that, it was published and promoted by my employers.[2] I started to get requests to talk about the economics of prejudice and my interest in the topic grew. Before I knew it, I was gripped with the insanity that takes hold of every economist from time to time: I should write a book. Several years later, here I am.

The economics of prejudice is a vast topic, and this book is the result of many discussions I have had with a large number of people over the years. My former bosses at UBS Investment Bank, George Magnus and Larry Hatheway, both deserve special thanks for not only putting up with me (a hard enough task) but also for championing my early research into prejudice. Mark Haefele, the chief investment officer at UBS Global Wealth Management, has been consistently supportive and has structured a team where lively debate and thoughtful challenges are the norm. Themis Themistocleous, UBS European chief investment officer, is a great sounding board for ideas and research direction.

There are many current and former colleagues who I should thank for their insights and debate over the years. In particular, Mark Andersen, Reinhard Cluse, Balthasar Marti, Carolanne Minashi, Richard Morton, Brian Rose, Mike Ryan, Andrew Sparks, Min-Lan Tan, Dean Turner, Tao Wang, Phil Wyatt and Geoffrey Yu all spent time listening patiently to my ramblings, then tactfully pointed me in the right direction on a diverse range of topics. Caroline Bhullar cheerfully sent files to me in various far-flung parts of the world and ensured that I had enough time to write. Julie Hudson (who did all the hard work of the two books we co-authored) is always a great source of insight; she and Stefano Nappo talked through several issues with me over several bottles of wine.

I interviewed many fantastic people for this book. Christopher Parr, Simon Miall, Chris Hessney, Erika Karp, Mike Johnson, Kyle Getz, Alexis Caught, Emily Benn and my mother, Sheila Donovan, all gave a generous amount of time and even more generous amount of insight – both in the interviews and in response to the many random emails with which I plagued them afterwards. A number of other people interviewed wished to remain anonymous, which shows only too well why a book on prejudice is still needed. They know who they are, and I am extremely grateful to them.

Over the years, many friends have contributed opinions, sources and recommendations. Many thanks to Bex and Danny Alexander, Barbara Burke, Nina Dobner, David O'Brien, Amy and Jeff Palma, Bhauna Patel, Michael Pollich, Charlotte Schraa, Mark and Trish Shepherd, Alison and David Wareham, Caroline and Steven Warner, and Ciara and Peter Wells for their support (and tolerance).

In terms of getting my thoughts structured into something coherent, I am extremely grateful to three people. My father, Roy Donovan, read the whole book from start to finish. (This proves it can be done, so please feel free to attempt it.) He always gave sensible advice and comment, as well as additional colour on references to the family history. Russell Comer also read through the text and provided constructive suggestions throughout, despite the additional work I was creating for him. Poilin Breathnach edited the work into its current form – a Herculean task, given my addiction to passive sentences, habit of forgetting to endnote sources and highly erratic writing style. She also generously dug out the sources I had forgotten about, tactfully indicated when I was babbling incoherently and snuck in a George Clooney reference.

Finally, a word of thanks to St Anne's College, Oxford. I am one of the college's alumnae.[3] I am perhaps biased (not prejudiced) in putting a great deal of emphasis on the value of education. But I do believe that the culture and environment of St Anne's and the way that it teaches its students did much to help me tackle some of my prejudices and gave me an enthusiasm for learning. Author royalties from this book will go to the college.

This book, therefore, is built on the views and skills of many people, expressed over several years. Any errors and omissions are down to me. There is a lot more to say on this subject and, in future, I hope to see many more people saying many more things about why fighting prejudice is so important.

Notes

1 See BBC (2013).
2 The article also appeared in the *Financial Times*. See Donovan (2013).
3 The feminine form is always used to refer to graduates of St Anne's – because why should the masculine form be the default?

1 Profit and prejudice

> I remember hearing you once say, Mr Darcy, that you hardly ever forgave, that your resentment once created was unappeasable. You are very cautious, I suppose, as to its being created?
>
> Jane Austen, *Pride and Prejudice*[1]

If this book has a main message, it is that prejudice is bad for business and the economy. And that is a message that matters more and more today.

Why is prejudice so bad for the economy? Prejudice throws away skilled workers for no good reason. Prejudice stops workers from moving to better jobs for no good reason. Prejudice prevents good decision-making. Prejudice weakens profits and economic strength. Prejudice wastes workers' talents. Companies and countries succeed if they make the most of their workers' talents.

Why does this matter more and more? The coming years are likely to be a period of major economic change. Indeed, it is set to be such a big period of economic change that economists are calling it the 'fourth industrial revolution'. Millennials, brought up on a steady diet of smartphone upgrades, tend to refer to this as 'Industry 4.0'.

Economies will survive and thrive in the fourth industrial revolution by having the right people, with the right skills, in the right job, at the right time. Prejudice puts the wrong people, with the wrong skills, in the wrong jobs, at the wrong time. Doing everything wrong at once is not often considered a winning economic strategy.

In the fourth industrial revolution, getting rid of prejudice (or at least fighting it) will allow economies and companies to win. The more a country or a firm can reduce prejudice, the more likely it is to succeed. The problem is that change is never very popular. Economic change often leads to political change and social change. In the past, economic change, political change and social change have led to a lot of prejudice. This prejudice has gone on to hurt economies, societies and people. The economic changes of the fourth industrial revolution are unlikely to be any different. More prejudice is coming, and it will be bad for economies.

In times of change, politicians can move to 'anti-politics'. As the name suggests, this involves being *against* something as a main policy platform. 'Anti' politicians pick a group to blame and make them the scapegoat for economic problems. 'Anti' parties pledge to reduce or remove that group's economic role. This, the politicians claim, will solve the problems. Being 'anti' or against a particular group is a simple and seductive solution to economic problems and a common response to periods of change. 'Anti' parties do not provide positive solutions to economic or social problems.

To an economist, the message that 'prejudice is bad' is clear. Economists have had a well-argued theory of prejudice for more than 75 years.[2] Sadly, it seems that the message is not clear enough. Economists have not convinced others of the damage that prejudice can do. In recent years, many of the world's most advanced economies have seen a rise in prejudice politics. Politics today echoes the prejudice politics of the past three industrial revolutions. And with that prejudice politics comes big economic risk.

Discrimination and prejudice

So, what exactly is prejudice? In this book, prejudice is not quite the same thing as discrimination. To discriminate just means to separate one thing from another. Discrimination is a way of making a choice. It can be rational. Rational discrimination is good for the economy. Rational discrimination should lead to the best option being chosen and, in turn, the best possible outcome. Discrimination can mean choosing the right person for the right job at the right time. The job interviewer who compares different candidates' skills comes to a rational decision. They discriminate in favour of the best possible person.

Economists like discrimination in this sense. The basis of economics is discrimination. Economics is all about choosing the best way to divide the limited things we have among our unlimited desires. Choosing the best way to divide things is known as the 'economic problem'. Most economic models assume that people make rational choices. The fact that people do not make rational choices in the real world is a big source of irritation to economists. It messes up our models.

Prejudice is a highly specific, very narrow form of discrimination. Prejudice is *irrational* discrimination.[3] It is the word 'irrational' that makes prejudice so bad. Irrational decisions destroy economies. If a person makes a decision based on irrelevant or illogical ideas, then we have prejudice. We want people to ignore what is not relevant when they make economic decisions. The moment people start listening to ideas that are not relevant, we get prejudice.

Prejudice does not have to be deliberate. People can be prejudiced without meaning to be. We often use 'rules of thumb' to make decisions. It is a complicated world. It is obvious that people want to make decisions as simple as possible. By using rule-of-thumb generalisations, people use prejudice without knowing it. 'Every economic book I ever read was boring, so economics is boring' would be a prime example. Clearly, economics is downright fascinating, so this rule of thumb would lead to an utterly absurd conclusion.

We can see the difference between discrimination and prejudice in an example. Women (on average) do not have the same physical upper-body strength as men (on average). A job requiring physical strength may employ few or no women. It is discrimination to refuse to hire someone who lacks the strength to do a job. It is prejudice to refuse to hire a woman to do the job. The employer should consider every woman's strength as an individual. Generalising – using a rule of thumb – about women may mean that the best person for the job is not hired.

A similar prejudice is unconscious bias. Unconscious bias is a slight variation on the rule of thumb. It comes from the assumptions people make. These assumptions are built by culture. They reflect what people see as normal. They tend to form rules of thumb. US Supreme Court Justice Ruth Bader Ginsburg famously said of the number of female Supreme Court justices: "I'm sometimes asked when will there be enough [women Supreme Court justices]? And I say when there are nine [out of nine], people are shocked".[4] Of course, as Ginsburg caustically noted, no one had been shocked when all nine justices were men. That was 'normal'.

Why should an all-female Supreme Court be shocking? The answer, of course, is the unconscious bias that creates prejudice in all of us. In the past, society did not let women take up their proper role in the law. Supreme Court Justice Sandra Day O'Connor, the first woman to serve on the court, was forced to start her career as a legal secretary. This was (obviously) not down to a lack of skill or qualification. Law firms simply did not hire women as lawyers. An all-female Supreme Court should be no more surprising than an all-male Supreme Court, but unconscious bias makes it so. I can remember being surprised when the UK had its first female prime minister. I remember being surprised at Ginsburg's suggestion of an all-female Supreme Court. Thirty-three years (and a lot of education) separated those events. Prejudice and unconscious bias can be hard to shift.[5]

As unlikely as it may seem, in the 1970s, sexism was common in the world's orchestras. There was a view that women could not play instruments (except, perhaps, the harp).[6] Then orchestras started to hold auditions for new members with a screen to hide the candidates from view. Women suddenly became a lot more successful at auditions. Before the screens, orchestral hiring decisions were irrational. A conductor who saw a female musician would decide she was an inferior musician. Introducing a screen forced a decision based on musical talent. Once prejudice was not allowed to thrive, the number of women in orchestras soared.[7]

The effects of this prejudice, unconscious or not, change how we behave with one another outside of work. The British psychologist and former US NBA basketball player John Amaechi, who is black, has commented on this. Amaechi has said that if he is sharing an elevator with a man, he will know where that man keeps his wallet.[8] This is because the other man will unconsciously touch his wallet when sharing a confined space with a large black man. For the same reason, Amaechi says he never has to queue at a cash machine. People in front of him are prejudiced about the perceived threat of a large black man queuing behind them. They move away as soon as Amaechi joins the queue.

Whether it is deliberate prejudice, a rule of thumb or unconscious bias, prejudice is irrational. Because it is irrational, it leads to bad economic outcomes. Refusing to employ the best possible worker for a job because of their gender or the colour of their skin is bad business. Gender and skin colour do not affect a person's ability to do a job. If prejudice stops the best person from being allowed to do a job, the company is not going to make the biggest profit it could make. If lots of people in an economy make lots of decisions based on prejudice, the result is bad for the economy.

As we will see, the decision *not* to do something can be just as economically damaging as the decision to do something. What an economy loses because of "the road not taken" can be highly significant. Economists, who occasionally have a less eloquent turn of phrase than the poet Robert Frost,[9] refer to "the road not taken" as the 'opportunity cost' – what might have been. If the "road not taken" was, in fact, the right road, then the individual, the economy and society at large are worse off.

Imagine that the legal profession was prejudiced against women, but the medical profession was not. If a woman had the skill to be a great lawyer, she might still choose not to go into law. To avoid prejudice, she could opt to be an average doctor rather than a great lawyer. Thus, the woman earns less money than she could, and the economy loses the talent of a great lawyer – all because of the "road not taken".

This is not a random example. Dr Ivy Williams was the first woman called to the English bar in 1922. Williams was an academic. She never actually practiced as a barrister. She completed her law exams at Oxford in 1903 and only received her degrees in 1920. Oxford University did not award woman degrees until then. Her success in being called to the bar was met with an editorial in the *Law Journal*, which declared that the admission of women "would never likely be justified by any success they will achieve in the field of advocacy".[10] The first female doctor in the UK, Elizabeth Garrett Anderson, qualified as an apothecary in 1865 (after finding a loophole), which allowed her to practice medicine. The Medical Act of 1876 allowed women to qualify directly as doctors.[11]

Prejudice can also hurt people who are not the direct targets of the prejudice. If someone sees prejudice against a different group and thinks, "I might be next", this fear can change how they act. They may behave differently at work. They may take a different road. Even if they are not subject to prejudice, they may choose to avoid certain careers.

The 1947 US government's anti-fascist propaganda film, *Don't Be a Sucker*, emphasised how easily prejudice against one group can easily morph into prejudice against others. The central character was attracted by a speaker promoting racial and religious prejudice. These prejudices did not affect him. He enjoyed being told that his life would be better were it not for the minority groups. Prejudice held out the promise of a better tomorrow by removing the minority groups from the economy. This was 'scapegoat economics' at work. It was when the scope of the prejudice broadened to include the Freemasons, of whom the central character was a member, that the risks of prejudice became obvious to him. An aim of the film was to make as many people as possible realise that they were at risk of prejudice politics.[12] The film became a social-media hit in 2017 after a white-supremacist rally in the US.[13]

Prejudice is irrational. That is what makes it so economically damaging. Prejudice is practically guaranteed to put the wrong person in a job. At the same time, it is seductively attractive. It can often come from a well-intentioned wish to simplify things. As the world becomes more and more complex, we crave more and more simplicity. That is where rules of thumb do most damage. Prejudice is also subtle. It can push people into careers that are less than ideal. It can change how people act – whether they are the targets of prejudice or in fear of being next. This raises the next important question. How far can prejudice spread and who can fall victim to it?

Who does prejudice target?

People often tend to think of prejudice as being about race or religion, as was the case in *Don't Be a Sucker*. These are blatantly obvious and very damaging forms of prejudice. People may also think to include disabilities, sexual orientation or gender as examples of prejudice. But prejudice is more than that. It is important to recognise that prejudice is *any* form of irrational discrimination.

Sometimes prejudice targets something that is considered visible, such as race or gender. Race and gender are generally visible, at least when people meet face to face.[14] At other times, prejudice can target something 'invisible'. People can hide their sexuality at work, for example, to avoid prejudice, real or perceived. Others may try to hide their religion. While certain disabilities are visible, others are not, and people can keep them secret. Hiding does not stop the economic damage of prejudice, however. An atmosphere of prejudice that forces people to hide who they are can do just as much economic damage as a direct, full-frontal attack of open prejudice. The strain of hiding who you are – of lying to earn a living – is economically costly.

There is also a grey area. If two people only use email to communicate, for example, there is no obvious reason why they would know each other's race or religion. However, if one person's name is Mohammed, the other person may assume they know Mohammed's gender, race and religion based on a rule of thumb. That person may then be prejudiced in how they deal with Mohammed.

A 2018 economic study put a price on this rule-of-thumb prejudice.[15] Researchers gave a group of Danish teenagers the choice of working with one of two people. The teenager had never met either of them. One of the people had a name that suggested they were from a similar ethnic/religious background to the teenager. The other had a name that suggested they were from a different ethnic or religious background.

The study showed that the teenagers were prepared to earn an average of 8% less if they could work with someone they thought came from the same ethnic or religious background. And this prejudice was not just evident among teenagers with ethnic majority names. Those with ethnic minority names were just as likely to take a pay cut to avoid a colleague with an ethnic majority name. The teenagers were blindly making assumptions about the race of their potential colleagues. They then applied prejudice to those assumptions, to the point where they actually allowed that prejudice to reduce *their own* potential income. The job required the two teenagers to work together for just *90 minutes*.[16]

Because prejudice is *any* form of irrational discrimination, the subject of the prejudice can be anything. The Sherlock Holmes story *The Red-Headed League* used the prejudiced hiring of red-haired men as a plot device. A character creates a fake job. The plot suggests the job was created by a man who,

> was himself red-headed, and he had a great sympathy for all red-headed men; so when he died, it was found he had left his enormous fortune in the hands of trustees, with instructions to apply the interest to the providing of easy berths [jobs] to men whose hair is of that colour.[17]

The story might sound somewhat silly to the modern reader. Why would anyone offer employment only to people of a certain hair colour?

The Strand Magazine first published *The Red-Headed League* in 1891. In the late 19th century, it was common to offer employment only to people with skin of a certain colour. Discrimination based on skin tone is a prejudice that continues, however silly its fictional parallel may seem.

As prejudice is irrational, it is often silly. Reality is as silly as fiction. In 2010, then deputy leader of the UK Labour Party Harriet Harman had to publicly apologise for calling then Chief Secretary to the Treasury Danny Alexander a "ginger rodent".[18] Suggesting that someone's skin or hair colour (or eye colour) makes a difference to how good they are at their job is prejudice. Alexander responded that he was "proud to be ginger".[19] He subsequently sent Christmas cards with a picture of a red squirrel and attended the launch of Cairngorm Brewery's Ginger Rodent beer.[20] The passage of time – and Alexander's good humour – may have detoxified the event. It was more serious when it happened. The comment led to the

Scottish National Party accusing Harman of an "anti-Scottish" attitude – another form of prejudice.[21]

There is also sometimes an idea that only the poor are the targets of prejudice. This seems to ignore gender prejudice, for example. Women can be rich. Religious or ethnic prejudice, such as anti-Semitism, often relies on the supposed wealth of its targets to foster prejudice. People in privileged circumstances can be just as much subject to prejudice as people in less fortunate positions. In fact, during the upheaval of an industrial revolution, prejudice and wealth are commonly linked. Of course, privilege and income may allow someone to deal with the negative consequences of prejudice more easily. That does not mean that the prejudice is not there.

One long-lasting example of prejudice against higher-income groups is rooted in the Battle of Waterloo (1815). In 1848, an anonymous pamphlet appeared, suggesting that Jewish banker Nathan Rothschild had profited from the battle by manipulating the London financial markets. The author of the pamphlet was Georges Dairnvaell, a left-wing anti-Semite.[22] Dairnvaell regaled readers with a tale of stereotypical greed and ruthlessness. He portrayed Rothschild as rushing from Belgium to the English Channel and, thence, to London. On arrival, Rothschild allegedly spread misinformation that caused the market to crash. Dairnvaell then claimed that Rothschild made "20 million francs" by buying the market at its lows, before the news of British victory.[23] The whole tale was designed to 'prove' the typical behaviour of a rich Jewish financier.

The story is completely untrue. It was 'fake news' in a world without Twitter. Rothschild was not in Belgium. There was no ruthless dash to London to profit from the outcome of the carnage at Waterloo. There was no London stock-market crash in the days before public news of the victory. Rothschild did receive news of the victory before the official communication, but so did several other people. The market conditions were not liquid enough to have allowed anyone to make a large sum of money by trading around the news of the Waterloo outcome. Nonetheless, the story fitted anti-Semitic prejudices perfectly. (Of course, it did. Dairnvaell wrote it specifically for that purpose.) The Nazis turned the story into a propaganda film (*Die Rothschilds*, 1940).[24] Books and articles were still repeating the prejudice over a century and a half after the pamphlet was first published. Nathan Rothschild's wealth offered no defence against this prejudice. In fact, his wealth made it worse.

The combination of prejudice against the Jewish population and wealth was so common as to be an everyday insult. The clergyman William Holland, writing in 1809, described a parishioner (obviously Christian) as being "as rich as a Jew".[25] The phrase was clearly meant as an insult. The irony was that most Jews in Britain in the early 1800s were extremely poor. Much of the Jewish immigration of the previous century had been from the ghettos of Eastern Europe. As is so often the case with prejudice, it did not matter that the stereotype of the wealthy Jew was wrong. As with Dairnvaell's 'fake news', repeating the stereotype is all part of the 'fake news' cycle. 'Fake news' promotes prejudice and prejudice keeps 'fake news' alive.

One secret of humanity's success is that everyone is unique. The problem is that our uniqueness can be used against us. Anyone can be a target of prejudice. All it takes is a group of scared, envious or resentful people to single out something that makes us different. We must fight back against prejudice in any way we can. Fortunately, economics is one way we can fight back.

Economists against prejudice

Economists have long understood that prejudice and economics are tied together. Slavery is perhaps the ultimate example of prejudice. A person's right to be treated as a human being is rejected on meaningless and irrational grounds. Before the 14th amendment in 1868, the US constitution (in)famously regarded slaves as being 'worth' three-fifths of a citizen.[26]

The British anti-slavery campaign of the 18th century relied as much on economic arguments as moral ones. Britain may have been able to end the extreme prejudice of slavery earlier than some other economies because of the country's changing economic landscape.[27] Industrialisation made material possessions more and more accessible. Social status became the result of owning *things* rather than *people*. The early 19th-century novels of Jane Austen signal how important possessions were. The books highlight the desire for shawls, muslin dresses or a 'capital' gun. Such possessions led to the realisation of the great social objective of being deemed to possess 'taste'. 'Taste' was essentially materialistic. 'Taste' was possible because materialism was cheaper. Materialism was cheaper because of the first industrial revolution. The feudal idea of serfdom and the idea of slavery (which survived after the feudal period) were no longer necessary to social status. Owning *things* became the more important driver of social position.

The British campaign against slavery was also an economic campaign and one in which women played a leading role. Some of the social changes associated with industrialisation gave middle-class women more free time, which they put to good use in women's anti-slavery associations. Those who wanted to bring an end to slavery boycotted slave-produced sugar. Women (who normally ran the household) led the protest. The aim was to prevent slavery from producing a profit. The campaign got attention. This was rational economics being used against the extreme of irrational prejudice.

The use of economics to fight prejudice was also part of the fight against racism in the US. In 1955, Rosa Parks, who was black, was arrested for not giving up her seat on a bus to a white passenger in Montgomery, Alabama. On the Monday that she appeared in court, black Americans refused to travel on the local buses. A flier calling for the boycott stressed the economics of the situation, stating that "if Negroes did not ride the buses, they could not operate. Three-fourths of the riders are Negro".[28]

Martin Luther King, who led the protests, was imprisoned for "interfering with a business".[29] The two sides initially fought using economic terms. Protests were aimed at making prejudiced businesses uneconomic to run. The bus companies were aiming to keep their customers – albeit in a rather peculiar fashion. The fight against prejudice was eventually won before the US Supreme Court, but economics played a role.

Just over 20 years later, economics played a role once again in fighting prejudice against the LGBTQ+ community. In 1977, the US Teamster's union was in the midst of a boycott of Coors beer.[30] Coors was an anti-union company. It was also anti-gay. The company explicitly refused to hire anyone who was gay.[31] The Teamsters approached gay politician Harvey Milk, who was still campaigning for office at the time. Gay bars in San Francisco joined the boycott. Coors's share of the Californian beer market went from 40% in 1977 to 14% in 1984.[32]

Clearly, economics can be used to great effect against prejudice. From the sugar bowl of the 1790s to the beer bottles of the 1970s, economics has played its part. But in the fight against prejudice, economics is needed now more than ever. The coming economic changes are unprecedented and carry the threat of greater prejudice than we have ever seen. We live in revolutionary times.

Changing times

We have established that prejudice is never good. It is, however, particularly bad right now. The changes the global economy is going through are significant and we need to get them right.

The world stands on the brink of the fourth industrial revolution. The technological changes of the next quarter century will cause massive economic disruption. Economists tend not to get excited by the technology itself. What is exciting about an industrial revolution is that it is revolutionary. Society will change. What we do, how we do it, where we do it – all these things will change. The social order will be turned upside down. Economic relationships will change. Parts of the economy will become much more efficient. Parts of the economy that were once valuable will become useless, destined for the scrapheap of history.

This radical change in economic relationships and social status will lead to a reaction. People will try to cling onto the status that they have. This is only natural. People feel very, very upset when what they have is taken away. Behavioural economists call this 'loss aversion'. This quirk of human behaviour means that people would far prefer to avoid a loss than to make an equivalent gain – three times as much, in fact. For humans, the effect of losing a thing is far more 'bad' than the effect of winning a thing is 'good'. Our ancestors ran from the sabre-toothed tiger three times as fast as they ran towards food. Thus, the loss of economic or social status is a major influence on economic behaviour.

Journalist Jacques Mallet du Pan famously observed that the French Revolution "devours its children".[33] People like Danton and Robespierre, who led the Revolution, died beneath the blade of the guillotine. Humans generally do not like change, and resistance to change can produce destructive impulses. The first industrial revolution in 18th- and early 19th-century Britain produced just such a wave.

A series of protests in between 1811 and 1817 saw riots, threats of physical violence and the destruction of machinery. The machines (large-frame weaving looms, for the most part) were the visible form of change – the physical manifestation of modern capitalism, which, in the eyes of the protestors, was destroying their way of life. The protests were spread out across the country. The media of the age quickly branded these largely unconnected groups as 'Luddites'. The term went viral. In fact, it was the branding of the 'Luddites' that made them distinctive. Previous protests, which dated back to the 16th century, had been localised. The branding created a sense of a national threat (even though there is little evidence of coordination). The government tried to rebrand the protestors to diminish their importance. The government, predictably, failed.

The fourth industrial revolution, too, contains self-destructive impulses. The Luddites of 21st century are not likely to roam the streets looking for 3D printers to smash. There is some hostility to robots, though. From time to time, there are suggestions of a 'robot tax'. Economically, this is pretty absurd. But the anti-robot ideas do echo the Luddite attacks of two centuries ago.

In the fourth industrial revolution, the real potential for self-destruction lies in attacks on people. What economists call 'human capital' – meaning people's skills – is likely to matter more than robots. We need the right person in the right job. Today's Luddites promote prejudice against people. They try to stop certain groups getting jobs. They put the wrong people in the wrong jobs. Today's Luddites also try to tell certain societal groups that they are worth less than others. Modern Luddites tell certain groups that they do not have the same rights as other people.

Twenty-first-century Luddites are trying to destroy human capital in the same way as earlier Luddites tried to destroy physical capital (machinery). The technology of the fourth industrial revolution can even help the modern Luddites in their endeavours. The prejudiced can cluster together on websites. Social media spreads 'fake news' faster and farther than the truth. Web cookies let companies charge different prices to different people, based on prejudice.

The changes of the next 20 years are going to be big. The fourth industrial revolution is likely to happen much faster than the first. The changes to society and the economy could be as great as, if not greater than, those of the first industrial revolution – and that means a lot of change in a short space of time. People will resent the change and try and find something or someone to blame. Prejudice is the natural result. Fighting that prejudice is something that I and many other economists are passionate about.

Why?

There are clear economic links to prejudice. But there is still an obvious question. Why is a white, middle-aged, male economist writing about profit and prejudice? The profit bit is perhaps easier to understand: I have worked in finance for my whole career. There is a casual assumption that people in finance know a thing or two about profit (despite repeated evidence to the contrary).

But what motivates an economist to investigate prejudice?

Part of my job is to predict where the economic winners will turn up – where we can find profit, perhaps. The fourth industrial revolution will change how the world works. Prejudice could be useful as a reverse signal of where we can find profit in that changing world. The less prejudice there is, the more likely you are to have found a fourth industrial revolution 'winner'.

Finance is a part of the economy that is driven by people. Finance must have the right people in the right jobs at the right time if it is to make money. When the wrong people are in the wrong jobs, events like the global financial crisis of 2008 happen. Economic analysis suggests that increasing racial diversity can have a big impact on finance. If we compare a relatively homogenous US state, such as South Dakota, with a more diverse US state, such as Tennessee, diversity adds about 30% to wages. Diversity has the right people in the right jobs, and it improves the decisions taken.[34] Perhaps more than any other part of the economy, finance has a reason to avoid prejudice and make the most of the people available.

The reality of the financial sector has not always lived up to the theory. The City of London, when I began work at the start of the 1990s, was full of prejudice. Race, gender, religion, sexuality, regional accent and educational background were all sufficient reason to single out a person for derision. The collective mind of a trading floor would use anything that made someone different as a reason to make someone 'less' than everyone else around them. It was a very, very unpleasant environment in which to work. Prejudice caused talented people to leave. The industry was hurt by the loss of their skills. Thankfully, finance has changed; if it had stayed unchanged, I would have left. However, the atmosphere of the financial markets in the early 1990s shows just how irrational and self-destructive prejudice can be.

The briefest glance at my background suggests that I am unlikely to be the target of prejudice. I am a man working in an industry (finance) and a profession (economics) that, despite some recent moves to diversify, are both still dominated by men. I am British, working in the UK. I am very unlikely to be subject to racial prejudice. However, prejudice is part of my family history.

I remember a visit from my grandmother when my brother and I were teenagers. We were both wearing the cutting-edge fashion of semi-suburban England at that time: black shirts and either flecked trousers or stonewashed jeans. This was the mid-1980s – and that alone must be our excuse. (My brother also had a 'mullet' hairstyle, which nothing on earth can excuse.) My grandmother was perhaps not quite so attuned to the nuances of mid-1980s fashion. Eyeing our outfits, she asked, "Have you joined the Black-shirts like your great-uncles, then?"

My grandmother's question was one of those remarks that teenagers are inclined to ignore. But it was, in its way, far more shocking than my broth-er's haircut. In 1930s Britain, members of Sir Oswald Moseley's British Un-ion of Fascists, or BUF, were known as Blackshirts because of their uniform. The party had a mixed support base across different classes of society. The British *Daily Mail* newspaper wrote approvingly about it. Many of its lead-ers came from middle-class military backgrounds. It found some support among the workers of East London. The BUF never achieved mass support, however. At its peak, membership was estimated at 20,000 people.[35] The BUF was an extreme political party, and to support it was unusual.

Prejudice politics was long established in London's East End, and not just a far-right issue. In 1906, a writer in *The Clarion* (a socialist newspaper) declared that "the number of these Jewish aliens in the East End is alarm-ing, and their increase is appalling … their presence is often a menace and an injury to the English working class". The same article described Jewish immigrants as "so much poison injected into the national veins".[36] A fur-ther article by the same author described the immigrants as "economically and socially a menace".[37] The prejudice was anti-Semitic and anti-foreigner (as many of the Jews in the East End were refugees fleeing the violence the second industrial revolution was bringing to Eastern Europe).

The BUF, like many similar political parties across Europe, developed a view that was both anti-Semitic and anti-foreigner. By the mid-1930s, the BUF ran on a fuel of prejudice. Its appeal lay in a simple promise of a better future for its followers. As soon as the BUF had rid British society of the influence of Jews and foreigners, a better future would begin.

Such was the economic logic of the BUF: clear, simple and complete nonsense.

To the BUF membership, it was plain that foreigners and Jewish citizens had caused all the economic problems that were hurting the country. Mass Observation, a somewhat Orwellian-sounding social monitoring organi-sation, reported in 1939 that 8% of men in the East London borough of Stepney and the surrounding areas thought that Jews deprived English-men of their jobs. Further complaints were made against Jewish landlords and business owners on economic grounds.[38] BUF supporters believed that Jewish employers forced down wages.

The changing membership of the BUF also hints at the link between economic circumstances and support for prejudiced political parties. Local branches reported that people would be members when unemployed, then become inactive or leave when they had a job.[39] There might be a number of other reasons for this – less free time or fear of what employers might think, for example. It is also true that a person could be just as prejudiced outside the BUF as in it. But these facts at least hint at a link between the politics of prejudice and bad economic times.

The BUF policy platform was a reaction to a time of economic change. It was a more severe form of the 'anti-politics' and 'scapegoat economics' that have started to emerge around the world today.

Were my great-uncles Blackshirts? This was the only time my grandmother mentioned the possibility, and her generation has now passed away. There are no public records of BUF membership. My grandmother's family were working-class East Londoners living in Duckett Street. They were poorly educated. Their jobs were not safe; their incomes were extremely low. My great-grandfather had been a contractors' carman – a cart driver. Duckett Street was at the centre of local BUF activity. Gladys Walsh, a party district leader, recalled, "Of course, the main street was Duckett Street, practically everybody in the street was a Blackshirt, and that's the truth".[40] A London council employee described Duckett Street as being "95% Fascist".[41] This was surely an exaggeration, but it gives a sense of the strength of local support for 'anti-parties'.

This was also a time when (at least for men) social identity was tightly linked to work. To lose one's job was to lose one's social identity. There was a social stigma of having to go and see 'uncle' – the local pawnbroker, who would make small loans against the pitiful security of clothing or household goods. Social status was also tied to a person's position as a consumer, so going see 'uncle' was a double social blow. Pawning possessions reflected the loss of social status as an employee and as a consumer. The recollection of that unstable existence meant that half a century later, my grandmother still fervently feared debt more than anything else.[42] In East London in the 1930s, with almost no social security, the social and economic descent from unemployment and debt would be very rapid.

The BUF attracted people who were just like my family into its membership. It was comforting to be told that your poverty was not your fault. To its members, the BUF offered the hope of identity in the promise of economic security. A sense of identity, perhaps lost through unemployment, was recreated by the 'us and them' nature of prejudice. Those who belonged to the BUF thought they belonged to a superior club – a group that could look down on others. The sense of identity was reinforced by the party's uniform – the black shirts. It was a uniform everyone wore, regardless of gender or class. Former members referred to the 'comradeship' of membership. In some cases, there was an almost religious fervour to belonging to a group that gave a sense of superiority, even if it was entirely self-created.[43]

The BUF was a prejudiced organisation that also thrived on prejudice. It was prejudiced because it discriminated irrationally against specific groups in society. It thrived on prejudice by building working-class support – just the sort of people that society, in turn, discriminated against.[44] The BUF appealed to those who were badly educated, poor and scared, because

British society in the 1930s was prejudiced against those groups. It is estimated that half the national membership of the BUF came from the East London boroughs of Bethnal Green, Stepney, Shoreditch and Hackney[45] – all areas of poverty. Some 15.5% of the population in Stepney, where my grandparents lived, were judged to be living in poverty.[46] The politics of the BUF are something I find abhorrent and reject utterly. However, I can also understand why the BUF might have drawn in my great-uncles.

There is an irony in that while my grandmother's family may have been attracted to social prejudice, my grandfather's family were still victims of it. My grandfather's family had emigrated from Ireland at some point in the mid-19th century and become dock workers in East London, where prejudice against the Irish was long established. In 1811, several brutal murders, known as the Radcliffe Highway Murders, were committed in East London. Suspicion fell on the Portuguese at first. It quickly moved to the Irish community, simply because they were Irish. Nationality was reason enough to be arrested.[47] My grandfather, several generations removed from his Irish roots, would still have been subject to prejudice in the labour markets. 'No Irish Need Apply' (or NINA) signs started to emerge in the 1820s. British satirical magazine *Punch* recognised it for what it was: in 1862, an (allegedly humorous) piece included the question, "Are they actuated by the prejudice which, in advertising a place, intimates that 'no Irish need apply'?"[48]

It was, in fact, a double prejudice. NINA tended to appear in adverts for domestic servants. This meant that Irish women were much more likely to be affected than Irish men. About half the Irish women in London at the time of the 1851 census were employed as domestic servants.[49] In the early 20th century, many Irish women ended up working as servants in institutions (e.g. schools or hospitals). They were more likely to be accepted there than in private houses. Irish prejudice has a long history in British politics. This prejudice was obvious at all levels, and on all sides of the political debate. In 1812, the Woolcombers' Union excluded Irish members.[50] Why? Because they were Irish. In a world of prejudice, no other explanation for so irrational an act was required. In 1836, years before becoming British prime minister, the author and politician Benjamin Disraeli described the Irish as a "wild, reckless, indolent, uncertain and superstitious race".[51] Clearly, he was not a fan. This was pure prejudice: irrationally giving negative characteristics to an entire country's population.

Being a Roman Catholic on low income with an Irish surname was sufficient reason not to employ a person in the minds of the prejudiced. Alternatives to NINA included 'No Catholics' and 'Christians only', which brought anti-Semitism and anti-Irish prejudice neatly together (the more extreme Protestants did not regard Roman Catholics as suitably 'Christian'). In 1938, one prospective employer looking for a servant set out her criteria in terms dripping with prejudice. She wrote, "We should be glad if she were a Protestant. We don't mind whether she is a Nazi, Austrian or Pole, but we would rather not have a Roman Catholic, as our experience with them has been disappointing".[52] The prejudice of the day characterised Irish workers as lazy and dishonest. At a time of high unemployment, there was no necessity for a prejudiced employer to hire anyone burdened with Irish ancestry. The NINA rule of thumb saved time when sifting through job applications.

NINA had been common in the 1850s and was still occasionally included in London job advertisements in the early 20th century. Indeed, the phrase was still used by owners of lodging houses (cheap accommodation) as late as the 1970s.[53] Public anti-Irish prejudice still prevailed in my lifetime.

NINA may have gone, but rule-of-thumb prejudice has not disappeared entirely. Today, my UK passport works in automatic machines in every country in the world – except the UK. I get extra scrutiny every time I come back home. As someone who travels 10 months of the year, this is a nuisance. The combination of my Irish surname and heritage, my travel patterns and the UK's history of terrorism trigger a rule of thumb when I travel. Prejudice casts a long shadow.

Something else suggests that both sides of my East London family were subject to another form of prejudice, namely, the fact that my grandmother and grandfather both spoke Cockney rhyming slang throughout their lives. This is a dialect found in a particular area of East London, where words are replaced with rhymes: 'dog and bone' for 'phone', for instance. Cockneys were subject to prejudice within London, characterised as a criminal underclass. This prejudice was particularly true for the London Irish community. Deceiving the authorities in such a way helped to protect them. To add to the deception, they often dropped part of the rhyme, so 'dog and bone' became 'dog'. This meant that rhyming slang, as spoken, rarely rhymed. And even when it did, it rhymed with Cockney pronunciation. 'Burnt cinder' could mean 'window', pronounced 'wind-err' in Cockney London.

Creating a coded language to deceive the authorities is nothing new among groups that are targets of prejudice. It is a both a defence mechanism and a way of building a sense of community. In the US, 'hobos' (normally men who travelled around the country looking for work) used slang words and a series of symbols to communicate in a way the social majority could not understand.[54] East London had used a coded language known as 'flash' to deceive in the early 19th century, until it became fashionable and lost its deceptive ability. As Chapter 10 will discuss, gay men in the UK developed a slang language (or cant) called "Polari," the remnants of which are still in use today. These languages were created for much the same reason that low-income dock workers in London used rhyming slang. They helped create a community of those who were targets of prejudice. They also helped to deceive those who persecuted them.

My family history shows how economics and prejudice work together. Economics and change and a climate of insecurity can build prejudice, but this works both ways. Prejudice also hurts the economy and very often hurts those who support prejudiced polices, particularly in times of change. The world needs to brace itself.

Profit and prejudice

The rest of this book tries to tell a story of what the world economy is likely to face in the years ahead. Enormous change is coming, and we are not talking about the flying DeLorean cars of a *Back to the Future* world.[55] This is about the changes to society that will follow technological change. Some of the technological changes may help build prejudice, and that prejudice may worsen the economic effects of those changes. Indeed, prejudice often causes more economic pain to those who support it. Economically, fighting prejudice is crucial. There are ways in which this can be done.

The story of profit and prejudice closely follows the philosophy of Jedi Master Yoda of *Star Wars* fame.[56] Economically, fear of change leads to anger and insecurity. Anger and insecurity lead to hate and prejudice. Prejudice leads to economic suffering – to the economic dark side.

Notes

1 See Austen (1813, p. 82).
2 See Becker (1957).
3 See Allport (1954). In *The Nature of Prejudice*, Allport does acknowledge the idea of misconception. This is when misinformation leads a person to make a prejudgement. It differs from prejudice, in that the person with a misconception will change their mind when presented with the correct facts. A person who is prejudiced will not. In modern times, prejudice thrives on the idea of "fake news" and the denial of facts.
4 See CBS DC (2012).
5 Such prejudice is a result of what one considers normal, of course. The UK journalist and broadcaster Jenni Murray recalled a remark by her seven-year-old son in 1990. He had only known one prime minister during his lifetime and asked, "Mummy, they said on the radio that John Major's going to be taking over from Mrs Thatcher. Is a man allowed to be prime minister?" See Murray (2013).
6 One reason may have been that instruments like the piano were designed for men. Men, on average, have larger hands than women. This led to a "rule of thumb" (that the average woman is not a good musician, as instruments are designed for the average man) and thus an unconscious bias (see Syed, 2019). The design of a harp does not (particularly) depend on hand size to play it. It could also be played without any 'unseemly' glimpse of a female harpist's legs.
7 See Goldin and Rouse (2000).
8 See Sweeney and Young (2019).
9 See Frost (1916).
10 See Twose (2014).
11 Ibid.
12 See Cooper and Dinerman (1951). The film was shown commercially and in schools.
13 See Gabbatt (2017).
14 A colleague once pointed out to me that for a transgender person, gender identity may not be visible. This is an excellent point, and my colleague was (very kindly) pointing out my biased way of thinking on this issue. It is perhaps best to suggest that gender is very often visible, but not always visible. This is also true with race. The 1999 film *East Is East* featured a mixed-race Anglo-Pakistani

family whose younger members successfully claimed to be Italian to avoid racial discrimination in Britain in 1971.

15 See Hedegaard and Tyran (2018).
16 Ibid.
17 See Conan Doyle (1891).
18 See Press Association (2010).
19 Ibid.
20 See BBC (2012a).
21 See Press Association (2010).
22 See Cathcart (2015).
23 Ibid.
24 See Waschneck (1940).
25 See Adkins and Adkins (2013, p. 160).
26 See National Archives (n.d.).
27 De Vries (2008) discusses the rise of consumerism in the UK economy, in particular over the course of the first industrial revolution. Sussman (2000) provides a detailed look at how women used economics as part of the abolitionist movement in the 18th and early 19th centuries.
28 See Robinson (1955).
29 See Stanford University (n.d.).
30 See Teamsters (2017).
31 The word "gay" is deliberately chosen here, as it was the term used at the time. The focus of this prejudice and the boycott was the gay community. Women were discriminated against regardless of sexuality, while bisexual and transgender people lacked even the limited visibility they have today.
32 See Cole and Brantley (2014).
33 See Mallet du Pan (1793).
34 See Sparber (2009). Sparber used a standard deviation of racial fractionalisation (a measure of diversity) – with a difference of one standard deviation being roughly the same as the difference between Michigan and Arizona, or South Dakota and Tennessee. The legal, financial and health professions all saw around a 30% wage increase for a more diverse workforce. However, Sparber points out that "industries heavily reliant on creative decision-making, problem solving, and customer service benefit from diversity" and experience this wage or value gain. Other industries (fabricated metals, non-durables, transportation and raw durables) do not benefit from diversity. These are industries that do not have the same requirements.
35 See Eichengreen (2018, p. 75).
36 See The Clarion (1906a).
37 See The Clarion (1906b).
38 See Linehan (1996, p. 78).
39 See Linehan (1996, p. 201).
40 See The Friends of Oswald Mosely (n.d.).
41 See Linehan (1996, p. 80).
42 The fear was such that this applied to any form of debt. Every week our telephone conversations would turn to the winning numbers of the UK government premium bonds. My grandmother's aim was for her numbers to come up so she could pay off the home mortgages of myself and my brother.
43 See Linehan (1996, p. 298).
44 BUF leader Sir Oswald Mosley said that shirts had been chosen for the BUF uniform because, "A shirt is the easiest and cheapest garment for the purposes of recognition, and the shirts had to be paid for by the men themselves, most of whom were on the dole [unemployed]". See Rawnsley (1980, p. 151).

45 See Thurlow (2000, p. 81).
46 See Linehan (1996, p. 58).
47 See Radzinowicz (1956).
48 See MacRaild (2013, p. 270).
49 See MacRaild (2013, p. 280).
50 See Burnette (2008, p. 247).
51 See Goodfellow (2019, p. 64).
52 See Delap (2011b, p. 38).
53 MacRaild (2013, p. 271).
54 See NSA/CSS (2008).
55 Zemeckis (1985).
56 Lucas (1977).

2 The revolutions we have had

Industrial revolutions are revolutionary. An industrial revolution is not a single event. It is not a narrow change. An industrial revolution, like any revolution, is far bigger than the changes that start it. Changes ripple out through the economy and society. The next two chapters look at these changes. This chapter looks at the ripple effects of the last three industrial revolutions. The next chapter looks at what is likely to change in the fourth.

As you might expect, many of the changes have economic consequences. This does not mean that the changes will show up in economic data. Non-economists have touching faith that economic data is accurate. It is not. Economic data is largely guesswork. Economic data is particularly bad at measuring the world if the structure of the world is changing. As the economy changes around us, we tend to know less and less about what is happening in it – at least in real time.

Economic data gives us a snapshot of the world by taking a look at the way it used to work. Economic data in a time of change rarely measures the world as it is. A good example is gross domestic product (GDP). GDP is very widely referenced, especially by politicians, as a measure of the size and strength of the economy. GDP was designed in the 1920s for a world dominated by manufacturing. Its aim was to maximise output for war. While GDP is often used as a measure of living standards, few economists would defend that use. In particular, the changes of the last century mean that GDP simply does not capture a lot of the changes that are happening today. What this means is that when thinking about the changes of an industrial revolution, we should focus on the trends and concepts and not get too worked up about the numbers. The numbers are sure to be wrong.

We are standing at the starting line of a new industrial revolution. Economists generally reckon this is the fourth one.[1] The 21st century is when everything changes (again). Thinking about how dramatically revolutions change the economy and wider society seems a good place to begin the story of profit and prejudice. How the economy and society change over the next 20 years will influence how and where prejudice occurs. We can look back at the last three revolutions to get a sense of how big the changes are likely to be.

The phrase 'industrial revolution' entered common usage long after the first industrial revolution had begun. Karl Marx's collaborator on *The Communist Manifesto*, Frederick Engels, used the phrase in German in the 1840s.[2] The phrase was first used in English by Arnold Toynbee in 1882.[3] The famous maker of cups and plates Josiah Wedgwood had come close. He had said that "a revolution was at hand" in the pottery business back in 1767.[4]

Once people began using the term, the phrase 'industrial revolution' was not used in a positive way. People saw the industrial revolution as an evil thing that hurt working people.

The past three industrial revolutions can be simplified as (1) steam power, (2) electric power and (3) computer power. This is, clearly, a significant oversimplification of the complex changes of each revolution, but we have to start somewhere. The first industrial revolution was mainly about steam power and began in the mid- to late 1700s in the UK. It brought with it the expansion of the factory system. There was also some urbanisation and other changes. The first industrial revolution suited the UK, as its political and social structure made more of the changes than other countries, at least at first.

The second industrial revolution was about electricity and the assembly line. Americans often date this revolution from 1870 to the 1920s or 1930s. This revolution saw the (slow) introduction of electric power into the global economy. How factories worked started to change. Electrical machinery allowed a different way of working to steam-powered machinery. As with the first revolution, the second included faster travel and more urbanisation. Globalisation accelerated. Economic events in one country had economic, social and political consequences on the other side of the world. The second industrial revolution arguably had a bigger impact on the US than anywhere else. Geography, the starting point of a still relatively primitive urban environment and limited earlier industrialisation, meant that the US was able to change more dramatically than other economies.

The third industrial revolution was the microchip revolution. Computer power started to develop during the Second World War. Initially, the use of computers was generally restricted to the government, with a military focus. Famously, in 1945, British Prime Minister Sir Winston Churchill ordered that the world-class computers of the top-secret code-breaking Bletchley Park be broken up into pieces no larger than a fist.[5] It took a while to recover from that destruction and commercialise computing. The practical application of computers in the economy began in the latter part of the 1950s. The third industrial revolution was most disruptive from the late 1960s to the 1980s, however. The introduction of computers changed work in the service sector, not just manufacturing. It was a more global revolution, but still biased to the more advanced economies. And as it was a revolution of the service sector, countries with larger service sectors were more likely to change.

It is often the technology of an industrial revolution that captures the popular imagination. It can be seen as a good thing or a bad thing, but it is the technology that is the focus. People get excited or scared about shiny new inventions. In the first industrial revolution, the steam engine was supposed to bring about world peace. (That did not work out so well.) The economic prosperity steam engines would bring was supposed to reduce taxation and debt. (That also did not work out so well.) But if it was new, it was exciting. Technology and inventors achieved celebrity status in Britain. A grateful nation commemorated the inventor James Watt with a huge and rather tasteless statue in Westminster Abbey in recognition of his work. It has since been removed.

The Great Exhibition of 1851, between the first and second industrial revolutions, is perhaps the greatest symbol of technological worship. People queued to gain access with the determination nowadays reserved for a new iPhone launch. The attention was on the machines. From an economic point of view, however, the worship of technology was not particularly significant. The technology was just the start of larger changes. In an industrial revolution, it is the larger changes that matter.

The larger changes

Back in 1833, Peter Gaskell wrote the enticingly titled book *The manufacturing population of England, its moral, social and physical conditions, and the changes which have arisen from the use of steam machinery; with an examination of infant labour.* In it, he observed,

> A complete revolution has been affected in the distribution of property, the very face of a great country has been re-modelled, various classes of its inhabitants utterly swept away, the habits of all have undergone such vast alterations, that they resemble a people of a different age and generation.[6]

Gaskell was not exactly a fan of change, factories or, indeed, very much at all about the time in which he lived. However, his complaint about the awfulness of existence is less about the technology of steam machinery. What got Gaskell so upset were its consequences for the way society was organised – the way steam engines and other technology changed the economy and how the ripples of change in the economy went on to change society.

A generation later, in 1860, that popular periodical *The Builder* cited John Giles on the same topic.[7] Giles saw the effects of the steam engine spreading out through society: "commercial community" leading to "wealth and power" leading to "political recognition". It was not just the technology that mattered. What mattered were the changes on society brought about by that technological change.

Over the next two chapters, we will look at the ripple effects of an industrial revolution in five areas. Of course, all of these areas are tied to one another. The primary focus of this book is employment. Employment has become linked with social status. Changing employment means changing social status. Changing social status encourages prejudice. The second focus areas are location and trade. These are linked concepts. As people change where they live and work, trade (domestic or international) must change to supply their needs. The third focus is communication. As communication changes, it brings people into contact with new ideas and other people. This can be good or bad for prejudice. Later chapters will expand on this. The fourth focus is politics. As society changes, politics will inevitably change too. This can be the result of prejudice arising from the revolution. It can be generated by changing location or communication. Lastly, there are various other changes that ripple out from each revolution.

Employment

The visible loss of jobs was one of the main reasons the first industrial revolution was viewed as an evil development. The Luddites, whom we met in the last chapter, smashed machines to defend their jobs. Importantly, this was about the loss of social status as well as the loss of employment. Being a weaver was a higher-status job until machinery changed all that. The job and its associated position in society were downgraded. This had significant implications, which we will explore in Chapter 4. Concerns about employment and status did not just apply to manufacturing. The knock-on effects of the industrial revolution spread to agriculture.[8] The technological changes in industry forced changes on the farm. Agricultural jobs were lost (even as industrial jobs were created). The result was the south of England 'Swing Riots' of 1830, when workers destroyed threshing machines in a futile attempt to save jobs.[9]

This focus on jobs lost was a repeated concern over history. By the third industrial revolution, computer companies had adverts promoting computers as reliable alternatives to unreliable employees.[10] They deliberately presented their products as a better way of doing business than employing people. Shockingly, the adverts were not fully accurate. In the end, total employment rose after the introduction of computers. Industrial revolutions do not destroy jobs overall. Jobs are created as other jobs are lost. The problems start because new jobs will often require different skills. Workers losing jobs often lack the skills to adapt to the requirements of the new jobs. Existing jobs may survive, but with different status. Again, it is this change in economic and social status that causes anxiety.

The first industrial revolution changed employment in a dramatic way. The immediate focus of the first industrial revolution was cloth and clothing. Women had traditionally spun and woven wool to make cloth for thousands of years, primarily at home. Herodotus's *Histories*, written almost two and a half thousand years ago in ancient Greece, tells of a woman in Sardis spinning, fetching water and leading a horse all at the same time.[11] This level of multitasking was designed to attract the attention of King Darius and prove how industrious the woman was. The importance of spinning was made clear. Indeed, before the industrial revolution, the most common job for women in England was spinning.[12]

The advent of spinning machines during the first industrial revolution changed this. First, there was the 'spinning jenny', a small machine that women still operated. This new technology stayed in the home in the early years. After the initial release (with 12 spindles), a 24-spindle version of the spinning jenny became standard. Women could buy them and use them at home, doubling their income thanks to the new technology.[13] Nothing much changed in society as a result. There was increased demand for the raw material to be spun, but that was about it. The first part of the industrial revolution was not revolutionary at all. It was a small upgrade – a new app rather than a new phone.

Within about 15 years, however, spinning jennies were considerably bigger. The revolution was underway. Eighty spindles were standard and 120 were possible. The cost went up. More space was needed. More power was needed. Spinning moved out of homes and into factories. The technology spread very, very quickly. Within 20 years of the spinning jenny going mainstream, the technology dominated the English textile industry. The effects of the technology were now rippling out from the spinner in her cottage to the economy at large.

As the technology advanced, men became spinners. 'Mules' replaced spinning jennies for spinning wool and cotton. But mules were really big and required considerable physical strength to operate. This meant spinners were likely to be younger men. It was all downhill for the male spinner after his early 30s. A parliamentary report of 1833 told the story of Alexander Pitcairn, a male spinner. Alexander was 34 years old. His weekly income had fallen 14% since his mid-20s. This was because the number of spindles he could operate (dictating the weight of the machine he was using) had fallen as he grew older. Fewer spindles meant less spinning, meant less money. A mule with 336 spindles weighed about the same as a Mini Cooper car (around 1,400 pounds). It had to be moved 3.5 times every minute.

This single industry, over 200 years ago, shows the pattern of employment change in an industrial revolution. It is repeated over and over and over. The first industrial revolution created jobs (for young men, in this example). It destroyed jobs (for women, in this example). Before the revolution, nearly all women in a textile district could have been employed thanks to the old-fashioned method of spinning. Women would shift between spinning and agricultural work, according to seasonal demand. Even part time, spinning was an important source of cash for women. With technology, the work was increasingly male and became full time.[14] It also relocated and became concentrated in the factories of northern England. Technology meant that the chance of a southern woman getting a job got a lot worse, very quickly. This changed local labour markets and wages. Eventually, it promoted urbanisation. It changed the economic realities of working families.

New jobs were created in factories, but that did not mean that the unemployed could fill them. Women became unemployed as spinners, but could not simply move to northern mill towns. Lower-skilled workers were unlikely to go much beyond 40 miles – a day or two of walking – in search of work. In the first industrial revolution, low-income groups had few alternatives to walking if they wanted to get somewhere. Under the law, anyone found wandering outside their parish without enough money would be sent back to where they had come from. To oversimplify a bit, the new mill workers were not unemployed women moving up from the south of the country, but men from the surrounding area. This lack of flexibility in the labour market meant at times that mills had a shortage of workers.[15] The female spinner replaced by machines was likely to stay close to home – and unemployed.

Other jobs were created in the first industrial revolution. The rise of the steam-powered factory led to demand for coal. British coal output more than doubled between 1750 and 1790, creating mining jobs. The proportion of male workers dedicated to mining doubled in the second half of the 19th century in both the US and the UK.[16] Meanwhile, in the factories, the mass production of consumer goods required mass employment. Machines still needed machine operators. Because automation often reduced the skill level required (in pottery or weaving, for example), lower-skilled jobs were created. That led to a problem of declining job status, however.

Technology also helped to bind social status to work more closely than before. The economist Adam Smith divided workers into 'productive' and 'unproductive' labour.[17] Productive workers used the new technologies to make things. Unproductive workers were 'menial servants' who added nothing to the economy. As the cost of fighting rebellious colonies in North America increased, the British government became ever more inventive in taxing the population. A tax on male servants identified them not by where they lived or who they worked for. The male servants who were taxable were categorised by what they did – butlers were taxed, farm labourers were not. The clear linking of social status to what a person did was a shift. Tying social status to the specifics of what one did was wrapped up in the new technologies.[18]

As traditional jobs for women disappeared in the first industrial revolution, the main career option remaining open to them was to become servants in towns and cities. The increase in supply of workers meant that female servants were relatively cheap. A British tax on female servants in the late 1700s led to an outcry. Critics pointed out that women would lose jobs as servants at a time when technology was taking away other options.[19] While the tax on 'unproductive' male servants lasted, the tax on women ended after a few years.

The second industrial revolution introduced electricity into factories and eventually into homes. Electricity generally led to the introduction of 'labour-saving' devices.[20] This was particularly true towards the end of the second industrial revolution. The fact that electric lighting did not need cleaning was a significant labour saving. The British electricity industry described its product as "the new servant in the home".[21] Some 'labour-saving' devices saved so much labour that jobs were lost. Long-established professions, such as the washerwoman, started to decline. Washing machines turned what had been a task of several days into a simple and quick job.[22] There was no need to outsource the work.

While technology did cost jobs, it also helped to create them. The washing machine, for example, allowed other people to work in different jobs. British computer entrepreneur Stephanie Shirley wrote about how important it was to her as a business owner to own a washing machine in the 1950s.[23] It meant that Shirley had the time to continue running her computer-programming business from home, despite having a young baby. (She also ran the business to the incomprehension of her mother and mother-in-law. Generational divides are common with new technology.)

Similarly, changes in the factory system (and the invention of sewing machines) changed the price of clothing. Cheaper ready-made clothing meant women did not have to make their own clothes at home. Throughout the first industrial revolution, making clothes remained a time-consuming process for women in all but the highest-income groups. With ready-made clothing, women had more time for leisure or work outside the home. The potential for new jobs was created by shifts in where things were made.

The move to 'labour-saving' devices also reduced the demand for servants. The supply of servants also fell as technology increased opportunities. After the Second World War, the ninth Earl of Shaftesbury lamented that it was impossible to find domestic servants, as girls would not take on the work. Without servants, living in a large country house was not practical.[24] Before the second industrial revolution, in rural areas, in particular, practically the only job option for a young, lower-income woman was domestic service. This, as we have seen, was a legacy of the ripples of change from the first industrial revolution. The second industrial revolution increased knowledge about opportunities, the ability to travel to find work and the range of jobs available. The second industrial revolution let women with enough education work in offices in clerical positions. The job of 'servant', into which women had moved after the first industrial revolution, went into decline over the course of the second industrial revolution. Technology changed both supply and demand.

As with the earlier changes, the third industrial revolution both destroyed and created jobs. While the computer companies advertised that they could replace workers, the reality was that computers could do new and interesting things with data, creating new jobs doing previously unimaginable tasks. The demand for workers often went up as computers opened up new possibilities. Interestingly, while new jobs in computing often required a good level of education, they were frequently categorised as relatively low-skilled, low-status jobs. Computer workers were seen as 'clerical' rather than 'professional'.

Job creation versus job destruction also had a global angle in the third industrial revolution. New jobs in new industries might be created abroad. Countries that were stuck with the infrastructure of the second industrial revolution had problems. The factories and ways of working of the past were not necessarily suited to the new opportunities the microchip revolution offered. This led to the 'newly industrialised economies' (NICs): countries such as South Korea in Asia or, arguably, Spain in Europe that were able to set up production that suited the computer-based age.

Japan's *kan-ban* or just-in-time system of ordering parts for production was very efficient and greatly helped by computer power. The US began to lag. *Kan-ban* was used in the car industry. In the second industrial revolution, the US car industry had led the world. The economic model is sometimes called 'Fordism' after the car company. In the third industrial revolution, computers made Fordism less profitable and the US car industry gave up its lead. The US was stuck in the old way of doing things. The third industrial revolution favoured making cars outside the US. Employment patterns shifted accordingly.

The textile industry was another area to change in the third industrial revolution. The fast-changing nature of the industry had kept relatively low-skilled jobs in developed economies. Labour was cheaper elsewhere, but it was too difficult to manage a long and complex supply chain without computer technology. The microchip revolution managed that problem and allowed production to shift to where labour was cheapest, or at least cheaper. In the 1970s, more than 70% of American clothing was made in America. In 1991, it was 56.2%. In 2012, it was 2.5%. Globally, jobs were not necessarily lost. Locally, employment in the industry was all but wiped out.[25]

Technology often changes how we work. The first industrial revolution had changed working life by shifting from self-employment to factory employment, at least for some jobs. In the second industrial revolution, there were hierarchies of managers. They made sure that their staff did what they were supposed to do and guided their work. In the third industrial revolution, there was a tendency to move away from hierarchies with lots of supervisors and middle managers. Collaboration and problem solving in teams is helped by technology.

A recurring problem in the first three industrial revolutions was the inflexibility of workers. Workers, understandably, wanted to defend the status and income of their jobs. Skilled workers by second industrial revolution standards were reluctant to change. In the third industrial revolution, these established workers were competing against new workers who had no need to change. These new workers were entering into manufacturing for the first time. They were already compatible with the new, computer-focussed way of making things.

The way in which car production changed is a good example of this problem, with parallels to the first industrial revolution. Economic structures and social status prevented unemployed workers adapting to new ways of working in the third industrial revolution. Two hundred years earlier, unemployed spinners in the south of England were unable fill the jobs available in the north of England because of the way the economy was structured. In the 1970s, unemployed car workers and dated assembly lines in the UK were unable to compete with the new designs of factories elsewhere.

The pattern of employment in past industrial revolutions has been quite similar. Jobs are lost. Jobs are created. Jobs go down in status. Jobs go up in status. The problem, time after time, is that the people who lose their jobs face many obstacles to finding work. The obstacles may be legal. Often the obstacles are cultural. People are unwilling to take a job they see as being lower in status. But industrial revolutions do not just change what jobs are available. They also change what jobs are done.

Location and trade

When *what* people do for work changes, *where* people work often changes too. As we have seen, the first industrial revolution moved spinning jobs away from the countryside and into towns. Jobs moved away from the home and into the factory. The second and third industrial revolutions began to reverse this. Stephanie Shirley was able to work at home, in the countryside, as technology gave her options, made her life easier and reduced the need to work in the same place as her colleagues.

As locations change, so patterns of trade will change. Before the first industrial revolution, most people lived in villages. Most of the things ordinary people consumed would be made close to home. Trade might take place in the local market town, but that was about it. This was the pattern of trade that had existed since the 10th century.

Technology changed all this. As machinery changed where people lived and worked, it became more important to bring things in from outside. As mass production increased output, firms looked for new markets to sell to. That encouraged more global trade, further impacting economies and societies.

Each industrial revolution has changed the built landscape. The mill towns of northern England, the slums of London's docklands, the rise of suburbia, the emergence of Asian megacities and the decline of America's 'Rust Belt' can all be seen as the result of technological change.

The first industrial revolution created more densely populated towns in the UK. Sir Frederic Morton Eden wrote *The State of the Poor* in 1797. He noted that Trowbridge, in Wiltshire, had rents that were "very high" and that the number of buildings increased every year. The reason was the rise of the mills. Wiltshire is home to a lot of sheep and thus wool. (Wiltshire is also home to a notable cathedral and some fairly notable economists.) Eden wrote that mechanisation had started after 1790. As the locals were "much averse" to the machines, their introduction was gradual. But the rise of the machines was relentless. As the machines came in, so the size and structure of the town changed.[26]

The urbanisation resulting from technological change is another example of how an industrial revolution created jobs. During the first industrial revolution, demand for bricks grew. More people were needed to make more bricks. British use of bricks grew a lot faster than the population.[27] Why was this? For one thing, towns and cities were more likely than villages to be brick built. Villages could use local stone. That was not normally practical for towns and cities.

In addition, people no longer worked at home. Working in a factory or mill meant one building to live in and another to work in. That meant more buildings per person. That meant more bricks. (Bricks were, of course, taxed. The government was not going to pass up the chance to tax something that was in demand.)[28] Technology meant more mills, more mills meant more bricks, more bricks meant more money for brickmakers. Brickmakers realised their market power and became more independent.[29] Technological progress, which had increased the demand for bricks, eventually started to affect the supply. In 1800, the way of making bricks had barely changed since Roman times. Over the following decades, technology allowed skilled brickmakers to be replaced with unskilled labourers of lower status, assisted by machines. The ripples that began with the spinning jenny changed life for skilled brickmakers.

As mentioned earlier, in the second industrial revolution, labour-saving devices invaded the home. Lower-skilled people could follow alternative careers to domestic service. Fewer servants meant that houses did not have to be so large. The middle class and upper class did not need to share their homes with so many people. Larger houses were subdivided or demolished. Apartment living became practical as electric devices replaced servants and the space they required. The physical landscape changed.

Skyscrapers are not possible without electricity. Electric-powered lifts (or 'elevators', as our American friends would say) are needed. It is not practical to be climbing endless flights of stairs. Electric lighting was revolutionary. The gloom of candles, oil lamps and gas lighting disappeared. Evenings could be spent more productively in bright light. The result of all of this was that more people could live in urban areas and make better use of their time.

Changing transport during the second industrial revolution encouraged urbanisation. The railways increased demand for horses at first, so railways started out by creating more horse-related jobs. Railways meant more people and goods could travel between cities. Once they got there, however, horses were needed to move people and goods around the town or city.

As internet retailers often comment today, the 'last mile' of delivery is the hardest. Moving stuff from city to city was easy. Getting it exactly to where it was needed gave a temporary boom to an old form of transport.

As technology advanced in the second industrial revolution, the horse became redundant. This, once again, changed the built environment. In the first industrial revolution, the size of a city was constrained by the distance from home to work. Commuting was a relatively new thing, but the distance travelled was limited. Houses had to be a walkable distance from factories (for low-income workers) or a horse ride away (for management). Cities could not outgrow these constraints. The result was that nearly every city before the first industrial revolution was no more than two miles wide from one side to the other. It takes about half an hour to walk a mile. People did not want to commute more than half an hour to and from work each day.

With the first railways (from 1836, effectively) and then the electrification of urban trams (in the 1890s in the UK), cities could become larger.[30] The motor car allowed the scale of cities to change even more. People could live much further from work, but still have just a half hour's commute by tram or rail.[31] Horses were relegated to exploiting tourists around New York's Central Park. The new technology of the second industrial revolution allowed people to commute longer distances than before. The technology of the second industrial revolution created suburbia.

In the third industrial revolution, the physical environment changed again as business started to do things differently. The rise of computers changed demand for office space. Computers needed large, clean, dry environments in which to operate. This was particularly true in the early years of the third industrial revolution. Office buildings from the previous century, even from a few decades earlier, were not suitable. The office had to be at the correct temperature. Too hot an environment and the vacuum tubes of early computing would break. Early computers were foiled by too much moisture. A damp punch card is a warped punch card. Computers said 'no' to warped input.

Opening a window to lower the temperature could spell disaster. One UK computer tried to read the flies that had flown in through an open window and settled on its punch-card input. This resulted in a data error.[32] It was also presumably fatal for the flies. The need for appropriate buildings changed office demand.

Computers also started to change working patterns yet again. This, in turn, started to change demand for buildings – and location – once again. In the 1960s, computer programming required a pencil and a piece of paper. Freelance Programmers Limited was set up in the UK with the initial aim of providing jobs for women with children. Originally, the company had no office space at all. Women could work at home as programmers – though the clients did not necessarily know that. Founder Stephanie Shirley marvelled that "the expensive, sophisticated, state-of-the-art computer programmes [clients] were buying from us were created at home by women surrounded by babies and nappies".[33] The labour-saving devices of the second industrial revolution freed up the time that let this happen. The changed technology of the third industrial revolution meant some jobs could be done at home. And this is a taste of what the fourth industrial revolution may offer.

Thus, each industrial revolution has changed the physical environment. The very shapes of buildings today depend on the application of technology from the late 19th century. Suburban sprawl and the endlessness of cities such as Los Angeles came about because of the second industrial revolution. Similarly, we can thank the technological changes of past revolutions for the skylines of New York and Hong Kong. However, as locations change, so do trade and transport. These changes, in turn, feed back into employment, health, politics and other aspects of society.

The first industrial revolution was accompanied by an increase in global trade. As mass production grew, so mass markets were needed. This meant more competition for raw materials and markets and can be seen as a key part of colonialism. But trade patterns within countries also shifted. Some countries had taxes on internal trade. Moving goods from one province to another would incur a tax or tariff. The industrial revolution emphasised the damage of such taxes.

Technology that led to changing locations forced more trade. A pre-revolution spinner working at home, even if using the early spinning jenny, could expect to sell all her work locally. A large steam-powered mill, producing huge amounts of thread on mules, could not possibly find enough demand locally. There had to be internal trade (at least) to find a market for the goods. Ideally, there would be external trade as well.

Large-scale movements of people took place. Steamships made it easier and cheaper to emigrate. This changed society, particularly in the US. As with the first industrial revolution, the ripple effects spread far and wide through the economy. Steamships made emigration cheaper and safer. Cheaper emigration prompted many Eastern Europeans to move to the US. Eastern European migrants included a disproportionate number of tailors.[34] More tailors lowered the cost of making clothes. As noted earlier, this freed women from the time-consuming chore of making clothes at home. Steamships meant more women could go out to work.

Better domestic transport allowed more trade within countries. In the US, in particular, catalogue shopping boomed in the second industrial revolution. Just like online shopping today, catalogue shopping needed a reliable delivery system to the customer's doorstep.[35] The changes of transport allowed this to happen. The decline of the high street, bemoaned by the British media and the subject of periodic French legislation, has its roots in the decline of the monopolistic general store in the US during the second industrial revolution. The location of the retailer became less important once trains could whisk goods and catalogues around the country.

Fast ships with cooled cargo holds could ship beef from Argentina to Europe. Argentina's cattle herds were far larger than the needs of the population for much of the 1800s. There were so many sheep that they were considered a pest, not a commercial resource. There was nowhere to sell the meat. Cattle were used for leather or fat (tallow, used in candles). Meat would rot before it got to any other market, so it was a waste by-product of the leather industry.[36]

Refrigeration changed everything. Argentina's economy benefitted from the possibility of exporting to Europe. Europe, particularly the UK, invested heavily in Argentina. Europeans could consume more meat because it was cheaper. For European farmers, this was not such good news. Cheap food from abroad meant less demand for expensive food grown at home. Refrigeration began a rural economic depression. The depression led to population shifts away from farms and into towns or to new countries. The depression also led to violence – the pogroms of eastern Europe can be linked to the economic changes that came from technology. The prejudice and violence encouraged emigration, which changed labour costs in other countries, which led to new prejudice. There is a link between the transport changes of the second industrial revolution and the prejudice of fascism in East London involving my family.

Communication

Each industrial revolution has seen some change in communication. Communication is obviously important: it is what spreads new ideas and technological innovations. Labour flexibility, in part, depends on being able to find out whether jobs are available elsewhere. People need to communicate for such knowledge to spread. Communication can change politics. As we will discuss in Chapters 5 and 6, communication can play an important role in reducing prejudice, or in making it worse.

Communication improvements in the first industrial revolution were quite limited. As locations shifted and trade started to expand, better transport links became more important. These allowed better communication by making it easier to move about a country. The move to towns may also have helped improve education standards. As people lived closer together, it became easier to set up a school with a sizeable customer base within walking distance. As more people were able to read, so pamphlets and newspapers could have a bigger impact. British literacy had been rising before the first industrial revolution but exceeded 50% of the population in the late 1700s.[37]

The anti-slavery campaigns relied on pamphlets to get their anti-prejudice message across. That meant that people had to read. Technology encouraged urbanisation, which allowed more people to learn to read, which improved communication, with political consequences. The combination of better literacy and railway travel influenced literature. The three-volume novel of 19th-century-Britain was the perfect length to occupy a long railway journey in the days before Netflix. And writers could use the rise of the novel as a means of pushing political ideas. Charles Dickens and Anthony Trollope, for example, both had political messages they wished to convey.

The Luddite movement that opposed the industrial revolution took advantage of the better communication it created. The common branding of the Luddites and the creation of the fictional 'General Lud' or 'King Lud' relied on written communication. The agricultural Swing Riots of 1830 were more likely to occur close to stagecoach stopping places, as this was a route that national news travelled (newspapers were sent by stagecoach). Again, this depended on the literacy the industrial revolution had created, although literacy was not as good in rural areas as in the towns.

Good communication led to good ideas. This helped to expand the industrial revolution. As the industrial revolution progressed, inventions became more complex. That meant bringing people with different skill sets together. The fact that mass production required better transport links to send out goods also allowed better communication of ideas. However, there were limits. One of the limits to good communication was differences in regional accent. Even today, these can be an obstacle to understanding, but in a world without television or radio, the differences in accent were more dramatic. People with different accents might not be understood, or even mistrusted.[38] The result was that where there was a common written and spoken language, there was more communication and more innovation. Three-quarters of the innovations of the first industrial revolution developed in relatively limited regions of the UK (London to Manchester) and France (Le Havre to Lyon). These were areas where people had similar accents. It was easier for people to communicate new ideas with one another.[39]

The second industrial revolution led to greater changes in communication. The railways and steamships brought news and information as well as people. The introduction of the telegraph, and later the telephone, changed the speed with which news was communicated. It also helped to globalise markets. If traders know the price of something in one part of the world, it will influence the price of that good elsewhere in the world, provided it can be traded. The exchange rate between the pound sterling and the US dollar is commonly called 'cable' in reference to the transatlantic telegraph cable that communicated the rate between London and New York.

The fact that internal migration was easier led to a standardisation of accents. Regional accents and dialects did not disappear, but they faded. That eventually made communication easier. International migration worked against this, however, with communities clustering together and only slowly integrating with the wider economy because of language barriers. This is still an issue in countries like the US today. Spanish-speaking Americans are less likely do well economically outside of Spanish-speaking areas.[40]

Communication also influenced travel. The telegraph meant that the US railway network did not need to have two tracks. If trains travelled towards each other on a single track, the telegraph could be used to put one train into a siding until the other had passed. The telegraph roughly halved the amount of rail track that needed to be laid.

The third industrial revolution brought television as a dominant communication tool. This produced a decline in national radio in countries like the US, but that, in turn, helped support local radio. This is something that has implications for prejudice, as catering to a smaller audience with less regulation can allow more extreme views to be heard. Television shifted the communication dynamic once again.

Technology has had the potential to change how people exchange information. The big change here was around the second industrial revolution. Nonetheless, the communication of the second industrial revolution depended (in part) on the rise of literacy. Better literacy came from the move to towns in the first industrial revolution. The communication of the second industrial revolution has roots in the 18th century. The intimacy of both radio and television changed how ideas were transmitted across the economy. This intimacy was a dramatic break with the past style of communication.

Politics

Any period of change in an economy and society is likely to alter the political landscape. One of the central ideas of this book is that the prejudice of 'anti-politics' is strongly tied to the economic changes of an industrial revolution. But the structural changes of an economy will also change the way politics is conducted.

The urbanisation that factories encouraged changed politics in both the first and the second industrial revolutions. Workers worked and lived in towns and cities. This meant they were forced into small areas where they could easily meet lots of people with similar problems. That helped the rise of trade unions. Trade unions were technically illegal in Great Britain until 1824, but they still existed. Political protests were a lot easier with people living close together. Despite former UK Prime Minister Theresa May's confession to the heinous crime of running through fields of wheat with friends as a child, it is generally easier to commit acts of riot in a city than in the countryside.[41]

As society adjusted to the new economy of the first industrial revolution, some parts of the UK went up in status. Some parts became less important. Traditionally prosperous areas (mainly rural areas) had declining influence. Areas no one had heard of before the 19th century, like Manchester, suddenly rose to prominence. These new areas demanded a voice in government. Political structures had to change. As John Giles noted in *The Builder*, the move from technology to commerce to wealth to political power was almost inevitable.[42]

This pattern was repeated elsewhere. In the US, Chicago was not particularly important until it became a railway hub. The transport and location changes of the second industrial revolution increased the city's relative significance.

As areas changed in terms of economic importance, demands for political rights shifted. The emergence of a wealthy manufacturing class, whose income was not tied to land or inheritance, led to demand for representation in government. The feudal system of political power gave way – sometimes relatively peacefully, or sometimes (as with France) more violently. Increased literacy meant increased awareness and, perhaps, increased understanding of political issues.

The structural changes and the rise of a manufacturing middle class helped to create political parties in the modern sense. The first industrial revolution shifted the focus away from court intrigues and personal or religious-based politics. Politics became more about economic ideas. The second industrial revolution took that further, as an educated working class began to use its political power. The rise of labour unions and class-based political parties changed the political landscape again.

The first and second industrial revolutions gave the emerging middle class more time to engage in politics. The first industrial revolution spawned cheap servants. The second industrial revolution bred machines that replaced human labour. People, especially women, had more free time available. This time could be directed at political campaigns. The role of women in the anti-slavery movement, mentioned in Chapter 1, is a good example of this.

The communication changes of the second industrial revolution also started to change politics. US populist politician William Jennings Bryan refused to accept campaign money from railway companies. That did not stop him using the railway extensively in his (unsuccessful) attempt to become US president in 1896. Bryan made over six hundred speeches, crossing the US by train to do so.[43] Towards the end of the second industrial revolution, US President Franklin Roosevelt made dramatic use of the radio to communicate with the population. The technology created a sense of intimacy with the electorate. The President used the radio to rally popular support for his policies. His marketing style caused concern among advertising agencies (trying to promote business, rather than the government).[44] Others saw the radio as a political threat – a narcotic, to which the electorate was becoming addicted.

The third industrial revolution changed politics in several ways. The rise of the computer gave rise to hopes of a more efficient state-controlled economy. Computers could manage huge amounts of data. UK politician Harold Wilson hoped for a Britain forged in the "white heat of the scientific revolution" in a party speech in 1963 (before becoming Prime Minister the following year). He even made an oblique reference to the first industrial revolution, declaring that there was "no room for Luddites in the Socialist Party".[45] This rhetoric did not amount to much in reality. The flaws in trying to run an economy as a computer system have already been mentioned: people do not behave rationally and economic data is not very good (especially in times of structural change). For a while, though, there was a real hope of a social and political change from being able to manage so much more data.

The technology of the third industrial revolution led to some surprising policy outcomes. President Richard Nixon imposed wage and price controls across the US in 1971. The technology of the third industrial revolution was pressed into the service of the government. The Emergency Management Information System and Reference Index was supposed to assist with the implementation of the controls and make the system work, but it did not do that.[46] The policy did not work.

As the industrial revolution progressed, a different sort of politics emerged around workers. The second industrial revolution had seen the rise of working-class politics. People (generally men) working in manufacturing were demanding and eventually getting a political voice. This was a group that was rising in power and knew it. Their concentration in urban areas, with the potential to protest or strike, gave these workers collective power. In the third industrial revolution, to oversimplify, this was a group in decline. Technological change was a direct challenge to the old way of doing things. Job security fell and the potential for an external challenge to the unions rose. There was an increase in political disputes over labour and the emergence of what economists call an 'insider-outsider' model. Unions sought to protect the interests of their members (insiders) through political action. The needs of outsiders (non-members) were not considered or were sacrificed to the needs of the insiders. This worked initially, until the problems of the outsiders exceeded the problems of the insiders. Nonetheless, the struggle over the changes of the third industrial revolution shaped politics for much of the 1970s and the 1980s in many countries.

Politics obviously changes as society changes. What industrial revolutions have tended to do is change the structure of how politics and government operate. The rise of the middle class, then of the working class, and the illusion that big data might mean better state control are all features of industrial revolutions. The actual political views of the different groups do not matter much to the argument – they are not the same in every country anyway. What matters is that the established political way of doing things is changed by each industrial revolution.

Other

The ripple effects of technological change are widespread, but employment has to be the main focus of any industrial revolution. It is employment that is most obviously affected and it is this that tends to shape the arguments around prejudice. Location, communication and politics are also fairly obvious changes. But the ripples of technological change will extend further still and some of the other changes are important.

Throughout the first three industrial revolutions, the whole concept of leisure changed. In the first industrial revolution, people could no longer work when it suited them (as they had done). Mills did not allow people to stroll in when they wanted to do a bit of work, then leave when they got bored. People now had to work according to shifts. This changed the importance of timekeeping in society and this created new jobs. People were employed to 'knock up' factory workers – to bang on windows or doors to wake factory workers in time for the next shift. As home spinning was replaced by factory spinning, the industrial revolution introduced the idea of commuting to work. Workers had to add the walk to and from the factory to their day, reducing their leisure time. The commute was no longer moving from one side of the family cottage to the other.

In 1930, the economist John Maynard Keynes famously predicted that people would be able to work just 15 hours a week within a hundred years.[47] That date is rapidly approaching and there are few indications that people are working a 15-hour week. Economists certainly are not. However, the labour-saving devices of the second and third industrial revolutions have reduced the amount of time spent doing unpaid (unrecorded) work. The amount of time spent doing housework has fallen significantly: some estimates have Americans spending less than a quarter of the time today that they spent in 1900.[48] Thirty-four hours of work have been taken away each week – it is just that the normal economic data we use is too inaccurate to measure that time as work.[49] GDP data does not recognise unpaid housework. (GDP effectively works on the principle that housework is magically done by *Harry Potter*-esque house elves, so does not include it in the national economy.) Some of that time has gone into other forms of work, of course. But it has also been used for leisure.

Moreover, people have chosen to keep working longer hours to be able to buy more stuff. It has been estimated that an average American would have had to work 17 weeks a year in 2015 to have the same standard of living as an average American in 1915.[50] Of course, few people would want to have the same standard of living as that enjoyed over 100 years ago. The point is that technology has increased leisure (by reducing time spent on housework) and could increase it further if it were not for the fact that people want to own more stuff. It is also worth noting that the increase in leisure time is often spent consuming. Shopping is still a leisure activity for part of the population. Eating at restaurants and watching films are also leisure. Technology has increased the time for leisure and the income available to spend on it. If you consider visiting a shopping mall to spend money on things you do not need to be an improvement in living standards, this is a good thing.

Changing where people lived changed how food was produced and how it was transported. Workers living in slums in cities could not grow food to feed themselves, at least not in the UK or Europe.[51] There were few opportunities to grow food in the shadows of the "dark Satanic mills" of the industrial revolution.[52] Food had to be moved from remote rural areas to the cities to feed factory workers. But more workers in town meant fewer workers in the country areas. Farmers had to find more efficient ways of growing crops. Farms got larger. Land was enclosed, which meant poorer people in rural areas had fewer options to get food for themselves. Farming technology again changed job security. As mentioned earlier, the threshing machine was a target of the Swing Riots of 1830. Packaging also started to change. If food was travelling to the consumer, it had to be packaged for the journey. Metal milk churns (for transporting milk rather than churning butter) were used from the 1850s. The railway companies, which were moving the milk to the cities, preferred to transport the stuff in churns.

The position of women in society changed with technology. In the first industrial revolution, women's jobs as spinners disappeared within a generation. Technological change cost them jobs in agriculture. Scythes are heavier than sickles, tending to give men an advantage. Agricultural work was 'piece rate' (paid by the area reaped, for example). That meant that a woman who did wield a scythe was likely to be paid less than a man for a day's work. The change to factories and shift work was something else that made it harder for women to work. Working at home had let women raise their children. That became a lot harder with shift work away from home. Until the 1960s in the UK, only a man's wages would be considered when applying for a mortgage. A woman's income was not considered reliable enough. Women still found it difficult to get credit without a male guarantor.[53]

Branding and advertising became important. If you were buying food or clothing from a distant location, from someone you did not know, you might be cheated. Before technology changed everything, people would buy what they needed in the relatively closed economy of a village or a small town. If you did not get what you expected, the whole economy would know. In a far larger economy, the advantage was with the producer. Bread could be adulterated, tea mixed with wood shavings and the consumer was too far away to do much about it. Customers bought goods from people and places that they did not know and did not wish to know.

Twinings, the tea company, was one of the branding pioneers. Building a brand meant that there was a cost for a company if its quality was poor. That cost was paid no matter how far the company was from its customers. That cost gave the company an incentive to be honest about its products and their quality. Consumers had trust in the brand. It also gave a company a competitive edge, of course. That was the point. Thus branding, advertising and eventually the alchemy of the 'spin doctor' was created as the ripples of technology spread. A whole range of professions sprang into existence as a result of technological change.

Health changed as urbanisation led to greater problems. People who live close to lots of other people catch communicable diseases more often. There was less fresh food. If you grew and made what you ate, you could control it. Once in cities, you did not know what you were eating. The problems of plumbing contributed to diseases like cholera. This led to changes in medicine. Treating people became more about science and less about super-stition and folklore. As communications technology improved, ideas could be exchanged more easily. Medical treatment could be based on scientific facts, not local superstition.

Eventually the second industrial revolution meant that fewer horses were needed in cities. Jobs associated with horses were lost. Looking after horses was a bad career move from the early 20th century onwards. Fewer horses also meant less fewer horses eating grain. There was more food for humans (at a potentially cheaper cost). Fewer horses meant less manure in cities. Fewer horses meant fewer dead horses in cities. All of these things helped to improve urban health.[54]

The different industrial revolutions have altered the gap in living stand-ards between towns and the countryside. In 1844, private baths had been banned in Boston, Massachusetts, because the basic plumbing system could not cope with the wastewater, but by the second industrial revolution, those days were long gone. Hot water at high pressure was readily available in the 1930s. Water was literally on tap. However, Lola Burster, who was living in rural Colorado in the 1930s, wrote that there was "not a bathtub in the community".[55] Electricity was the power of the second industrial revolution, but not for everyone. Lola lived in the middle of nowhere, with no electricity. No electricity meant no electric pumps to draw or heat water. That meant no baths without considerable effort.

Different hygiene standards meant different health issues. Here, the sec-ond industrial revolution was a reversal of the first. Then, living in a town meant increased health risks. Now, the country dweller was at higher risk. Differences in access to electricity between town and country also meant different lifestyles (particularly for women). The urban woman had free time. The rural woman was still standing over the washtub. The rural-urban divide is still significant almost 100 years later. In fact, the urban-rural di-vide is one of the more important explanations of prejudice in politics.

Technology meant there could be variety in what people ate. You no longer had to eat the narrow range of what could be produced locally. Americans may have had enough to eat in the 1800s, but it was all pork and corn. The lack of fruit in parts of the US and Europe caused health problems. Refrig-erated railcars could move fresh food around the country cheaply. People could eat new, different foods. (Whether they chose to was a different issue.)

The ripple effects of the third industrial revolution can take an economist down some very strange routes. The first industrial revolution changed how things were sold with branding. The second industrial revolution introduced catalogue selling. Both moves are essential to companies like Amazon to-day. The Amazon brand is trusted as a marketplace. The Amazon customer cannot see the goods in person. The Amazon customer knows (because of the brand value) that they will be refunded if the goods are not as expected. The distribution system of Amazon is little changed from the mail-order catalogue four generations earlier.

The shopping environment was also changed by the third industrial revolution. Barcodes, which came along in 1974, changed how we buy food. The first item scanned was a 67-cent 10 pack of Wrigley's Juicy Fruit chewing gum.[56] This was not a great start. Scanners were expensive and only about 200 items had barcodes on them. The technology really took off in the 1980s. Barcodes allowed supermarkets to grow.

In the early 1970s, a US supermarket operator could claim to know the price of every item in the store. Given the rapidly changing prices of the Nixon era, this was quite an accomplishment. Every item had a price tag. Every price was manually typed into the register. The customer would often check the bill to make sure no errors had been made.[57] This series of manual operations put a practical limit on the size of a supermarket and the range of goods it could stock.

Barcodes changed this. Stores could become larger. They could stock more goods. Barcodes allowed stores to manage their inventory more efficiently. Stores were less likely to run out of things if they knew exactly how much had been sold every day. The risk of holding too many items was also reduced. Barcodes meant that there was no need for employees to put price labels on every single item. That meant it took less labour to stock the shelves. Checkouts were faster, which meant fewer operators were needed.

The barcode allowed superstores or hypermarkets to exist. The transport network had to change to fit this. Superstores required more frequent deliveries (because inventory was managed daily). Because superstores were larger, there was enough demand across a range of products to justify daily deliveries.[58]

However, there is also evidence that the growth of large food stores has had health consequences. When supermarkets were first introduced into the US, shoppers would often find themselves at the checkout without enough money. The supermarket encouraged people to buy. People bought more than they intended.[59] The superstores of the 1980s encouraged that trend even further. It has been argued that there is a link between large supermarkets and obesity.[60] In other words, barcodes may make you fat.

It's the economy, stupid (but also society and politics)

In the first industrial revolution, the spinning jenny changed far more than the productivity of the cloth industry. The spinning jenny changed employment, social status, urbanisation, brickmaking, leisure, home life, food, branding, health, politics and society. Peter Gaskell's complaints about "people of a different age and generation" may sound like the grumblings of a grumpy old man, but it does not alter the fact that change was everywhere.[61] Changing technology was like dropping a stone in the middle of a pond. There was a splash, which caught a lot of attention. Technology is like that – lots of noise and excitement. But it is the ripples that spread out from that initial impact that are most interesting. The entire economy and society were changed by these ripples. The technology of the spinning jenny and the mule were perhaps the least important things about the change.

The second industrial revolution, like the first, was about far more than technology. How and where people lived changed. Free time changed. Health changed. Some of the changes of the first industrial revolution changed again. Spinning was the largest employer of women before the first industrial revolution. As technology destroyed those jobs, women became servants. Domestic service was the largest employer of women in the UK at the start of the 20th century. Technology and the opportunities technology presented destroyed those jobs. Change rippled out further and further.

There was more upheaval with the third industrial revolution. The introduction of computers changed the built environment, working practices and the status of different jobs. The technological splash produces waves that affect far-flung parts of the economy.

To borrow from former US President Bill Clinton's 1992 campaign, "it's the economy, stupid".[62] The common theme of all this history is obvious. Technology has a direct impact on the economy. The effect extends far beyond the initial area that technology is changing. A lot of these effects have implications for employment. The changing built environment of the first industrial revolution changed the jobs of brickmakers. The changing transport environment of the second revolution created and then destroyed jobs in the horse industry. Technology in the third industrial revolution changed the jobs in the retail sector.

Economic data may not measure this properly. Economic data is often stuck in the past. Today's data is attempting to measure the modern economy by trying to make it fit into the structures of the 1930s. This is why technology tends to show up everywhere except in the economic numbers.

New products are created or existing products are made more efficient. That can reduce the size of the economy, even as it raises living standards. Using a washing machine rather than a washerwoman will lower GDP over time, for example. But what really matters are the ripple effects of that technology on the wider economy. An industrial revolution changes the social order. An industrial revolution affects politics. As society and the economy adapt to new technology, new opportunities arise. Old ways of doing things decline. The fourth industrial revolution is likely to follow the same pattern.

We do not really need to ask what your next smartphone can do for you. What matters to the economics of prejudice is what new things you do with your next smartphone.

Notes

1 There is some dispute about this. Some merge the third revolution (the microchip revolution) with the current set of changes. However, the World Economic Forum distinguishes between the third and fourth. The social changes caused by the third and fourth industrial revolutions seem to be sufficiently different as to consider them separate events. See Schwab (2016).

2 See Griffin (2013).
3 Ibid.
4 See Mokyr (2009, p. 79).
5 See Chown (1999).
6 See Gaskell (1833, p. 33).
7 See MacLeod (2007, p. 136).
8 It is worth noting that every industrial revolution has had an accompanying agricultural revolution.
9 See Aidt et al. (2017).
10 Hicks (2017, p. 202) shows an advert from computer company ICL titled, "It's a waste of money paying people like this". The picture is of three people at work, but not working. The two female employees are prominently positioned at the front of the picture in what certainly seems to be a deliberate form of prejudice.
11 See Boas (1949).
12 See Burnette (2008, p. 40).
13 See Allen (2007).
14 This is not to say that the work was exclusively male. Women worked in factories too. However, women were generally excluded from the highly paid jobs, because these were the jobs that required physical strength. Where women were employed, there was a strong reaction. The Broomward Cotton Mill of Glasgow employed only women in 1820. Female workers were attacked and there was a fire at the mill. Eventually, James Dunlop, the owner, fired the women and employed only male spinners. See Burnette (2008).
15 See Adkins and Adkins (2013, p. 201).
16 See Mokyr (1977).
17 See Smith (1776).
18 See Brown (2007).
19 Ibid.
20 'Labour-saving' was a phrase coined in the US, which had spread to the UK by the early 20th century.
21 See Delap (2011b, p. 115).
22 Leto (1988) notes that laundry had more patents for technological innovation than any other form of housework. Washing clothes took a third of a woman's working time before the 1800s. While better methods of heating water and better detergents should have reduced the time spent washing clothes, the fact that laundry became easier increased demand for clean clothes. Higher standards of cleanliness increased the frequency with which clothes were washed. It was only with the introduction of the washing machine in the second industrial revolution (requiring a ready supply of water and power) that the demand for people to clean clothes started to fall. Outsourcing laundry did not end the role of the washerwoman entirely. The musical *Hairspray*, set in 1962, has the character Edna Tumblad working as a laundress at home (see O'Donnell and Meehan, 2002). This was not the norm, however.
23 See Shirley (2019, p. 75).
24 See Ashley-Cooper and Knox (2018).
25 See Thomas (2019, p. 5).
26 See Eden (1797, ed. 1928, p. 348).
27 In the first half of the 19th century, British brick supply grew about one-third faster than the population.
28 See Watt (1990).
29 See Watt (1990). There were riots by brickmakers in Liverpool and Manchester in the 1840s.
30 See English (2019). The London and Greenwich Railway opened in 1836. The first part of what is now London Underground opened in 1863.

31 A steam train could cover 10 miles or more in half an hour. This, of course, meant that cities of 20-mile diameter were viable.
32 See Hicks (2017).
33 See Shirley (2019, p. 90).
34 From the 1880s, there were a large number of Jewish immigrants from Eastern Europe, particularly Russia. Historical restrictions on where Jews could live in Russia meant that they were more likely to be urban and to have urban professions, such as in the garment industry. It has also been argued, as in Weinryb (1955), that better transport led to exports of American grain to Europe, lowering prices and impoverishing the local populations, encouraging the pogroms that forced the Jewish population to leave.
35 The two big American mail-order catalogue companies were Sears and Wards. Both were based in Chicago. Chicago was, of course, a national railway hub. It made sense to be based there.
36 See Jones (1929).
37 See Boucekkine et al. (2007).
38 See Hall (1939). The diarist, Miss Weeton, recounts of a visit to the Isle of Man in 1812: "I met two men, who appeared for some time not to understand my question ... I called at a farm house. The woman within could not speak English".
39 See Dudley (2017).
40 See Tran and Valdez (2017). The poorer performance is partly due to a lack of bilingual infrastructure.
41 See McCann (2017).
42 See MacLeod (2017).
43 See Harpine (2005). Bryan typically travelled by private railcar, paid for by the local Democratic party.
44 See Trentmann (2016, p. 287).
45 See Francis (2013).
46 See Tou (1974, pp. 263–289).
47 See Keynes (1930).
48 See Worstall (2015).
49 Ibid.
50 See Autor (2015).
51 Gordon (2016) notes that working-class residents of smaller cities in the US did have small yards attached to their houses where they could grow food. Most people in US cities lived in houses rather than tenements. European cities and older US cities were more likely to have tenements, with several families living in one building. These people did not have access to land to grow their own food.
52 See Blake (1804).
53 See Kerley (n.d.).
54 The US horse population continued to increase in the 1890s but began to decline in the early 20th century.
55 See Cannon (2000).
56 See Gordon (2016, p. 451).
57 See Terkel (2004, pp. 282–285), interview with Babe Secoli.
58 See Holmes (2001).
59 See Packard (1961).
60 See Courtemanche et al. (2015).
61 See Gaskell (1833).
62 See Luce (2019).

3   The revolution has started

As the last chapter hopefully made clear, the effects of an industrial revolution ripple out beyond the initial, limited splash of new technology. Society experiences a series of significant changes. In considering the changes of the fourth industrial revolution, it would be a waste of time to concentrate on the specific technology. There are very few things that an economist can be certain about when it comes to technology, but the general way in which the fourth industrial revolution will influence social and economic trends is clear.

There is a fascinating aspect to the fourth industrial revolution. (At least, it is fascinating if you are an economist.) The ripple effects of the changes that are coming seem likely to reverse at least some of those of the previous three industrial revolutions. In some ways, the trends of 250 years are being uprooted. We are not going back to some pre-industrial age. However, the social structure and infrastructure of the future economy may have more in common with the time before the first industrial revolution than might be supposed. This may make the changes ahead even more dramatic. And that may make the reaction to the changes ahead even more dangerous.

Similarly to the last chapter, we will break down the changes of the fourth industrial revolution into employment, location and trade, communication, politics and other issues.

Employment

As with the past three industrial revolutions, the biggest change in the fourth industrial revolution is set to be the change to employment. It is, perhaps, inevitable that employment is the main story in a book focussed on labour-market prejudice, but it is the main story for all of us. Jobs matter In modern society, the job a person does is what sets their social status. The first industrial revolution tied social status and employment status more closely together. In the modern materialistic world, jobs pay the income that further sets social status. Income from jobs often sets our living standards. Conspicuous consumption is even more conspicuous in a world where cameras are everywhere. Instagram and Facebook feeds show photo after tedious photo of food, drink, clothes and holidays. When honestly come by, these things cost money. The fourth industrial revolution ties consumption (and thus income) to status even more than in the past. Who a person is should be about more than their job; but a person's job is still a big part of who the person is.

And now the robots are coming. And lots of people worry that robots will steal our jobs.

The fear that some combination of robots, artificial intelligence and automation will destroy most jobs is very, very common. In fact, this has been a persistent fear for at least two-and-a-half centuries. The Luddites smashed spinning machines because they were going to replace humans. They did replace humans. Even so, more people have jobs today than when the Luddites were breaking machinery. In 1964, US President Lyndon Johnson set up the 'blue-ribbon'[1] National Commission on Technology, Automation, and Economic Progress. This ponderously named body was created because President Johnson worried that automation was going to destroy jobs. The Commission, very sensibly, told him not to worry. Jobs were destroyed, but in the end, more people have jobs today than when the Commission was meeting.

Modern jobs are complex. The founder of modern economics, Adam Smith, famously wrote about the advantages of specialisation – specifically, breaking down the process for making a pin.[2] An individual doing one task again and again is likely to become good at that task – and so more efficient. Smith wrote approvingly of splitting pin-making into its different stages. In fact, he suggested 18 stages. Apparently, 18 things need to happen to make a pin. Having one person specialise in each of the stages should allow pins to be made more quickly and more cheaply. However, there is a problem. One person doing one task again and again is also likely to become very bored. That makes it difficult to keep them in employment. Most jobs today are not mind-numbingly repetitive tasks. Jobs are more complex than cutting the wire for a pin 48,000 times a day. People do multiple tasks. Those tasks are different. This collection of tasks is called a 'job'.

The past industrial revolutions have made today's jobs more complex. It is inefficient to have people do the same task again and again. Machines can and will perform repetitive tasks better than humans. The first pin-making machine came along in 1832.[3] From that point on, there was no longer any need to have people repeating one of 18 tasks 48,000 times a day. Thus, we have robots repeating the same tasks in factories. We have computers repeating the same tasks in offices. That robots and computers do the repetitive stuff does not mean humans are useless.

This means that before we give up and hand the planet over to our robot overlords, we should think about what is actually likely to change. The robots will not *take over* many jobs. The robots will *change* many jobs. This is an important difference. We need to separate a job into the different tasks that make the job what it is. If over half the tasks that are done in a job could be done more efficiently by a machine or artificial intelligence, then the overall job is more likely to be taken over by a robot or automated out of existence in some other way. However, it is also important to remember the positive: robots do not just take over or change jobs, they also create jobs.

Losing jobs

The fourth industrial revolution will threaten jobs when it makes economic sense for automation to replace a person. Automation is good at repetitive tasks. Jobs that have lots of repetitive tasks are threatened by automation. Economists estimate that over the next 20 years or so, perhaps 10–15% of jobs will be lost to automation.[4] These are the jobs that are likely to be directly lost as a result of the fourth industrial revolution.

Certain industries may be hit hard. In 1900, for example, two in every five working Americans worked on a farm. Today, fewer than two in every hundred working Americans work on a farm.[5] Automation of agriculture led to a collapse in agricultural employment. Agricultural workers had to move into new roles.[6] They also had to move to a new place. When one industry is hit hard by automation, a geographic area can suffer. Industries often cluster in certain geographic areas.

What sorts of job will be lost in the future? It is tempting to suggest that it is the low-skilled worker who will be affected. This is not necessarily true. Jobs at risk of automation tend to be defined by the routine nature of the work. A low-skilled job may deal with people. This job is likely to work *with* robots and automation, not be *replaced by* robots and automation. A semi-skilled job that is repetitive, like that of a legal clerk, can be automated away. Other office support functions are also considered to be high risk.[7] It is not just manufacturing jobs that perform repetitive tasks.

Sometimes the jobs that are lost may be subsets of a role. One question often asked is, 'What will happen to truck drivers?' Self-driving vehicles seem to suggest that truck driving is a bad career move. That may not be true, at least at first. Sure, long-haul truck driving across a country like the US could be replaced by self-driving vehicles. It is less likely that the complexities of delivering in a city will be automated away as quickly, however. Driving anything around the streets of a major city is not easy. It is not repetitive. It is a bit like the initial impact of railways on the demand for horses during the second industrial revolution. Similarly, some food-service jobs will be lost. Other food-service jobs will stay. Automated ordering in fast-food outlets is increasingly normal. However, it seems relatively unlikely that a robot will take your order at a Michelin-starred restaurant.

A problem is that some of the job losses will be concentrated in certain areas of society. This could be based on where people live. Industrial clusters (as with agriculture) have already been mentioned. A study by McKinsey warns that different regions of the US are clearly moving apart (economically speaking). The report estimates that automation could destroy over a quarter of all jobs in more than 500 counties of the US.[8] This is far worse than the 10–15% of jobs that will be automated away globally. These hard-hit counties are mainly rural. The job losses from automation are geographically focussed. That has implications for prejudice. It also has political implications, as the US electoral system is biased in favour of lower-population rural areas.

We have seen this happen before. In the first industrial revolution, northern England and Wales boomed at the expense of the south. In the third industrial revolution, the south boomed at the expense of northern England and Wales. In both industrial revolutions, certain sorts of job were clustered in certain areas. This was good for northern England and Wales in the 1790s. This was not so good for northern England and Wales in the 1970s.

Job losses may also be concentrated by skill level and age. Although it is not only lower-skilled jobs that are set to be lost in the fourth industrial revolution, it is more likely to be lower and low- to mid-skilled jobs that are lost. These jobs are more likely to have a lot of repetitive tasks that can be automated. In many countries, this will add to the geographic pattern of lost jobs. Lower-skilled workers tend to live in lower-cost areas. Lower-cost areas are hurt more by change. It is worth noting here that skills are not necessarily the same as education. Some of the skills required in the fourth industrial revolution can be taught. However, the flexibility that any industrial revolution needs is something that can be learned outside of the classroom.

Older workers may also suffer more from job losses. Younger workers are also likely to suffer from job losses. However, younger workers tend to find it easier to change. They have fewer things tying them to a location. They have invested less time in their careers. That makes it easier to accept the loss of investment that a change of job would mean. Younger workers may still lose jobs but should find it easier to adapt. They can get new jobs. Thus, while older and younger workers may both suffer from job losses, unemployment is more likely to be serious and long-lasting for older workers.

This concentration of job losses in certain parts of society is something that plays an important role in generating prejudice. We will explore this in the next chapter.

Job losses are not as simple as a robot marching in to replace a person. Job losses can be indirect. Digitisation has destroyed most of the retail-sales jobs associated with the music industry, for instance. People used to buy compact discs from shops. Now more than 70% of the world's music sales are digital.[9] The compact disc has become a relic. Technological change directly affected jobs making compact discs, as computers replaced people. Technological change directly affected jobs selling compact discs. Here, computers did not replace people; compact discs were just not sold anymore. In my youth, selling music was one of the most sought-after Saturday jobs for a teenager. Selling music naturally made someone cool by association. (I did not have a Saturday job selling music.) Despite all that, in most advanced economies, retail-sector jobs selling music have become highly specialised today. Jobs in music retail are all but destroyed.

The fact that, overall, a relatively limited number of jobs will disappear outright in the fourth industrial revolution does not minimise the impact of job losses on the people affected. Social status is affected by the loss of a job. Social status is hit by the loss of income and the loss of spending power. Sometimes, the job losses will be directly down to technology. But the indirect impacts are important, too. They are also less easily understood. Potentially, from the perspective of prejudice, the indirect impact is more important.

Changing jobs

The absolute loss of jobs will be very distressing to the people involved. The most important economic impact of technology on employment is not job losses, however, but job *changes*. Around half of the jobs that exist today are likely to *change* because of automation. It can help to think about this in terms of tasks rather than jobs. Some of the tasks that people currently do will disappear. But if robots or automation can do fewer than half the tasks that make up a job, that job will probably still exist. It will be different, but it will still be there.

I know this from experience. My job has changed radically over 30 years. Starting work as a junior economist covering Japan in the early 1990s, one of the most time-consuming tasks I had to do was to enter data from the Bank of Japan's monthly statistical bulletin into a Lotus 1-2-3 spreadsheet. It was time-consuming, repetitive and very boring, indeed. There was, however, no other way of being able to draw a chart of Japanese money supply. The data was simply not available in electronic form.

The idea of doing this nowadays is absurd. Today, the Bank of Japan's own website will allow you to download the same data in a fraction of a second. No economist has to manually enter numbers into a spreadsheet. The single most time-consuming task I was employed to do has disappeared. I am, however, still employed as an economist.

The role of an economist has changed and adapted. While we no longer have to spend hours entering data into spreadsheets, we do have the ability to analyse more data than ever before. There are more opportunities and ever more need for economists to communicate. Economists now spend time on social media. This is a new task for economists (and they are not necessarily very good at it).[10] It was not possible for an economist to tweet in the early 1990s, because Twitter did not exist in the early 1990s. It is possible for economists to tweet today.[11] Thus, while some tasks economists used to do have disappeared, other tasks have taken their place. The job of economist still exists, but it is not the same as it was.

This does not mean that the change is easy for the people who have to change. People do not generally like change that much. But it is wrong to suggest that if robots take over one task, people have nothing to do. People will carry on doing some of the tasks that they do today. People can learn new tasks to earn a living. People will need to change with changing times. If people *fail* to change, their job will still exist, but they are unlikely to be doing it for much longer.

Changing jobs may mean a change in what someone does for their job (different tasks). It may also mean changing the way in which one gets their income. There are new(ish) ways of earning income. This is sometimes referred to as the 'gig economy'. It may mean having more than one job, several different careers, different income streams, contract work, agency work or zero-hours contracts. In fact, like many made-up words associated with economics, the 'gig economy' means whatever one wants it to mean. For the purposes of economics, it can be assumed to mean a changing way of working.

In a changing economy, it is possible for people to have many careers, not just one. My grandfather worked as a warehouseman for one company for his entire life. After the second industrial revolution, this was not very unusual.[12] People had one job and they carried on doing that job. This approach is less sensible in a world where tasks may be automated away and jobs will change. Having more than one job could be a good insurance policy.

Having multiple jobs, or multiple sources of income, was quite normal in times past. Single careers are unusual, historically speaking. Before the first industrial revolution, and even after it, it was quite normal for people to have several different jobs. In a family, the man (typically) might work at one career, have some investment income and, with the help of his wife, take in lodgers to earn an additional income.

In the UK today, about 3.5% of workers have a second paid job. The number moves between 3.5% and 4.0%. That seems quite low, albeit at a time of full employment.[13] The reality is that more people have more than one income stream. We have to question what a 'job' is. The fourth industrial revolution is changing our ideas. A global study across developed economies suggests that between 20% and 30% of people have independent work. Independent work may be selling goods online, or offering accommodation, for example.[14] The family offering rooms for let in the 19th century is today's Airbnb host. This gives a different income stream but would not normally be classed as a job in official surveys.

This is a good example of how economic data fails to capture the changes in an industrial revolution. The way people think about 'jobs' is not necessarily the same as 'employment that earns an income'. Selling on eBay is 'employment that earns an income' (assuming you do it correctly). But 'eBay seller' does not necessarily appear in economic data on employment. Today's economic data is stuck in the world of the second industrial revolution. The multiple incomes of the fourth industrial revolution reverse some of the social and economic effects of the second industrial revolution.

Multiple income streams did survive the first industrial revolution, albeit in a somewhat battered form.[15]

Independent work can also be contract work. There are also 'jobs' (in the sense of employment earning an income) for car-ride services, courier companies and so forth. Often these jobs have no set hours. In some economies, zero-hours contracts are also an independent form of work (where there is no commitment on the hours a person will work in a week). Zero-hours contracts remain a very small part of the workforce, however. They are also more concentrated among students, who are earning while studying.

None of these ways of working is necessarily new. There have always been short-term, flexible jobs in the economy. My family's work in the London docks a century ago was contracted on a daily basis, with no certainty of employment the following day. What the technology of the fourth industrial revolution is doing is changing the ease with which these jobs can be done. It is a lot easier for employers to find the right sort of labour, with the right level of skills. It is a lot easier for workers to find offers of work. The costs for both sides are a lot lower than they used to be. It is logical for there to be more 'independent work' than in the past.

A lot of the independent work means self-employment.[16] This may be self-employment alongside paid employment. (For example, I have paid employment as an economist and self-employment as an author and a farmer.) It may be the more traditional 'freelance' work, where a self-employed person chooses to work a series of fixed contracts. Self-employment has grown rapidly in several economies. In the UK, the proportion of older workers in self-employment has seen a significant increase.

The final aspect of changing jobs that is worth mentioning is the change in location. This will be covered more in the trade and location section, but the new ways of working may mean working outside the office. This changes how people interact with colleagues. It can make it easier for some people to work. The cost of commuting, in terms of both time and money, could fall to zero. When I work at home, I do not have to pay roughly GBP 5 to stand on a London Underground train for half an hour to get to the office. My commute when working from home requires me to stumble from bedroom to home office in 10 seconds. The Covid-19 pandemic is likely to accelerate this location shift. While public health concerns forced people to work from home where they could, the crisis also prompted companies to look at shifting to home working over the longer term.[17]

There are potential negatives to changing job location. This can create tensions when some people work in the office in a 'second industrial revolution' manner, and some people work outside the office. Unless carefully managed, the two types of workers may resent each other. There is also a risk of home workers being 'always on' and losing the boundaries between personal and professional life. It is harder to 'clock out' when working from home. This is another way in which the changes take us back to the social patterns of the pre-industrial period.

Changing jobs in the fourth industrial revolution is likely to make people worry about the future. This is particularly true for workers who have enjoyed job security in the past. The changing nature of work is another important factor in the rise of prejudice.

Keeping jobs

Amid the fear of automation and a future robot dictatorship, it is worth noting that just because a job can be done by a robot, there is no guarantee that it will. Economically, people will pay to be able to deal with other people. Coffee shows this very clearly. Coffee vending machines have been around for more than 70 years. Modern coffee vending machines can make high-quality cups of coffee, yet the number of coffee baristas in the US has continued to increase. The pay of coffee baristas in the US has continued to increase.[18] Why is this? Because while it is perfectly possible to automate the process of making a cup of coffee, that is not what people want to pay for. Customers at coffee shops are paying for human interaction – for the brief conversation, their names being misspelled on the side of a paper cup, and so on. Coffee shops could simply be spaces with sofas and sophisticated vending machines, but they would almost certainly be economic failures.

Creating jobs

Industrial revolutions do create jobs. The first industrial revolution factory system introduced shift work. In a world before alarm clocks, someone was paid to go around and knock on workers' windows to wake them up. That was a new job. The second industrial revolution created car manufacturers, mechanics and salespeople. Car accessories were made and sold. Fuel was sold. These were new jobs. The third industrial revolution invented computer programmers. The new jobs started out using the language of the second revolution. The people (mainly women) working computers were 'machine operators'. Employment changed faster than language. The fourth industrial revolution is likely to be no different. The technology of the fourth industrial revolution will create jobs both directly and indirectly.

Direct job creation basically means new jobs. Technology creates new products. Those new products will have new jobs associated with them. The job of app designer was unimaginable 20 years ago. Apps did not exist, so how could they be designed? In 2018, the median app programmer earned over a USD 100,000 a year.[19] The new jobs directly created by technology are likely to require relatively high levels of skills. The jobs may be creative or mathematical – but they are unlikely to be low-skilled, repetitive tasks. A low-skilled repetitive job is more likely to be destroyed by the fourth industrial revolution.

Most people agree that new jobs will be created. It is hard to argue with the evidence that new jobs are being created. The fear that is most often heard is that 'there will not be enough new jobs created'. This was US President Johnson's fear. It was the fear of the 19th-century Luddites. There is no evidence that this has ever been true. In 1980, 8.5% of Americans were doing jobs that did not exist in 1965.[20] In 1990, 8.2% of Americans were doing jobs that did not exist in 1977. The third industrial revolution created new jobs that were simply not thought of in 1965. In 2000, 4.4% of American workers were in jobs not recorded in 1990.[21] The 1990s were a less dramatic period of change. Change happened, but economists would not generally say this was a revolutionary period. Therefore, fewer people were working in newly invented jobs.

Technology therefore can directly create a number of new jobs. Past periods of revolution have led to substantially more than 8% of people working in new industries. This is not a small number. Of course, we have to set the new jobs in past revolutions against the idea that 10–15% of jobs will be lost through automation in the years ahead. Those are the jobs in which at least half of the tasks can be automated away. Assuming the new jobs that are directly created are similar to past revolutions, the direct effects of the fourth industrial revolution may leave a number of people out of work.

Industrial revolutions do not only create new jobs directly, however. More jobs are created indirectly. These are types of jobs that already exist (not newly created by technology). Indirect job creation happens in two ways.

The first form of indirect job creation comes from changes in consumer behaviour. Changing consumption patterns will create more jobs in existing professions. Hotels and coaching inns existed long before the second industrial revolution. As cars increased travel, the demand for roadside accommodation increased. That increased employment in what economists call the 'lodging' category, such as motels. Technology indirectly created these jobs, and they were not necessarily high-skilled jobs. Today, the automation of the fourth industrial revolution is increasing employment in warehouses, for example. Companies like Amazon do use robots in their warehouses. However, they still rely on humans as part of the distribution system. Humans are better at certain tasks. Humans are more cost-effective at certain tasks. As e-commerce grows, retail jobs will be destroyed, but the technology of computer programming and e-commerce will indirectly create warehousing jobs.

Similarly, social media and the sharing economy have created new incomes for people. Podcasters are paid to advertise to listeners. Instagram influencers are paid to promote products to their followers. As mentioned earlier, people have independent income from letting out their spare rooms. These may not be jobs in the way of the second industrial revolution. People do not 'clock in' and 'clock out' of a place of work. But this is not the second industrial revolution anymore. In the modern economy, the fact that people can earn money as entrepreneurs is a job. It is not a particularly new job – product endorsement certainly predates the first industrial revolution. King Louis XVI and Queen Marie Antoinette of France were early product endorsers, even without the advantages of an Instagram account. (They promoted potatoes.)[22] The technology of the fourth industrial revolution is making advertising or letting accommodation easier to do. If it is easier to do, more people will do it. This grows employment in the advertising and accommodation sectors.

The second way jobs are created indirectly is through demand. This is not about the direct impact of technology, but the impact of the industrial revolution on economic output and the incomes of some people. As long as technology raises real economic output – either by lowering prices or by increasing output – there will be more income in the economy. The distribution of that income may be uneven; that is a separate problem. However distributed, more income means more spending. That will raise demand for anything that has positive income elasticity. (Positive income elasticity means people spend more on it as their income goes up.)

This also means that there may be more jobs in the very industry that is being automated. If automation lowers the cost of production of something, the price should go down. If the price goes down, people can afford to buy more. If they buy a lot more as the price goes down, higher demand will create jobs even as technology destroys jobs. The balance between creation and destruction depends on the extent to which demand changes and on how job-destructive the technology is.[23]

The tension in creating jobs in an industrial revolution is that the new jobs may need different skills from what the jobs that have been lost would have required. If you cannot change, the creation of new jobs is not of much use. The situation is little different from the fate of the unemployed spinners in the south of England in the first industrial revolution. The women lacked the flexibility to take the new jobs in northern mills.

Employment in the fourth industrial revolution

What matters for jobs in the fourth industrial revolution is less the actual job losses. Some jobs will disappear. In the long term, the losses are likely to be in fairly manageable numbers. New jobs and greater employment in existing jobs will offer new employment opportunities. What matters in the jobs market of the fourth industrial revolution is that jobs themselves will change. This means that the ability to change – the ability to be flexible – is hugely important.

The story of employment set out here perhaps has more in common with the labour markets of the 18th than the 20th century. We are moving to a world with more self-employment. A world with more flexibility of working – not necessarily clocking in and clocking out every day. A world where income is earned by doing something not conventionally considered a job. The security of employment weakens. My grandfather had a lot of certainty about his job, at least later on in his life. That certainty is increasingly rare today.

The employment story matters a very great deal in the story of prejudice. The new employment of the fourth industrial revolution is focussed on status changes and insecurity. People lose status if they lose their jobs. People lose relative status as new jobs (better than theirs) are created. People lose or gain relative status as the tasks they do in their job change. People become less secure as the way of working shifts. Historically, there is nothing very unusual about any of this. It is a problem for those who grew up expecting the stability and security of the 'Fordism' model that emerged from the second industrial revolution. That is where the risk of prejudice comes from.

Location and trade

The fourth industrial revolution is doing a lot to change where things happen. Where we work, where we consume and where things are made – all of these are starting to change. This has implications for the structure of individual economies and societies. It also has implications for the structure of the global economy and society.

Where we work

Technology is freeing jobs from being tied to a physical location. This is not something that applies to all jobs, of course. Some jobs need people to be in a certain place at a certain time. But economies have become more service-sector based in recent years. It is suggested that nearly half the population of the Irish capital, Dublin, and its surroundings 'telecommute'.[24] Commuting times in Dublin are horrible. Working from home cuts the wasted time of travelling to work. This use of technology to work from home changes both transport and building needs.

For someone who has the option to work from home for most of their job, the decision to live in a city becomes a lifestyle choice. In past industrial revolutions, people wanted reasonable commuting times. Changing transport technology increased the distance one could travel, allowing cities to get larger. But it was generally still necessary to live in the same city as one's job. If a person can work from home, the commuting time becomes (basically) zero. The 10-second stumble from bedroom to home office rarely requires much transport infrastructure. Since 2014, the number of vehicles paying London's Congestion Charge to travel into or around central London has been falling. In 2014, the average was nearly 70,000 vehicles per day. In 2019, it was fewer than 50,000. The charge targets peak commuting hours for work. Of course, this does not mean that 20,000 people per day are working from home. There are alternative modes of transport that people may be using. But at a time when London has had a rising population, it is at least indicative that technology is changing working patterns and, through that, transport.[25]

If a person can work from home, the demand for real estate shifts. There is less need for the additional workspace that inspired the construction boom (and changes to brickmaking) of the first industrial revolution. Just as working from home returns the economy to a pre-industrial pattern of working, so too it returns us to a more pre-industrial pattern of building demand. In the extreme case of someone working from home all the time, there is no need for office space at all. If a company has people working from home part of the time, flexible or agile working can reduce the amount of office space required. The number of people employed by the company per square metre of floor space will go up, because the assumption is that a significant number of employees will be working outside of the office at any moment in time. It is not that firms are forcing people to work closer together (although there is some aspect of that as well); technology allows for smaller offices. Fewer (or smaller) office buildings are therefore required.

One aspect of this location shift is that economic data gets it wrong again. Someone working from home will provide their own office space, desk, chair, internet connection, electricity and heating. The company will not have to provide any of those things, or (if people work in the office some of the time) will have to provide fewer of those things. If a person buys a desk for their home office, it is almost certainly classed as consumer spending. If a company buys a desk, it is investment spending. Working from home means that the official data on investment in an economy will fall. In fact, things are just being used more efficiently. Before the fourth industrial revolution, a worker could have a desk at home that was unused most of the day. But they would also have a desk at the office that was unused for up to six days a week. (A desk in a traditional office is normally occupied for around 24 hours a week.)[26] Working from home full time would mean only one desk would be needed, not two. The output of the worker is unaffected by having only one desk.

The willingness and ability to work from home is not just a matter of what job someone does. The culture of a country (or a company) can impact whether flexible working becomes the norm. In 1991, at the start of my career, I was an intern for a Japanese financial company in Tokyo. The culture of the company (and much of the economy) was that you did not leave until your boss had left. This was not a rule I followed. The idea of *presenteeism* – of being seen to be at work, often for longer than necessary – can be powerful. There is also a social aspect to working. When I started in the financial markets, people still went out to lunch on a regular basis. Not being in an office would mean missing out. The London culture of lunching seems to have faded, helping the UK to adopt flexible working. But that culture does linger in other economies.

The fourth industrial revolution may finally free us from living near the office. But the fourth industrial revolution does impact where we live in other ways. Telecommuting requires internet access, for example. It is becoming more and more common for home buyers to check the speed of internet access before buying a property. The cost of housing is also being affected by the fourth industrial revolution. Evidence from Europe and the US suggests that the arrival of Airbnb to a location will increase rents in the neighbourhood. Landlords appear to prefer short-term lets over longer-term tenants.[27]

Where we consume

If the location of where people work changes, consumption patterns change. People working from home will shop differently (certainly for food and maybe for other items). Lunch is no longer a trip to a nearby sandwich shop, but more likely to be made at home. That part of the retail industry that caters to office workers is likely to be reduced if working from home continues to become more common. Working from home can also simplify one of the other big location changes that arises from the fourth industrial revolution: the rise of online shopping. As online shopping requires delivery, working from home makes that a lot easier to arrange.

Shopping as a leisure activity (loosely defined) was an invention of the first industrial revolution. People like potter Josiah Wedgwood (who we heard talk of a "revolution" in the business of making cups and plates in Chapter 2) pioneered shopping as fun. Before industrialisation, buying things was something servants of the middle and upper classes did. The poor rarely bought anything at all. Wedgewood and others got the growing middle class to visit shops in person. Serving tea to the middle class in a tea service they could buy, while a string quartet played in the background, was innovative. Shopping as a leisure activity continued to spread. The shopping mall is not an American invention. The Burlington Arcade in London was built in 1819, and it still exists.

As industrialisation spread, the cost of buying things declined. The time or inclination to make things at home declined. Consumers of all income groups bought more and more of what they needed, and that meant more and more shops. Shopping was not just a fun thing to do. Shopping was also a chore to get what was needed. When the middle class had servants, the servants could do the boring stuff. The middle class could still pursue shopping for leisure purposes. As the supply of servants started to fall at the end of the second industrial revolution, the chore of shopping became universal. Other domestic tasks performed by servants could be automated away (or made substantially less labour-intensive). Shopping could not be automated very easily. A maid could clean and shop. You cannot send a dishwasher out to buy bread.

The internet has changed this, of course. Where shopping is a chore, the internet steps in. The internet acts in the way the servants of the middle class did 100 years ago. The pace of consuming online has varied from country to country. Logistics do make a difference. The competitive advantage of a physical shop is instant gratification. You can buy something and take it home to consume immediately. A country like the UK is relatively well suited to delivering goods in a short space of time. Twenty-four-hour delivery reduces the competitive advantage of instant gratification in a physical shop. The US has the challenge of larger geography. In 2019, UK online retail sales hovered around 19% of total retail sales, rising to more than 20% in the Christmas shopping period. Korea's online retail sales are 24% of all retail sales. US online retail sales are around 11% and Australia's are around 9%.[28]

Just as catalogue shopping changed American consumer spending in the 19th century, so the rise of online retail sales is changing today's retail landscape. Just as in the 19th century, this requires financial changes. The credit or debit card is key to buying online. This financial innovation is also dependent on technology.

Buying online means not being able to see and touch the goods before buying. This can make it hard for the consumer to decide what to buy. When Amazon just sold books, this was not necessarily a huge problem. As a physical product, a book is fairly standardised. The quality of the content is not something a reader can understand by stroking the cover. As online retailing now sells a wider and wider range of products, not being able to see and feel the product before it is purchased may be a problem. This is again increasing the power of the brand – by two routes. Either the product makers need to build a brand as a trustworthy, high-quality company, or the online store needs to build a reputation as a trustworthy retailer that will deal with any product-related issues.

This means that changing where we consume things is yet again increasing the power of branding. It is possible to argue that this is fuelling the rise in Instagram influencers and other social-media advertisers. People believe that they 'know' the people they see online (something we will cover in more depth in Chapter 5). As a result, they trust their product endorsements as a 'word-of-mouth' recommendation. They may well know that the endorser is being paid for the endorsement, but they ignore it. The brand is built and online sales gain ground. The technology that creates online sales will create brand-building 'jobs'.

Changing the location of retail sales to the online world will cost jobs in old-fashioned retail. This is often viewed as a crisis by the media. Stories about the destruction of town centres sell newspapers. They appeal to the sense of insecurity that the way of life we know is changing. The way of life we know *is* changing. It is changing in a very visible way. People notice when shops close. But one of the reasons shops are closing is that people do not like taking time to shop for the boring stuff. There are other arguments about pricing and whether online retailers have an unfair advantage (either through tax payments, or the lack thereof, or by using their size as buyers to get lower prices from suppliers). Even so, this does not mean there will be no shops in future. Rather, the pattern of consumption is changing back to mirror that of the 18th century.

It seems plausible that the future of retail will be far more online. Goods may be purchased direct from suppliers (with strong brands). Alternatively, they will be purchased from online retailers whose branding gives customers the confidence to buy products without seeing them first. But this shopping is likely to be the 'chore' shopping. There is still room for shopping in physical stores where that form of shopping is a leisure activity. The weekly food shopping may be done online, but that does not mean you cannot visit an artisanal cheese shop or speciality delicatessen on the weekend. Thus, independent bookstores have been increasing in number in the UK (slowly, and only recently), despite the ease of buying books online. Independent bookstores try to entice people by offering more than just books. Coffee shops are common in US bookstores. In the UK, bookstores are obtaining licences to serve alcohol.[29] Buying a copy of this book could turn out to be a pleasant leisure activity, undertaken in a real-world book shop – if accompanied by a glass of wine.[30]

Jobs are created in online retail, lost in 'chore' retail and possibly created in what might be termed 'leisure' retail. Retail employment in the US as a share of total employment has fallen from its peak in 1987. But there are *more* people employed in the retail sector than there were 10 years ago (this includes online retail). It is just that employment in retail is growing more slowly than employment in the economy as a whole. The growth in the number of people employed comes despite the increase in online retail market share.[31]

The retail situation, again, returns to the 18th century – with the internet replacing the servants of the middle class.

Where things are made

The employment section of this chapter noted that jobs in the service sector were shifting with the rise of home working. Where services are performed is changing. But it is also true that where things are manufactured is changing. One of the most obvious ways this is happening has already been introduced: entertainment is being manufactured in the home. Entertainment was historically made in the home (singing around the family piano, for instance). Today, the process is a little different.

Streaming and downloading entertainment converts what was a manufactured product into a service. This shift from good to service is yet another problem for economic data to capture. But most people no longer buy manufactured music products. Fifteen years ago, when music was bought, it was made all over the world. While the intellectual property of the music itself could come from the UK, the compact disc might be made in one country, with the components coming from another. The plastic casing could be made in yet another country, using plastics made from raw materials from several countries. The paper insert could be printed in a different country. And then the product would be shipped back to the UK to be sold. Today, the user 'makes' the music by downloading or streaming it at home. The compact disc is now produced in the home, just without the compact disc.

The entertainment industry tipped into localised production as soon as the technology allowed. This led to an upheaval and more employment change. Music retailer HMV failed twice as music moved online and streaming replaced downloads. A chart comparing the revenues of the video rental store Blockbuster with the revenues of the video streaming company Netflix is quite famous in investing circles. (For non-investors, the chart is fairly obvious: Blockbuster's revenue started to fall sharply in 2008 and collapsed in 2010; the company failed in 2013. Netflix's revenue continued to move higher throughout this period).

The abruptness with which the entertainment industry shifted to 'local production' is worth bearing in mind. The idea that we can make everything at home with a *Star Trek*-style replicator machine seems like a science-fiction fantasy.[32] However, it is possible to imagine a future shopper buying and downloading computer code that they send to a 3D printer in the basement. The printer could then make the desired product. We already do this with entertainment, after all. In this scenario, a physical product is the end result. That means the raw material used by the 3D printer would have to be brought in from outside. Otherwise, manufacturing is now a cottage industry again.

Printing in the basement (or any other room) is possible. It may not be a good idea in terms of cost. People will have to think about the capital cost of acquiring a printer, the cost of printing an object and how many different objects can be produced. Small-scale home production may not make sense. But one does not have to scale up much. Technology is allowing more and more things to be made locally. Onshoring is on.

There are two key reasons technology is encouraging onshoring or local production: cost and small-scale production. Here, the clothing and textile industry provides an interesting case study. Where our clothes were made was subject to radical change in the first three industrial revolutions. It is likely to be subject to radical change in the fourth industrial revolution, too. The first revolution shifted thread production from homes to factories. The second revolution shifted clothing production from homes to factories. The third industrial revolution shifted clothing production from close to the consumer to low-cost economies.

The outsourcing of the third industrial revolution led to a dramatic decline in clothing production in advanced economies. Only where there was a quality brand did clothing cling on (Italian fashion, Savile Row suits). As the last chapter showed, the US clothing industry was effectively wiped out by 2012. The reason was that clothing was still a relatively labour-intensive industry. Lower labour costs meant lower prices. Lower prices meant more sales. Producing in low-cost (generally Asian) economies was viable. The computers of the third industrial revolution made controlling long and complex supply chains easier to do. However, that competitive advantage starts to fade with further automation.

The first reason technology encourages onshoring is cost. It is difficult to completely automate the sewing process. Robots are not particularly good at sewing. They are getting better but are not there yet. However, other elements of making clothes are easier to automate. And as more and more of the process becomes automated, it makes less and less sense to outsource just the sewing part to a low-cost country. For the non-sewing part of the industry automation removes the advantages of lower labour costs. Producing locally then significantly reduces transport costs. Conceivably, it can lower the cost of movements in the currency markets.[33] It can also reduce the cost of reputational damage. Outsourcing reduces the control a company has over environmental and labour-market practices. If something goes wrong in either of those areas, it can do a lot of damage to a company's brand. Arguably, technology may be increasing the cost of reputational damage. Technology increases the importance and the visibility of the brand. If bringing production closer to home increases control, it reduces the risk of future costs to the brand.

The other advantage of producing locally is that production can quickly respond to changes in demand. This is one reason clothing is moving to onshore production. To generalise, most manufacturers have labour as their largest cost. But the second-largest cost is inventory – the stock of unsold stuff. If a manufacturer overestimates demand, they are left with a lot of unsold stuff (which is a loss). If a manufacturer underestimates demand, they are left with unsatisfied customers (and less profit than they might have made). The problem with outsourcing is that while it may incur lower labour costs, it increases inventory risks. It can take six weeks to ship goods from Asia to Europe; on the other hand, it can take two days or less to ship goods from Europe to Europe. The ability to respond very quickly to changes in demand lowers risk. It lowers the costs associated with that risk. This lowers the price. At an extreme, the response to demand can be personalised. Thanks to technology, it is almost as cheap to buy a made-to-measure T-shirt as it is to buy a generically sized T-shirt from the mass retailer Gap.[34]

What automation does is reduce enough of the labour costs to make onshoring at least a viable option. Clothing production is starting to increase in the UK, Europe and the US. Jobs are created in these economies. Jobs are potentially lost in the low-cost labour economies. The number of jobs created through onshoring is likely to be far lower than the number of jobs lost. The point of automation is that labour-intensive work overseas is replaced with capital-intensive work locally.

Other industries also benefit from the lower costs of automation, of course. My local village has fewer than 1,000 residents, but it supports its own baker. The baker is an automated robot that sits in a room behind the convenience store. It bakes bread several times a day. The shop has less waste, as the supply of bread can respond to daily changes in demand. Transport costs are lower. (Bread is relatively heavy and bulky to transport. Flour and yeast are lighter and take up far less space than bread).

The second reason technology is shifting where things are made is that technology may be making it easier to be a small-scale manufacturer. The entertainment industry has taken this to extremes. But in other areas, the fourth industrial revolution is making it easier to be a small business.

Manufacturers can sell directly to the public. The options for building a brand via social media have increased. What used to be called 'word-of-mouth' advertising can now 'go viral' to a far larger audience, far more quickly than in the past. Inventory management and cost control are easier to achieve with modern technology. There is evidence that small businesses have improved their inventory cost control significantly in the last decade.[35]

For a small business, there are more incentives to produce locally. There are costs to managing overseas production (negotiating, legal fees and travel costs). A company with a turnover of less than USD 10 million is more likely to keep production close to its customers.[36] If the fourth industrial revolution does lead to the creation of more small-scale manufacturers, those manufacturers are more likely to be local. The location of global production starts to shift.

Trade – the return of the imperial model?

As technology starts to change production, it will change trade. The outsourcing of the third industrial revolution encouraged an explosion of globalisation. This was a very different sort of trade from the past, however. In the late 20th century, global trade rose dramatically as a share of the world economy. But most of this trade was not between countries. Most of this trade was inside *companies*. A company would have subsidiaries around the world and move parts between those subsidiaries. Most of the world's trade takes place inside these multinational companies.

This is why the introduction of new trade taxes (or 'tariffs') in recent years is often resisted by local producers. A tax on imports into the US hurts a US manufacturer that uses those imports as part of their production process. As supply chains have become longer and more complicated, taxing trade does not necessarily help the local industry. Badly constructed trade taxes could easily make things a lot worse for local manufacturers.

As technology changes where we produce, the pattern of trade is likely to change. In the past the outsourcing trend made supply chains more global and more complex. Each supply chain had more links in it as time went on. Any move to onshoring reverses that. The trade of the future is more likely to follow what might be called the 'imperial model' of trade. During the first industrial revolution and much of the second industrial revolution, trade was about importing raw materials to make things locally. Often those raw materials came from a colonial empire. Finished goods were then exported. All of the parts for the finished goods would be manufactured locally, however.

The modern imperial model will be a variation on that. Raw materials would still be imported. Intellectual property would also be imported.

Music for a download, computer code to run a 3D printer, or the pattern to be used in cutting out a suit are all intellectual property that can be traded. The actual production combines raw materials, intellectual property and automation in a process that takes place close to the consumer.

This is still disruptive. The modern imperial model will cost jobs that service the global supply chain. Container shipping may not be a growth industry. There may be more transport jobs in local distribution. Manufacturers that have to export (because they make more than their local market can absorb) may need to restructure. That will cause more disruption in the labour market.

Location and trade in the fourth industrial revolution

We are already seeing technology start to disrupt location and trade. We are not going to go to a future where everyone works from home. There will always be jobs that require people to come together. But economies today have larger service sectors. That gives a lot more flexibility to a lot more workers. Companies, culture and the workers themselves will all have to be flexible to take advantage of this. Changing location may mean less trade. Localisation of production is already happening. The imperial model of the 18th century does seem to be making a comeback. Trade in raw materials must continue. Trade in intellectual property becomes a lot more important. Trade in manufactured products becomes a lot less important.

Therefore, globalisation of trade may have peaked. This does not mean globalisation is dead. Communication has globalised in a way we have never seen before.

Communication

Communication is probably the most immediately visible change of the fourth industrial revolution. People hunched over smartphones are one of the biggest obstacles to walking down a street. The feverish scrabble to turn on a smartphone as soon as a plane has landed shows our addiction to modern communication. This change is something that has significant implications for the development of prejudice.

The ripples of the fourth industrial revolution have made several obvious changes to the way we communicate. Communication is faster. It is potentially more visual. It is certainly more global. But communication is also potentially more anonymous. An economist would also say that while the barriers to entry to receiving information have come down, the barriers to entry to communicating information may have increased.

Faster communication

Each industrial revolution has increased the speed with which information travels around the world. The fourth industrial revolution is no exception.

When I started work in the financial markets in the early 1990s, daily mass communication to clients was by fax. The original copy of the fax was sent to an external bureau. The fax bureau had the technology (many fax machines) to enable mass distribution. Even with this, it still took time for every client to receive the information. Remarkably, if the fax was delayed, clients would telephone to ask where it was. This is a method of communication that must seem almost medieval to the younger generation in financial markets. Today, my daily mass communication is through email, websites, social media and podcasts. An iPad will accomplish nearly all of this in seconds. I rarely get called about unsent emails.

Getting the news first has always mattered in the financial markets. Dairnvaell's 'Rothschild libel', mentioned in Chapter 1, was all about getting information quickly by carrier pigeons and fast-sailing ships. The fact that it was not true does not disguise the importance of speed to the financial markets. Each industrial revolution since the Battle of Waterloo has increased the financial importance of speed. In 2012, a trader in London, dealing in Chicago, was at a disadvantage. Their trade was at least 0.04 seconds behind the market. That is how long it took to transmit and receive the information, before accounting for additional router delays.[37] Even now, algorithms run by computers that are physically closer to the market can trade faster and have a competitive advantage. The speed of communication, in financial markets at least, has actually increased the need for localisation. If every nanosecond counts, every metre counts.

Fast communication can also change the quality of communication. This is basic economics. There is a cost to writing a letter. Writing letters takes time. A letter writer is likely to write about things that matter and is likely to think about the content. Automation led to junk email – mass-produced letters or circulars with little content value. The internet, however, led to spam email. In 2010, it was estimated that 88% of emails sent were spam.[38] Spam email costs money. People and firms pay other people to develop software to stop spam. Email providers spend a lot of money employing people to stop spam. (Communication technology creates new jobs to protect us from the abuse of the new communication technology.) The spam that does get through takes time to delete.

The ease and speed of communication reduce the amount of thinking that goes into non-spam communication. A study suggested that it commonly took less than two minutes to reply to an email.[39] Older users take longer to reply to emails. The difference between those in their 50s and those in their teens is significant. Older people take more than three times as long to reply. This may in part be due to the sort of technology used. People reply to email over mobile phones far faster than they do when writing on a computer. The more email people receive, the more they check their inbox, and the faster they reply. But it may also be the social norms. Older people are used to writing letters and taking time over them. I had to memorise how to write a formal letter for my English O-level exams (state exams typically taken around the age of 16). It was all about knowing when to sign off 'Yours sincerely', when to use 'Yours faithfully'[40] and where to put commas. It took time to do. That meant the content of the letter had to be worth the time it took to write the letter.

The fact that the reaction to a communication is now so fast has created the 'viral' message or story. American political activist Cleve Jones has talked of viral communication in the third industrial revolution:

> This was pre-internet, and yet I was able to turn out thousands of people within an hour or two just by going to a payphone with a pocketful of dimes with a list of people. And I would call everyone and ask them each to call 10 people, and they would each call 10 people. It was incredibly effective.[41]

The model was what is known as a telephone tree.

While an impressive political tool in its day, the telephone tree is nothing compared to modern communication speeds. The telephone tree took time – calls had to be made and conversations repeated. The modern viral message can be sent rapidly over email and social media with little repetition to a far larger audience. Jones had to know the people he called in the first instance. An 'influencer' posting on Instagram cannot possibly know more than a tiny fraction of their followers. To retweet or repost a comment does not require thought. It can be an accidental slip of the finger.

Truth may also be one of the first casualties of a viral retweet. A viral message spreads out faster and further if it is 'fake news'. 'Fake news' here means something that is not true. Analysis of 12 years of Twitter activity shows that 'fake news' is around 70% more likely to be retweeted than actual news. 'Fake news' is retweeted more often. And 'fake news' is spread significantly faster than the truth. This is particularly true of fake political 'news'. Fake political 'news' will reach 20,000 people three times faster than a true political story reaches 10,000 people.[42] The analysis also shows that 'fake news' tends to be new information. People are interested in new information, so pass it on. 'Fake news' tends to lead to responses of surprise and disgust. These are powerful emotions that people often want to share.[43] Although not tested in the analysis, anyone with even a passing knowledge of the UK media might add that sensationalism sells. 'Fake news' can be put into sensational language. This becomes what is known as 'click bait'. If the author is not worried about the truth, it is easy to sensationalise the story. That attracts readers and speeds up the sharing of the story.

The fact that the fourth industrial revolution encourages faster and broader communication and that it is especially good at telling lies obviously has significant implications for any work that looks at prejudice.

Visual communication

The fact that every smartphone is a camera and video recorder has also changed communication. Communication is more visual than in the past.

There is a potential threat in this. Many people today have been brought up to believe what they see on television. There is trust in 'the evidence of your own eyes'. Technology is now catching up with that. It is increasingly possible to change video images in a way that will distort what is shown. When combined with the viral speed of communication (which allows little time to question whether what is being shown is realistic), this can produce a strong reaction. That is potentially dangerous, particularly in emotional areas like prejudice.

Images have power. People understand them quickly. In 2006, the government of Bahrain blocked Google Earth.[44] The satellite images allowed the local population to compare land owned by ordinary Bahrainis and land owned by the elite. The comparisons led to protests at a time of housing shortages. The differences in land ownership were nothing new. Rather, it was the visibility of the differences and the fact that the comparison was very simple to understand that led to the protests.

There are clear positives from a world where visual communication is the norm. The Peek Vision organisation uses videos in smartphones to conduct sight tests.[45] The tests do not need to be done by a health professional. The app shows the tester the difference between normal vision and the vision of the person being tested. The technology is using visual communication to conduct the test. It is also using visual communication to stress the results of the test. In schools, this is powerful. Teachers can see and understand the problem of their student's poor eyesight. A standard eye test is time-consuming and requires a professional. Key people like teachers may be unaware of how bad the problem may be. Visual communication changes that. The impact on human capital could be huge. Catching problems with vision early on can change a child's education.

Global communication

It is also worth acknowledging the globalisation of communication. In the early 1990s, travel abroad left me cut off from friends and family at home in the UK. Calls would be from hotel phones at prearranged times. The introduction of mobile phones did little to change that. European and US travel involved a complicated juggling of different phone systems. Japan or Korea had completely incompatible systems. A European mobile phone was useless in those countries. This segregation has largely gone. We can talk and see each other around the world.

There are still obstacles. Governments attempt to censor access to websites and communication platforms, for example, in the Middle East and parts of Asia. I have become so used to the global nature of communication that the shock of not being able to access Bloomberg, Twitter or Facebook in some countries is a jolt to the system. However, global communication is a lot easier than it used to be. In my childhood, making friends in different countries was done through organised 'pen-pal' schemes, whereby physical letters were exchanged. Now, any chatroom, game or social-media feed provides the opportunity to interact with people from different cultures.

The globalisation of communication, where it is allowed to take place, can reduce the isolation of minorities in a country. For example, the presenters of the *Gayish* podcast have noted that they are listened to in countries where not being heterosexual is dangerous, is criminal or carries the death sentence.[46] The social media around their podcast has created a strong sense of community among people who have never met in person and who live on different continents.[47] Being part of a virtual community can be as helpful as being part of a real-life community, particularly if a person lives in a country where a real-life community is difficult or dangerous to find.

The combination of global communication and speed can have positive or negative effects. Ordinary communication can echo around the world as never before. An individual's social-media post can have greater reach than *CNN* or *Fox News* in terms of the speed of transmission and the global reach.

Anonymous communication

It seems odd to suggest that modern communication can be more anonymous. We can be tracked by our phones. We can be monitored in our homes by a piece of Amazon technology. This seems to deny privacy. And yet, at the same time, we can hide behind the technology. Communication is also potentially more anonymous.

The obvious, negative example of this is the 'troll'. Trolls are normally anonymous individuals who attack others online, generally through social media.[48] Depending on the platform, the person can hide behind a pseudonym. Arguably, this anonymity allows the troll to be more outspoken and offensive. They may not be in the same country as the person they are attacking. It is unlikely that they will be personally known to their victim. This encourages more abusive attacks.

On a more positive note, anonymity in communication can lead to more positive outcomes. Prejudice can be tackled by anonymity. If someone forms a friendship online in a chatroom or on a computer game, they may become friends with a pseudonym or an avatar. Interactive online games rarely show the person's actual face or name. Ethnic background, religion, gender and sexuality are all hidden. (Americans can, it is true, generally be identified by their inability to spell words like 'labour' correctly.) Prejudice is hard to achieve in such an environment. Anonymity in communication can also create freedom. The escapism of anonymous gaming is that the players can be whoever they want to be.

Communication and control

The popular image of the fourth industrial revolution is that it makes communication more democratic. Anyone can post an opinion, or a video, or an article. The barriers to entry for communication have plummeted for anyone with the price of a phone and a data plan. It is often forgotten, in the positive hype, that there are many people who cannot afford that price. The democratisation of communication only applies to those above a certain income level.

Even for those with access, there are still some limits. It is true that views can be posted. But at the same time, the process has given more editorial control to the platforms on which views are posted. Not everyone on social media is created equal. Algorithms give preference to some social-media users. They also will censor others. Government censorship was commonplace 300 years ago. The private-sector equivalent is the demonetisation, downgrading or banning of published content.

Given the volume of communication that flows across social-media platforms, monitoring and censoring content is often delegated to algorithms. Algorithms are not neutral. There is a risk that the creator of an algorithm will allow bias into the process of promoting or demoting different content. This is an area where the robots may be taking over – at least for lower-level social-media users. Those who are sufficiently popular are likely to be handled by a real person, not an algorithm. This reduces the risk of automated bias.

Communication and the fourth industrial revolution

Communication is already changing. This is very visible. It is easier to communicate quickly, with anyone. We can see and experience things around the world more than ever before. As we will see in Chapter 5, that is a powerful thing. But at the same time, fast communication cuts the quality of what we are saying to each other. Fake news is sent faster and further than the truth. That will have some big implications for prejudice. It also has implications for the structure of politics.

Politics

Political *views* will be changed by the fourth industrial revolution. In this chapter, however, the focus is not on political views, but political structures. The *structure* of politics is likely to change in the fourth industrial revolution, too. The first industrial revolution expanded democracy. The second expanded party politics, seeing a divide based on economics rather than culture or religion. The third industrial revolution challenged the economic division of politics as 'labour versus capital' faded.

The fourth industrial revolution may change party politics once again. The communication changes, in particular, are encouraging the rise of single-issue politics.

The decline of the political party

Since the first industrial revolution, voters have had to compromise their beliefs. Political parties offer a range of policies. These are packaged up into party manifestos. The chances of someone agreeing with the entire contents of a party manifesto are relatively low. You might like the tax policy but disagree on gun control. You might agree on immigration but disagree on education. People end up supporting the party that comes closest to their views. The party that is in line with your thinking on the issues most important to you is the party that you are likely to support.

Modern politics is moving away from that. Changing how we communicate allows changes in politics. The first change is that political parties do not need members as much as they did. Getting votes used to be labour-intensive. Knocking on doors, giving speeches to rallies, sending out leaflets or operating a telephone-calling system all needed people. Parties had to have members if they were to get votes. Modern technology makes all of these methods less relevant. Communication is easier and can be accomplished with fewer people. The use of automatic 'bots' to communicate means that a message can be spread without human action.

It is also possible to be highly specific in political advertising. US President Barack Obama encouraged supporters to give his campaign information from their social-media accounts, which enabled focussed campaigning – a new, concentrated way of getting votes. In 2018, Cambridge Analytica revealed a more negative way of using technology. The company had obtained information from Facebook accounts that could potentially be used for political advertising.[49] The Facebook users would not necessarily know that this was what the information was being used for. All of this was possible without a large political party. A small group of political activists, with finance and external help, could create a focussed appeal for votes. This form of politics was not possible before the fourth industrial revolution.

Membership of political parties is falling. A political party that uses technology may not care very much that its membership is falling. Instead of using members, a core group can control things via electronic communication. Across Europe, membership of political parties has been falling for some time. Party membership as a share of the electorate almost halved in the three decades after 1980.[50] Technology seems to be helping to cut party political membership.

Political parties may not need so many members, but the members still influence the policies that the party will follow. Parties are not attracting younger members. The average age of political parties' membership is getting older and older. That means that political parties are less and less likely to represent the views of the population as a whole. The views of political parties – all political parties – are more likely to represent the views of a subset of the population. In short, if you are a member of a political party today, you are somewhat unusual.

The rise of the single issue

Communication change is not just affecting demand for party members. The technology of the fourth industrial revolution is also changing the supply of party members. Younger people are still engaged in politics; they just tend not to be engaged in *party* politics. Social media is encouraging the rise of single-issue politics. Joining a party means compromising, as it would be very unusual to share all the views of a political party. Joining a campaign means less compromise. Single-issue politics is not new: there have always been single issues that have motivated people. What is different is the fact that single-issue politics has broadened. Social media allows 'low-cost' involvement in single-issue politics. Support can involve following a campaign on social media, or liking and retweeting about it. Support can be attending a social media-arranged rally or event.[51] Before social media, single-issue politics involved big efforts by passionate people. Now, lots of smaller efforts by people with some interest can make a lot more noise.

We can see patterns of this in recent political history. The 'Arab Spring' movements in 2011 were essentially single-issue politics (against corruption). Social media started the protests in a small way. The ease of communication then made it easier to escalate them. The UK referendum on EU membership divided parties but was a single issue that dominated social media. It could be argued that US President Trump mobilised the single issue of immigration and ran a campaign in defiance of the Republican Party and not as part of it. The September 2019 Global Climate Strike was dependent on social media, focussed on a single (if broad) issue.

Single-issue politics changes politics and may make politics more difficult. Political parties offer manifestos that are, at least in theory, 'joined up'. The policies that are being offered are supposed to work together to produce the desired outcome. The risk with single-issue politics is that governments will end up with a series of policies that do not sit well with each other. Governments that have a 'shopping list' of single issues people feel passionate about may not work. The 'economic problem', the very thing economists exist to solve, is that we have unlimited wants but limited things to satisfy those wants. This means that economic policy and hence government policy is essentially about rationing compromise. Single-issue politics recognises the unlimited wants but does not recognise the limitations to satisfying those wants.

Boycotts? There's an app for that

The fourth industrial revolution changes how political pressure is applied in other ways. As mentioned earlier, the power of economics is often used to achieve political ends. That includes the fight against prejudice. The late-18th-century consumer boycott of sugar in Britain aimed to end the slave trade. Sugar was served in bowls that declared the sugar inside was "East

India sugar not made by slaves".[52] Guests could take sugar guilt free. Now, there is an app for that. In fact, there is a variety of apps for that, depending on the particular issue the person wishes to influence. The technology of the fourth industrial revolution is trying to simplify the politics of spending money. The Gender Fair app assesses companies (and thus their products) on their treatment of women.[53] The Human Rights Campaign (HRC) Buyer's Guide does the same based on policy on sexuality.[54] A consumer can boycott companies that do not agree with their political position. Apps can even suggest alternative products with better scores.

Unlike the slogan on the sugar bowl, the politics of gender and sexuality are complex. Sugar was either made with slave labour or not. It was a clear thing to boycott. A consumer looking to spend on the basis of policy on gender or sexuality is focussing a broader topic. They are also spending on many products, not just one commodity. This makes things difficult. The consumer is giving up their political judgement to an external organisation. The apps will use different tests to decide how a company should be ranked on gender or sexuality (or whatever the topic is). The consumer may not be aware of those tests and just focus on the score. Scoring on social policies is set by a person's opinion. With an app, the opinion that works out the details is someone else's opinion. It is not the user's opinion. Anyone who has spent even a short while in the field of socially responsible investing knows that a company can rank high on one index and low on another. If the shopper has different priorities to the app designer, they may spend in areas they do not actually support.

The possibility of reverse boycotts is also real. China's social-credit system relies on the technology of the fourth industrial revolution to be effective. The aim is that Chinese citizens will lose social credit for various things – playing music too loudly, for example. All businesses will have a social-credit code; all citizens will have an identity number. Without a sufficiently good social-credit score, the citizen may not be able to book a flight or get a bank loan. In theory, it could happen without modern technology. In practical terms, technology is necessary to coordinate data in real time on such a large scale. This is the reverse boycott. The app is telling companies to boycott consumers.

Politics in the fourth industrial revolution

All industrial revolutions have changed the structure of politics. The fourth industrial revolution is no different. Much of the period since the first industrial revolution has been about the rise of parties. The founders of the US wanted to oppose 'faction', or parties, and completely failed to do so. The way the economy shaped societies lent itself to 'faction'. Now, however, the need for mass parties is fading. A charismatic media presence and good control of information can get a message across. Voters are less likely to campaign on an integrated platform and more likely to focus on single issues. They can use technology to help in this regard. The risk is that politics becomes less coherent. A shopping list of issues that appeal is not the same as a set of policies that work together.

This new political structure may exacerbate the risk of prejudice. The defences against prejudice were built as elegant weapons for a more civilised age. They may not adapt so well to the new way of politics. Technology offers some new ways to mobilise against prejudice with more coordinated boycotts. But while the boycott has traditionally been an action of the many against the few, technology also allows that process to work the other way.

Other

The other changes that will ripple out of the fourth industrial revolution are more difficult to forecast. Many of the changes in employment, location, trade, communication and politics have already started. The general direction of travel seems set. Other changes will ripple out from these changes but become harder to predict.

The era of more visible consumption has extended to some services. Holiday photographs were a punishment that was once handed out personally. With social media, people can display holidays and other experiences in as public a way as possible. This may change demand patterns. From the first industrial revolution, having 'things' became increasingly important. Possessions bestowed 'taste'. The fourth industrial revolution may make experiences more important in the future – provided, of course, those experiences are documented on Instagram.

The new way we are entertained has implications for the family. For centuries, family life was centred on something. Initially, this was the fire. There is good reason why the hearth was such a focus from Greek mythology onwards. The practical use of fire was replaced by central heating and electric lighting. This removed the focus for the family. No one stares at a radiator the way they stare at a fire. The family focal point was swiftly replaced by the television. This focus drew the family together in the evening and provided a topic of conversation afterwards.

The episode titles of the US comedy show *Friends* all begin with the words, "The one with ...".[55] People rarely remember the title of an episode, but in talking about a television show will tend to describe it as 'the one with ...' followed by a key feature or plot point. It seems a little old fashioned now. These days, entertainment is 'on demand'. The opportunity to stand around the coffee machine or water cooler at work and discuss the previous night's entertainment is giving way to binge-watching and streaming on demand. Patterns of social interaction start to shift.

As mentioned earlier, every industrial revolution has also been accompanied by an agricultural revolution – generally out of necessity. The fourth agricultural revolution is already starting to emerge. The rise of plant-based protein, vertical farming and other innovations are already with us.[56]

Change and the fourth industrial revolution

As an economist, I have no way of predicting what the next smartphone will look like. Neither do I care very much what the next smartphone will look like. I have no hope of being, nor desire to be, a smartphone *fashionisto*. But even at this early stage of the fourth industrial revolution, we can start to see some of the social and economic changes that are taking place. These changes will cause pain, problems and, of course, prejudice.

We have been through this sort of upheaval before, however, and the end result has always been better for the world. I believe that this industrial revolution can result in a higher global standard of living. I believe that efficiency and changing patterns of behaviour from this revolution will help with the environmental credit crunch. Eventually. It is that caveat of 'eventually' that is the problem. The changes to the labour market are likely to take us back to a more flexible, less secure (but possibly more interesting) employment future. Some people will enjoy that. Those who have become used to the security blanket offered by the end of the second industrial revolution will not. And they will probably react. The longer it takes to get to 'eventually', the worse it will be.

Change is coming. We cannot hold back the tide, any more than the Luddites of the first industrial revolution could prevent the swell of mechanisation. The question is how much damage it will cause before we see the benefits – and what the Luddites of the fourth industrial revolution will attack.

Notes

1 A committee of exceptional people appointed to study or investigate a particular issue.
2 See Smith (1776).
3 See ConnecticutHistory.org (2018). Simplistically, the automation of a pin-making machine will cost 18 people their jobs.
4 See Nedelkoska and Quintini (2018).
5 See Osborne and Frey (2018).
6 One of the reasons every industrial revolution to date has had some form of agricultural revolution is that there is a need to move workers from agriculture into industry. Thus, this shift from automation should be seen as both a supply and a demand issue for jobs. The supply of agricultural jobs fell as automation took hold during the second industrial revolution. The demand for workers in industry rose, *eventually* absorbing these workers. In the interim, there was a lot of pain and dislocation, as fictionalised in books like John Steinbeck's *The Grapes of Wrath*.
7 See McKinsey Global Institute (2019). Exhibit E5 indicates the education level, risk from automation and current share of employment in the US of different categories of jobs.
8 Ibid.
9 See IFPI (2019). Digital is, essentially, streaming and downloads.
10 Economists have done an analysis of Twitter that has suggested that physicists are better at communicating than economists. This is not something economists are proud of. See Royal Economic Society (2018).

11 Please follow me on Twitter @PDonovan_econ. Increasing my number of fol-
    lowers makes me feel trendy and cutting edge. I am an economist, so, of course,
    I am neither; but I like to try and maintain the illusion.
12 It should be noted that he also had a second weekend job on a garage forecourt.
    My grandmother held down three cleaning jobs. There were elements of the gig
    economy even in the wake of the second industrial revolution.
13 See Taylor (2017).
14 See McKinsey Global Institute (2016).
15 Recall that before the first industrial revolution, women spinners would often
    spin part time, alternating with agricultural work when that was available.
    After the first industrial revolution, spinners spun and labourers farmed. There
    was no real prospect of pursuing both jobs side by side. Nonetheless, in the first
    industrial revolution, there were many more middle-class people who pursued
    multiple careers. Paul (2017) recounts several cases, including Edmund Harrold
    of Manchester, who was a barber, buyer and seller of hair, maker of wigs, book
    dealer, auctioneer and money lender. He lent money at 10% interest.
16 At least in the UK, someone working on a zero-hours contract is not self-
    employed, but employed with the same legal rights as any other employee.
17 See Conger (2020) for Facebook's idea of moving half of its employees to a
    home-working model. My view is that Covid-19 is likely to accelerate the two
    great structural changes of the next 20 years, namely, the fourth industrial
    revolution and the environmental credit crunch. These were in motion anyway,
    but the strains in the global economy arising from the pandemic add urgency to
    the implementation of the changes.
18 The US Bureau of Labor Statistics Occupation Employment Survey reports em-
    ployment of "Counter attendants: Cafeteria, Food Concession, and Coffee Shop"
    under the code 35-3022. The number of people in this category increased more
    than 6% from 2000 to 2018, with (nominal) median income also increasing 6%.
    This is a broader definition than that of 'barista' (See US Bureau of Labor Statistics,
    2019a).
19 See US Bureau of Labor Statistics (2019b), occupation code 15-1132.
20 More accurately, people were in 'new' jobs that had not been catalogued in the
    earlier period. Some people may have been employed in these jobs at the earlier
    date, but too few to be worth identifying. The analysis of new jobs and the
    impact on employment is from Lin (2011).
21 See Lin (2011).
22 The King and Queen of France were persuaded by Antoine-Augustin de Par-
    mentier to wear potato flowers. The product endorsement by the leaders of
    fashionable society meant that before long, everyone was talking about pota-
    toes. See Hudson and Donovan (2014).
23 For those who like economic jargon, this is essentially about the price elasticity
    of demand for the product in question. Bessen (2019) notes that price elastic-
    ity of demand may change with product saturation. He uses the example of
    clothing. Initially, clothes are handmade and expensive. People own few items
    of clothing. Automation (in the second industrial revolution) lowers the price
    of clothing and demand soars. Further automation lowers the price of clothing
    even more. As people already have lots of items of clothing, they do not increase
    demand so dramatically. I have three nieces who might serve as a counterex-
    ample to that final point, and fast fashion per Thomas (2019) is also a counter-
    point. But the basic argument of shifting price elasticity would give changing
    reactions of employment to new technology over time.
24 O'Keefe et al. (2016) suggest that 44% of the greater Dublin area telecom-
    mutes at least once a month. The average commute time is roughly 50 minutes

each way, which is substantially longer than other areas of the Republic of Ireland. Other areas have a commute of just under 30 minutes. As mentioned in Chapter 2, the size of cities tended to be constrained to commutes of half an hour; hence, ancient cities did not exceed two miles in diameter. Most of Ireland fits this model, but the greater Dublin area does not. This may help explain the attractions of telecommuting.

25 Cars entering a 21-kilometre zone in London are charged a fee (one payment per day). Residents of the zone are also required to pay a fee if they use their cars, at a substantially lower rate. The charge operates between 07.00 and 18.00 each day, which captures the peak commuting times into and around the city. Data on the number of vehicles paying the London Congestion Charge can be found at https://tfl.gov.uk/corporate/publications-and-reports/congestion-charge.

26 The British Council for Offices (2018) suggests that in a conventional office without flexible working, desk space will be unused for around 40% of the core working day. In other words, an office is typically used for three days of every working week. In fact, allowing for an eight-hour core working day, this could be taken to mean that office space is typically used for one day in every seven. Weekends and other times outside working hours, and desks that are simply not occupied, account for the equivalent of six wasted days a week.

27 See Garcia-López et al. (2019) for evidence from Barcelona and Barron et al. (2017) for evidence from the US.

28 UK data is from the Office of National Statistics. Korean data is from Euromonitor International. US data is from the Census Bureau. Australian data is from the National Australia Bank.

29 See Flood (2019).

30 Some people might suggest that drinking a glass of wine could also make reading this book a more pleasant leisure activity. Or, at least, a less painful one.

31 The Bureau of Labor Statistics reported 15.3 million Americans working in retail trade in 2008 and 15.8 million in 2018. The share of employment went from just over 10% to just under 10% of all US employees. Over the same period, online retail sales went from a little over 3% to almost 11% of total retail sales.

32 See Roddenberry (1966).

33 This is more likely to apply to clothing production in Europe or the UK than to clothing production in the US. For now, the US dollar is the global invoicing currency, so movements in the dollar are not likely to hurt US producers who have outsourced parts of their production. This may change if the dollar's role as a global currency is undermined.

34 In 2019, a T-shirt custom-made to a client's personal measurements cost £45. A premium-collection T-shirt from Gap was £35 – although there are lower-quality products available at a lower price.

35 In the US, for example, the 2008 credit crisis led to a change in the amount of inventory that small businesses held. It became more difficult to find the credit that financed inventory. This hurt small businesses, in particular, because they depended on credit from their suppliers to fund inventory. The abrupt ending of that inter-company credit coincided with advances in computer software and technology for inventory management. Small companies were therefore given a push to cut inventory (lack of credit) and the tools with which to do that (technology).

36 Thomas (2019, p. 125) offers anecdotal evidence to support this. In the UK, the Office of National Statistics reports that only 2.2% of businesses large enough to register for value-added tax had more than one location. See Office for National Statistics (2019).

37 See Coates (2012, p. 78).

38 See Rao and Reiley (2012).

39 Kooti et al. (2015) found that 90% of all emails received a response within a day. Half of all emails received a response within 47 minutes. This, the authors note, is roughly the same rate as people retweeting on Twitter. The most common response time to email is two minutes.

40 For the benefit of the younger generation, 'Yours sincerely' is used if the letter is addressed to someone by name. 'Yours faithfully' is used if the letter is addressed to a generic honorific (someone you do not know), such as 'Dear Madam'.

41 See Lytal (2008). The telephone tree Jones described was featured in the political biopic *Milk* (see Van Sant, 2008).

42 See Vosoughi et al. (2018). The article refers to 'false news'; I have used 'fake news'. The rationale for using 'false news' in the article is clearly explained, but for a global audience 'fake news' is probably the more widely recognised term.

43 Ibid.

44 See Wallis (2006).

45 See Peek Vision (2019).

46 Author's interview with Mike Johnson and Kyle Getz, 25 August 2019.

47 See Johnson and Getz (2017).

48 Trolling is generally assumed to be a general attack; who is being attacked is not important (although their views may be). Cyberbullying is the repeated online attack of an individual, where the person being attacked is important. You can troll anyone but cyberbully one person.

49 See Confessore (2018).

50 See Van Biezen et al. (2012).

51 Margetts et al. (2016) suggest that a successful political campaign on social media involves a lot of 'micro-donations' of time and money, scaling this up into a mass mobilisation. Social media is the mechanism for collating lots of small contributions, which before social media would have gone unnoticed.

52 See ageofrevolution.org (n.d.).

53 See Gender Fair (n.d.).

54 See HRC (2020).

55 See Crane and Kauffman (1994).

56 See Hudson and Donovan (2014). In fact, I would urge you to not only see Hudson and Donovan (2014) but buy multiple copies of the book. An ideal gift for friends and family.

4   Change and prejudice

As a species, humans are where we are because of change. Whatever the world throws at us, we find a way to change and cope (at least, we have done so far). Our ability to change has taken us to a position of evolutionary dominance. Whether that dominance is a good thing is something economists prefer not to think about.

The last two chapters showed that an industrial revolution means a lot of change. The change ripples out through society. The fourth industrial revolution may have more change than the second or the third. The effect of that change will, arguably, be as big as that of the first industrial revolution. Some of the trends which the first industrial revolution set in motion (such as urbanisation and set working hours) are already turning around. Changing things that have been normal for generations is going to cause a reaction.

One of the odd things about humans is that while we have won the race of life by being able to change over the ages, most people do not like too much change in the short term. We prefer what we know. The fact that we cling to what is familiar is highly relevant to prejudice. Periods of economic change encourage prejudice. The more dramatic the economic change, the greater the risk of prejudice. When the present and the future are uncertain, we will tend to look to the past to provide security. This is nostalgia. It is dangerous. It encourages prejudice.

There is a depressingly large number of ways in which change can lead to prejudice. To try and simplify things, this chapter will look at four layers of change and prejudice. There is the bottom layer, on which the politics of prejudice rests. It is made up of two very simple ideas: nostalgia and loss aversion. The next layer builds on that. The world today is complex. Most people do not understand how most of the things around them work. That encourages rule-of-thumb thinking. The third layer is inequality and 'scapegoat economics'. This is the real focus today. The foundation of the first two layers supports the fear and anger that inequality breeds. We then want a target for that fear and anger, which produces the top layer: the rise of prejudice politics and the 'anti' parties.

The bottom layer – nostalgia and loss aversion

The Swiss invented nostalgia (the term, if not the concept) in the late 17th century.[1] Originally, it represented a longing for the home of one's younger years. Nostalgia was considered a form of mental illness. During the American Civil War, soldiers could be hospitalised for nostalgia.[2] The idea was not positive. Nostalgia prevented people from functioning properly.

Nostalgia today is a more general yearning for the past. It carries a sense that things used to be better than they are now. The word can still have negative connotations, however. In the UK, few politicians or people will admit to nostalgia. Some current British politicians may have the appearance and world view of characters in a 1920s P.G. Wodehouse novel, but actually using the word 'nostalgia' is seen almost as admitting defeat in the face of change. A reluctance to accept change means that while the *idea* of nostalgia is frequently used as a political rallying cry, in the UK, the word itself is rarely mentioned.

Other politicians have turned nostalgia into a baseball-cap slogan. US President Donald Trump's campaign cry of 'Make America Great Again' is pure nostalgia. In fact, Trump was making a direct appeal to what is known as 'restorative nostalgia'. The baseball caps suggested that there were glories in the past. Change had taken away those glories. There was a political way to restore those glories. In this case, the political way to restore those glories was, supposedly, to vote for candidate Trump. That action would reverse the glory-destroying changes of modern life. It was quite a lot of information to pack into four words emblazoned on a red baseball cap. It worked.

Psychologically, fear and uncertainty trigger nostalgia, which is why it tends to be fuelled by periods of change. In some cases, the nostalgia may lead to a desire to stop or slow change. This is the case with straightforward nostalgia – we want to keep things as they are. Trying to stop or slow change leaves us worse off than we could be. Trying to stop change is the "road not taken," or opportunity cost, as mentioned in Chapter 1. We could accept change, adapt and enjoy the good things that change can bring. By choosing not to accept change and to avoid the uncertainty or risk of change, we deny ourselves the potential reward. In economic terms, plain nostalgia preventing change is not good. But it could be worse.

'Restorative nostalgia' is worse. This takes basic nostalgia a step further. It is no longer about keeping things as they are. Restorative nostalgia is about reversing change that has already happened. Restorative nostalgia deliberately seeks to go backwards to an earlier time. Like most nostalgia, the earlier ideal probably never existed. Politicians who use restorative nostalgia offer a heavily edited version of the past.

It is logical that a dislike of change will encourage a desire to do more than change slowly: it will try to reverse change. There is lots of evidence of this happening in the world today. For example, a huge majority of white evangelical Americans supported US President Trump in the 2016 election. It is worth remembering that Trump lost the popular vote. In that context, to win more than 80% support from a specific group is astounding. A huge majority of white evangelical Americans believe that the US has changed for the worse since the 1950s.[3] The reasons people vote for one candidate rather than another are many and complex. For this particular group, the link between dislike of past change and the promise to restore the glories of old by reversing that change would seem to be a factor. President Trump's restorative nostalgia appealed very strongly to this group. This is not about stopping new things happening. This is about reversing things that have already happened. In this case, presumably, the wish is to reverse almost every change that has happened since the 1950s.

Restorative nostalgia was what drove the ever grumpy 19th-century author Peter Gaskell, mentioned in Chapter 2. Gaskell did not like the world he lived in. He thought the world he had previously lived in was better. Gaskell forced his inexcusable prose style onto the world to try and persuade people to turn back to the past. Clearly, this did not work.

Restorative nostalgia was used by British campaigners who wanted to leave the European Union. Michel Barnier, the EU's chief negotiator, blamed the British decision on "nostalgia for the past".[4] The then leader of Britain's Liberal Democrats, Sir Vince Cable, described those supporting the Leave campaign as driven by "nostalgia for a world where passports were blue, faces were white, and the map was coloured imperial pink".[5] Neither commentator is, perhaps, entirely neutral on the topic. But both make it clear that (in their views, at least) some voters who wanted to leave the EU were motivated by a desire to return to times past. In a world of economic and social change, voters (particularly older voters) wanted to return to the familiarity of their younger days.

The restorative nostalgia that has been set out so far does economic damage, but it is not something that *has* to result in prejudice. There is a sinister part of restorative nostalgia – wrapped up in the desire to restore past glories. The sinister part is that the story will often include conspiracy theories and fantasies as to *why* the past glories were lost. This is where prejudice comes bubbling to the surface. Nostalgia can be used, and often is used, to blame a specific group for why things are not as good as they were. Once blaming a group has begun, prejudice against that group will almost always follow.

Very often, the nostalgia used in politics is not a desire to return to a real past. No sane person, however much they dislike the EU, would want to return to the Britain of the 1950s. Surely no sensible American voter could want to return to the social climate that existed in the US in the 1950s. Restorative nostalgia in politics is a nostalgia for a misremembered past. 'Fake news' sells political ideas. It seems 'fake nostalgia' sells political ideas, too. The reason that fake nostalgia works so well has a lot to do with the economic idea of loss aversion.

Loss aversion

Loss aversion is an important foundation for prejudice politics. It works in two ways. Loss aversion fuels anxiety about loss in the future. But loss aversion also helps make us believe that the past was better than it actually was.

Change involves the threat of losing something. If things are changing there is always going to be anxiety that something you have will be swept away by the tide of change. It does not have to be economic. It could be social status. It could be cultural. But it could be economic. It could be your job. As we have seen, some people will lose their jobs in any industrial revolution. Even more people will fear that they could lose their job as tasks change and they struggle to keep up. Anxiety and insecurity about income may lead to a fear of loss of status, or loss of possessions. Can you pay the mortgage if your job is lost in the changes of an industrial revolution? What if your skills (acquired with time and effort) become irrelevant? The investment a person has put into their career is lost.

Fear of future loss is strong in the fourth industrial revolution. The actual threat of robot overlords taking over everything is limited, as the last chapter showed. But the fact that some people will lose their jobs creates loss aversion. The fact that jobs change and that some tasks people do today will be lost also creates loss aversion. A 2017 PEW survey found a majority of older Americans felt automation to have done more harm than good for the economy. Workers with less education felt the same. These are groups that tend to be most afraid of change. These groups are more likely to see loss coming from the change of the fourth industrial revolution.[6] Younger workers were more likely to say that they had experienced loss (a job, pay, or hours) as a result of automation. However, the younger generation is generally more flexible in the face of change.

I have faced the risk of losing my job at various times in my career (for various reasons). This has generally been as a result of events outside my control. As someone who has, basically, worked for one firm since leaving university, the threat of loss has always been very powerful. As I have aged, the threat of loss has become larger: the financial threat mixed with the fear of losing my 'brand'. Having been in my job for a very long time, I (somewhat egotistically) assume a lot of people at work know who I am. In moving to another job, my 'brand' would be lost. The fact that I have jobs outside of my regular employment count for little. The reassurance of friends that I would find other work if I needed to count for little. That is how loss aversion works.

The Luddites of the first industrial revolution were protesting the loss of jobs *and* the loss of status. There were still some spinners and weavers. For those still employed, the loss was that their job eventually became low status. The Luddites of the first industrial revolution were being told that all the time and effort they had put into becoming skilled workers was lost, wasted. Rioting is an understandable reaction.

Fear of losing status is very powerful. Society often puts pressure on men to have a certain status. In the 1980s, the traditional industries of the second industrial revolution died out in the UK. The miners and steelworkers (nearly always men) lost their jobs. They also lost social status. After the initial recession, employment rose in the UK. But the new jobs were not seen to have the social status of the old jobs. Men who had lost their skilled jobs remained long-term unemployed. Men did not want jobs that were 'beneath them'. Female participation in the workforce increased. Women saw the new jobs as opportunities and did not care what other people thought about status. The 1997 film *The Full Monty* was based on this.[7] It showed men struggling with the loss of high-status jobs. Women had disposable income and economic power without any of the old ideas about what status meant.

People who worry about losing income tend to support mainstream, left-wing parties. These parties offer financial help. People who worry about losing social status are more likely to support extremist groups – the 'anti' parties that lead to prejudice.[8] This is particularly true for men. It also means that just throwing money at the problem may not help. Government handouts do not solve the loss of status.

Fear of future loss is clearly very influential. It can affect our political and economic decisions. But loss can also be backward looking. Nostalgia generally includes a sense that something has been lost. Restorative nostalgia definitely includes a sense that something has been lost. People who believe things were better in the 1950s, by definition, believe that they have lost something in the years between then and now. Sometimes, this may be a feeling of absolute loss: 'I earn less now than I earned then'. Sometimes this may be a feeling of relative loss: 'I earn less than my neighbour now and I earned more than my neighbour then'. It does not matter if the sense of loss is true or not. All that is needed is a *belief* that something has been lost. After that, loss aversion will kick in.

As explained in Chapter 1, loss aversion is an evolutionary trait. We are programmed to put more emphasis on loss than on gain. It is safer to put more effort into running away from the bad things. Being reminded of bad things, as powerfully as possible, helps humans avoid them in the future. The result of this rather caveman-esque genetic coding is that humans dislike losing things a lot more than they like getting things. If you look back over the past you are more likely to emphasise the losses that you suffered than the gains that you made. It is supposedly safer to think this way. This means that we tend to look back on change as making things worse. We remember the bad points. It means that future change is likely to be seen as being worse than it actually is.

Because loss aversion is so powerful, it is easily exploited. The nostalgia for the past is not nostalgia for a past reality. It is nostalgia for a lie. Restorative nostalgia is arguing for a carefully presented costume drama. Nostalgia is a Jane Austen adaptation, delicately avoiding the early 19th-century riots, discomfort and disease. Loss aversion helps with that carefully edited presentation. In looking at the past, we misremember what has changed. We naturally forget (or at least downplay) the good changes between then and now. We remember (and exaggerate) the bad changes. This is loss aversion at work.

Thus, our nostalgic view of the past is not realistic. We think that we can return to the past, but with the good changes kept and the bad changes gone. Importantly, loss aversion means we think the bad changes are three times as bad as they actually were. The power of a loss is three times the power of a gain. If nostalgia lets you reverse the bad losses, you will reverse more bad news than actually happened. The past looks much better than it ever was.

Change, plus nostalgia and loss aversion

Change and uncertainty naturally make us anxious. Uncertainty and anxiety encourage nostalgia. This easily becomes a process of regarding change as negative. Life was always better in the past because loss aversion messes with our minds. We are programmed to remember the bad effects of change, not the benefits. Change plus nostalgia plus loss aversion equals a strong foundation for prejudice.

The second layer – complexity and rules of thumb

To make our lives simpler, we make everything more complicated. Before industrialisation, washing clothes meant finding a river and a rock and indulging in some therapeutic bashing. It was time-consuming. And exhausting. Different stains required different treatments. You might use French chalk, or boiled milk, or buttermilk, or half a tomato.[9] You had to know which thing to use for which stain, but the treatment that was used was fairly simple. There is nothing complicated about boiled milk. Lots of simple solutions were used on a case-by-case basis. Now we throw clothes into a washing machine with a single liquid capsule and press a button. One washing capsule cures all laundry ills. For us, the action of washing clothes is simple – reduced to a single liquid capsule. But behind that simplicity is a massively complex electronics industry. Alongside that, there is an equally complex chemicals industry. These industries need to combine lots of different elements in just the right way. If something goes wrong with just one of those multiple elements, the clothes are not cleaned as they should be.

This means that although our lives are filled with labour-saving devices, we are surrounded by things we do not understand. Most people would struggle to explain how a television works, or how wireless internet can penetrate walls. We rely on the simple outcome and do not worry how we got there. This is often the case with the global economy.

In any industrial revolution, the economy is likely to become more complicated. The new technology offers new opportunities. But we rarely understand the new technology. We rarely understand the impact of the new technology on the economy. It is new. There is no reason we would understand it. We tend to cling to the old way of thinking about things. After all, if you have spent a lot of time learning how the world works, you do not want to throw that away and have to learn again.

The first industrial revolution is a good example of this. Before the industrial revolution, most people lived in relatively simple economies. Most of the things that ordinary people bought were made locally. One person would tend to make a product from start to finish. Things an ordinary household owned at the start of the 18th century would not have been radically different from the things an ordinary household would have owned 100 years earlier.

With the first industrial revolution, things started to get a lot more complex. People were able to own more things, but industrialisation also meant that a lot more people were involved in making those things. How would a person know that something did what it was supposed to, when they did not personally know the maker? In a pre-industrial village, you could trust the blacksmith or the baker because you knew them. You lived with them in the same village. In a city, you would not know the blacksmith or the baker in the same way. Just as importantly, the process of making the bread or the cooking pot involved more than one person (or one family).

More and more relationships are used to make the goods and services that we buy. The washing machine today or the bread of the early 19th century is more complicated than someone from the 18th century could imagine. In just the same way, the overall economy today is more and more complex. We cannot be sure how everything comes together to create the modern economy. We do not know how one economic policy can ripple out, causing changes across society. Add in the fact that the economic data we use was designed for a different time and the potential for general misunderstanding is even greater. The causes of the Great Depression that threatened the jobs of my grandparents' generation in East London were many and complex. Even today, economists argue about the relative importance of the causes.[10] My great-uncles did not understand the complexity of what was going on around them and sought simple solutions.

Modern trade is massively more complex than it was even two decades ago, never mind in the 1930s. Two-thirds of global trade is by multinational companies. Most trade in goods involves firms moving things from one subsidiary to another. It takes over 2,500 different suppliers, from all over the world, to make a single Samsung mobile phone.[11] For anyone who has not studied trade in depth, it will be hard to understand the links. An economist might suggest that many of the world's trade policies today are promoted by politicians who do not understand the full effects of what they are proposing.

Equally, it seems likely that many of the cryptocurrency enthusiasts who buy the 'coins' fail to understand the technology behind them. Experience would suggest that many also fail to understand the economics of money and value.[12] To an economist, Bitcoin looks like something designed by a competent mathematician who knows nothing about how money works. And yet some people are prepared to spend real money on something that they do not properly understand. Indeed, such people are almost fanatical about something they do not properly understand.

The point here is that change increases complexity but reduces understanding. This is not a criticism of anyone's education or intelligence. It is simply not possible for one person to understand everything around us.[13] The problem is the same as with washing clothes in the washing machine. Washing machines and detergents are lots and lots of different things coming together. If something goes wrong with just one of those multiple elements, the clothes are not cleaned as they should be and we do not understand why. The changing world economy is becoming more and more complex. If something goes wrong with just one of the multiple elements that allow us to have jobs and buy things, the economy does not work as it should and we do not know why. The damage is unpredictable.

The people whose lives are damaged when something goes wrong may not understand the cause of their pain. In fact, they are very unlikely to understand the cause of their pain. In such a situation, there is a temptation to fall back on rules of thumb to simplify the complex world around them. This raises the risk of prejudice still further.

Rules of thumb

No one likes feeling out of control. No one wants to believe that they are being pushed around by the complex forces of the universe. Whenever we are confronted with complexity, we try to find things to make life simple. The 'rule of thumb' that was introduced in Chapter 1 is a great way of simplifying things. If there is a simple rule, based on fact, experience or prejudice, it narrows down the complex range of choices. Prejudice arises almost by accident. Someone who does not conform to the rule of thumb suffers irrational discrimination.

Simple sells. Manufacturers worked this out and have tried to make a rule of thumb for their stuff. Can any normal person really tell the difference between one brand of soap powder and another? Soap powder (or a liquid detergent pod) is a complex product. Those of us who have not studied chemistry since school (or at all) are at something of a disadvantage. Can any non-chemist really know which soap powder is, in fact, better? This is where product branding comes in. Product branding is basically a rule of thumb. 'Trust our product, don't trust their product.' 'Our product is better.' The assertions of the marketing department may or may not be accurate. The fact that advertising regulation has to exist suggests that the art of the 'spin doctor' may not be naturally honest. But accuracy is not essential to product branding. The aim is to create a simple rule that 'this is the best brand'.

The cryptocurrency bubble is another simplification. You do not need to understand what Bitcoin is to trade it (evidently). As the economist Robert Shiller points out,[14] Bitcoin traders just need to know it is 'the future'. Traders do not even have to know why it is supposed to be 'the future' (evidently). Traders just need to use that simplifying rule. Cryptocurrencies are the future – and economists who point out that this is not necessarily so[15] just 'do not get it'. More complex arguments are unlikely to work because no one likes complexity. Keep the explanation simple and the idea can be sold.

The prejudice risk in all of this comes when complexity, loss aversion, nostalgia and change pile up on top of one another. Things are changing. People feel things were better in the past. People feel that they are being hurt by the changes. People do not understand why the changes are happening. People do not understand what it is that is causing them pain. People use a simplifying mechanism like a rule of thumb to cut through all of this. A general rule, which may or may not have a basis of truth, makes decisions easier. It avoids trying to understand the complexity of the world. That rule of thumb often involves trying to reverse the change. It also often involves blaming someone else for causing the change. Saying 'it is all your fault' is a wonderful simplification.

The problem is that simplifying rules is rarely rational. Remember, prejudice is being irrational when making decisions. The NINA (no Irish need apply) attitude of the 19th and 20th centuries was a general rule of thumb. It was irrational. It was based on generally untrue assumptions. But it did make decision-making simpler. It is all too easy to move from 'Protestants are hard-working' to 'there is a Protestant work ethic' to 'Catholics are lazy' to 'don't employ anyone Irish'. That becomes a rule of thumb, irrationally applied to an entire nationality.

The Danish students this century who refused to work with other students because of their names were making a (slightly) complex decision using two rules of thumb. The first was that 'this name means this person is from a different ethnic background'. The second was, 'I will not like working with someone from a different ethnic background'. Applying those two rules of thumb led to a very simple decision. It was also a costly decision. The students were paid less money.

The balance is not a fair one. It is hard to argue against simplifying rules of thumb. The arguments against are often complex. In a complex world, a rational, factual argument is likely to be complex. A series of bullet-point slides explaining the principles of monetary economics do not work against a crypto-fanatic crying 'it's the future'. Arguments about the intensely complex global trading system are naturally at a disadvantage against the meaningless simplicity of 'a level playing field'. The complexity of the modern economy means rules of thumb win out.

Rules of thumb tend to focus on people who are different from the rule-maker. Chapter 2 mentioned how collaboration on new ideas in the 19th century happened when people spoke with similar accents. People with different regional accents were harder to understand. They were also, it seems, less likely to be trusted. They were different – 'other' sorts of people. That pattern is similar to NINA in the 20th century. The Irish had different accents, traditions and religion. If they were from East London, they (effectively) had a different language. The pattern is the differences of a class system.

The London weekly newspaper, the *Saturday Review* (not exactly a bastion of inclusion), declared in 1864 that the "Bethnal Green poor are a caste apart, a race of whom we know nothing, whose lives are of quite different complexion from ours, persons with whom we have no point of contact".[16] Ideal scapegoats, in other words. This pattern is repeated with the Danish students in the 21st century. We feel comfortable with people who are like us. We are comfortable with people who look like us – who have the same cultural references as us, who talk like us and who think like us. That makes dealing with these people simple.[17] That encourages us to build rules of thumb about those who are different from us. That, in turn, helps us to build prejudices about other people.

Complexity and rules of thumb

Complexity is an inevitable part of change. Human progress has nearly always made things more complex. The complexity confuses us. It becomes harder and harder to understand the world around us. It is only natural to try and simplify things. But this encourages the use of rules of thumb, which are generalisations. Rules of thumb will nearly always depend on some irrational assumptions. It is nearly always irrational to generalise. People are unique. It is unwise to assume that all people in a certain group act or think the same way.

Change makes things more complex. We react to that complexity by trying to create simple rules. These rules often mean trusting what is familiar and rejecting what is different or 'other'. That helps to make sure that the rule of thumb is a way of spreading prejudice.

The third layer – inequality and 'scapegoat economics'

Inequality and prejudice are often linked. Before looking at the ties, we should narrow down what inequality is. What normally matters is inequality of living standards. We want to have as comfortable a life as those around us.

The media often fail to separate income inequality from wealth inequality. The two are different. As a rule, it is income inequality that is more important. Income is what sets our day-to-day standard of living. If we ignore credit and inflation for the moment, the level of income is important to setting how much stuff we can buy. Wealth, which is the value of assets, has less of an impact on the standard of living. Generally, you have to sell the asset, or borrow against its value, to be able raise your living standard. If my house rises in value, it does not make any difference to what I can afford to buy or to the standard of living I enjoy.[18]

This does not mean that wealth can be ignored entirely. Wealth inequality can lead to envy. This is especially true if society tells you that you should own assets. Housing is the obvious example. High house prices mean that some groups in society cannot afford to own their own home. If society puts a value on owning rather than renting a home, that can cause problems. It is not particularly rational to value owning a home over renting a home. Again, human beings have an irritating habit of not being rational when economists tell them to be.

Wealth inequality can also easily lead to 'scapegoat economics', which we will go into in more detail. Wealth inequality can contribute to the sense of being 'left behind', which is an important step in building prejudice. Normally, wealth inequality involves bigger numbers than income inequality. That makes for more sensational headlines, which may be why both media and politicians use wealth inequality when they are actually talking about income inequality. As a general rule, it is income inequality that determines differences in standards of living.

Over the course of the last 30 years, income inequality has collapsed. It has also increased a lot. It all depends on how you look at it. Today, the world has fewer people in poverty than ever before.[19] In 1981, 44% of the world lived in poverty. By 2015, that number was 10%. This collapse in poverty has never happened before in human history.

While global inequality has collapsed, inequality has risen within economies. Over the past 30 years, the gap between the highest and the lowest levels of income has increased in almost every major economy. The change brought about by the fourth industrial revolution is likely to increase that inequality. Of course, a country may have policies that reverse this through income redistribution. Inequality is the starting point. It does not have to be what a country ends up with. But rising inequality and the fear of being left behind threaten more prejudice.

Income inequality may be disguised for a time. This is through the use of credit. Credit can be thought of as income in disguise. Credit is about using tomorrow's income to raise today's standard of living.

Credit, to state the obvious, allows us to buy things with money that we do not have today. This can lead to what economists call the 'credit illusion'. To quote the mighty economic guru Madonna, "we are living in a material world".[20] We therefore tend to judge our relative standard of living by what we own. Generally, our incomes are only visible through what we have. Income inequality plus credit (using tomorrow's income) can result in consumption equality today. If our neighbour has a new car and we have a new car, we feel equal. We do not stop to think that our neighbour paid cash and we paid using credit. While the credit still flows, inequality in living standards and social status is not visible. But, like the story of Willy Loman in Arthur Miller's *Death of a Salesman*,[21] at some point, the credit stops. Bills have to be paid. The inequality of living standards becomes very obvious if we have to live within our income.

The credit cycle can therefore disguise income inequality. But an abrupt end to credit can make inequality very visible, very suddenly. This is what happened with the global financial crisis of 2008. Income inequality had been building for some time. It was not exactly hidden, but the impact was softened by credit. In the years before the crisis, credit had been extended to lower-income groups. This was politically approved, even promoted. A Boston Federal Reserve 1993 manual encouraged US mortgage lenders to extend credit to people on lower incomes. It also warned about the financial costs of prejudice (banks could be fined). The implication was that a bank that did not lend to lower-income groups could be accused of racism.[22] Lower-income groups in America are disproportionately from ethnic minorities. Lending to lower-income people increased. Consumption was more equal than income as a result.

With the crisis, the credit stopped. That meant that consumption inequality was suddenly visible. The living standard of someone on a low income who had been using credit fell. Low-income people could not use tomorrow's income to raise today's standard of living. Worse still, low-income people had to lower today's standard of living to repay yesterday's credit. Those were two separate forces widening the gap to people who did not depend on credit. The loss of credit invoked loss aversion at once. We know the power of loss aversion.

Not everyone experienced a loss of living standard as credit ended. People who had not used credit could maintain their living standards. Thus, the gap in living standards (or consumption) between a low-income family and a high-income neighbour opened up almost overnight. And in the years that followed, the gap was made even worse. As economies recovered, regulation of the banks (and the experiences of bank managers in the crisis) meant a more cautious approach to lending. Credit has generally not been made available to lower-income groups, but has been restored to higher-income groups. That increases the potential for more consumption inequality.

Alongside income and credit, inflation plays a role in creating inequality. How much stuff we can buy is driven by both our income and the prices we must pay. There is a tendency to think of inflation as a single number. Most governments present consumer inflation as a single number (or a couple of numbers). However, everyone has a different inflation rate. An older person is more likely to spend more money on healthcare. A younger person is more likely to spend more money on education. Spending patterns also differ by income group.

Inflation inequality has been a feature lately. Lower-income people tend to spend more of their income on food, energy and housing. Higher-income people spend more of their money on services and consumer goods. If the prices of food, energy and housing rise more rapidly than the prices of services and consumer goods, low-income people will have higher inflation. High-income people will have lower inflation. This is what has tended to happen in recent years. Most major economies have had inflation inequality. The official data on income inequality do not adjust for inflation. When that adjustment is added in, the inequality in standards of living becomes more significant. People realise this and that helps to support 'scapegoat economics' and, ultimately, prejudice.

Inequality in living standards and the abrupt realisation of inequality in living standards brought about by the end of credit have built a foundation for prejudice. A period of rapid economic change is likely to increase inequality. This, in turn, increases the risk of prejudice. The economic change of an industrial revolution can make people suddenly rich. It can also make people suddenly poor. Rapid change creates the fear of inequality through the fear of being 'left behind'. That is a very powerful fear.

Having the right idea at the right time can give people sudden and unexpected income or wealth. This is the reward for innovation, with some acknowledgement for luck and marketing. Inventing things does not always make money, however. In the first industrial revolution, inventors did not always benefit from their ideas. The patent system was primitive. Lawsuits defending patents went against the inventor more than half the time.[23] Today, patent laws provide more financial protection for inventors. The more sophisticated financial system also allows people to cash in on their innovations more quickly.[24]

The other thing that helps make people rich is having skills that rise in value as a result of the rapid economic changes. In the first industrial revolution, brickmakers saw a sharp rise in income as technology increased demand for bricks. As we saw in Chapter 2, this went wrong in the end. But at first, the skills required to make bricks led to richer brickmakers. In the third industrial revolution, sports stars saw huge income gains, because their skills were made more valuable by television. The effect of this on income inequality has been big. In many advanced societies, the rise of income inequality has been driven by the growth in incomes not of the top 10%, nor even the top 1%, but the top 0.1%. This is a group whose 'star quality' has combined with the changing technology of communication. The result is more income.

Periods of dramatic change can mean dramatic shifts in how skills are valued. Some skills go from zero commercial value to very high value indeed. In the fourth industrial revolution, computer gamers and Instagram influencers have skills that are now in demand. When I was growing up, parents would tell their children that they could never make a living from playing computer games. That turns out not to be true. Skills that were previously thought to have zero value now earn high incomes.

At the same time, rapid change can make people rapidly poor. Industrial revolutions can quickly make jobs obsolete or less valued. The women who spun yarn at home before the first industrial revolution went from being relatively well paid to having no income, almost overnight. The brickmakers' fall from relatively high income to poverty was just as fast. One technological change can make people richer and poorer at the same time. Introducing robots into a factory could lower the income (and status) of workers doing routine jobs. The value of creative and managerial skills may increase. Normal economic forces mean that the pay of a manager will increase relative to the pay of a routine worker.[25]

As mentioned, income inequality is just a starting point. A country can chose to challenge inequality through taxation and welfare spending. But policy rarely changes as fast as the economy. Politicians may also be unwilling to tax those who are leading the change. There is sometimes a fear that higher taxes will damage 'entrepreneurship' and stop the leaders of the fourth industrial revolution from using their skills in the domestic economy.

Rapid economic change will tend to produce inequality of income, wealth and inflation. Society is rarely quick enough in addressing the issue. The result is that rapid economic change will build a sense of being 'left behind' for a part of society. That group can potentially be quite large. 'Left behind' is a phrase that is increasingly heard in the fourth industrial revolution. It carries with it a sense of impotence. Events are moving too fast for some people in society. People are powerless to stop what is happening to them.

How people see opportunity is relevant. If people feel that there is equality of opportunity, the sense of being 'left behind' is less damaging. Being 'left behind' is still very unpleasant. But if there is a belief in equal opportunity, then you can *hope* to raise your income and status. Hope is a powerful force. It is the belief, not the reality, that matters. Giving a group hope of a better future can help to undermine the role inequality plays in prejudice. It is helplessness in the face of the way things are that fuels prejudice.

It is easy to use inequality without hope as a way to move towards prejudice. All it takes is envy. In fact, envy requires inequality. As the moral philosopher Gabriele Taylor says, "Envy rests on interpersonal comparison. The envious person thinks of another as being in some way better off than she is herself".[26]

Times of change often mean that the economics of aspiration are replaced by the economics of envy. The economics of aspiration mean that people want things they do not have, but they think they might be able to get them. Credit relies on the economics of aspiration. The whole advertising profession is pretty much built on them. But if the inequality gap is too wide, the object becomes 'out of reach'. There is no point wishing for what you cannot have. This encourages the economics of envy. Envy can take several forms, but three, in particular, are relevant to the story of prejudice.

'Object envy' focusses on the thing, not the person owning the thing. This is the envy of the school playground – if you envy someone's new smartphone, perhaps. It is not personal. Because it is not personal, it is not likely to fuel prejudice. However, object envy can turn into 'state envy'. This is when the person who owns something is, in some way, seen as being the reason you do not own something. You want to close the gap, remove the inequality. The gap can be closed in two ways. One way is for you to be better off. The other way is for the other person to be worse off ('destructive state envy'). By making envy about the other person, prejudice is allowed to build.

Then there is 'sophisticated envy'. This is more about status. Someone has something that gives them status. You want to reduce their status. It does not necessarily mean you want to take their status. It does mean that you want to reduce the gap between you and them. This is a personal form of envy. Again, it is something that easily fuels prejudice.

Income inequality has grown and is likely to keep growing in a period of change. Policy can change its effects, but the starting point is that there will be groups 'left behind' by the process of change. As higher living standards are seen as being out of reach, the economics of aspiration will be replaced by the economics of envy. That is a very solid foundation for 'scapegoat economics'.

Scapegoat economics

'Scapegoat economics' is the next, easy step in building up to prejudice. It is helped by state envy and sophisticated envy (though it is possible to have scapegoat economics without envy). The story is always simple. Start by pretending that things were better in the past. Things changed. Those changes caused people losses. It is too hard to try and understand what actually caused the losses. The world is a complex place. The risk of prejudice increases when change becomes more complex. If the reason behind a change is simple, then the true cause can be easily identified.

If the true cause behind the changes cannot be identified, make something up. Finding a simple solution that seems to explain a complex world is politically seductive. The easiest solution – the rule of thumb – is the one thing that caused all those changes to happen. This one thing is the 'scapegoat' of 'scapegoat economics'. People can then be persuaded that they must remove the influence of that scapegoat. People are told that by removing the scapegoat, the changes can be reversed. If the changes can be reversed, then it would be easy to arrange a return to the glorious past. The fact that the whole thing is built on layers of lies does not matter. 'Fake news' sells. 'Fake news' sells nostalgia really well.

'Scapegoat economics' is often focussed on jobs. Increased income inequality can be blamed on a group 'driving down wages'. Immigrants are an obvious group that can be targeted in this regard. Whether or not it is true is irrelevant.[27] But scapegoat economics can be about anything that is seen as affecting someone's standard of living. Income is just the most obvious example. Thus, foreigners may be blamed for the wealth inequality that high house prices can create. Some parts of the British tabloid media are very fond of accusing immigrants of 'health tourism' and using the resources of the health system at the expense of the local population. The reality is that immigration does not drive down average wages. Low interest rates generally have more to do with wealth inequality than foreign investors. And immigrants make British healthcare function. Over a quarter of British doctors are of Indian origin.[28]

Perhaps the biggest attraction of scapegoat economics is the seduction of saying, 'it's not my fault'. With complex changes, it is rarely obvious why an individual is affected. My great-uncles almost certainly did not understand the complex forces that led to trade protectionism in the 1930s. That protectionism led to unemployment in the docks of East London. My relatives were very unlikely to associate their low pay and job insecurity with monetary and fiscal policy in the US, movements in currency markets or credit bubbles. They were doing their jobs as they had always done. In their view, there would have been no reason why their wages and job security were threatened. Why should things change? There was no reason for pay to go down or job insecurity to go up. The problems they faced were not their fault.[29] But if it was not their fault, whose fault was it?

It helps if the scapegoat can be identified in human terms. In 1787, rioters in Leicester in the UK chanted, "No Presbyterians, no machines".[30] The Presbyterians, as a minority Protestant religious group, were convenient scapegoats at a time when automation was threatening jobs. The Presbyterians were not obviously connected with the machines. But having a group of people to attack made it easier. In London, the Gordon Riots of 1780 targeted Catholics. The riots had economic causes (price increases were blamed) and Catholics were a convenient group to blame. They were excluded from mainstream society by their religion, but a group that could be identified and targeted.[31] In the early 1800s, women became the target. As wages and status fell, trade unions began to exclude women, or try to confine women to lower value work.[32]

In the US in the 1870s and 1880s, farmers were under pressure. Tying the value of gold to the dollar was blamed. Global trade was blamed. But so were immigrants. In 1882, the Chinese Exclusion Act aimed to prevent Chinese immigration.[33] Economic difficulties had a human face. The downturn in agricultural prices was 'not my fault'. Blaming the immigrants was an easy next step. This was followed by restrictions on Japanese immigration in 1907.[34] The 1920s saw limits on Italian immigration. Italians were not seen as being sufficiently 'white' and they made suitable scapegoats.[35] The Italian population tended to cluster together in certain city areas. 'Little Italy' gave immigrants a sense of community, but it limited their contact with non-Italians. It is easier to have a scapegoat that you do not know very well. Immigration quotas specifically favoured northern European migrants, who tended to integrate more readily into existing American culture.[36]

The uncertainties of the second industrial revolution fed scapegoat economics. The notorious US Ku Klux Klan saw its membership peak in the 1920s (at around 4,000,000 people). While the organisation is best known for its attacks on African Americans, there were as many attacks on immigrants, Catholics and Jews.[37] Attacking immigrants and Catholics captured anti-Italian feeling.

As the Great Depression progressed and standards of living fell, extremism increased in the US. A radio preacher, Father Charles Coughlin, had an anti-Jewish agenda. In 1935, he received more mail than President Roosevelt.[38] British fascism in the 1930s also tried to make scapegoats of the Jewish population. This was a visible minority. It was easily targeted. The largely untrue stereotype of the wealthy Jew added to the story. Income inequality was rising. It was easy to claim that one group was wealthy and then blame that group for all the problems of East London's dock workers. This scapegoat economics reached its most terrible conclusion in Nazi Germany. But the Jewish population of Germany had been scapegoats before – the economic weakness of the 1870s had led to the Jewish population being singled out for attack.

It is noticeable that some of the British Union of Fascist's propaganda distinguished the local (poor) Jewish population from the wealthy Jewish one. Dock workers would probably know local Jewish neighbours. They were more likely to realise their Jewish neighbours had nothing to do with their problems. It helps if the scapegoat is an identifiable, human group. But it also helps if the scapegoat is not personally known to the prejudiced.

The anti-immigration sentiment that was partly behind the UK's 2016 decision to leave the EU was focussed in areas with very little immigration. A white British person living in an ethnically diverse area is likely to become less prejudiced over time.[39] The chants of "build that wall" during US President Trump's 2016 election campaign were heard in areas with little immigration. Votes for Trump in 2016 had an almost perfect inverse relationship with the size of the city a voter lived in. Voters who lived in or near large cities, which were generally more ethnically and socially diverse, did not support Trump. Voters in smaller cities (less diverse) or who lived a long way from cities were more likely to support him.[40] The largest swing in favour of Trump occurred in the Midwest – an area that has a lower concentration of foreigners than most of the rest of the country.

This is tied up with trust. It is easier to trust people we know and relate to. It is easier to make a scapegoat of someone we do not know (or do not know well). Scapegoating and prejudice rely on dehumanising the target. Pretending a group is somehow less than human makes that group an easier target for 'scapegoat economics'. The attacks of 'scapegoat economics' are easier to justify if the group that is being attacked is 'less than'. The anti-Semitic propaganda of Nazi Germany relied on caricatures and grotesque images to make the Jewish population scapegoats. Racial abuse directed at black football players today explicitly seeks to dehumanise them. A French slang term for a gay man is *PD* *(pédé)*, meaning pederast or child molester. Anti-immigration language today uses words more often associated with animals than people. This is all deliberate. Prejudice works if we know enough about the group to fear them, but not enough to realise that we are all human.

If different groups cluster together in separate places, trust between groups is difficult. Tensions between groups build, be it in the suburbs of France or the different neighbourhoods of the US. Different groups in the US 'stick with their own' when it comes to where they live. Different groups living in different areas help create the hostility of 'scapegoat economics'. Different groups will lobby against government assistance if it is seen helping other groups in society. For example, white Americans may blame ethnic minorities for 'draining' government resources they feel could otherwise go to them. This also ties in with income inequality. There is a tendency to dehumanise lower-income groups, as it helps higher-income groups to justify using lower-income groups as scapegoats.[41] Emotional language is often used to describe lower-income groups. They are seen as enjoying a lifestyle funded by the tax payments of higher-income groups. In doing so, they are blamed for lowering the living standards of the higher-income groups and thus become scapegoats.

Prejudice is reduced when we know people who might otherwise be targets of prejudice. A diverse neighbourhood helps break down the stereotypes or rules of thumb that feed into 'scapegoat economics'. We get to know members of the other groups and realise that they are human, too. It is easier to realise that 'scapegoat economics' is a lie when a person can see first-hand that prejudice is irrational. It is a lot easier to fear the unknown.

The final layer – prejudice politics

Prejudice politics rests on a toxic mix of nostalgia, loss aversion, complexity, rules of thumb, inequality and 'scapegoat economics'. Prejudice politics pretends to tackle each of these issues in turn:

- There is no need to be nostalgic. Prejudice politics can take you back to a mythical, glorious past.
- There is no need to worry about loss. Prejudice politics will restore everything to you.
- There is no need to fear complexity. Prejudice politics has a simple solution.
- Your rules of thumb were right all the time. Prejudice politics confirms them.
- Your feeling of being left behind can be reversed. Prejudice politics will make you equal again.
- Your fear of the unknown is a valid fear. Prejudice politics tells you it is right not to trust that which seems different.

Needless to say, the story of prejudice politics is the ultimate 'fake news'. However, any politician can exploit these issues with the right message of prejudice. 'It's all the fault of the foreigner' or 'the ethnic minority' or 'the gays' or 'the Muslims'. 'Vote for me and I will put them in their place.' 'That one simple solution will make everything right again (for you)'. Of course, that is a seductive message. It is a message that has deceived people for centuries. Of course, it is a simple message – one cause behind the complexity of all of your problems. And, of course, it is a message that is extremely hard to defeat. The arguments against prejudice politics tend to be complex. They are complex because the world is complex, and complex problems rarely have simplistic solutions. The argument against prejudice politics is hard to condense into a slogan that fits neatly onto a baseball cap.

Thus, it is not true that immigrants drive down wages and put local people out of work. Economic migration is generally in response to demand for labour. Migration follows economic strength. But it takes a lot of data and analysis to show that. A supporter of prejudice politics can simply point to the house of an immigrant and state, with no evidence whatsoever, that they are the cause of low wages. No one wants to hear complicated arguments when a simple explanation is at hand.

Prejudice politics appeals to a specific group in society. In country after country, supporters of prejudice politics tend to be older, lower-skilled, lower-income, ethnic-majority, male and rural, not urban. There are exceptions, but these are common traits. This fits with the layers that build prejudice politics.

Older voters will naturally tend to nostalgia. It is harder for a millennial to be nostalgic. By definition, their past is recent. Older people, on average, will have more loss. Analysis in Europe[42] suggests that prejudice politics is more likely in areas that have experienced long-term economic decline. The older populations of such areas will obviously have experienced more of that decline than the younger people. Older people potentially also have more to lose (or fear losing) in future. Ethnic-majority men are also more likely to fear loss, having had a privileged social status in the past.

Lower-skilled workers are less likely to accept or understand the complexity of economic change. A lower-skilled worker will generally have a narrower view of their industry. Higher-skilled workers tend to be further up in the hierarchy, giving them a better overview of the changes hitting their industry.

Lower-income workers have been hurt by the growth of inequality. This group is most likely to have experienced a loss of consumption equality.

Rural voters are generally less likely to know people from minorities. That helps scapegoat economics. It makes it easier to present minorities as being a threat. Rural areas are more at risk of relative economic decline. This feeds back into the inequality arguments. Social status also plays a role. There are negative associations with the 'flyover' states of the US. The term implies that these are places to fly over on the way to somewhere else, not places to visit.[43]

Politicians can be seduced by using prejudice politics as much as voters can be seduced by the message it offers. Prejudice politics gives politicians a wonderful escape route. Marissa Begonia, a founder member of The Voice of Domestic Workers advocacy group, has said, "They [politicians] always use migration as the scapegoat, when all their policies, all the things that they're doing failed in terms of economy, they blame migrants".[44]

If politicians mess things up (by ignoring the advice of economists), there is a 'get-out-of-jail-free card' to be found in prejudice politics. Blame a suitable minority. Your policies would have worked, if it were not for the actions or existence of this one group. The simplicity of the message has attractions for politicians as well as the public.

Prejudice politics naturally ties in with scapegoat economics. Scapegoat economics identifies a fake cause to problems. Prejudice politics identifies a fake solution to the fake problem. Prejudice politics claims that by introducing irrational discrimination, the fake cause of the problem can be removed. This is dangerous enough. But prejudice politics can then promote even more prejudice. This makes prejudice politics even more dangerous.

Any society has its rules of behaviour. The rules are different in different cultures. But the rules can also change over time. The British television series *Life on Mars* saw a police officer transported from 2006 to 1973.[45] The sexism, racism and homophobia of the earlier era are shown to be alien to someone from the modern world. What was normal behaviour and language in the past is not normal behaviour and language today.

We tend to assume that societies have become more inclusive and less prejudiced over time. The World Values Survey, which asks people all over the world their views on a range of issues, shows that younger people are nearly always less prejudiced than their parents.[46] But change is not always in one direction. Social attitudes could move towards more prejudice in the turbulence of an industrial revolution. Prejudice politics can help to breed prejudice by changing what people consider to be socially acceptable.

People do not have to agree with a more extreme form of prejudice to be influenced by it. A society can agree that racism is bad. An extreme racist will not attract much support. But if more extreme forms of prejudice are visible, people may feel more comfortable about moving away from the social norm. In this case, it could become okay to be 'a little bit racist'. It is quite common to hear that 'political correctness has gone too far' or 'it's just a joke'. An attempt to be present on both sides of an argument, however worthy, may make prejudice seem more normal. Making prejudice mainstream may encourage more prejudice.

When social rules are strong, people will tend to obey them. This is what is called 'social desirability bias'. We want to fit in with what society expects or considers normal. Playing by the rules may mean people deliberately hide their true prejudice. When society expects people to be more inclusive, if asked, people will lie about how prejudiced they are. This makes survey evidence very unreliable. In the US, this has been seen in politics. The 'Bradley

Effect' refers to the fact that black candidates for Congress did notably better in opinion polls than they did in reality. People stick to the rules when answering a question face to face. The privacy of the ballot box is less likely to be influenced by social rules.[47]

When prejudice is out in the open, the social rules can start to shift, changing what society considers to be desirable. This, in turn, reduces the ability of social desirability bias to steer public behaviour away from prejudice. Why does this matter? People are prejudiced anyway, after all. It matters because, as we shall see in a later chapter, public prejudice carries additional costs. Those costs are both social and economic. Public prejudice is more intimidating for the targets of prejudice. It can be harder to defeat. A sense of shame associated with prejudice, caused by social desirability bias, can help to defeat prejudice. A sense that it is alright to be 'a little bit' prejudiced loses that force for inclusion.

Prejudice politics is dangerously easy to slip into.

Economic change and prejudice

Economic change does not *have* to lead to prejudice. But the layers that build up to support prejudice politics are easily encouraged by economic change. Change builds on our fears. Change exaggerates our insecurities about the future. And in a world that only gets more complicated, we look for the simple solution. Prejudice politics is the equivalent of the one-type-cleans-all laundry detergent. Prejudice politics seems to solve all our problems without our having to understand how complex the world is – or to make further, painful changes to our skills, how we live or what we do to earn a living.

After a long period of decline in prejudice, we are now starting to see it rise again in developed economies. This is the pattern of previous industrial revolutions. The anti-Presbyterianism of the first industrial revolution, the anti-immigration sentiment and anti-Semitism of the second industrial revolution and the nationalistic racism of the third industrial revolution have foreshadowed what we are now experiencing.

Change can easily fuel prejudice. The question is whether this period of change is better or worse than past industrial revolutions. And this is what we will explore in the next two chapters.

Notes

1 Johannes Hofer, in 1688, came up with the term to describe the desire of Swiss mercenaries to return to their homeland. See Gaston and Hilhorst (2018, p. 27).
2 See Roper (2011, p. 431).
3 Exit polls from the 2016 US presidential election suggest that 81% of white evangelical Americans voted for Trump. A 2016 poll by the Public Research Religion Institute suggested that 74% of white evangelical Americans felt that the US had changed "mainly for the worse" since the 1950s. See Gaston and Hilhorst (2018).

4 See Matlak (2019).
5 See BBC (2018).
6 See Geiger (2019).
7 Cattaneo (1997).
8 Gingrich (2019) covers this in detail.
9 This example is shamelessly abridged from Donovan and Hudson (2011, p. 143). It is one of the better-researched parts of our book, which means it is almost certainly Julie who wrote it.
10 I realise that many people will be shocked to learn that economists disagree with each other. It is not something we tend to advertise, but it has been known to happen from time to time.
11 See World Bank and WTO (2019).
12 I was once referred to as a 'Bitcoin pundit', which is either an accolade or a gross insult, depending on your perspective. I am sure my mother was very proud of my achievement. I feel reasonably qualified to talk about the rather obvious failings of cryptocurrency as a currency, as someone who knows something about monetary economics and monetary history. I would not claim to have in-depth knowledge of the details of the technology behind cryptocurrencies.
13 Obviously, economists will pretend to understand everything around us, as that is what economists do. But if we cannot understand the world, we will always have a very good reason why the world failed to do what we forecast.
14 See Shiller (2019).
15 Please note, this is an excellent example of British understatement.
16 See Malik (2001).
17 In my day job, I interact with a lot of different people from different cultures, all over the world. However, these people tend to have similar, higher-education backgrounds and are (often) of a similar age to me. They have a direct interest in economics and finance. It is relatively easy – and thus comfortable – to interact with them. Most years, I also present to a group of 16- and 17-year-old students at a school in East London. It is without doubt the most terrifying presentation I have to make all year. The students are articulate and intelligent. They are not necessarily interested in economics. The gap in age and differences in culture reduce the common ground that we have – despite my East End ancestry. The result can be a high level of discomfort for me (the students are generally at pains to put me at my ease, I should note).
18 Economists do recognise the 'wealth effect'. This happens when rising asset values persuade people that they do not need to save as much money. There is a belief that their more valuable assets can replace savings. In this sense, there may be a change in living standards (measured by consumption) as asset prices rise – but this rests on the choice to reduce saving. That choice may not be a rational one if asset prices are especially volatile or there is a bubble in asset values.
19 I use the World Bank definition of poverty here, namely, having an income per person of USD 1.90 per day (using purchasing power parity exchange rates at the 2011 value of the dollar). This what the World Bank defines as the income required to provide the most basic standard of living. See World Bank (2020).
20 See Madonna (1985).
21 See Miller (1949).
22 See Norberg (2009, p. 31).
23 See MacLeod (2007, p. 186).
24 This can present different economic challenges. The technology sector in Israel, for example, has a reputation for innovation. However, the innovations tend to be sold to existing companies or via an initial public offering on the financial

markets. The inventor achieves a considerable amount of wealth. The development of the innovation may move elsewhere, meaning Israel may not receive the economic benefit.

25 This is a statement of economic forces. There is no judgement about whether this is a 'good' or 'bad' thing. That is something for society to decide and (if it chooses) to adjust through taxes and benefits or, in the longer term, through education and training.

26 See Taylor (2006, p. 41).

27 As mentioned in Chapter 2, in the late 19th century, immigration from Eastern Europe helped push down wages in the US clothing industry. Modern immigration does not appear to have an overall negative effect on wages. Rather, immigration has tended to complement the activity of the existing population. However, immigration may still result in lower wages in some sectors of the economy.

28 See MacKenzie (2015, p. 23). This does not mean over a quarter of doctors have migrated from India, although some may be first-generation immigrants. It does mean that over a quarter of doctors are working in the UK because they, or previous generations of their family, have migrated.

29 Ascribing blame is not very helpful. The fault lay with global forces, a period of change in the global economy and the relative inability of my relatives to adapt to change and find other work. Of course, the reason behind their inability to adapt can be tied to their very low skills and education, which can be blamed on the social policy of the era.

30 See Wykes (1978, p. 44).

31 The Bank of England discovered a "Papist" employee in 1746 and banned Catholics from that point on until 1829 (when the Emancipation Act was passed). This is pure prejudice, of course. There is no reason why a Catholic clerk should be any worse than a Protestant clerk. It is all the more notable because the Bank of England was somewhat more meritocratic in employment than other parts of the government at the time. Of course, hiring on the basis of ability did not extend to giving women clerical jobs. See Murphy (2015).

32 The Bookbinders Trade Society excluded women in 1810. The Manchester Spinners' Union excluded women in 1818. The Stockport Hatmakers' Society excluded women in 1808 and agreed to strike if women were employed. See Burnette (2008).

33 See Chinese Exclusion Act (1882).

34 See Rodrik (2017).

35 Staples (2019) shows the dire consequences of this. Italian immigrants were demonised in grotesque caricatures in the American media (including the now rather more liberal *New York Times*). In 1890, 11 Italians were lynched by a mob in New Orleans, an action that met with approval in the media. A grand jury declared the killings to be "praiseworthy". The use of anti-Italian slurs, as recorded by Google Ngram in English language books, peaked in the 1930s, coinciding with the Great Depression.

36 See Abramitzky and Boustan (2017).

37 See Eichengreen (2018).

38 Ibid.

39 See MacKenzie (2015).

40 See Eichengreen (2018, p. 125).

41 See Valentine and Harris (2014).

42 See Dijkstra et al. (2018, p. 18).

43 Dijkstra et al. (2018) reference the risk of relative geographic decline for Europe. McKinsey Global Institute (2019) identifies the same risk for the US.

44 See Goodfellow (2019, p. 133).
45 See Kudos and BBC Wales (2006).
46 See World Values Survey (2020).
47 Economists have other ways of getting groups of people to reveal their prejudices. See Margalit (2019) and Coffman et al. (2013) for more on this topic. Margalit cites a study of American non-Hispanic whites. When asked directly, 42% said they were not opposed to cutting off all immigration to the US. When asked indirectly, in a way that would not reveal identify any one person's prejudice, 61% were not opposed to cutting off all immigration to the US. This gives an indication of the scale of hidden prejudice.

5 Does technology make prejudice worse?

The good news

The change of any industrial revolution is more than technology. Technological change creates social change. Social change causes uncertainty. Uncertainty fuels prejudice. The lesson of history is that we should expect prejudice to rise in the years ahead. The reality of modern politics and economics is that prejudice is already rising. We can watch this happening. But there is also a very important question – does today's technology make things worse?

The answer is 'yes and no'. Most economic questions can be answered 'yes and no'. Some of the changes we are living with will help to reduce prejudice. Some of the changes will increase prejudice by feeding irrational behaviour. This is the 'fake news' problem. Some of the changes will create new ways people can be prejudiced. Some of the changes just make it easier to be prejudiced.

As Chapter 3 pointed out, a lot of the changes of the fourth industrial revolution are about communication. Past industrial revolutions have also changed communication. This is certainly true of the second revolution: film, radio, television and the telephone were all big changes in how people communicated with each other. Do the mobile phone and Twitter really compare to that? They do. This comes back to one of the central ideas of this book. In an industrial revolution, it is not the technology itself that matters, but what people do with the technology. It matters for the economy. It matters for society. Communication and data are driving bigger changes in the society and economy of the fourth industrial revolution than in the previous three. These changes set up the opportunities and the risks that matter to prejudice.

This chapter looks at the good news – the ways in which technology reduces prejudice. The next chapter will look at how technology makes prejudice worse – the 'fake news' and the bad news.

The good news

There are two big ways in which today's new technology and communication help to fight prejudice.

- Technology brings together people who are targets of prejudice. This helps people to fight against prejudice and the effects of prejudice.

- Technology brings together people with different backgrounds. It is easy to be prejudiced against a person you do not know. It is harder to be prejudiced against a person with whom you are friends.

There are three different ways of bringing together people who may be targets of prejudice. Groups can be shown what they might be able to achieve if they beat prejudice and do not do what society expects. In other words, role models can help fight prejudice. Groups can form virtual communities that give each other support in the face of prejudice. Groups can mobilise to tackle prejudice through campaigns. All of these things were possible before the fourth industrial revolution, but they were a lot, lot harder to do. Social media and changes in entertainment have made these connections much easier. That helps to overcome prejudice.

Showing what is possible

One of the problems with prejudice is that it can turn into a form of self-censorship. Groups subject to prejudice may not be aware of what they could do in life. If they are aware of the opportunities that exist, they may feel that they do not exist for 'the likes of us'. To believe that a job or education is 'not for the likes of us' is common among those subject to prejudice. This is an economic negative. It is the "road not taken".

If you cannot see people like you doing something you would like to do, it is hard to believe that you could do it. If you do not know what is possible, you will not try. If people do not try, then they do not achieve their full potential. That is bad news in economic terms. It is terrible news for the individuals in question.

I was very lucky to have parents who helped and supported me going to university. My parents wanted me to aim high. This was by no means automatic. In the UK in the 1970s, many families did not aim for university. I had no role models in my immediate family. No one had gone to university before. My father went to university after I did. My grandfather's highest qualification was the leaver's school report he received when he was 14. Future employers were told that "at woodwork, he is 'good'". That was thought to be all the qualification he needed. I clearly remember, on a walk with my family, aged six or seven, my father telling me it was okay to choose to read a book rather than play football. He told me it was fine to ignore friends telling me what to do and just do what I wanted to do. This was very sound advice, not least because I have no coordination and was – and still am – terrible at football.

Other people with no family history of going to university may not have the same sort of support. I heard a student from a similar family to mine tell how their mother reacted when they got a place at Oxford University. Her reaction was not one of joy, but (literally) "that's not for the likes of us". That reaction was in *this* century. Self-censorship by the target of prejudice could have helped keep the prejudice alive. The student in question went to Oxford, despite their mother's view.

The effects of self-censorship can be just as economically bad as prejudice. Socially, the damage is, perhaps, even worse. Self-censorship can build the idea that the system is against you. That, in turn, destroys ambition. The "road not taken" wastes talent. The "road not taken" means the right person is not in the right job.

Technology helps by letting people know what they can do. Technology lets us see people just like us as role models. This helps to build ambition. Ambition strengthens the argument against self-censorship.

In 1933, a 17-year-old African-American high school student said of the film *West Point* (1927) that it "stirs within me a desire to go to college or some military or naval school ... and serve my country".[1] (The US Military Academy, known as West Point, admitted black students from the 1870s. The movie did not show this). Diversity was not the point of the film, which can best be described as a corny romance.[2] Even so, the film brought possibilities to life, building ambition in the high school student. The new technology of film was showing what might be possible and this was enough to spark ambition. It would have been even more powerful had it shown African-American students at West Point.

Movies could also challenge self-censorship through a sort of negative effect. Seeing what you did *not* have could create a negative sense of dissatisfaction with life as it was. The same report had another African American saying, "Often I get ideas of how much freedom I should have from the way in which fellows and girls are given privileges in the movies".[3]

The US television sitcom *Will and Grace* was first shown in 1998.[4] Will was gay, as was a second leading character, Jack. While a comedy, *Will and Grace* could be argued to show that it was possible to be non-heterosexual. The show was focussed on white, gay men. As such, it may not have been as relevant for large parts of the non-heterosexual community. Nonetheless, television was showing an accepting environment for white, gay men. Will was a successful lawyer. He had a nice apartment. He had a good social group. He had a generally good life.

In 1995, only 0.6% of the US *television* population was homosexual. The share of the overall population that is not heterosexual is many times higher than that.[5] The fact that a popular television show was showing gay men doing well was rare. It showed that it was possible to be a minority, to be accepted (generally) and to succeed in 1990s America.

The media of past industrial revolutions have shown people what is possible. But the media of the past were not that good at giving the targets of prejudice direct role models. In the past, film, radio and television were controlled. The control may have been by regulation; it may simply have been economic. It did not matter. The result was media that were biased to the majority view. Showing the lives of the majority attracted the largest audience. That meant the most profit for the least risk.

Even 20 years ago, the music people listened to, the television people watched and the books people read were chosen by other people. Entertainment was chosen by 'gatekeepers'. I grew up in the UK of the 1970s. We had three television channels. The excitement of Channel 4 being launched in 1982 was huge. Our choice grew by a third. What I saw on television was decided by what the commissioning editors of those television channels wanted me to see. Such people were gatekeepers to what a country watched. The music I listened to was dictated by what record companies selected or what the main radio stations chose. If an agent or a publisher did not accept a book proposal, it was very unlikely that the book would be published.

The global business of entertainment was driven by profit. (There were some exceptions, such as the British Broadcasting Corporation, or BBC.) Risks were not generally taken. The cost of producing a television programme or an album or a book or a film meant that there had to be some certainty about the profit. Gatekeepers tended to keep to the mainstream. If it had made a profit in the past, it would probably make a profit again. Minorities would be ignored as a risk to profit.

The US Motion Picture Production Code (known as the Hays Code) shows how control helped prejudice and stopped positive role models.[6] The Hays Code was established in 1930. It lingered on until 1967. Films that did not follow the code were simply not shown in American cinemas. The need for profit forced film makers to obey the code. The original code prevented films showing inter-racial relationships. That ruling lasted until 1956. The code also did not allow non-heterosexual characters to be shown unless they were shown to be evil. No *Will and Grace* could exist in this world. It is worth pointing out that something not far from the Hays Code exists in public schools in the US state of South Carolina today. South Carolina teachers may not legally discuss LGBTQ+ relationships, except in the context of sexually transmitted infections.[7]

The control of the code kept prejudice alive. Other media had similar controls. The US Comics Code Authority (CCA) banned "sexual perversions". What was a "sexual perversion" in the world of US comics? Anything other than heterosexual behaviour. Although not part of the CCA code,[8] the head of the CCA tried to prevent a comic hero being black. It has been suggested that it was not felt right to be showing black people as heroes.[9] Stores did not stock comics that did not follow the code. If you wanted to make money, you did as you were told. The need for profit stopped positive role models yet again. The CCA code was established in 1954 and remained in place until 2011. (It was effectively ignored from 2001.)

All this has gone. Technology has taken media control away from the gatekeepers. Digitisation, streaming and social media have changed the economics of media. This is also a risk, as we will discuss in the next chapter. But the loss of control has helped to fight prejudice. Of course, some changes happened earlier. Radio helped local languages and cultures to survive from the 1930s. Television helped – not by promoting local language, as such, but by partially replacing national radio programming and encouraging local radio. This, in turn, helped to promote local cultures.

Digitisation has taken this process further. The role of gatekeepers has almost gone. Online, anyone can sell anything. The cost of selling one more album (what economists call the 'marginal cost') is zero. Once a music album is recorded, there is no further cost to making it, if the music is streamed or downloaded. From the seller's point of view, it does not matter if the number of sales is very small. It makes economic sense to sell products that are of interest to a small minority. Sellers are financially free to sell any product. Creators can create any product.[10] There is no need to get the approval of a gatekeeper to write a book or make a movie. E-books have made self-publishing viable since 2007. YouTube allows anyone who has the talent to be a film maker to make a film. YouTube also enables those with no talent as film makers to inflict their output on the world – see my YouTube channel for a practical example of this.[11]

The economic barriers to entry for books, films, TV and music have come down. There is more minority content. People who are targets of prejudice can read, see or hear about people like themselves. Digitalisation is not perfect. There are concerns about how content is controlled on YouTube, Facebook and other social media. But, overall, it is a lot easier for people to find role models today. Someone who is a target of prejudice can follow a successful YouTuber or Tweeter who is like them. They see at once what is possible. It is hard to imagine the Hays Code existing in a democratic country today. The technology of the fourth industrial revolution is weakening prejudice by giving ambition or hope to those who are victims of prejudice.

Building communities

Technology has clearly helped to fight self-censorship by showing more positive role models. Building a community is not the same as creating role models. Role models say 'anything is possible' to targets of prejudice. A community says 'you are not alone' to targets of prejudice. This can be very important psychologically. This also matters for the economy.

For the role-model story to work, technology had to be cheaper and more easily available. Those things also matter to community-building. Perhaps more important, however, is the fact that we have new ways of talking to each other. Instant communication is easier. Both of these things matter.

When I started my career, a business trip to Asia was a very lonely experience. Mobile phones would not work. If I am being strictly honest, at the start of my career, mobile phones did not really exist. To speak to friends or family at home meant a carefully planned call using the hotel telephone. That call would cost a fortune. Maybe there was an English-language newspaper with out-of-date news. Maybe there was an English-language channel on the hotel television. As a business traveller, it was easy to feel alone. This feeling only lasted a short time, of course. Short-term loneliness is easy to forget in the excitement of foreign travel with access to a hotel minibar. For a migrant, the sense of being cut off from home was more overwhelming. It was also longer lasting.

Technology has changed all of that. Staying in touch with home is simple and cheap. The almost audible sigh of relief when a plane lands and the mobile phones can be turned on again is proof of that. But social media means that modern communication goes far beyond the two-way flow of a phone call or text message. The 21st century marks the rise of the virtual group.

Social media builds virtual groups that are hard to build in the real world. Virtual groups have risen as real-world groups have declined. In the US, membership of churches, bowling leagues and similar real-world social groups has fallen in recent years.[12] People now find friends online. There is a clear difference. With a physical community, like a bowling league, like-minded people need to be physically close in order to share experiences. Building a community is easier if you live next to people like you. But living next to people like you may not be possible for targets of prejudice, who are often minorities in their neighbourhoods. A virtual community does not care where you live. Online gaming can build global networks. Chatrooms link people with shared interests. Facebook groups and Tumblr posts bring people together over geographic borders and across time zones.

In the 1930s, radio spread new styles and cultures across countries. It allowed small groups a wider audience. Today, websites, chat rooms and apps offer direct proof to isolated people that they are not alone. Any forum for shared experiences is helpful. A lot of modern communication can also be anonymous (like chat rooms). This makes it easier for people to ask complete strangers for advice or information. That can be very helpful to targets of prejudice. Families with disabled children, for example, can use technology for support. A question in a chat room can give answers and practical guidance based on the experiences of others.[13] The help can come from someone in the same situation, anywhere in the world. Community does not depend on the person living next door.

What is really different about how we communicate today is interaction. A community is about sharing, not about being lectured by a single voice. With a common language, anyone can communicate. Even with no common language, video and photographs can get a message across. Translation software helps to lower the language barrier (though the risks of mistranslation are still quite high).

Social media is a particularly powerful tool that lets people who share something find each other. Mike Johnson and Kyle Getz, who run the podcast *Gayish*,[14] have built up a community around their show over various forms of social media. The aim of the podcast is to break down stereotypes about the LGBTQ+ community. The style is wide ranging and, at times, a highly personal discussion of issues in the community. Their interaction with their audience has shown that they have a particular impact in rural areas, where the sense of being part of an LGBTQ+ community is limited by conservative social values, religion and the basic probabilities of numbers.[15] The podcast and associated social media help to bring a sense of community to those areas. They also have an audience in countries where being anything other than heterosexual lies somewhere between dangerous and deadly.[16]

Radio and television have had more limited effects on community-building than social media. Nonetheless, they have had an impact. In the 1930s, radio 'friends' were considered reliable in a way that people in the real world were not. 'Parasocial interaction' is how psychologists describe the way people identify with characters on radio and on television and consider them to be people they know. They become the equivalent of friends – even though listeners and viewers do not directly interact with them. Thus, mass media creates the illusion of a face-to-face relationship.

YouTube and podcasting have even more 'contact' than television and radio. People feel they are 'in the room' with the broadcasters. What social media does, and what radio and television could not do, is allow interaction. Social media encourages interaction with the 'friends' on the screen or through the loudspeaker. We have gone from shouting at the television or talking back to the radio to chatting in the comments section. This may result in a conversation with the broadcasters. It may result in a conversation with other members of the audience. Either way, a sense of community is built. You are not alone if you are talking with someone just like you. Shouting at the television does not lead to a conversation. Commenting on social media often does.

Social-media broadcasters use this. The style of social media is rarely the traditional, scripted broadcast of views to an audience. The style of social media is more like chatting with someone. Johnson and Getz say their first aim was to be authentic on the podcast. Their very personal (and, at times, brutally honest) style helps to build a sense of intimacy with their audience. They have noticed that the more honest and painful the subject, the more the audience responds.[17] Similarly Alexis Caught, who co-presents the Qmmunity podcast, deliberately set out to find a middle ground. A key aim of this podcast was to build a sense of community.[18] That podcast has other social-media channels. Qmmunity also uses real-world events to promote public debate, offering a range of views. Indeed, the rise of podcast festivals allows real communities to operate as a junior partner to the virtual community of social media.

Virtual communities do have 'lurkers'. These are people who observe but do not interact with others in the community. This can still be very valuable for those who are targets of prejudice. Just observing can build the sense of not being alone. However, the evidence is that those who interact and build virtual friendships will spend more time in the community – because, for them, it is more like a real-life community.[19]

The value of community in fighting prejudice is huge. A lot of the economic damage of prejudice comes from telling people that they are 'less than' others in society. That is very destructive – something that will be explained in Chapters 7 and 8. Having role models helps to attack this prejudice. But there is also value in being able to talk to people in similar circumstances. Targets of prejudice can build on their advice and encouragement. And, of course, there is strength in numbers. A community will find it easier to fight back.

Rallying against prejudice

Online communities have helped to give the targets of prejudice a stronger and louder voice. Chapter 3 showed how the changes of the fourth industrial revolution have changed the structure of politics. Single-issue politics has risen as interest in party politics has fallen. In some cases, this may mean little more than 'liking' a social-media post. A marginally more engaged person may perhaps repost a social-media post. But more serious changes are also taking place.

It would be wrong to suggest that prejudice is driven by a single issue. This is clearly not true. It is a key argument of this book that the complexity of the modern world is helping the rise of prejudice. Complex causes can rarely be summed up as a single issue. However, prejudice can be the focus of single-issue politics. Modern technology can help attack prejudice.

There are two ways in which modern technology can help fight against prejudice. The first is a general attack on specific forms of prejudice. The second is to fight against the supporters of prejudice. Such fights often use economics. Technology can help with that.

The general attack on prejudice

The impact of modern technology allows messages to be communicated more strongly than in the past. The #MeToo[20] and #BlackLivesMatter[21] groups show the power of this. These were not online communities in the sense mentioned earlier. The #MeToo movement was about sexual harassment, mainly against women. It came to social-media prominence from October 2017. The hashtag had been around for some years before that. The #BlackLivesMatter group was about the killing of unarmed African Americans by American police. The group started in 2012. It had a major social-media presence from 2014.

Both the female and the African-American groups are vast. The groups are both internally diverse. It is hard to call either group an 'online community' as such. This is not about bringing together targets of prejudice for support. Rather, these groups have sought to tackle narrow areas of prejudice through wider political mobilisation. Technology makes this easier.

Technology can help to make people aware that prejudice exists. The focus of a social-media campaign will highlight facts and data. The #BlackLivesMatter group is a good example of this. The group makes use of disturbing video footage. Videos are recorded and sent out with no help from traditional media. There is no controlling editor deciding what content should be distributed. The group sends out its own media. There was a disproportionately large number of African-American deaths at the hands of the police in the US long before *#BlackLivesMatter*. The data on this got little attention in the traditional media. Data is boring. Unreported data is boring and invisible. What changed? It was not the data. The data was nothing new. What changed were the communication and the technology. Videos can be shocking. Videos sent direct to your mobile phone can be shocking and visible. Cameras on smartphones changed the political debate.

Technology can also motivate a lot of people, fast. Eric Garner was an African-American New Yorker who died after being put in a chokehold while being arrested. A video of his arrest showed Garner saying "I can't breathe" 11 times. In December 2014, the arresting police officer was not indicted. There were 13,000 Tweets in the hour after this decision.[22] Within a week, social media was being used to arrange large-scale public protests. The protests went global. The scale of the protests became 'news'. That led to the traditional media reporting the issue. To get so many people involved this fast was not possible before modern technology. The 'telephone tree' of Harvey Milk's era could hardly have had global reach. Even nationwide protests were hard to arrange quickly before the fourth industrial revolution.

Social media has brought more people to politics. In traditional media, it is reporters and editors who shape the political debate. With the *#BlackLivesMatter* group, it was youth of colour. Young African Americans had never directed politics before. Now they were directing political protest using Twitter. Technology broadened the fight against prejudice.

Gender prejudice gives a similar example of technology rallying a lot of people, fast. The largest one-day political protest in US history was on 21 January 2017. Half a million people went to Washington, DC for the Women's March. A retired lawyer's Facebook post started the protest. The lawyer, Teresa Shook, had no history of arranging protests.[23] The size of the protest was all due to the 'viral' nature of her post and the speed of social media.

Alongside this, technology can make it easier for people to report prejudice. The *#MeToo* movement has become so powerful simply because of the number of women recording past sexual harassment on social media. Such harassment was not often talked about until recently. There was a social stigma around it. As a result, victims tended to suffer in silence. Harassers relied on this silence to get away with what they did. In effect, sexual harassment is a double prejudice. There is the prejudice of harassing someone based on gender (normally). There is the additional harassment of social expectations, which say that the victims of harassment should not complain.

The technology of the fourth industrial revolution has helped to break the silence. In doing so, it has attacked both forms of prejudice. Generally, social media puts the user in control. There is no journalist to interpret (or misinterpret) your words. Social media does not filter what the user wants to say. The user is telling their story directly. Critically, the user has the power to decide how much detail to give. That power is very important when there is a social stigma around what is being discussed.

Numbers also help break a social stigma and demand a response. A sign of the success of the #*MeToo* movement was that it went viral. Large numbers of people used the hashtag to share their stories. That was a direct strike against the social stigma. If a large number of people defy the social norms, the stigma has to be weakened. A social stigma relies on a conspiracy of silence from a large number of people.

Use of new technology was helpful in showing how big the problem was. The speed with which #*MeToo* went viral in 2017 led to a larger debate about sexual harassment. Tweets on the topic were retweeted more often and liked more often than normal on Twitter.[24] It is doubtful that this would have happened without social media. The only real way of getting a sense of the harassment problem would be by using an opinion poll or a survey. The problem is that people often lie in surveys. This is particularly true when it comes to surveys on all forms of prejudice or social stigma. It is very unlikely that an opinion poll would give anything like an accurate answer on a topic like harassment.

The changing way in which we communicate makes it easier to attack prejudice. It is easier to find out about prejudice today. The negative effects of prejudice have a bigger impact. We watch videos; there is no need to fall asleep over boring statistics when we can see and share emotions about prejudice over social media. It is easier to realise how many other people are victims of prejudice. It is easier to overcome social stigma. Today's technology has built the power of protest. It has particularly built the power of protest against prejudice.

The economics of protest

Chapter 3 introduced the idea of modern technology helping with boycotts. Apps today can tell you what to buy according to some rough idea of your political principles. There were boycotts of sugar produced by slave labour over 200 years ago. Technology was indirectly used to get the message out. The new English porcelain was made into sugar bowls that carried political slogans.[25] In the early 1900s, gramophone records were used to rally the Bengali community in a boycott of British goods.[26] Mixing technology and consumer power is hardly a new idea. Chapter 1 highlighted the boycotts of Alabama buses in the 1950s and Coors beer in the 1970s. Both used the economic power of the consumer to attack prejudice. But the fourth industrial revolution may increase the power of the boycott. That will raise the economic cost of being prejudiced.

Chapter 7 will go into the economic costs of prejudice for a company. Traditional economic analysis of the costs has looked at the damage to labour markets. That is very important. But today, the internet and virtual shopping have raised the power of the brand. If you buy online, you cannot physically inspect the goods you are buying. It is the reputation of the seller or the marketplace that gives the shopper the confidence to buy.

Anything that damages a brand can be a problem. A focussed campaign using social media can be very damaging. But boycotts have been around for centuries. What is new about social media? Why does this make economic protests more powerful?

There are two ways social media increases the power of a boycott. A social-media protest is democratic. There does not need to be a big organisation. Before social media, many boycotts were arranged by an organisation. The boycott of slave-made sugar was part of a campaign set up by churches. There was also a national anti-slavery society. As mentioned in Chapter 1, the campaign was largely orchestrated by women.[27] More recently, large organisations, such as Greenpeace, have orchestrated boycotts.[28] An arranged boycott takes time and effort. They are relatively expensive to set up. An arranged boycott has to connect a lot of unconnected consumers.

A boycott set up over social media is quick and cheap to do. Social media lets unconnected consumers connect to each other without any central bureaucracy.

The second way social media increases the power of the boycott is visibility. A boycott works only if enough people say, 'no'. One consumer refusing to buy a product will not be noticed. Social media is transparent. It is a bit like the 'building community' function. With traditional media, it is hard to know how many people join you in refusing to buy something. The act of boycott is a private decision. Other people cannot see you not doing something. Now, a consumer knows how many other people have liked a boycott message on social media. A consumer gets an idea of how big the boycott is. Perhaps more importantly, a company will have a sense of how big a boycott is.

The low cost and high visibility of a modern boycott combined to great effect in 2011. This boycott was not about prejudice. Nonetheless, it shows how today's technology can increase the power of a boycott. This is the legendary tale of Israel's great cottage-cheese boycott.

Israelis eat a lot of cottage cheese, and prices had been rising for several years. Consumers were unhappy. A Facebook event called on Israeli consumers to stop buying cottage cheese. Within a day, more than 30,000 Facebook users had signed up to the boycott. Within two weeks, more than 105,000 users had signed up.[29] Demand for cottage cheese fell 30% as a result. Demand fell most in the areas of Israel with the highest social-media use. Firms lost money with the loss of demand. Firms also worried that so public a protest might lead to political regulation of the price of cottage cheese. Social media won. The price came down and has stayed down ever since.

There was no central organisation backing the cottage-cheese boycott. Consumers came together without help. The numbers backing the boycott were very visible. This made other consumers aware of the boycott. It made firms aware of the scale of the protest. This was true even before demand started to drop. It made politicians aware of voters' views, which made firms aware of the risk of political interference.

Boycotts have also been used in the field of prejudice. American fast-food chain Chick-Fil-A was the target of a social-media campaign after the company's charitable arm funded a number of anti-LGBTQ+ entities. This led to a campaign to boycott the chain. In October 2019, the company announced "a more focused giving approach".[30] This was a coded message. It meant that the anti-LGBTQ+ entities would no longer be funded.

A broader social-media campaign trended under #BoycottBrunei, aimed at the Dorchester Collection of hotels. The hotels are owned by the Brunei Investment Authority. The campaign was started after the introduction of strict Sharia law in Brunei in 2019.[31] The mere possibility of enforcement threatens women and the LGBTQ+ community. Targeting a country via a company is a less direct boycott; the law has not changed. The campaign has caused the Dorchester Collection to retreat from social media, however. That comes with an economic cost; social media is important to advertising.

Fighting against things

Obviously, people should fight against prejudice. It is right to attack anything that tells a group of people that they are 'less' than everyone else. A lot of the fourth industrial revolution is about communication. Thus, the fourth industrial revolution shapes how prejudice is attacked. Technology makes it easier to talk about prejudice. We are able to show the effect of prejudice more clearly. People are better able to mobilise against prejudice. Consumers do not have to wait to be organised to protest. Consumers are doing it for themselves. Technology today helps to build anarchic grass-roots protests.

Winning a fight does not just mean attacking the other side. Winning a fight, especially one about prejudice, depends on *winning over* the other side. Today's technological change can help with this. Technology can help to bring together people on opposite sides.

Bringing people together

The modern world makes it easier to support targets of prejudice. It is easier to find role models. It is easier to talk to similar people. It is easier to rally against prejudice. This helps to reduce the bad effect of prejudice on people. It helps to reduce prejudice itself. But a lot of prejudice is against a minority in society. Real success in fighting prejudice comes by getting the majority to take a stand against prejudice alongside the minority.

Technology makes it easier to bring people from different groups together. This is part of the fight against prejudice. If people from different sides of prejudice can be made to talk, it can help to reduce prejudice.

There are two different theories that work side by side with technology to help reduce prejudice. The first is parasocial interaction, mentioned in the section on community. People form emotional bonds to people they do not actually meet.[32] The second is contact theory.[33] Contact theory says that if we know someone, we are less likely to be prejudiced against them. If we know people, we tend to realise that they are not vastly different to us. We get to like them. This was why the British Union of Fascists changed their anti-Semitism to target wealthy Jews, not the local Jews of the East End of London. Prejudice will not work if we realise it is a lie when we talk with our friends and neighbours. It helps to explain why anti-immigrant views are less likely in integrated cities and more likely in places with few or no immigrants.

Putting parasocial and contact theories side by side, if people feel that they 'know' characters from the media or social media, they are less likely to be prejudiced against them. Media gives us the friends we want, not the friends we have. Media gives us friends from groups we may not otherwise meet. Those media friends shape our prejudices.

It is not a guarantee, of course. Gary Hailes, who played a gay character in UK television soap opera *EastEnders*, met with a very hostile reaction after an onscreen gay kiss in 1987.[34] He said of the hostility: "I think what was so frightening ... was that the two gay characters were quite real. They were like the people you sit in the pub with. They could be your mate or your brother or your son".[35] The analysis is telling. Prejudiced people in society feared the power of television. Television was seen as promoting inclusion. The fear, fortunately, was justified. Parasocial and contact theory made the gay community less threatening. *EastEnders* gave British people gay friends. Those virtual gay friends helped cut prejudice as a result.[36]

We have already seen how the television programme *Will and Grace* helped create role models through parasocial activity. It also helped reduce prejudice. The show made people more familiar with LGBTQ+ people. Viewers came to like the characters. If viewers watched the show a lot, they were less likely to be prejudiced against homosexuals.[37] People who did not know anyone who was LGBTQ+ in real life were the most likely to have a decline in prejudice if they watched the show a lot. The media of the second industrial revolution let people have 'friends' from groups they did not know in real life. People had contact with targets of prejudice. It was just contact through the television screen rather than over the office cubicle wall or the garden fence.

Contact with people who might be targets of prejudice has been developed further with television shows like *Queer Eye*.[38] The show's male cast (who are all members of the GBTQ+ community) have spoken about the impact they have tackling prejudice with the people they meet. Contact theory is a key part of the show's success. The format plays very much on emotion. This builds intimacy between the audience and the cast. It is reinforced by the use of social media to promote the show.

The same effect is seen with racial prejudice. A 1999 survey of Japanese students visiting the US is one example. The surveyed students were more likely to have positive views of African Americans if they saw positive images of African Americans on television. The students did not have much direct contact with African Americans. (If they did, the contact was reported to be positive.) Television was shown to be changing stereotypes. Stereotypes are the 'rules of thumb' that help to build prejudice. African-American television 'friends' helped to change any negative ideas the students had about race.[39]

It does not have to be film and television that fight prejudice. If people feel a connection, the connection can fight prejudice. The *Harry Potter* books by J.K. Rowling show this (acknowledging that the books are also films, computer games and myriad other media forms). The central message of the books is inclusion. The Millennial generation grew up reading the books and identifying with the characters. They have reacted to this. Readers of the *Harry Potter* series are more open to diversity and more inclusive than those who did not read the series.[40]

The *Harry Potter* series was not presenting real-world examples of prejudice. Although some adults appear to believe the books' magic spells are real, the series was a work of fiction.[41] The point is that readers identified with characters in the books as being similar to themselves. They absorbed the message of the costs of prejudice. No one is suggesting there is actually prejudice against 'house elves' in the real world. It is enough to identify with the sort of character who is a target of prejudice. Children are clever enough to spot the analogies.

The examples so far are all very much part of the second industrial revolution. Television and physical books are very 'last century'. How does technology change this? In part, it is an extension of the community-building enabled by the fourth industrial revolution.

Today's technology can change who controls media. Today's technology can change the sense of intimacy of media. Fujioka noted (in 1999) that the main concern of African Americans about how they were shown on television was that "these images are developed and controlled by dominant (white) decision makers".[42]

The gatekeepers of media in the second industrial revolution were not diverse. The gatekeepers were mainly white, middle-aged, often bald men. (As gatekeeper of this book, I fit that role to perfection.) The choices they made were biased by who they were. The choices were also biased by economics. Obviously, the gatekeepers wanted to make money from the shows, films, music and books that they chose. Making money meant aiming for the majority audience. To aim for a minority audience would be a financial risk. Getting rid of gatekeepers in the fourth industrial revolution has increased the diversity of both new and old media. New media, such as YouTube, and streaming television shows that represent diversity make money. That has left old media trying to catch up.[43]

In the US, television has had a sudden surge in the number of ethnic minority and LGBTQ+ characters. The change came around 2014. In 2018–2019, LGBTQ+ scripted characters were almost 9% of the total on US broadcast television (old media). As mentioned earlier, that figure was just 0.6% when *Will and Grace* was first shown. In 2018–2019, ethnic minority groups were 44% of the total. Gender diversity still lags. In 2018–2019, 43% of television characters were women, even though women are 51% of the US population. People with disabilities are also still badly represented.[44]

By getting rid of the gatekeepers and changing the economics of modern media, parasocial and contact theory have become more common. They have also become more powerful. If there is more diversity in the media we see or hear, there are more chances for us to have our stereotypes challenged. There are more opportunities to make 'friends' outside of our social comfort zone. This applies equally to old and new media. But the new media bring an additional bonus in tackling prejudice. New media also deepen the friendship.

Intimacy online

Social media takes the parasocial relationship a stage further than television ever could. Someone my age may have felt a parasocial friendship with the cast of television show *Friends*. It was easy to identify with them. Everyone knows someone a little like Monica Geller.[45] But over social media, the parasocial link is even stronger. A secret of being a successful 'influencer' on social media is the direct relationship the influencer has with their followers. Social media stars have question-and-answer sessions with their followers. They react to comments. They can respond to direct messages. It is a more intimate relationship than television could achieve.

The language of the comments sections of influencers shows this intimacy. The influencers share details of their personal lives. Their followers respond. Reading the comments sections on the social-media sites of someone such as British diver Tom Daley shows how being a fan of a celebrity has changed with modern media.[46] This intimacy helps build a community for people who are targets of prejudice. The same intimacy helps form deeper virtual friendships between targets of prejudice and the rest of society. This all helps to strengthen the anti-prejudice reaction of the audience.

The virtual world of friendships can go beyond podcasts and YouTube. Virtual direct contact can also make a difference. Megan Phelps-Roper is a good example of this. Phelps-Roper was a member of the Westboro Baptist Church and the granddaughter of its founder. Westboro is an American organisation that could be said to practice extreme prejudice. Anti-Semitism and homophobia are high up on its list of preferred prejudices, but the irrational discrimination is pretty broad. The philosophy, according to Phelps-Roper, is "the good was my church and its members, and the evil was everyone else".[47] The group achieved notoriety by picketing soldiers' funerals to promote its world view. Phelps-Roper came to leave the church after interactions with people over Twitter.

Phelps-Roper had taken to social media to present her group's views. The group met with protests when they picketed. It could be said that its members were exposed to alternative viewpoints in public. However, social media provided Phelps-Roper with a chance to get to know people on the other side. She talks of "genuine curiosity on both sides". The interactions over social media were (eventually) not the shouted abuse of the pickets and protests, but a proper conversation. Phelps-Roper even suggested that online conversations had an advantage over real-world conversations. An online conversation has what she calls "a buffer of time and space". People can more easily walk away from a conversation in a virtual setting and return to it later.

Modern technology meant that Phelps-Roper was exposed to views in a way that was not otherwise possible for her. Being trapped in a bubble of prejudice can be just as isolating as being a target of prejudice. Very extreme forms of prejudice are normally minority views. As a result of being exposed to views and questions that she was not exposed to in real life, Phelps-Roper left the group. She now campaigns against the prejudice it promotes.

Sometimes technology can supplement real-world experiences. Derek Black is another American, whose family believed in white supremacy. Black was a radio-show host on the white supremacist *Stormfront* website. Black's godfather is David Duke, former 'grand wizard' of the Ku Klux Klan. Black was described as a future leader of the far-right movement but now researches and campaigns against racism. He attended a small college in Florida, hiding his extreme views. He was 'outed' as an extremist after someone had searched for his name on Google. The college had an online community for students. As Black recalls,

> I could sit there and just read post after post on this 1,000 page message talking about how I was not welcomed there, how I didn't represent them, how they didn't understand how I could be a part of this place that they were trying to build ... seeing people that I respected saying that what I was – I was espousing was hurting them ... that was a different kind of feeling from every other condemnation I had ever had.[48]

Black abandoned his extremism following direct personal discussion with fellow students. However, technology played a role in getting him to a point of self-doubt. This allowed him to challenge prejudice and, ultimately, to fight against it. Phelps-Roper is perhaps a more extreme example of how modern technology can force people to change their views. Black was isolated in a family environment that only allowed one world view. College forced him to engage with other views – with technology helping that process. Phelps-Roper was arguably more isolated, and technology was her escape from her wider family's bubble of prejudice.

Using technology to fight prejudice

The technology of the fourth industrial revolution is helping to attack prejudice. Technology has changed communication in the past. But this is different from the film and television of the second industrial revolution. The fourth industrial revolution gives us a more democratic technology. This is especially true in communication. The economics of entertainment used to create a form of censorship. It may not have been the aim, but decision makers decided on what would appeal to the majority. That made money. It did little to fight prejudice. Taking away the decision makers has changed how we see the world.

The ease with which a sense of community can be built is also important. This may be especially true when the targets of prejudice are spread out. Religious and ethnic groups often live close to one another. That makes a real-world community easier. People who are targeted because of the sexuality or disability are less likely to live in groups. At least while young, these targets of prejudice are evenly spread out across a country.

The ability of technology to bring people together has had two further benefits. First, people can organise against prejudice. The single issue of single-issue politics can be prejudice. The combination of online communication and economics can be particularly powerful in changing corporate or social views of the world. Second, bringing people together can help change views. Prejudice often targets a minority in society. It is important to win the support of at least a part of the majority if prejudice is to be defeated.

This creates a relatively positive view of the way in which technology can tackle prejudice. But, as I made clear at the start of the chapter, technology is both good and bad news when it comes to prejudice. The good can be very, very good. But the bad can be terrible, as the next chapter explains.

Notes

1 See Blumer (1933, p. 257).
2 It is unlikely that the high school student was aware at the time, but the lead actor in *West Point* was gay. William Haines's career ended after a fight with MGM boss Louis Mayer. Mayer wanted Haines to end his relationship with Jimmie Shields. Haines had a second and very successful career as an interior designer. The prejudice of self-censorship that Haines was unwittingly defeating with his film was ultimately undone by a different form of prejudice – although Haines could not be accused of self-censorship and did not hide his homosexuality.
3 See Blumer (1933, p. 156).
4 See Kohan and Mutchnick (1998).

5 It is generally assumed that at least 8% of the population is non-heterosexual. This will be explored in more detail in Chapter 10. Regardless of the true number, it is clearly not 0.6%.

6 See The Hays Code (1930).

7 See Hagemann (2020).

8 See Kiste Nyberg (n.d.).

9 See Diehl (1996). The comic in question was *Incredible Science Fiction* and a story called "Judgement Day". The hero removes his space helmet in the final panel to show that he had distinctly African features. Al Feldstein, the writer, recalled, "I went in there with this story and [CCA head Charles] Murphy says, 'It can't be a black man.' But ... but that's the whole point of the story". The story ran in its original form.

10 Waldfogel (2017) suggests that the quality of media content has increased overall. This is because, in the past, gatekeepers mistakenly rejected good-quality content, either because it did not appeal to the mainstream or because they simply misjudged the quality of the product they were being offered. Removing the gatekeepers has allowed for that quality product to be published or broadcast.

11 Yes, I actually have a YouTube channel. See Donovan (n.d.).

12 See Ridings and Gefen (2004).

13 Ibid.

14 See Johnson and Getz (2017).

15 British comedy television show *Little Britain* had a character named Dafydd Thomas, who claimed to be "the only gay in the village". The humour was derived from the fact that this was clearly and repeatedly shown to be untrue. While statistical probabilities mean it is quite unlikely that any community with a population of more than 20 people has only one person who is not heterosexual, it is certainly possible that LGBTQ+ residents will not be 'out' and public about their sexual orientation in such a small community, particularly if social desirability bias is firmly against being out.

16 In an interview I conducted on 25 August 2019, Johnson and Getz suggested that around 0.2% of their podcast audience came from Saudi Arabia and almost 0.4% from Russia. The podcast is only broadcast in English.

17 In the same interview, Getz cited an episode talking about depression, which he found a very difficult topic to discuss, but which led to a significant response from the audience.

18 Interview by the author, conducted 8 October 2019. Qmmunity focusses on rediscovering a middle ground, which Caught believes is at risk of being lost in the 'niche' focus of some online interaction.

19 See Ridings and Gefan (2004).

20 See Me Too (2018).

21 See Black Lives Matter (n.d.).

22 See Carney (2016).

23 See Gomez and Kaiser (2019).

24 See Manikonda et al. (2018).

25 See The Abolition Project (2007).

26 See Trentmann (2016, p. 267).

27 The word 'boycott' was not used at this time. The term was named after Captain Boycott, a land agent in Ireland in the 1880s. Boycott was told to lower rents and tenants felt that he had not done enough. There was a rent strike, local firms refused to do business with Boycott and local workers refused to work for him.

28 For example, Greenpeace was part of the high-profile 'Stop E$$o' boycott aimed at the Esso oil company. See Gill (2002).

29 See Hendel et al. (2017). Cottage cheese is a food staple in Israel, which is why consumers are so sensitive to the price. The price of cottage cheese had been deregulated from 2006 to 2009. The price had risen significantly during and after deregulation. At the time of the boycott, a container of cottage cheese cost around NIS 7.00. It fell to NIS 5.50 as a result of the boycott.

30 See Chick-fil-A (2019). The group has also been criticised for its lack of an anti-discrimination employment policy, which was not addressed in this move.

31 See Clooney (2019).

32 See Schiappa et al. (2006).

33 Contact theory was proposed by Gordon W. Allport in the 1950s. Allport suggested that contact was one of the most effective ways of reducing prejudice between members of different groups. See Allport (1954).

34 The *Daily Star*, a tabloid newspaper, filled its front page with the word 'SCUM' and a photograph of Gary and his fellow actor Michael Cashman (see Flynn, 2017, p. 51).

35 See Flynn (2017, p. 51).

36 Michael Cashman, who played the other character in the on-screen kiss, was the first gay character on the soap opera. He recalls that there were questions asked in parliament about why a gay character was being introduced into a 'family show'. Cashman is now a member of the British Parliament, sitting in the House of Lords as Baron Cashman. His citation as a member of the House of Lords (part of the process of being ennobled) specifically mentioned this on-screen kiss. See Cashman (2020).

37 The show did not show transgender people and rarely showed lesbians. Thus, the contact theory was most likely to be about prejudice towards gay men.

38 See Collins (2018).

39 See Fujioka (1999).

40 See Gierzynski and Eddy (2013).

41 The Reverend Dan Reehill, pastor of St Edward Catholic School in Nashville in the US, banned the books. The explanation to parents was "The curses and spells used in the books are actual curses and spells; which when read by a human being risk conjuring evil spirits into the presence of the person reading the text". See Sommerlad (2019).

42 See Fujioka (1999, pp. 54–55).

43 A television show like *EastSiders* (not to be confused with *EastEnders*), created by Kit Williamson, is an example of the use of technology and new media. The show is focussed on the LGBTQ+ community in the US. It was first broadcast on YouTube and was funded by crowdfunding – both obvious examples of new technology being used to finance and promote inclusion in the wider media. The show was then shown on streaming service Netflix.

44 See GLAAD (2019). The data here refer to scripted US broadcast TV programmes and count the number of regular characters (857). New media forms, such as streaming services, have only been added to the GLAAD survey more recently. Comparing 2013–2014 with 2018–2019, the number of female characters has gone from 43% to 46% of the total. The number of characters representing people of colour has gone from 23% to 47%. The number of characters representing people with disabilities has gone from 1% to 3.1% (note, though, that the actor portraying the character may not have a disability).

45 Ciara, you know it is true.

46 Daley has more than 830,000 followers on YouTube. He has used his social-media presence to promote inclusion, particularly on LGBTQ+ issues.

47 See Phelps-Roper (2017).

48 See Hunter-Gault (2019). Further information was taken from Capehart (2018).

6 Does technology make prejudice worse?
The bad news

Modern technology can help against prejudice. Isolated, minority groups can easily find help and support. This was often not possible before the fourth industrial revolution. But, as the last chapter hinted, prejudiced people are very often also an isolated, minority group. The worst forms of prejudice are views that are rarely held by a large number of people. The things that allow persecuted minorities to come together also allow *persecuting* minorities to come together. By strengthening the persecuting minority, the technology can strengthen prejudice.

The American white supremacist David Duke summed up this approach. In a radio broadcast he said, "There are hundreds of millions of us [which is obviously not true – ed.], and we now have a tool ... the internet".[1] He was talking with the founder of *Stormfront*, a white supremacist website. White supremacists are a very small minority. Like other minorities, they often do not live close to one another. Duke lives in Austria but uses technology to address supporters across the US. They use the same tools as other minorities. Such groups use these tools to promote prejudice, not to defeat it.

There are six broad ways in which the technology of the fourth industrial revolution can build prejudice. Three trends are often discussed: people seem to be more vicious online than they would be in real life; 'fake news' spreads faster and farther online; and people may get a distorted world view by not being challenged in their views. But there are other, less obvious ways in which modern technology is building prejudice. Modern communication is increasing the influence of some companies. Those companies may also introduce prejudice. Technology chauvinism (techno-chauvinism)[2] assumes that algorithms will give fair results. The reality is that computers can be prejudiced if their programmers are prejudiced. And, lastly, technology creates brand new ways for old prejudices to come out.

If the last chapter created a sense of optimism about what technology can do, this chapter is designed to depress.

Saying things differently

The fourth industrial revolution allows us to say things differently. The cost (and benefit) of what we say has shifted. Social desirability bias was mentioned back in Chapter 4. Society has unwritten rules. For example, making a racist joke will hopefully be considered socially unacceptable. Anyone who makes a racist joke will be criticised by people around them. People who are racist will therefore keep quiet. Being racist has a social cost. In a workplace, it can have an economic cost. Fear of criticism stops people being publicly prejudiced. Over time, this can work to lessen private prejudice.

Modern communication changes the social cost. Social media allows pseudonyms and avatars. People can hide who they are online. That means that if a person is prejudiced, but is only prejudiced in the virtual world, the social cost in the real world is zero. People have always been rude. Plato's Euthyphro has Socrates complaining of political incivility.[3] That was almost 2,500 years ago. But people today will say things online that they would never dream of saying to a fellow human in person. It only goes wrong for the prejudiced person if their virtual identity is leaked in the real world. This is why people are quick to claim that their social-media account has been hacked if prejudiced comments leak into the real world. Denying ownership is the main defence against the social cost of prejudice on social media.

The fact that people believe that they are anonymous in the virtual world reduces their inhibitions (or self-control). The speed of communication can make this worse. Alongside 'my account was hacked', 'I was drunk' is the other common defence when online prejudice leaks into the real world. Alcohol reduces inhibitions.[4] Social desirability bias is an inhibition. The fear of social consequences stops or inhibits prejudiced comments. The combination of alcohol with the instant nature of modern media makes drunken prejudice common. The speed of communication does not allow time for sober reflection.

The Roman politician Cicero used social media extensively. In the dying days of the Roman Republic, social media came in the form of letters that were intended to be passed around or read aloud to others. But letter writing is more time-consuming than tweeting. Alcohol is less likely to affect the contents of a letter. Unless permanently inebriated, a letter writer would be more likely to conform to social rules. Before social media, the only way to 'troll' someone was by anonymous letter. That takes effort. You also had to know enough about the person to have an address to send the letter to. Even the era of email meant trolls needed to know their target's email address. With social media, no such knowledge is required. Views can be broadcast to a public platform within seconds.

There is also evidence that prejudiced people are more likely to be on social media in the first place. Trolls, who often use prejudice to attack other people, tend to be narcissists.[5] Narcissism (self-love) is also something that may encourage people to use social media.[6] Social media reaches a bigger audience than writing letters in ancient Rome. That feeds the ego of the prejudiced tweeter. Thus, this means that as the costs of being prejudiced go down, the benefits of being prejudiced (an ego boost) go up. Prejudiced people do not necessarily object to criticism – what they are interested in is the attention. Trolls can easily dismiss critics, as we will discuss later.

There is a further way in which the virtual world makes prejudice easier. When face to face with someone, it is harder to deny their humanity. When people are "behind the keys of a message board" (to quote the singer Macklemore), that reminder of humanity fades.[7] The targets of prejudice are not seen as individuals. They are seen as part of a group. As the British Union of Fascists learned in the East End of the 1930s, it is a lot easier to be prejudiced against a group you do not know than an individual you do know. It is also easier to stereotype people you do not know. Being away from the person or group you are being prejudiced against allows trolls to dehumanise their subjects. This is the very heart of prejudice. If you are dehumanising a person, you are saying that they are 'less than' other people – including you. If someone is face to face with the target of their prejudice, they are more likely to accept that their target is human.

What is particularly troubling about prejudice online it that it can change things in the real world. As already described in Chapter 4, it is dangerously easy to slip into the idea that 'a little bit of prejudice is okay'. If people become used to anonymous prejudice online, they may start to believe that this is okay in the real world. Standards slip. Social desirability bias is then less powerful in the real world. The fact that extremely prejudiced people are a minority is also part of this. Coming together in an online group changes what is socially desirable. One extremist in an inclusive community has one set of social pressures. A cluster of extremists in a like-minded virtual group has a different set of social pressures.[8]

Prejudiced talk is cheap

The fourth industrial revolution changed the cost of being prejudiced. People can talk to a large group while staying hidden. That allows prejudice to explode, without any real-world cost. As social desirability bias falls, prejudice rises. Saying on social media only what you would say to someone's face is an ideal. It is not a reality. US President Obama urged people to disagree without being disagreeable. This worthy ambition is not, perhaps, being followed in all areas of politics and social media today.

Specifically, social media has changed the cost of prejudice. But it also increases what fuels prejudice. 'Fake news' is an essential part of prejudice. 'Fake news' is not new. The 'Rothschild libel' mentioned in Chapter 1 was pure 'fake news' from start to finish. It has survived for over a century and a half. But modern technology has taken 'fake news' to a new level.

Feeding 'fake news'

'Fake news' is part of modern life. This matters for prejudice. Because prejudice must be irrational, 'fake news' can be important to building prejudice.

Prejudice is based on things that are not true. The internet does not care if things are true or not. If a story that is not true is repeated and believed, it can become a basis for irrational decision-making. That, by definition, is prejudice.

Modern technology makes 'fake news' easier to spread. Modern technology spreads 'fake news' faster than the truth. Modern technology spreads 'fake news' farther than the truth. On Twitter, 'fake news' reaches people six times faster than the truth. On Twitter, 'fake news' is 70% more likely to be retweeted (on average) than the truth.[9] Someone with no media qualifications and no commitment to the truth can reach as many readers as *CNN* or the *New York Times* or *Fox News*. There are no barriers to entry on social media – anyone can post if they stay within some loose rules.[10] On Facebook, fake news is shared more often than the most popular accurate news stories. Fake news websites depend on social media for readers far more than actual news sites.[11]

All of this is despite the fact that people who tweet 'fake news' tend to have fewer followers than people tweeting the truth. 'Fake news' tweeters were less active and have been on Twitter for a shorter period of time (on average). All of those things should make their tweets less likely to spread. They still spread faster and farther.

Why is this? The great advantage of 'fake news' is that it can say whatever you want it to say. The truth can be boring. There is no need for 'fake news' to be boring. 'Fake news' can be made as interesting as the writer wants it to be. 'Fake news' can be sensational and is nearly always new information. Certainly, 'fake news' *appears* to be newer information than the truth.[12] That makes it something people want to read. Having new news that other people do not know gives a person some kind of social status. It makes the sharer of 'fake news' interesting to other people. People are – perhaps obviously – more likely to express surprise when receiving a 'fake news' story. People are also more likely to be disgusted by 'fake news'. These are powerful emotions and may encourage a reply to the sender. As social-media trolls tend to be narcissistic, that reply feeds their egos. It does not matter if the reply is a criticism. Criticism is still attention. That is what the troll wants.

Analysis of anti-immigration groups in Sweden suggests that selective use of facts or outright 'fake news' is an important strategy for building support online.[13] 'Fake news' mixes well with prejudice, because it can be used to present the persecuting group as the victims. 'It's not my fault I lost my job' can be backed up with 'fake news' that 'proves' someone else is to blame. People desperately want to believe that it is not their fault. The truth is often complicated, particularly in economics. 'Fake news' is a simple story that sounds convincing. 'Fake news' can then easily blend with 'scapegoat economics'. If the 'fake news' uses pseudo statistics or selective information to blame the scapegoat, it feeds the prejudice. This is why 'fake news' is so popular with some politicians. A simple message, repeated often enough, will be believed by some people even when it is clearly not true. 'Fake news' is willingly read, believed and retweeted.

'Fake news' also relies on using information out of context. Social media is very good at doing that. An argument on a social-media site can link to part of a story or an edited video clip. Taking something out of context often makes the story simpler. The world is complicated, which is why context is often complicated. Presenting a simple single fact that fits with a story of prejudice is why 'scapegoat economics' works so well.

This is not to say that everyone accepts 'fake news'. Social media is generally less trusted than mainstream media. Almost two-thirds of Americans get news (including 'fake news') from social media. Only 14% of Americans cite social media as their most important news source.[14] That does not mean that 86% of Americans ignore the 'fake news', of course. It is estimated that during the 2016 US presidential election, 'fake news' was read around 760 million times.[15] Of course, some of those shares may have identified the 'fake news'. Sharers may comment along the lines of 'isn't this absurd, how can anyone believe this?' It seems unlikely that everyone was sharing 'fake news' in order to ridicule it, however.

Making and faking news

The fact that 'fake news' is more common online is an important part of the next stage of technology and prejudice. This is often called the 'echo chamber'. Once you are online, the news and information that you receive is the news and information that you want to receive. It does not matter whether that news is fake or true. The risk is that once online, your views are just confirmed by what you hear.

The echo chamber

News is rarely neutral. Long before the internet, news was presented with a spin. Newspapers gave a world view that their readers would enjoy. With the rise of political parties after the first industrial revolution, people tended to support one party's view or another. The newspapers followed the lead of their readers and presented the news in a way that would fit with their readers' prejudices. It is the same with other forms of media.[16] Journalists are biased, just like everyone else. That bias is likely to come through in their work. Even the best training cannot remove all bias.

Modern technology allows the bias in news to fuel prejudice in a stronger way. Everyone can become a journalist in the modern world. That means everyone can add their own personal bias to the news. The extremely prejudiced can cluster together on the internet, just as other minority groups do. They can share news and 'fake news'. Hearing the same bias in news again and again is likely to build prejudice. The idea of an echo chamber is that a person hears their views repeated back to them, confirming what they already think.[17]

Evidence suggests that the people who are most active on social-media news sites tend to focus on a smaller number of sites.[18] In other words, if you are glued to the news on your smartphone, you have a small number of 'go-to' sites that you will check every day. It can become a matter of routine.[19] Moreover, the same sort of people will visit the same sort of sites. What that means is if you are visiting one particular news site, you are likely to visit another site with a similar view. And you are likely to find the same people in the comments section of the second site as you did in the comments section of the first site. People cluster together online. Their views are also likely to cluster together. Thus, the echo chamber is born.

However, the fourth industrial revolution is supposed to give us access to information like never before. How, then, can people be exposed to only a single viewpoint? However fanatical the prejudiced person is, it is almost impossible to escape other opinions in the virtual world. The answer is obvious: people do not escape other opinions.

If people cannot be stopped from seeing other opinions, the simplest way to keep them in your news cluster is to tell them the other opinions are fake. We are back to 'fake news'. This time what is branded 'fake news' may actually be true. If you are told that different views are part of a conspiracy against you, you will not believe those views. Any counter-argument can be dismissed with the line 'well they would say that, wouldn't they?' Because the world is getting more and more complex, we have less and less ability to fact-check everything we hear. To be able to dismiss a large swathe of news as being wrong simplifies your life. If the news you dismiss is news that does not fit your personal prejudices, you feel even better about it.

This process can add another level of prejudice. It is easy to go from saying that the opposing views are part of a conspiracy against you to saying that the authors of those views are part of a conspiracy against you. This is what is known as an *ad hominem* attack.[20] You go after the person, not the idea. In terms of convincing people, attacking the person is just as good as attacking the idea. As someone who has spoken out against the lunacy of cryptocurrencies, I am highly familiar with this tactic. I do not think I have ever been challenged on the economics of cryptocurrencies. This is mainly because the economic evidence is overwhelmingly on my side. These things are not and never can be currencies. I am attacked as being ignorant, or a dinosaur (a particular favourite), or corruptly promoting some kind of global banking conspiracy. If you cannot attack the argument, attacking the person is the obvious alternative.

Personal attacks by crypto-fanatics are just silly. But attacks by other sorts of fanatics can be a lot more serious. It is a perilously short step from saying 'this news is a conspiracy' to 'this is a Jewish conspiracy'. I have heard intelligent people in the 21st century declare that Jews run America, or large corporations, and that they are controlling the 'mainstream media' and thus the news that we read. The 'homosexual agenda' is another example of this sort of *ad hominem* attack. The idea is that LGBTQ+ people are controlling the media to 'twist' the general public's perceptions. This phrase was used, in all seriousness, in the 21st century by a US Supreme Court Justice.[21] The arguments are not being attacked. The people making the arguments are being attacked. *Ad hominem* attacks work. If you want to discredit a point of view, attacking people is as effective as attacking arguments.

Hearing your own voice

The fourth industrial revolution amplifies echoes of prejudice in two ways. First, it reinforces your views by encouraging you to read similar views. People are told what they want to hear. Second, it creates an environment where alternative views can be ignored. So, how big a problem is this? The evidence seems to suggest that some people have their prejudice strengthened. Other people have their prejudice challenged. But the fourth industrial revolution builds on existing prejudice.

People who want to keep things as they are seem more likely to live in an echo chamber. People who value diversity are less likely to live in an echo chamber. This is perhaps obvious. If you do not like change, you do not want to hear that your views should change. You want to hear that your views are right. People who are open to different views are more likely to look for those views online. At the very least, they are not likely to resist other views when they come across them. To return to the subject of Chapter 4, the fourth industrial revolution will bring change. This cannot be stopped. People who are scared of change are the most likely to be prejudiced. People who are scared of change want to keep things as they are. People who are scared of change are more likely to live in an echo chamber. The fourth industrial revolution creates the basis of prejudice by changing society. It then reinforces that prejudice through echo chambers.[22]

Prejudice is irrational discrimination. By definition it is based on 'fake news'. Modern technology makes getting information ridiculously easy. To survive, prejudice needs to defeat the facts. In a more complex world, we crave simplicity. Rather than using complex arguments against the facts, it is simpler to attack the person. *Ad hominem* attacks have been around for ever. The Latin phrasing hints at that. But modern technology is promoting them. The spread of information through technology almost forces these personal attacks. And once *ad hominem* attacks have started, 'scapegoat economics' and prejudice politics are in control.

Because the extremely prejudiced are generally a minority, the technology that benefits the persecuted will also benefit the prejudiced. Online anonymity encourages extreme behaviour. You get the high of attention without the hangover of real-world condemnation. 'Fake news' is, by definition, a vital part of prejudice. Prejudice is built on lies, and those lies need to be repeated. Nothing promotes 'fake news' like modern social media. And social media sites are controlled by companies.

Company control and other censorship

Technology can be seen as democratic. Anyone can broadcast their views. There are lots of different forms of social media. Anyone can be an entrepreneur. There are lots of different sharing websites. But social media and sharing sites are run by companies. Companies can control what appears on their sites. Free speech generally applies to governments, not the private sector. This gives the potential for corporate censorship. That may result in prejudice.

Facebook has a policy that people should only use the names by which they are generally known on its site. The aim is to reduce bullying and fraud.[23] However, this policy may encourage prejudice. Originally, the policy was that people had to use their legal names. This led to a protest by drag queens and transgender people, who were being banned from the site. However, the new policy still places a burden on certain groups to prove that the name they use is the name that they are generally known by. Native Americans also protested, accusing Facebook of disproportionately targeting and banning their accounts.[24]

Whether or not the results are intentional, it is clear that access to modern communication is under the control of companies. Companies decide who can communicate. If their policies exclude one group for no rational reason, that is prejudice.

The technology of the fourth industrial revolution is also being used to help with customer selection. Where a platform has a dominant market position, the rules of that platform can exclude certain groups in society. Who decides which groups are excluded is down to the company, not to society.

The accommodation-sharing website Airbnb has filed an application for a European software patent. The software will search the web for information about a person, which will then be used in "assessing behavioural and personality traits of a person".[25] This means what is on your social-media accounts could stop you getting somewhere to stay. What you have posted in the past may affect your ability to find somewhere to sleep in the future. The point here is that Airbnb will decide which social traits are desirable in a person and which are not. Airbnb may not be prejudiced in deciding which social traits it thinks are good, but clearly it raises risks.

A variation on corporate censorship comes with recent accusations against YouTube. Many people who post to YouTube aim to make money from advertising. However, YouTube has the power to demonetise videos (whereby adverts, which earn the video maker money, are no longer posted with a specific video). The producer obviously does not make money from that video. The video still appears on the site. This process happens if the title or content contain certain themes. There have been accusations that adding the word 'gay' or 'lesbian' to a title will trigger demonetisation. YouTube changed its procedures in 2017 after earlier complaints. However, analysis in 2019 suggests that a third of titles with LGBTQ+ content were demonetised.[26]

The direct risk is that if some groups tend to use certain words, the output of those groups may be demonetised. This is another way for prejudice to creep in. Making good social media takes time. Making good social media may also take money. In theory, a podcast or a YouTube video can be done at relatively little expense. Increasingly, the most widely accessed social media is produced using more expensive equipment. (Blogs are, perhaps, the exception). This is why many YouTube videos need the monetisation of advertisements. It is why podcasts have adverts and pleas for sponsorship.

Social media already puts lower-income groups at a disadvantage. Posting to a site is free. The technology and time required to make quality content is not free. There is a direct cost for technology. There is an opportunity cost (the "road not taken") in posting on social media rather than working. Either way, middle- and higher-income groups will find it easier to post higher-quality content on social media.

Prejudice and low income often go hand in hand. This is the subject of the next two chapters. But prejudice stops people achieving their full potential. If you are the target of prejudice, you are more likely to be low income. A middle-income person can still afford to produce social media if they are demonetised. A low-income person is more likely to depend on the money they make online. Demonetising can silence certain groups in society.

Corporate control

The changes of the fourth industrial revolution give firms more control than in the past. Companies have dominant positions in certain markets. This means that companies control access to certain parts of the new economy. Whether intentional or not, bias can creep into the rules of access.

Many of the examples of corporate bias come about because companies use computer algorithms and programs. People believe that computers make bias less likely. The truth is that modern technology can enable prejudice. What makes this more dangerous is the fact that people believe technology is not prejudiced. Prejudice becomes accepted because of technological chauvinism – the belief that computers are better than people. This allows prejudice to hide.

Algorithms, artificial intelligence and admitting prejudice by stealth

There is a belief that bringing in a computer removes humans from a decision-making process. Removing humans would remove human prejudices. Of course, bringing in a computer still brings in humans. It is just that you cannot see the humans anymore. Their prejudice is disguised in a halo of technology. The prejudice may be unintentional. Unintentional prejudice disguised by a computer is perhaps one of the most dangerous forms of prejudice. Prejudice that is not obvious is harder to fight against.

When I studied computing in the 1980s, one of the main ideas of programming was summed up as 'GIGO'. That meant 'Garbage In, Garbage Out'. If you put nonsense into the design of your computer program, nonsense will come out of your computer program. In the modern world, we might add 'PIPO'. If you have prejudice in the assumptions of your computer-program design, prejudice will come out of your computer program.

The *Pokémon Go* game that surged in popularity some years ago is an example of this sort of prejudice.[27] The game uses smartphones and the real world. The game's players are rewarded for visiting certain real-world places. Analysis of Washington, DC showed that the whiter the neighbourhood (ethnically speaking), the greater the number of places *Pokémon Go* players could be rewarded. It seems that the choice of places was driven by an earlier game, *Ingress*. *Ingress* used suggestions from players to choose reward places. Players of *Ingress* were disproportionately white (and young and male). The choice of reward places was therefore biased towards places visited by white (young, male) players. There is no suggestion that there was racial prejudice, either by the *Ingress* players, or by the creators of *Pokémon Go*. Nonetheless, racial prejudice was the result. If you did not live in a mainly white neighbourhood, you were less likely to do well at the game. *Pokémon Go* attracted people to certain geographic areas. Shops near reward sites would benefit, for example. Shops with no reward site nearby would be worse off, relatively speaking. *Pokémon Go*'s unintended bias created a real economic cost.

The virtual voice assistants Alexa and Siri do not, it seems, assist the Scots very much. The more sophisticated voice-recognition software depends on datasets to work out what is being asked. Those datasets depend on humans to work out what is what in the first place. The voice assistants are generally able to work out the difference between an English accent and an American accent. They fail to understand regional accents and dialects. Regional accents are not as great a barrier as they were in the first industrial revolution (as described in Chapter 2). However, they are still strong enough to defeat voice assistants.[28]

The reason that the voice assistants fail is that the datasets on which they rely are biased to less accented English. The human input into the programming has created an outcome that irrationally discriminates against certain sorts of accent and dialect. It is not just the Scots that are affected.

There are some real economic problems when a game as popular as *Pokémon Go* is biased in favour of certain communities. It is unfair that programmers think everyone in the UK speaks a certain way. But far more serious damage can be done when people believe that computer-generated results cannot be prejudiced.

Parts of the US use algorithms in the judicial process. Computer programs give people a score. This score is supposed to indicate how likely the person is to commit a crime. This can influence decisions about giving an accused person bail. The scores are available to judges when passing sentences. There has been intense debate about the use of such programs. There is a concern that racial bias may occur. The scoring system means that 60% of white people and 61% of black people given a score of seven (out of ten) are likely to commit another crime.[29] A higher score signals a higher risk of committing another crime. But the same system also means that black Americans are more likely to be classified as medium or high risk. The data for Florida, for example, showed that 58% of black Americans were medium or high risk, compared with 33% of white Americans.[30]

One of the main algorithms used is run by a for-profit company. The company will not give out details of its model. However, the scores are based on answers to a number of questions. The computer generates the final score, but the computer does not choose what questions to ask. Humans choose what questions to ask. It should also be noted that humans are answering those questions as well. Race is not one of the things used in making the decision. However, the answers to the questions may favour one racial group or another.

The risk with algorithms like these is that 'rules of thumb' are encoded into computer programs. The demands on the US criminal-justice system are huge. Time is limited. The information needed to make a decision is complicated. There is a natural craving for simplicity in an increasingly complex world. The combination of a rule of thumb and technology is very seductive.

This debate highlights the risk of prejudice built into modern technology. It can be hard to prove whether an algorithm is built on prejudiced assumptions. The lengthy and heated debate in the US about using these algorithms for bail setting and sentencing is proof of this. But there is the possibility that technology is allowing prejudice to creep in.

Hiding prejudice in plain computer code

The problem with computers, algorithms and artificial intelligence is that they create an illusion of impartiality. People with prejudice can hide behind this illusion. Unintended prejudice can often be overlooked. There is a tendency to underestimate the influence of programmers on computer-code outcomes.

Computers are generally allowing existing prejudices to creep into the modern world, hidden in the program code. But users of technology can also find new ways to be prejudiced. People can find themselves excluded or targeted by the new ways of doing things in the fourth industrial revolution.

New ways to be prejudiced

The big economic impact of technology is that it changes how we live now. Social and economic structures will change in the fourth industrial revolution. We will do things in new ways. Of course, we like to focus on the exciting changes. The ability to buy things online has made my life a lot easier (if more expensive). I have met people who have designed smartphone apps to diagnose eyesight problems remotely. From the trivial to the life changing, we can do things in new ways.

We can and should emphasise the good changes that technology can bring. But the fact that technology allows new ways of doing things also means that technology allows new ways to be prejudiced. Some of this may be because laws have not changed. Technology changes faster than the law does. But the effect is to increase prejudice.

Sharing prejudice

The rise of the sharing economy has been a big change for economies. In particular, this is true of developed economies. We have greater efficiency. The accommodation-sharing site Airbnb makes more efficient use of the stock of housing. We have more opportunities to earn an income from our assets. The shared-ride site Uber gives people a way to earn money part time or full time. Car drivers can make money out of an expensive asset.

The sharing economy relies on sharing information. This is quite logical. Sharing information helps to build trust between the buyer and the seller. The sharing economy is less regulated. The initial contact is rarely face to face. Trust is very important to make the thing a success. Online rating systems perform just the same function as the branding of Twining's tea in the first industrial revolution. The value of the Twining's brand gave 18th-century buyers confidence that there were no rat droppings mixed in with their tea leaves. The value of having a high 'star' rating on a sharing website is the modern equivalent. The star rating is the same as being a trusted brand. It reassures people that you are worth dealing with.

Both sides know that a bad rating does damage, so there is an incentive to behave well when doing a deal. The shared data help the platform refine its service, which helps the platform make more money, which is the point. Information is very important to the sharing economy. But by sharing information, prejudice can creep out. It might be unconscious bias. It might be deliberate. But economic research shows that it is definitely happening. This is not the same as the earlier examples of a site or application itself exerting censorship. This is about the users of the site finding new ways to be prejudiced.

The shared-ride service Uber allows a two-way rating. The passenger rates the driver. The driver rates the passenger. This is all very democratic. It is supposed to let both sides make a judgement about whether they want to take a ride together. But what happens if the person making the rating is prejudiced? The Qmmunity podcaster Alexis Caught saw his Uber rating fall after a perfectly normal trip. The only plausible reason, he says, was that he was holding hands with his boyfriend.[31] It seems that public displays of affection may seriously damage your Uber rating – if you are LGBTQ+.

Receiving a low rating as a customer means that you have a lower chance of being accepted as a customer in future. Taken to an extreme, prejudice could lead to people being excluded from the sharing economy.

It is not that Uber (as a firm) is prejudiced. It is that the technology used gives a driver a new way of expressing their personal prejudice, as appeared to be the case here. It is also extremely hard to police this. A hotel or a taxi company is (in most economies) subject to regulation on prejudice. Firms that refuse service based on racial prejudice will be prosecuted.[32] Proving prejudice against an individual who submits a subjective rating on another person is very difficult to do at an individual level. If economists can show prejudice as a systematic trend across a sharing platform, that suggests that society has a new way of exhibiting prejudice.

There is also evidence that shared-ride services may allow racial prejudice by drivers. Surveys in the US suggest that customers with African American-sounding names may have to wait longer than customers with white-sounding names. They are also more likely to be cancelled on.[33] Prejudice based on someone's name is quite common. Chapter 1 introduced the case of the Danish students who would willingly take a pay cut rather than spend 90 minutes with a co-worker with an ethnically different name.

One study of shared rides in Seattle and Boston suggested that a customer with an African American-sounding name may have to wait 35% longer than a customer with a white-sounding name. On Uber, men with African American-sounding names were more than twice as likely to be cancelled as men with white-sounding names. However, the cancellation rate was the same for those passengers if they used the Lyft platform. The difference between the two platforms is simple. Uber drivers get the name and photograph of their passenger after accepting the job. Lyft drivers get the name and photograph of their passenger before accepting the job. If an Uber driver wishes to be prejudiced, they have to cancel. A Lyft driver can be prejudiced by not accepting the work.[34]

Prejudice preventing people from accessing the marketplace is also evident in shared accommodation. Airbnb has been investigated by economists several times for different forms of prejudice. One test in the US again relied on what people assume when they hear a name. In a test, possible renters with African American-sounding names received a positive response from hosts 42% of the time. If your name was a typical 'white' name, the chance of getting a positive response was 50%. This gap held, whether the host was sharing the space with the renter or not. It did not matter whether the host had multiple listings, what the cost was or what the location was. It made no difference whether the property was in high demand or not.[35]

The economists checked whether the property was booked by someone else. If prejudice means that the property is standing empty, it puts a price on prejudice. Over a quarter of the properties were empty after rejecting a possible customer, while other properties were removed from Airbnb.

Using this information, the price of prejudice would seem to be somewhere between USD 65 and USD 100.

The suggestion is that a 'rule of thumb' about someone's name led to someone with an ethnic minority name being rejected. The property owner was prepared to pay quite a large sum to be prejudiced.

A different study in Dublin found a slightly different form of prejudice existed in the shared economy. This time, the focus was on sexuality. Sexuality is not often visible in economic transactions, but with accommodation, it is more obvious. Airbnb hosts were 20% to 30% less likely to take a male same-sex couple.[36] The sexuality of the couple was implied by using the booker's name and then 'boyfriend' or 'girlfriend'.[37] A typically male named booker would thus reference their 'boyfriend' or 'girlfriend'. The most common way of applying prejudice was simply to not reply to a male booker and his boyfriend who were looking for somewhere to stay.

It is worth noting that these results are for the period after Ireland had voted to legalise same-sex marriage.[38] The Republic of Ireland has shifted to support LGBTQ+ people. But prejudice is still able to hide behind the anonymity of a website.

Airbnb Chief Executive Brian Chesky called discrimination (prejudice) "the greatest challenge we face as a company".[39] Users are now required to agree to a non-discrimination policy (as of November 2016). Photographs of the visitor are only shown to the hosts after the booking has been confirmed (as of 2018).[40] There is also a hotline for people who feel they have been victims of prejudice. The challenge for a sharing platform in addressing prejudice is that it is not the firm's decisions that are giving rise to prejudice. It is individual *users* on the platform who are creating prejudice.

The sharing economy offers a slightly more subtle version of the boarding-house 'No dogs, no Irish'[41] sign. The prejudice is hard to regulate (because it is hard to prove in a specific case). It may even be that the prejudice is coming from unconscious bias. The seller may not be aware that they are being prejudiced. The sharing economy needs trust and shared information to work properly. The fact that people feel that they can be prejudiced over a smartphone app means that the sharing economy is not working properly. Of course, it is not working properly: prejudice is irrational. Sellers are prepared to give up income to indulge their prejudice. Buyers are not able to buy the services that other people can buy.

It is not just the sharing economy that allows prejudice. Once it goes on-line, there is an opportunity for the more traditional economy to become quietly prejudiced as well. Modern technology allows for price discrimination.

Pricing prejudice

Every young economist, when they start out on their studies, learns how to draw a supply and demand curve. It is one of the rites of passage of the profession. As prices fall, fewer sellers will sell. As prices fall, more buyers will buy. In a normal market, supply and demand will find a happy point where price and quantity match. One price will be set for everyone who wants to buy and sell. The market 'clears'. Sellers do not know much about the individual buyers. The market sorts out one price at which everyone can get together and swap cash for goods or services.

There have been attempts to charge different prices for different people. In the US, doctors tried to charge the rich a different price to the poor in the early 20th century.[42] The idea was to make more money, of course. But in the past, it has generally been too difficult to separate customers (or patients) into different groups.

Technology can really change this. Websites know who you are. Even if the website does not know exactly who you are, it may know more about you than you think. The 'cookies' policy everyone agrees to in their rush to get to the good stuff online gives away information. There are two ways in which that can allow prejudice.

Most obviously, the more a website 'knows' you, the more it can set a price specific to you. We have always had some kind of price discrimination.[43] Children travel on trains and planes for a lower price than adults, for example. The sellers hope to make a profit by persuading families to travel. That is fairly broad discrimination. If a seller can get even more information about their potential buyer, they can make more money. Estimates suggest that profits could increase by more than 12% if companies could really discriminate.[44]

Consumers probably will not realise that online price discrimination is taking place. It is hard to know that other people are paying a different price to you. The aim of the seller is to make more profit by charging different people different prices. It is unlikely that the seller is deliberately being prejudiced. The danger is that price discrimination becomes price prejudice anyway. This is an indirect form of prejudice.

We know that websites may already charge different prices for the same item, depending on where the customer lives. The sellers believe people in different areas will be willing to pay different prices for the same things. But this may result in, for example, discriminating between buyers on the grounds of race. If neighbourhoods are not racially integrated, where you live signals what race you are. That means that what appears to be discrimination by location is actually discrimination by race.[45]

What is happening here is pricing by rule of thumb. Rather than one price for everyone, there is price discrimination. Despite the hype about artificial intelligence, modern algorithms are not good enough to identify each individual person. Based on the data they work with, they use rules of thumb. If one group is often prepared to pay more for a good or service, modern technology allows a higher price to be charged. However, everyone in that group is charged the higher price.

There is then an additional risk. Consumers may not find the cheaper prices. As the online world becomes more and more complicated, we rely more and more on search engines to find our way around. This gives power to the search engine, as already discussed. This may also create risks. A search engine may push certain people towards certain websites. The advertisements that appear at the top of your search list are not placed there at random. If your search characteristics suggest that you are a member of a certain group, search engines will promote sites that are supposed to 'fit' with that group. One group is pushed to one set of sites. Another group is pushed to a different set of sites. The rule of thumb is biasing what the searcher sees, and it is a new form of prejudice.

Technology-enhanced prejudice

In a sensible society, prejudiced people are a minority. Extremely prejudiced people are an extreme minority. But this means that the help that technology offers to persecuted groups will also help prejudiced groups.

Technology makes it easier to 'dehumanise' our fellow humans. Technology makes superheroes (or supervillains) of us all. Our real-world lives sit side by side with secret identities online. People feel that hiding behind a keyboard means that social rules do not apply. As social rules are important to contain prejudice, that is a problem. The new rules of communication also have a different relationship with the truth. Because prejudice is irrational, the truth is a powerful force against prejudice. The truth shows prejudice to be wrong. But the truth is often boring. The truth is often repetitive. The truth is not an easily retweetable idea. If clicks are the only thing you care about, you will sell 'fake news'. 'Fake news' fuels prejudice.

Not everyone believes 'fake news'. It is not even a majority, most of the time. But the problem is that prejudiced people will hear what they want to hear. Everything else will be dismissed as a conspiracy theory. As the prejudice is repeated back to people online, it starts to change their behaviour in the real world.

Modern technology does not just promote prejudice but creates new risks. Constitutions guaranteeing free speech have less power when it is companies rather than governments that decide who gets to be heard. Companies may or may not be prejudiced – the next chapter argues that there are strong reasons for companies to avoid prejudice. But society is not setting all of the rules anymore.

The wonderful thing about the fourth industrial revolution is that we find new ways of doing things. The terrible thing about the fourth industrial revolution is that we find new ways to be prejudiced. Computers can lull us with fake impartiality. 'Prejudice In, Prejudice Out' is the reality of today's computing. And even if the programs are designed without prejudice, the changes that the sharing economy and big data bring can let prejudice express itself in new ways.

As the world changes, the ways in which we can be prejudiced change. The new technologies change the way in which the world economy works. Similarly, the new ways in which we can be prejudiced will change the way the world economy works. This is the focus of the next two chapters.

Notes

1 See Saslow (2018, p. 237).
2 As coined by Broussard (2018a).
3 See Bejan (2017).
4 Farrington et al. (2015) offer specific examples of drunken online attacks against sporting personalities.
5 Ferenczi et al. (2017) examined the use of Facebook, concluding that narcissism predicted trolling behaviour. Research suggests that men are more likely to use Facebook for promotion. Narcissists are less likely to value community traits such as reasonableness.
6 Please follow me on Twitter @PDonovan_econ.
7 See Macklemore and Lambert (2012).
8 Sites like *Stormfront*, Facebook groups and other fora bring together the extremist minority. That can change their idea of what is socially acceptable.
9 See Vosoughi et al. (2018).
10 Again, I would urge you to follow me on Twitter @PDonovan_econ. This will clearly demonstrate how low the barriers to entry can be on social media.
11 See Allcott and Gentzkow (2017).
12 See Vosoughi et al. (2018). This is perhaps inevitable. The truth, particularly in areas of prejudice, is often repeated. 'Fake news' is new because it can be custom made to fit the distributor's particular prejudice.
13 See Merrill and Åkerlund (2018).
14 See Allcott and Gentzkow (2017).
15 Ibid.
16 In one episode of British political television satire *Yes, Prime Minister*, fictional Prime Minister Jim Hacker complains about the bias of the national television channel covering his tour of the North West of England:

> The BBC didn't describe it as 'the Prime Minister touring the North West', they said it was 'Jim Hacker visiting the marginal constituencies'. Both versions are perfectly true, but in my opinion it shows that the BBC is biased against me ... I explained that they don't have to report *all* the facts.
>
> See Lynn and Jay (1989, p. 474, Episode 17:
> The National Education Service)

17 In behavioural economics, this is known as 'confirmation bias'. People hear what supports their own pre-existing position and ignore any counter arguments.
18 See Schmidt et al. (2017).
19 In my day job, I produce a podcast every morning. I comment on the economic and market-relevant news that took place over the past 24 hours, with thoughts on what might happen in the day ahead. Inevitably, as I start preparing this around 5am, I tend to visit the same media outlets to get my basic information. I am dealing with the economic problem of finite time and infinite demands on that time (or, in this case, near infinite sources of information). Aware of the issue of confirmation bias, I deliberately try and check media sites from

different sides of the political spectrum when a news event has an obvious political interpretation.

20 In full, *argumentum ad hominem;* Latin for 'argument against the person'.

21 Justice Antonin Scalia referenced "the homosexual agenda" when dissenting in Lawrence v. Texas (539 US 558) in 2003. This case ruled that the prohibition of consensual homosexual activity was unconstitutional. Scalia wrote,

> Today's opinion is the product of a Court, which is the product of a law-profession culture, that has largely signed on to the so-called homosexual agenda, by which I mean the agenda promoted by some homosexual activists directed at eliminating the moral opprobrium that has traditionally attached to homosexual conduct.
>
> See Scalia (2003)

22 A Bail et al. (2018) study demonstrated that in the US, Republicans who followed a liberal news feed in an experiment were likely to become significantly more conservative in their views, while Democrats who followed a conservative news feed became modestly more liberal. Those with conservative views at the outset were likely to favour certainty and tradition (and thus dislike change) and seek to have their certainties and traditions confirmed in the views that they read.

23 See Levin (2017).

24 Ibid.

25 See European Patent Office (2019).

26 See Romano (2019).

27 Within three weeks of its launch, *Pokémon Go* had more daily users than Twitter. See Kooragayala and Srini (2016).

28 See Broussard (2018b).

29 See Feller et al. (2016).

30 Ibid.

31 Interview with the author.

32 This is not necessarily the case with sexuality, particularly in the US, as will be discussed in Chapter 10.

33 See Ge et al. (2016).

34 Ibid.

35 See Edelman et al. (2017).

36 See Ahuja and Lyons (2019).

37 There were thus four possible combinations: female booker with a 'boyfriend' or with a 'girlfriend', and male booker with a 'boyfriend' or with a 'girlfriend'. Interestingly, the study did not show the same rate of rejection for prospective same-sex female renters. The authors suggest that the term 'girlfriend', when used by a female booker, may not have been associated with a romantic relationship. In modern English, the term 'boyfriend', when used by a man, would suggest a romantic relationship, but 'girlfriend', used by a woman, could suggest either a romantic or a platonic relationship.

38 In 2015, a referendum to amend the constitution of the Republic of Ireland saw 62% vote in favour of marriage equality, on a turnout of more than 60% of the population, making it the first country to do so by popular vote.

39 See Wong (2016).

40 The pledge reads, "I agree to treat everyone in the Airbnb community – regardless of their race, religion, national origin, ethnicity, disability, sex, gender identity, sexual orientation, or age – with respect, and without judgment or bias". See Airbnb (2019).

41 A variation of NINA, used in the housing market.

42 See Gordon (2016).
43 There are three degrees of price discrimination. Third-degree discrimination is different prices for different consumer goods. Second-degree discrimination is discounts for bulk purchase. First-degree discrimination is charging the maximum price possible, varying the price consumer by consumer.
44 See Merler (2017).
45 Larson et al. (2015) found that Asian-Americans were significantly more likely to pay a higher price for an online tuition service. This held even after controlling for differences in income level. The seller charged different prices according to where people lived, justifying this by saying that the pricing reflected "differential costs of running our business and the competitive attributes of the given market". Higher-income areas and areas with a higher Asian-American population were both charged higher prices. This presumably reflected the price sensitivity and level of demand.

7 The economic damage of prejudice – part 1
Firms

The first half of this book has looked at how the economy has influenced prejudice. We are about to have an age of major economic change. The fourth industrial revolution is probably going to involve more social change than either the second or the third. It will reverse some of the trends put in place in the first revolution. But, as Chapter 4 made clear, people do not like change. Change gradually builds up prejudice. And, as with every past industrial revolution, the fourth industrial revolution will naturally encourage prejudice.

The technology of the fourth industrial revolution can work against prejudice. Unfortunately, it can also encourage prejudice. We can see this happening today. So, while economic change may create prejudice, prejudice is also going to influence economic change. The greater the level of prejudice, the greater the economic damage to a firm or country.

Chapter 1 established that winning in the fourth industrial revolution will depend on people. The technology is useless without people who make the most of it. New ways of doing things come from people and technology, not from technology alone. It is vital to get the right person, in the right job, at the right time. Prejudice stops that from happening at a firm level and at an economy level. The next two chapters look at the economic damage of prejudice.

This chapter looks at the damage prejudice causes to firms. The focus is on the economic cost. This is the 'profit' in 'profit and prejudice'. Or, rather, it is how profit is lost because of prejudice. There are three broad problems. Two are about higher costs, and one is about lower income. The first is what economists (ever eloquent with a turn of phrase) call 'misallocation of resources'. This is a cost. It is the result of either not employing the right people or of damaging the people you have already employed. The second is also a cost. It is the impact of prejudice on ideas and risk taking. Prejudice cuts the number of views used in decision-making. It narrows the corporate mind. This is not a good thing. Lastly, there is the reputational risk of being prejudiced. This is about the income a firm can get. Social desirability bias and obvious prejudice can cost firms customers. Fewer customers mean fewer sales. Fewer sales mean lower profits.

Cost: wrong person, wrong job, wrong time

As a reminder, prejudice occurs when irrational choices are made. Prejudice is a big risk when people make choices about who to hire for a job. In most firms, the biggest cost is the people that work there. On average, labour costs are about 70% of a firm's total costs. It varies a bit from sector to sector. But, clearly, people are the expensive part of being in business. If the wrong people are hired, the firm will be less profitable than it could be.

New technology alone does not guarantee profits. When electric power was introduced into factories in the late 19th century, it did little to improve productivity or profits. This is because factories were designed for steam power. Workers were using electric power as a substitute for steam. This was highly inefficient. Steam-driven equipment tended to have one central source of power. Electric power could be localised. Not everything had to be connected to a central drive. It was only when humans adapted the working environment to make the most of the new technology that the profits started to flow. The point here is that the right people had to adapt the working environment to make the most of the new technology. It emphasises the importance of getting the right people in place.[1]

Hiring the wrong people

One of the earliest modern economic books on prejudice was Gary Becker's *The Economics of Discrimination*, first published in 1957. This pointed out what now seems obvious – people and firms have to pay a price to be prejudiced. We saw a this in miniature with the Danish students in Chapter 1. The students were put in the position of being employers. They got to choose who they worked with. This mimics a hiring decision. They knew that refusing to work for 90 minutes with someone they thought might be of a different ethnic background would cost them money. They were still prepared to pay 8% for the privilege of being prejudiced. The situation was designed so that the person who seemed to be ethnically different was clearly the better person for the job. The person who seemed to be ethnically similar was clearly worse at the job. Because of that, the seemingly ethnically similar co-worker was worse for the employer's 'profit' (wages for the job). It made no difference. The lost profit was clearly a price worth paying.

Becker, as an American living in the 1950s, was, naturally enough, focussed on racial prejudice. Most American surveys of prejudice are still focussed on race.[2] But the analysis applies to any form of irrational discrimination. Employer prejudice hurts profits twice. The prejudiced firm owner is paying more for poorer-quality workers. That is fairly obvious. But the prejudiced firm owner is letting good-quality workers go and work for the competition. That puts the prejudiced firm at a competitive disadvantage.

Why would a firm be prejudiced in hiring? There are three explanations: the person making the hiring decision is prejudiced, existing workers are prejudiced, or customers are prejudiced. With prejudice, someone loses. Either the firm owners lose profit, employees lose wages, or customers lose by having to pay a higher price. The critical point is that these losses are likely to become larger in the fourth industrial revolution.

If the employer is prejudiced, then (as we have already seen) they will have to accept lower profit. They know that they have the wrong person in the job. They know they could make more money having the right person in the job. They choose not to employ the right person.

A firm that is trying to make as much money as possible will hire the best person it can find. If employees are prejudiced, they have to find a way of persuading their firm to follow their prejudice rather than make as much profit as it can. One way to do that is through a 'closed-shop' trade union. The employer is effectively given no choice but to hire from only one group. In the first industrial revolution, the role of women in the workforce was a cause of a lot of anxiety. It was the male workers who were anxious. It was often the employers who fought for the right to employ women. It was the early trade unions that first excluded women from their associations. Having done that, they could threaten to stop working unless employers agreed not to use women.[3] This is not just some historical oddity. During the Second World War, British women had succeeded in a huge range of jobs. Economic necessity had meant that there was less time for prejudice. Having the right person in the right job was a matter of survival. At the end of the war, the head of the Trades Unions Congress Women's Conference said, "Women should go back to the home, whatever that might mean".[4] Efficiency surrendered to prejudice.

The other way for prejudiced employees to persuade employers to accept their bias is for workers to accept lower wages. That would be the price of not working with a person against whom they are prejudiced. The lower cost of hiring prejudiced workers offsets the lower efficiency of not having the right person in the job.

If it is the customers who are prejudiced, they have to accept higher prices. The difference in price (prejudiced firm versus non-prejudiced firm) is the cost of prejudice to the customer. The higher price compensates for the damage that prejudice does to profits. At the right price increase, an employer may then find it rational to be prejudiced. Customers and prejudice will be covered later in this chapter. For now, it is the prejudiced employer that is the focus.

Some very clear evidence of the cost of prejudice comes from the world of American baseball, a popular pastime in the US. Like most US sports, it is big business. Up until the late 1940s, it was also racially segregated. The racial barrier had prevented baseball teams from hiring the best people that they could. With the lifting of segregation, major baseball teams had the opportunity to hire black baseball players with a proven track record. These players were substantially cheaper than the cost of developing an existing player. Employers knew what they were getting in terms of talent. Black players had played in their own leagues before segregation ended.

American baseball was still prejudiced. Prejudiced firms were knowingly paying more for poorer-quality players. Those teams that did hire black players won more games. They had more spectators. They made more money. It has been calculated that in the 1950s, each black player hired by a team increased the number of games won by two per season.[5]

This is a very direct example of how hiring based on talent produces results. The teams that hired based on prejudice by excluding black players did badly. Their poor sporting performance also put them at a disadvantage financially. The 'customers' (spectators) wanted to see good baseball. Prejudice did not seem to stop people from watching good, black baseball players.[6]

The baseball example makes clear the double cost of prejudice. Teams ('firms') lost out on talented players. Black players were disproportionately 'superstar' players. But those talented players then went to play for the less prejudiced competition. Their talents were put to work against the prejudiced team. Prejudiced teams thus suffered twice.

There is a more recent US example of employers throwing away talent, although not in the business world. The former US armed forces policy of 'don't ask, don't tell' shows how costly prejudice can be. From 1994 to 2010 (yes, really), LGBTQ+ military staff were fired if they were open about their sexuality. They were allowed to continue to serve if they were not open about it. This is pure prejudice. The policy itself was an admission that LGBTQ+ personnel were just as highly skilled as non-LGBTQ+ personnel (because they were allowed to serve if they were silent). The policy led to around 14,000 military personnel being discharged. Around 40% were classed as having a critical occupation. The cost of each discharge was put at just under USD 53,000.[7]

This example shows, again, the direct costs of refusing to employ people because of prejudice. Ultimately, the US government (taxpayer) paid a high price by rejecting highly qualified staff. The personnel continued to be fired while the US was fighting wars in Iraq and Afghanistan. Losing trained personnel when there is a war on raises the risk of substantial non-monetary costs. Those fired included Arabic language specialists.[8] It is unlikely that the fired personnel went to work for 'the competition'. It is still an unnecessary cost and loss of competitiveness.

The rapid changes of the fourth industrial revolution mean that skilled workers will be in short supply. This is natural. It takes time for people to get new skills. When change is rapid, skills will be learnt on the job. It takes a certain sort of person to learn while they are working. Rejecting skilled people on irrational grounds will be more costly in the fourth industrial revolution. Firms that are prejudiced are always going to risk lower profits. That risk of lower profits is more likely in the fourth industrial revolution. The loss of profit is also likely to be larger. As the value of skilled workers goes up, unprejudiced firms will have a greater competitive advantage as they employ the workers irrationally rejected by prejudiced firms.

Not hiring other people

So far, there has been an assumption that a prejudiced firm would not hire the targets of prejudice. A prejudiced hiring policy would reduce the pool of workers the firm could choose from. Targets of prejudice would not apply, or not be considered. But the cost of prejudice may be even higher. A firm that is prejudiced may not be able to hire people who are *not* the targets of prejudice. The pool of workers may be even smaller.

Prejudice in hiring is what economists call a 'signalling effect'. Prejudice signals something about a firm's culture and values. For anyone who is at risk of prejudice, that may be a problem. It raises the fear that 'I may be next'. A firm that has or seems to have a racist hiring policy may stop someone LGBTQ+ from applying. Even if there is no evidence of anti-LGBTQ+ prejudice, if a firm is prejudiced against one group, it may be prejudiced against another group. The prejudiced policy is a negative signal about the values of the firm.

This keeps shrinking the pool of potential workers from which a firm can hire. The chances of hiring the right person at the right time keep dropping. But there are even more problems. People who are not likely to be targets of any form of prejudice may chose not to work for prejudiced firms.

The World Values Survey[9] is a global survey of social attitudes. It includes a number of questions about prejudice, covering race, religion, sexuality and gender. The survey is conducted in 'waves,' some years apart. This allows us to see how attitudes evolve over time. The World Values Survey shows that younger generations tend to be less prejudiced than their parents when it comes to most forms of prejudice. Each survey wave shows less prejudice. This trend is generally the same in different countries. The results also fit with what different age groups value when looking for a job. Research suggests that younger generations value diversity in the workplace.[10]

This adds to the cost of being prejudiced in hiring workers. Younger workers tend to be cheaper. If younger workers are not applying to work at a firm, the cost of hiring workers will tend to go up. Younger workers may also have flexibility or skills that are useful. This is particularly likely to be true in a time of major economic change. If a firm cannot attract younger workers, it will find it harder to get hold of those skills. This is not to say that all older workers lack flexibility or the needed skills. To say that would be prejudice. But if younger people tend to be flexible or skilled, deterring younger workers will reduce the pool of qualified people applying for a job.

If a firm is signalling that it is prejudiced, it risks missing out on three groups. First, the targets of prejudice, who are not hired. Second, people who might be targets of prejudice, who fear 'I may be next'. Third, the younger generation, who tend to be more opposed to prejudice. The pool of talent from which a prejudiced firm can hire is made smaller and smaller by these effects. Shrinking the pool of talent will cost more and more in the fourth industrial revolution. Shrinking the pool of younger workers by signalling prejudice is likely to be especially costly. But having lost out on potential talent, a prejudiced firm will then do more damage. Prejudice weakens the talent a firm does manage to hire.

Damaging the people you have already hired

Prejudice clearly reduces the pool of talent from which firms can hire. Talented workers will head off to competitors. This hurts the profits of the prejudiced firm even more. But large modern firms cannot be a monoculture. The supply of white, straight men is falling in many economies. This means that prejudiced firms may still have a diverse workforce. Simply hiring a diverse group of workers does not solve the profit problem, however.

Firms that have some diversity among their workers can still lose profits to prejudice. This is because people will not work as hard if a firm has a culture of prejudice. If prejudice stops some groups of workers from being able to get the higher rewards that other workers are getting, the obvious question is 'why bother trying?'

This can become a downward spiral. If a group in society expects prejudice at work, they will not spend time and money getting qualifications. If that group does not have qualifications, our old friend, 'rule-of-thumb' prejudice, will start to work.[11] Employers will take a short-cut in the interview process and tend to reject people from that group. The right person does not get the job. This also becomes a problem for firms that are not prejudiced. Their pool of skilled workers is being reduced unnecessarily, as people are not achieving their full potential. This is the 'it's not for the likes of us' mentality of Chapter 5. If people give up on trying to get skills they could get, good firms will also find it more difficult to hire the right people.

Prejudice can make this even worse. (Prejudice seems to be able to make everything worse.) Black Americans are more likely to be promoted when employers look at what they have achieved (measurably). Education is an important part of this. White Americans are more likely to be promoted as a result of informal ties. It is a case of 'who you know'.[12] Prejudice deters some groups from getting the right education. Prejudice also increases the importance of education for people from those groups to getting promoted. The question 'why bother trying?' gets harder to answer.[13]

Prejudice is therefore stopping people from reaching their full potential. If people do work to get the necessary qualifications, prejudice stops people from using their skills. In the US, women, black men and Asian men are more likely to have a degree in a job that does not need a degree.[14] This suggests firms are throwing away potential profit by having the wrong people in the wrong job.

This problem also applies when the targets of prejudice are not obvious. People do not necessarily reveal their sexuality, religion or disabilities at work. Some disabilities are not visible. Where this is the case, people may feel that promotion and pay opportunities are still open to them. At the same time, the worker will have to spend time and effort disguising who they are. That effort appears to make people less effective as employees. Stress makes people less productive. Stress-related illness means workers take time off work. If they are at work, their mind may not be on the job. Hiding who you are all the time is stressful. If people are not working to their full potential, the firm they work for is missing out on profit.

There is a suggestion that gay men 'hiding' in heterosexual marriages earn less than straight men in heterosexual marriages.[15] This idea fits with the idea that the stress of hiding makes workers less effective. It is not only that stress has been shown to make workers less productive. Stress also tends to make for poorer-quality decisions.[16] As the productive jobs of the fourth industrial revolution will involve making more complex decisions, this is a problem that is likely to grow in the years ahead. Having to lie to make a living comes at an increasing cost.

A more subtle version of hiding who you are is 'covering' at work. Covering occurs when people downplay something that they think makes them different. This applies to people who may be visible targets for prejudice. Thus, a woman might avoid talking about her family at work for fear of playing up to a gender stereotype. People might avoid similar people in groups at work for fear of being identified too strongly with their race, sexuality or religion. The stress of distorting who you are will also impact your efficiency at work. In addition, people who have to cover at work are less likely to feel loyalty to their firm.[17]

Prejudice weakens how well workers work. If firms are clearly not using merit to decide how to pay people, then people who are targets for prejudice have little incentive to work harder. If people feel they either have to hide or 'cover' who they are at work, they will be under additional stress. That reduces the quality of the decisions they take. None of this is going to improve a firm's profits when confronted with the complexity and uncertainty of change in the fourth industrial revolution.

These are all costs of having the wrong person in the wrong job. But there is an extra cost of prejudice. Even if the workers hired are individually good at what they do, they can still be a bad team. Getting the right person in the right job at the right time will be about more than the individual. Most successful modern firms are team efforts. The level of prejudice helps dictate whether those teams are effective or not.

Cost: narrow thinking

With each new economic era, the world economy becomes more and more complex. The solutions to economic problems become more and more complex. More complex solutions have more complex inputs. Humans tend to want simplicity in a time of economic change, but simplicity is harder and harder to get.

The simpler economy of the past did not need this. If a job was simple, there was no need to have lots of opinions about how to do it. Until the first industrial revolution, wheat was harvested with a sickle. That technique had not changed since ancient Greece. There was no need to have a variety of views on how to use the sickle. In fact, debating the best way to harvest corn with a sickle was a waste of time.

This remains true today. There are simple tasks that do not require debate and discussion. These tasks generally do not benefit from a diversity of views. But these are the tasks that are most at risk in the fourth industrial revolution. There is no need to employ humans to do repetitive simple tasks. Whether it is basic factory work or clerical work in a lawyer's office, automation is likely to take away the job. Simple and repetitive is what computers and robots are extremely good at. These are the tasks that are automated away.

People do add value in the fourth industrial revolution. Sometimes, this will be through complex decision-making. At other times, it will be through dealing with other people (as other people tend to be complex). More complex decisions are generally better if there are a range of different views in the decision-making process. More views improve decisions by considering the options, combining different ideas and increasing our understanding. Because people are different, any customer-servicing role needs to reflect the range of experience and views of the population. If workers understand customers properly, the customers are likely to be happier.

Considering all the points (or, how not to bankrupt the bank)

Good decisions happen when all the implications are considered. If someone did not think of all the possible implications of a decision, losses could be made. US investment bank Lehman Brothers found this out with rather disastrous consequences in 2008. The US commission into what went wrong concluded,

> Lehman's failure resulted in part from significant problems in its corporate governance including risk management ...[18]

Putting it another way, Lehman Brothers messed up. And one of the reasons it messed up was that its decision-making process helped it to make bad decisions. If decisions are all being taken by people of similar backgrounds, then questions that seem obvious to someone from a different background will go unasked. Obvious risks will be overlooked.

It is important to recognise that good decisions come from diverse *thinking*. I was once on a three-person panel discussing diversity and financial markets. An audience member subsequently tweeted a photo of the panel. This was accompanied by a sarcastic comment about the lack of diversity of the panel; all the panellists were men. The tweeter saw three panellists of the same gender and assumed that we were all from one homogenous, over-represented group. There was an assumption that three men would share the same ethnicity, educational background, disabilities, social background and sexuality. That assumption was not true. In spite of the lack of gender diversity, this was an extremely diverse panel in ideas and outlook. That probably reflected the different backgrounds and professions of the panellists. It was one of the livelier discussions that I have had. It may well have been true that gender diversity would have added new opinions. But I have also sat on gender-diverse panels in the past which have produced bland, mono-cultural views. A panel of men and women of similar backgrounds is more likely to share the same ideas. Sharing the same ideas will overlook the risks.

A group without diversity may also create an 'echo chamber'. Chapter 6 looked at the echo chamber on social media. But an echo chamber can also happen in a firm's boardroom. Views are reinforced when like-minded people get together. Everyone hears their own views repeated back to them. The certainty builds that these views are correct. Why wouldn't you believe the views are correct? No one is arguing against you. This builds a false sense of certainty. It can lead to higher risk, with more extreme decisions being taken. The group uses opinions and information from within the group to come to a decision. If some of the group like the high-risk option, they can influence the rest of the group. Views are echoed back to the group, so everyone feels more confident that what is, in fact, an extreme position is sensible and normal. There is no dissenting voice to bring people back to a more reasonable view.[19] Someone needs to declare that 'the Emperor has no clothes'.[20] If that voice is not in the room, the point cannot be made.

One of the best examples of the success of having different ideas was Bletchley Park. This was the British government's code-breaking centre during the Second World War. Breaking a German code would seem to require knowledge of the German language. Mathematics is also a logical requirement. However, relying purely on professors of German and mathematics might give a rather narrow range of ideas. Particularly in the 1940s, professors of mathematics and German might be expected to have similar social backgrounds. They were also very likely to be all male.

Recruitment for Bletchley was deliberately diverse – up to a point. The centre included professors of art, ancient history, the Renaissance and law. A crossword competition was created as a recruitment drive. This brought in people outside the university system. Post Office engineers were essential, and generally also outside the university system. Women were badly underrepresented in code-breaking but dominated what would be considered computer programming in today's world. Alan Turing, who played a critical role at Bletchley and is regarded as the founder of modern computing, was generally known to be gay when recruited, as were other crypto-analysts.[21] The range of views led to innovative thinking. Innovative thinking created modern computing, broke the supposedly unbreakable Enigma code and probably shortened the war by two years. It all rested on diversity in decision-making. British Prime Minister Winston Churchill was a strong supporter of the results Bletchley produced. On one occasion he visited Bletchley and gave a (presumably) rousing speech to the diverse group of staff. He is alleged to have remarked afterwards, "I know I told you to leave no stone unturned to get staff, but I didn't expect you to take me literally".[22]

Diversity of thinking – leaving no stone unturned – increases the chance that risks will be spotted. Decision-making is less likely to overlook facts when there is a diverse range of experience. Amid the dramatic changes of the fourth industrial revolution, leaving no stone unturned may be the difference between a firm succeeding and a firm going bust. But there are additional advantages. Genuine diversity of thinking can merge ideas together. When this takes place, the sum is often greater than the parts. In other words, two productive ideas combined can create a super-productive idea.

Different ideas, better outcome

Undergraduates cannot study pure economics at Oxford University. Instead, most aspiring economists at Oxford over the past 100 years have studied Philosophy, Politics and Economics (PPE).[23] The idea behind this is that, to understand economics one should also understand the moral and political issues that influence economics. But it is also about using ideas outside of a narrow specialisation. Combining ideas that may at first seem unrelated can produce a new and more productive idea.

Bringing together different views will help with innovation. We can innovate by making small changes, a little at a time, to an existing idea. But the explosion of innovation – and thus efficiency, and thus profit – comes from putting different ideas together. Technological innovation often comes from pulling together different ideas, often in unrelated areas. This has been described in rather vivid terms as "ideas having sex".[24]

If you are reading this book in paper format, you can thank the wine industry. The wine press was an idea that helped to produce the printing press. That only worked when combined with other ideas (like soft metals to create movable letters). But the printing press needed more than the press itself to succeed. Printing on vellum (animal skin) is not practical. It took around 300 sheep to make enough vellum to print a parchment edition of the Gutenberg bible. The ideas behind modern paper production also had to come together. If any one of the ideas required had been ignored or not properly communicated, then modern book publishing would never have happened. Mixing different ideas from very different sections of the economy led to a major invention.

Failing to mix ideas works against good ideas. Specialisation without diversity may limit innovation. As the world gets more complex, there is a tendency to specialise. Without focus and specialisation, it becomes harder to understand more complex subjects. But this specialisation also produces narrow results. If there is no attempt to connect with other groups, possible research benefits are lost.[25] Today, 90% of academic papers in science and engineering have more than one author.[26] Of course, that does not guarantee diversity of thinking – but bringing teams together to study a problem at least increases the chances of diversity and innovation.

Personalised medicine is a good example of how complexity requires diversity. Personalised medicine is about getting the right treatment to the right person at the right time. The echoes of economic diversity are already being heard. This relies on genetic information to customise treatment to a specific patient's needs. This customisation is also very much in sympathy with the fourth industrial revolution. But this is not something that geneticists can do alone. Personalised medicine involves genetics and medicine. It also needs to consider ethics and the social impact. There are legal questions. There are economic questions. Oxford University's Centre for Personalised Medicine, therefore, brings together all these groups to advance personalised medicine – combining as many diverse ideas as possible.[27]

Combining ideas also means that people do not have to remember everything. That is impossible anyway. Even the best chief executive cannot know everything that is happening in a large, modern firm. To attempt to do so would (literally) be to behave like a Neanderthal. Early humans were able to adapt to significant change because they shared information. A species that moved from Africa to the Arctic met with some pretty dramatic changes. Homo Sapiens lived in groups and shared information. They overcame the changes they had to face. Neanderthals, it is believed, were more solitary and, thus, did not share information. Humans did not have to remember everything. Humans just had to remember to share their expertise. Learning from someone else is always more efficient than teaching yourself through trial and error.[28]

This meant that although Neanderthals may have had larger brains than humans, they were limited. Humans, by pooling information, had huge capacity to store and use information. It is the difference between getting information from a computer disk and getting information from the internet. This is what firms need to do. Sharing information from lots of different sources tends to lead to the best outcome. This seems to be especially true in the face of change. And, for firms, the fourth industrial revolution is a huge change.

The collective brain

Prejudice does not allow good decision-making. Risks are overlooked. More extreme views may be reinforced by the lack of anyone to declare that the 'Emperor has no clothes'. As the world gets more and more complex, we run the risk of specialising too much. Forgetting to take ideas from a wide group undermines what allowed humans to evolve.

The fourth industrial revolution increases the value of broad thinking. Narrow, simple jobs do not require a lot of debate. There is little value in having a variety of opinions about simple tasks. But this is exactly the sort of task that the fourth industrial revolution will automate. It is the creative, complex tasks that humans will do. This is where the interaction of humans and technology will add most to the economy and to corporate profits. It is exactly these tasks that require broad discussion and different opinions. Prejudice blocks this from happening. That increases the costs for a firm. Any new technology will be less effective than it should be if no one thinks properly about how to use it.

However, prejudice does not just affect a firm's costs. Prejudice can threaten a firm's income. As the interaction of income and costs is what drives profit, this is also going to matter.

Income: customers

Becker's work on prejudice[29] included analysis of customers. Customers of a prejudiced firm will pay a price. This is either in the form of a higher price or lower quality (or some mix of the two). If it is prejudiced customers who are causing the firm to have a prejudiced hiring policy, it is presumably deemed to be a price worth paying.

The racial divide of 1950s America meant that customer prejudice was still a real issue. Customers did not want to be served by people from a different ethnic group. It still exists in some societies and industries today. But as society has shifted, firms increasingly face consumers who oppose prejudice. Customers are not a single group with single ideas. Customers can disagree violently with one another.

For a global firm, the division of consumers into prejudiced and anti-prejudiced groups can be a huge problem. Take, for example, the issue of marriage equality. A global firm may wish to support marriage equality. It signals that it considers its staff to be equal. That boosts productivity. It makes moving staff around the firm easier.[30] It is a positive signal to customers who support marriage equality. However, in many parts of the world, marriage equality is not supported. Some groups actively oppose it. This means that customers in some parts of the world may object to the firm taking a position on this point and stop using the firm.

The technological shifts of the fourth industrial revolution have made this a powerful economic issue. As discussed in Chapter 5, the power of the boycott has increased in modern times. It is easier to organise a corporate boycott. The success of a boycott can be a lot more visible. Social media rallies support. As already mentioned, the Chick-fil-A restaurant chain ended its support for anti-LGBTQ+ groups after protests. But that decision then met with a reaction. The governor of Texas tweeted disapproval of the decision, along with photographs of his meal at a rival restaurant. There were calls from anti-LGBTQ+ groups to boycott Chick-fil-A.[31]

It might seem logical for a firm to take a neutral position. But as politics has become more polarised in the fourth industrial revolution, neutrality on social issues has become more difficult. Being neutral on an issue of prejudice may undermine a firm's productivity through the impact on its workers.[32] There is also a risk that opponents of prejudice see neutrality as being the same as support for prejudice. South African Archbishop Desmond Tutu said,

> If you are neutral in situations of injustice, you have chosen the side of the oppressor. If an elephant has its foot on the tail of a mouse and you say that you are neutral, the mouse will not appreciate your neutrality.[33]

Modern communications mean that silence on issues of prejudice is very obvious. With social media has come an expectation of instant opinion. This is not necessarily a good thing. There are times when a period of thought is useful. But the reality is that silence is increasingly seen as unacceptable. As the fourth industrial revolution raises the value of a firm's brand, the values that are associated with that brand become increasingly powerful. A brand is a way of simplifying a lot of complicated information. But that does push firms to have clear positions, rather than silence, on the issues that matter to their customers. A brand has to stand for something.

Show me the money – what is the cost of prejudice?

Prejudice raises a firm's costs and can cut a firm's income. Both these things will hurt profits. So, how much does prejudice cost a firm?

A 2011 study found that nearly all of the top 50 American firms and top 50 government contractors believed that diversity policies were good for business.[34] But the idea is not expressed in hard cash terms. This brings us back to a problem mentioned right at the start of this book. Economic data is poor quality in normal times. Economic data in a time of structural change is even worse. Economic data about something so personal as prejudice (with the potential for added legal problems for firms that admit to prejudice) leaves economists wringing their hands in despair. But there are some signs that can be used.

With staff accounting for around 70% of corporate costs, firms that fail to make the most of their workers should have some negative effects. One estimate from the US suggests that losing staff to prejudice costs around 0.4% of the economy each year.[35] That is just the cost of having to replace people fleeing prejudice. It does not include the fact that firms with prejudice are less efficient. On top of the hiring cost, a prejudiced firm is not hiring the best people. The people who are hired may not be working as hard as they could. The decisions being taken by a prejudiced firm are likely to be lower quality in many industries. All of those will do a lot of damage to a firm's profit.

Analysis of racial diversity between the different US states yields some very large numbers. An increase in diversity may improve productivity by around 25% to 30% in certain professions.[36] Higher productivity is potentially higher profit for a firm. Productivity will include the quality of the people hired. It will include how hard people at the firm are working. It will include any improvement in decision-making.

The firms with the 25–30% productivity gains are those that depend on creativity. They tend to have complex decision-making. Parts of the economy with high customer service also do better with diversity. There are no gains in productivity for parts of the economy that do not need creativity. Transportation, for example, does not gain from diversity. A long-haul truck driver will have to make decisions at work. However, these are unlikely to be complex decisions that would benefit from multiple points of view.

This stresses why diversity in the fourth industrial revolution is so important. Automation, digitalisation and robotics will replace jobs in the less creative parts of the economy. If a job does not require too much thought, a robot can do it. If a job does not involve much customer service, it can be automated or digitised. The parts of the economy that grow in the fourth industrial revolution are the parts that make most profit when there is diversity.

Even in sectors where prejudice is less damaging, like trucking, there will still be some jobs that require creativity or more complex decision-making. The management of a haulage firm will be making decisions that could benefit from diverse input. The risk is that if a firm is generally prejudiced, the signal that sends will make it more difficult to attract the right people into the jobs where diversity is important.

Investors seem to be reacting to the cost of prejudice. The diversity of a firm's board is often reflected in its share price. The focus tends to be on gender diversity. But if prejudice weakens the productivity of workers, it is not just diversity at the top of a firm that will matter. Productivity is only going to be maximised if firms minimise prejudice at all levels. One study of technology firms suggested that 1% female employment (across the firm) increased average equity performance by 0.1%.[37] That is a meaningful amount.

A firm that runs on simple repetitive tasks, without much interaction with customers, may not benefit much from diversity. Such a firm may not have much of a future in the fourth industrial revolution. Otherwise, the evidence is that diversity will increase profits.[38] Investors are increasingly noticing this and rewarding firms that are diverse. For firms, profit and prejudice do not go together.

Why would firms be prejudiced?

The profit motive for not being prejudiced is strong. This raises an obvious question. Why do market forces not stop prejudice? Rationally, firms are supposed to maximise profit. It is in the interest of firms and their profit margins not to be prejudiced.

To come back to the original definition – prejudice is *irrational* discrimination. The rationality of economic theory is attacked by prejudice. Prejudice is also something that can happen at an individual level. A firm's board may realise the cost of prejudice – but a firm's board rarely takes every decision within the organisation. Decisions, especially about hiring, are made all the way down a firm's hierarchy. Personal irrational bias can easily creep in.

The prejudice of American baseball teams, discussed earlier, shows this irrationality at work. By the early 1950s, it was very, very clear that baseball teams that were racially segregated were underperforming. The five teams that employed the greatest number of black players were five of the six top winning teams. Teams that were racially segregated had fewer star players. They lost more games. They made less money by attracting fewer spectators. They had higher costs. (Black players were normally paid less than the players they replaced). As a sports team and as a business, the only possible rational thing to do would be to desegregate. And yet, five years after desegregation was allowed, fewer than half the teams had desegregated.[39] Irrational prejudice triumphed over rational logic. Market forces were not working. Converting the losses into 2020 values, the average prejudiced team had between USD 20million and USD 25million of lost profits.[40] It was not until 1965 that all major-league baseball teams had at least one full-time black player.

Even in the modern, changing economy, we still spend a lot of time with the people we work with. More of that time may be virtual, as the Covid-19 crisis accelerates some of the changes of the fourth industrial revolution, such as home working. Even so, working together still needs us to trust our co-workers. We need to be able to talk to them. We may even want to like them. In fact, these things may be more important in a world with more virtual and remote working. The problem is what is known as 'in-group bias'. People feel comfortable with people like themselves. Being challenged can be socially awkward or irritating. That means that people hired may look and sound like the person hiring them. What is more troubling is that people hired will think like the person hiring them.

People may not know that they are being prejudiced. 'Unconscious bias' refers to the fact that adult humans come pre-programmed with a whole set of 'rules of thumb'. These prejudices and generalisations start very early in life. It means that there is a gap between what people say and what they do. In economics, of course, it is the action and not the intention that matters.[41] Whether people know that they are being prejudiced or not, if their actions are prejudiced, the economy will suffer. Just to complicate things, a lot of people will deliberately hide prejudice. Social desirability may mean that people claim not to be prejudiced, but are still prejudiced in reality.[42] This makes it very difficult for an economist trying to model prejudice. We can only see it in the outcomes (the wrong people in the wrong job at the wrong time).

There is evidence that larger firms with formal hiring processes can reduce this prejudice. If there is a formal process for hiring, personal bias is less able to work. The rules of thumb that encourage unconscious bias are challenged. Having to justify each decision in a rational way can cut the amount of prejudice in a process. But if the hiring process is too complicated, managers may move to more informal hiring methods. That then allows the bias to come back in. If a firm's hiring policy slips into 'who you know,' there is a huge problem. As mentioned earlier, in the US, the informal network of who you know plays a more important role in the hiring and promotion of white men. That does not guarantee the right person in the right job at the right time. To get diverse thinking, hiring really needs to be a case of 'who you don't know'.

A manager might view hiring a worker who might be subject to prejudice as a risk. A workforce that gets along is a workforce that does not require so much management. Research suggests that risk-averse managers are more likely to be prejudiced in their hiring policies.[43] This may not be because they are prejudiced, as such. It is simply because they like 'a quiet life' and are putting their own interests ahead of those of the firm. Having a quiet life is rational for the manager. It is not rational for the firm, as it does not lead to a profit maximising outcome.

In the rational world of an economic model, firms would not be prejudiced. Prejudice cuts profits. Investors notice this. However, firms are still prejudiced. The simplest explanation is that we do not live in a rational world. The reality is that people who make decisions in a firm will have prejudices. If the culture and structure of the firm do not overcome those prejudices, the actions the firm takes will be subject to prejudice.

Prejudice and profit

We can say that prejudice will lower profit. We cannot say, with any credibility, that prejudice lowers profit by a certain percentage. Economics is not precise. People do not admit to being prejudiced. People may not know they are being prejudiced. There is no good index for prejudice that can be plotted against profit on a chart. More importantly, any number trying to itemise the profit lost would be out of date in months. The cost of prejudice to a firm is not stable; it will change over time. It will increase during an industrial revolution. The fact that the world's leading firms are trying to encourage a diverse culture does suggest that the damage of prejudice is being understood. The fact that investors are reacting to crude measures of prejudice is also a sign that the profit lost to prejudice is likely to be significant.

The fourth industrial revolution will increase complexity. Complexity, by default, requires more complex decisions. Those decisions need to be taken by a more diverse group if they are to avoid obvious errors. Simple, repetitive tasks that do not involve complex decisions are most likely to disappear in the years ahead. The share of a firm's employees that will *need* diversity to make the best decisions will rise. A firm that is prejudiced will be at a competitive disadvantage.

Firms are a key part of the overall economy. If prejudice hurts the profit of firms, that is one signal that there may be problems in the wider economy. A lot of the damage of prejudice takes place at the level of the firm. However, prejudice can also be considered a cost to the economy at large.

Notes

1 Harford (2017) notes that, in 1900, electric power accounted for less than 5% of the mechanical drive of US factories. Steam still dominated, despite the fact that electric-powered motors for commercial use had been around since the early 1880s. It is also worth noting that the first steam engine was actually invented by Hero of Alexandria in the first century CE. Hero, sadly, did not have people who would implement the technology in a productivity-enhancing way. The people needed to implement the technology did not come along for another 16 centuries or so.
2 See Rogers (2006, p. 61).
3 For the male workers, this had a double advantage. They were reducing competition for employment by cutting out half the population. In addition, they were able to play up gender stereotypes ('a woman's place is in the home') as a justification for higher wages – a 'family wage'. See Burnette (2008).
4 See Hicks (2017, p. 42).
5 See Gwartney and Haworth (1974).
6 Ibid.
7 See Keyes (2011).
8 Ibid.
9 See World Values Survey (2020).
10 See Gibson et al. (2009).
11 See Rogers (2006).
12 Baldi and Branch McBrier (1997) did a detailed study. As with most US studies on prejudice, the focus is on race. However, it seems reasonable to suppose that similar issues will apply to any group that is the visible target of prejudice.
13 Sexuality is possibly an exception to this. As we will see in Chapter 10, sexuality is relatively unusual among targets for prejudice, in that it is rare that the prejudice is shared with family. As such, LGBTQ+ people may strive harder to show that they have something to 'prove' to their families. Andrew Tobias, the financial writer, wrote two books –*The Best Little Boy in the World* and *The Best Little Boy in the World Grows Up* – referencing this desire to outperform in order to win approval from one's family (See Tobias, 1973; 1998). It is also true that gay men have higher educational levels than straight men from similar family backgrounds (Blandford, 2003; Rogers, 2006).
14 See Rogers (2006, p. 84).
15 See Blandford (2003). The analysis is focussed on whether being unmarried contributes to a sexuality pay gap. The research predates equal marriage in the US, of course. The sample of 'masked' lesbian and gay workers – workers in heterosexual marriages, while behaviourally LGBTQ+ – is based on a small sample. Because this is a self-identification survey, the reported number of LGBTQ+ people (masked or not) is almost certainly lower than in reality.
16 Coates (2012) cites research on this, with specific reference to the financial sector. Hedge funds are now more inclined to separate decision-making from trading in order to insulate the decision makers from stress as much as is possible.

17 See Deloitte (2019).
18 See Financial Crisis Inquiry Commission (2011, p. 343).
19 See Sunstein (2019).
20 See Andersen (1837).
21 See Smith (2015). Bletchley Park was not an LGBTQ+ utopia. Alan Turing, Angus Wilson and other gay men were recruited because they had unique skills (and at a time of national emergency, any prejudice that denied those skills could have had dire consequences for the war effort). Two more junior female staff were fired for an inappropriate relationship. This was seen as disruptive and their work was not valuable enough to suspend prejudice.
22 See Smith (2011, p. 137).
23 There are other undergraduate joint honours degrees involving economics, but economics is not taught as a single subject.
24 See Ridley (2010).
25 Jones (2010) and Kellogg School of Management (2011) cover this with regard to the scientific community.
26 See National Research Council (2015).
27 See Centre for Personalised Medicine (n.d.).
28 Boyd et al. (2011) give a detailed example of this, focussing on the need to pool information to survive in the Arctic.
29 See Becker (1957).
30 Prior to the Obergefell ruling in the US (see Chappell, 2015), a firm may have had difficulties moving people around the country. Asking a married man with children to move from, say, New York to South Carolina would have been high risk if the man were married to another man. Their marriage was recognised in New York, but not in South Carolina. The rights normally associated with marriage – including guardianship over the children of the marriage – would not have been recognised. The lack of marriage equality posed a considerable additional cost to the person contemplating the move. Under certain circumstances, a father could theoretically lose his children, simply because he lived in the wrong state.
31 See Ennis (2019).
32 Failing to visibly oppose prejudice is a signal for potential employees. It may also be viewed as tacit acceptance of prejudice, changing the working environment.
33 See Younge (2009).
34 See Badgett et al. (2013).
35 Burns (2012) estimated that the additional recruitment cost was USD 64bn per year in 2012. That equates to 0.4% of US GDP (author's calculations).
36 Sparber (2009) suggests that a standard deviation increase in racial diversity leads to an increase in productivity of approximately 30% across the legal, financial and health sectors, for example. A standard deviation improvement in racial diversity is the equivalent of moving from the diversity of South Dakota to the diversity of Tennessee.
37 See Kellogg School of Management (2020).
38 Burns (2012) notes that 48 of the Fortune 50 firms had non-discrimination policies for sexuality, for instance. This is a clear signal to investors that the firms' management teams value diversity.
39 See Gwartney and Haworth (1974).
40 See Lanning (2010), adjusted by the author for 2020 values.
41 Bayer and Rouse (2016) surveyed the US economics profession, which has significant underrepresentation of both women and ethnic minorities in academia. They argued that unconscious bias plays a role – although acknowledging the lack of specific studies focussed on economists. They also noted bias (whether

unconscious or not) among students about their teachers when assessing the quality of tuition. This is a reminder that what might seem to be an objective measure of performance (review by the 'customers' in the form of students) may not be objective. As soon as people are asked to give their opinion, irrationality and bias can be introduced – just as with the biases of computer programs discussed in Chapter 6.

42 Coffman et al. (2013) look at this with specific reference to the LGBTQ+ community. Using a veiled elicitation method, they found that 67% more people were likely to disapprove of an openly LGBTQ+ manager at work than would admit to being prejudiced if asked directly. Further, 71% more people were likely to say it should be legal to discriminate against LGBTQ+ workers than would admit to the prejudice if asked directly.

43 See Baert (2018).

8 The economic damage of prejudice – part 2

The economy

It seems fairly logical to conclude that if prejudice damages firms, it must also damage the overall economy. Private-sector jobs account for 85% of employment in the US.[1] If firms are prejudiced, this will damage their profits by reducing the productivity of their workers. The damage to profits and employees will affect the standard of living in the economy. Workers will earn less than their skills would justify. Savers will have a lower return than they could achieve.

Prejudice in society will also damage the economy directly. This is not the same as prejudice in a single firm. Single-firm prejudice will affect the shareholders, employees or customers of the firm. Those groups must 'accept' the cost of their prejudice. Prejudice in the wider economy will hurt the profits of all firms. It does not matter whether the individual firm is prejudiced or not; society's prejudice will damage their profits.

Economy-wide damage from prejudice is most obvious in the labour market. Firms that have employed the wrong people will feel the pain in their profits. Similarly, if prejudice means that economies cannot employ the right people, in the right jobs, at the right time, the economy will perform below its potential. The two key labour-market concerns revolve around labour mobility and productivity. Social prejudice stops workers being where they are needed most and stops them working as hard as they could.

The other common form of economy-wide prejudice is prejudice against foreigners. Prejudice often attacks the free movement of labour, goods and capital. Immigration has become central to 'anti-politics' today. As Chapter 4 identified, the policy of 'scapegoat economics' naturally tends to attack foreigners. Linked to such attacks on foreigners is the rise of trade protection. Trade protection is often prejudice based. There are times when trade barriers or taxes are justified. But accusing foreigners of 'unfair' trade practices helps 'scapegoat economics'. Lastly, foreign ownership of firms can be resisted through prejudice. People can get quite emotional in opposing the idea that foreigners own 'our' firms.

These forms of prejudice limit how well an economy can perform. And they are all likely to be bigger problems in the fourth industrial revolution.

Labour – moving around

Being able to move to find work is important if an economy is to work properly. If the whole aim is to have the right person in the right job, if that person is on the other side of the country, they need to be able to move.

Prejudice is a barrier to people moving about. Chapter 2 mentioned the unemployed female spinners of southern England in the first industrial revolution. These women were not able to move to find work in the new northern mills because of prejudice. There was suspicion about poor people moving around the country. If you were poor, you were seen as a potential troublemaker. Worse, you might cost the local parish money. As the rich made the laws, the laws could be used to prevent labour mobility. The result was a shortage of workers in the north. This hurt the efficiency (and profit) of the northern mills. There was extreme poverty in the south – again, an economic loss. It was not the northern mill owners that were prejudiced. Indeed, the northern mill owners were eager to employ women if they could. If they were low-cost (poor) workers, so much the better. The prejudice was from the rate payers (taxpayers) of the parishes between the south and the north. That prejudice hurt labour mobility in the wider economy.

The years after the American Civil War saw prejudice hurt the US economy. Geographically, it was a mirror image of what had happened in the UK. The southern states experienced a significant labour shortage. A combination of prejudices prevented people moving south. The racial segregation that continued in the post-war southern states meant that ethnic minorities would not choose to transfer from the less prejudiced north. This is not to say prejudice was absent in the north. Four Union states had been slave states at the start of the Civil War. But moving south made little sense unless you were white.

Similarly, immigrants to the US faced prejudice in the south and did not tend to locate there. Southern states were active in trying to encourage immigrants to avoid the north and come south. It did not work. As noted in Chapter 4, Catholics were early targets of the Ku Klux Klan. Why move to an area of the country where your religion could mean you may be physically attacked or killed? The South Carolina Commissioner for Immigration and former Confederate General John Wagener wrote,

> ... it is the circumstance that native residence looks with coldness and suspicion upon new comers. I must confess that the apprehension of your [southerners'] prejudices against the foreigner discourages me more than anything else ... strong opposition [to immigration] was based on nothing other than bare prejudice.[2]

The south continued to suffer a labour shortage: immigrants who were brought in soon moved north and west.[3]

The prejudice that prevented people moving to the southern US meant that the southern economy suffered. There was a shortage of labour, including skilled labour. The economy lagged. But it was not just the south that suffered. Workers in the north had lower standards of living than they could have had. The prejudice that created a labour shortage in the south meant a higher supply of labour in the north than would otherwise have been the case. Wages and living standards were therefore lower than they would have been in a country with less prejudice and more mobility.

In 1902, the Federal Industrial Commission recommended that immigrants be encouraged to move out of the 'crowded' northern cities and relocate to the south. Yet by 1910, only 2% of people in the southern states were foreign born. In the rest of the country, it was 20%.[4] The migrant share of the population of the southern states actually fell in the aftermath of the civil war, as the *relative* prejudice of the south increased. The whole US economy suffered. If workers are not where they are most needed, the economy as a whole has a lower standard of living.

The impact of prejudice on labour mobility persists. Until a Supreme Court ruling in 2015,[5] the US was divided over marriage equality. Same-sex marriages were legal in some states, but not in others. This prejudice limited labour mobility and employment. Same-sex couples were both more likely to be employed in states with same-sex marriage.[6] That increased the costs of moving to a prejudiced state without same-sex marriage. Even if it was a good idea (economically speaking) for one partner to make the move, there was a higher risk of the other partner not being employed. The prejudiced state would also reduce other rights. Tax, inheritance, rights as next of kin and rights as a parent could be fewer or non-existent in a state without same-sex marriage. The cost of a same-sex couple moving state went up. The higher cost lowered labour mobility. The lower labour mobility hurt economic efficiency. The right person could not be employed in the right job.

It is not just the individual who has to consider the costs of moving in a prejudiced society. Firms' profits are hurt, so they also have to consider the costs. If firms worry about being able to move people around, they may not invest in certain places. From 2016 to 2019, North Carolina had what became known as the 'bathroom law,' which prevented transgender people from using the correct bathroom.[7] Local governments within the state were also prohibited from passing anti-discrimination legislation on sexuality. Further new legislation meant that the state could overrule any local regulations that made it illegal to fire someone for being LGBTQ+, for example. The payments firm PayPal changed its plan to open a centre in Charlottesville in response. The firm specifically cited the prejudice the laws implied.[8]

The PayPal decision may have been about more than moving employees around the country. It is likely to have reflected the risk to the firm's brand of being tied to such prejudice. The impact on staff morale must also have been a factor. But PayPal had (presumably) decided that the best place to locate its new centre was Charlottesville. The introduction of prejudice *in the economy* forced PayPal to move to a (presumably) second-best site. Prejudice in one part of the economy hurt the ability to move people around. It resulted in a second-best economic outcome for a firm.

It is important to be able to move someone who has the right skills to the place where they can do most good. The fourth industrial revolution may reduce the importance of where we work. Nonetheless, legally, people have to be employed in a certain place. Their employment is governed by the laws of that place. If people do not want to work under prejudiced laws, they will work less effectively somewhere else. The whole economy suffers.

Labour – being productive

It is all very well to keep saying that we must get the right person in the right job at the right time. But what makes a person economically 'right'? Economists, with their ability to answer any question, would say that it all comes down to productivity. The right person is the person who works hardest (or is most productive). If prejudice hurts productivity in the economy, then the whole economy will suffer for it. Prejudice damages productivity by stopping people from using their talents. There are three ways that happens.

As Chapter 7 explained, within a firm, people will stop trying to work hard if the working environment is one of prejudice. Why bother trying if you will not be rewarded for your efforts? But the effect of this can go beyond an individual firm. If one group is the target of prejudice, the whole group may stop trying to succeed.

The second way prejudice hurts productivity is more subtle. This is prejudice against outsiders. By extension, this becomes prejudice against change. Resistance to change is very damaging to innovation. If prejudice stops people challenging how things are done, change is likely to be more painful.

The third way prejudice hurts productivity is by preventing entrepreneurs from being entrepreneurial. New ideas normally cost money. If some groups find it hard to raise money, their new ideas are likely to be lost to the economy.

These forms of prejudice create a negative operating climate for firms. The result is likely to be lower productivity. That means lower profits.

Arrested development

Targets of prejudice have to work harder to prove themselves. We have already seen that white Americans are more likely to be promoted through informal networks. Other ethnic groups need to prove themselves through their skills. This bias has been around for a long time. US mathematician Katherine Johnson noted that in 1930s Virginia, black teachers generally had to have a higher level of training than white teachers. They were, of course, paid less.[9]

Firms do train their staff. Indeed, in the fast-changing world of the fourth industrial revolution, training on the job is likely to be ever more important. The world is likely to change faster than the formal education system. But the decision to hire someone will still use formal education as a guide. Some jobs require certain qualifications. In the modern world, a doctor needs a degree in medicine, for instance.[10] Most professional economists will have a degree in economics.

Prejudice can stop a group from getting education. This will shut off parts of the labour market to that group. The prejudice can be a formal ban. It can be informal. It can be voluntary (the 'it's not for the likes of us' argument). But if people are not able to get the skills they need, the result is that people cannot work where they would work best. The effect of that is to damage the economy as a whole. Firms that are not prejudiced will miss out on the skills that could be available.

The most obvious way prejudice damages productivity is through an outright ban. Marie Curie won two Nobel prizes. She could not be a member of the French Academy of Sciences.[11] Women were not allowed. Curie achieved great things in spite of the prejudice. The question is whether she could have achieved more if the prejudice had been less? Oxford and Cambridge Universities would not admit women to degrees until the 20th century. The pool of talent available to the UK economy in the 19th century was halved by the failure to allow women to be educated.[12] There is no question that the standard of living of the UK economy would have been higher if this prejudice had not existed.

Prejudice does not have to be as formal as a ban. Social norms can be an effective weapon for prejudice. In 1960, 60% of American women dropped out of college, often because they were married. Married women were expected to support their husbands.[13] Prejudice pushed people who were clearly capable of taking on higher-skilled work into lower-skilled roles. This was prejudice feeding prejudice. Prejudice in society meant that men were supposed to make the most money. Women's careers came second. That reinforced the idea that women were second-class citizens. Women gave up their education, denying themselves the chance of more successful careers. This reinforced the prejudice that women were not 'suitable' for jobs requiring higher levels of education. The result was the economy was denied the skills of highly intelligent people.

Before US schools began to be integrated after 1953, prejudice relied on economics to keep African Americans out of education. In parts of Virginia, an African-American child might have to travel nearly 270 miles to be educated beyond the age of 13. (At the same time, white children could go to high school in their hometown).[14] In practical terms, that meant that a family would have to move to educate their children. Economically, that was often not realistic. Prejudice kept people in low-skilled jobs, and the low incomes of parents stopped the next generation from getting the education they needed to obtain higher-skilled jobs. These barriers were very hard to overcome. When someone did climb over the barrier, it demonstrated the sacrifice of talent of those left behind. Katherine Johnson, who did the mathematical calculations for the Apollo 11 moon landing, moved with her family so that she and her siblings could receive higher education.[15] Prejudice made this a very challenging process. If her parents had not had the strength to overcome those challenges, the US would have lost a valuable mathematical skill. The US undoubtedly did lose other skills due to its racial policies. People with skills equivalent to those of Johnson were never discovered because of prejudice. The US economy (in particular, the economy of the southern states) suffered accordingly.

Education and skills can also be affected by more subtle prejudice. In 2004, France enacted a ban on religious symbols in schools. This was not specific to any one religion, but the effect was particularly felt by Muslim girls who were not able to wear a veil. A high proportion of Muslim girls wore *hijabs* and the legislation banning religious symbols had been prompted by a court case over Muslim women wearing the headscarves. The result was that more Muslim girls dropped out of school at the age of 16 (the earliest they could drop out). Muslim girls also took longer to complete their education than had been the case before the ban.[16] This drop-out rate was not always religiously motivated (it was not just an unwillingness to attend school without a scarf on religious grounds). Girls reported increased discrimination at school in the aftermath of the ban. This discrimination caused them to leave education as soon as they could. Although the ban only applied to schools, some university professors also reportedly adopted the ban. This then became an additional obstacle to higher education. The French economy wasted the talent available.

Lastly, there is the obvious risk that prejudice will affect the judgement of people awarding qualifications. There was a hint of this back in Chapter 1, when we saw female musicians doing far better in 'blind' auditions. An audition is not that far removed from an exam for a qualification. An audition is an attempt to find the best person for the role. Qualifications are supposed to do the same thing. They act as an economic signal. The problem is that some qualifications, like music auditions, depend on the opinion of another person. That person may be prejudiced – whether they realise it or not. British schools assess students using both the views of their teachers and externally marked exams. For some ethnic groups, the exam results give clearly better grades than the coursework assessed by the students' own teachers. The teachers obviously know the students personally. The exams are marked by people who do not know the students.[17]

Whether through a formal ban or not, stopping people from reaching their potential is destructive to the economy. Education that is not based on merit will shrink the pool of talent that the economy as a whole can use. Prejudice would have made it difficult for me to go to university a generation earlier. Prejudice would have made it impossible for me to go to university in my grandfather's generation.

Resisting change

Chapter 4 showed that nostalgia is part of prejudice politics. People cling to the past as a 'comfort blanket'. People want things to stay as they are or return to an unrealistic idea of the way things used to be. It is a central theme of this book that fear of change is something that drives prejudice. It is therefore logical that prejudice will work against change. This generally takes the form of prejudice against 'outsiders'. An 'outsider' is anyone who thinks differently from the established way of doing things.

Innovation is a new way of doing things. To come up with a new way of doing things, people need to be able to challenge the old way of doing things. Some economic historians argue that this is part of the reason why the first industrial revolution happened in Britain. The UK political system of the 18th century allowed challenges to authority (up to a point). There was an opposition to the government in parliament. Public criticism of the government was allowed, within certain limits.[18] This meant that challenging the established way of doing things was allowed. What applied in politics applied in the country at large. One could be an inventor and try new ideas without fear of political persecution. Outsiders were heard. This even extended across class. While the working class was still subject to prejudice, artisans and skilled workers were important as inventors. There was prejudice against them, but not enough to stop them from contributing to the economy.[19]

This was not necessarily the case in continental Europe. Changing the established way of doing things was more difficult in an absolute monarchy. If the monarch did not like the change, things could go badly wrong for the outsider. When the UK started to become more oppressive and less tolerant of criticism in the 1790s, innovation weakened. Prejudice against new ideas, or the people who had the new ideas, was sufficient to kill innovation.

This remains the case today. Democracies tend to be better at innovation than dictatorships. This is not necessarily about democracy as such. This is more about the ability to disagree. Challenging things is what innovation is all about. Some technology firms try to encourage their staff to challenge what management wants, to become innovative in a fast-moving part of the economy. Google (now known as Alphabet) is known for allowing some of its staff a fifth of their working time to pursue their own interests.[20] The ability to challenge is especially important in academic circles. If there is a bias to keeping things as they are, or a prejudice against new ideas, then research will be restricted. It has been suggested that academic research can be particularly important in the early stages of innovation.[21] Where there is a prejudice against disagreement and outside opinion, innovation is harder to achieve. If the prejudice is social or led by government policy, the damage extends to the whole economy.

Lack of cash

Prejudice obviously makes it difficult to get the right person, in the right job, at the right time. But what happens if the right job is that of 'boss'? If prejudice in society stops people getting the cash that they need to start their own businesses, the economy will suffer.

A legacy of prejudice can do a lot of damage. Entrepreneurs often use their own money or their family's money to finance their businesses. This means that if your parents are poor, it will be harder for you to start your own business. Money breeds money, in effect. If a country has a history of prejudice, the victims of prejudice are usually poorer over the different generations. That means that the victims of prejudice are less able to set up their own businesses. This loss of entrepreneurial talent is a cost to the economy.

For example, Americans that are ethnically black or Latino are significantly less likely to own a home than white Americans. If they do own a home, the value is likely to be lower.[22] Mortgages are one relatively cheap way of raising capital to start a business. No home, no mortgage, no business. In the US, wealth differences explain most of the difference in business ownership between different ethnic groups.[23] This means that even if prejudice declines in the US, ethnic minorities will remain less likely to set up a business. The legacy of prejudice is felt in lower inherited wealth.

Similar problems exist when it comes to gender. Women are nearly always less likely than men to set up a business. In the 50 economies covered by the Global Entrepreneurship Monitor, only three have more women than men starting businesses. Saudi Arabia, which is one of the three, is an interesting case. Changing regulation has made it easier for women to establish businesses in recent years. The result has been a very dramatic rise in the number of women setting up businesses. However, that explosion of female entrepreneurship also reflects what Saudi Arabia was missing when its policies were biased against women.[24] At the other end of the spectrum, in five economies, twice as many men as women set up a business. That group includes developed economies, such as Japan, and emerging economies, such as Pakistan.[25] The businesses owned by women were also likely to have a lower value.

Analysis of German entrepreneurs shows that lower access to finance limits the ability of women to set up their own businesses. If women are given a bank loan, it does more for their business than a similar loan does for a male-run business.[26] This strongly hints at bias in the system. The fact that women's businesses outpace men's businesses when given money suggests that women have bigger barriers to getting the loan in the first place. If the standards that women's businesses have to reach are set higher, they will naturally outperform poorer-quality businesses run by men, even if both get the same amount of money.

The 'right job' will include business ownership. But business ownership depends on more than a good idea and a determination to succeed. Cash is needed to start a business. If prejudice in society means that cash is harder to get for some groups, fewer people will be in the right job.

The damage to economic productivity

Prejudice damages productivity and the economy by stopping people from doing things. That might be by stopping people from learning, or by not giving their skills the recognition they deserve. It might be by stopping people from challenging the existing way of doing thing, or not letting them build alternative ideas. It might be by not giving funding to allow people with good ideas to develop them further. In each case, the economy as a whole will suffer. A firm that is not prejudiced will still have to deal with the negative consequences of the wider prejudice in the economy.

The economic damage so far has been mainly a domestic issue. But foreigners are one of the most frequent targets of prejudice. Trying to stop any movement of people, goods or capital is a common aim of 'anti-politics' around the world.

Foreigners – labour

As Chapter 4 detailed, the role of immigrants in modern society is one of the most controversial political issues of the fourth industrial revolution. This is nothing new. In the year 996 CE, the citizens of Cairo rioted against Italian merchants, killing over 100 of them and looting their goods. The Italians seem to have been particular targets – an English poem from 1436 entitled *Libelle of Englyshe Polycye* blamed the Florentines for England's economic ills, in rhyming couplets. In the 1590s, London rioted several times against immigrants (mainly from the Netherlands and France). The US began racial profiling for immigration with the Chinese Exclusion Act in 1882.[27] In 1972, the British city of Leicester paid for adverts in the Ugandan Argus newspaper saying that they were "full up" and could not accept any more immigrants.[28] History is littered with prejudice against immigration.

The irrationality of the prejudice against immigrants is often tied up with exaggeration of their numbers. Immigrants are often easy to identify as having a different appearance or accent. This makes them stand out. That, in turn, means that they are remembered and their numbers tend to be exaggerated. Surveys in the UK suggest people think the number of migrants is two-and-a-half times what it is in reality.[29] Media attention on immigration also adds to the prejudice. In 2016, the British *Daily Mail* newspaper ran an average of three immigration stories every day.[30] The stories did not normally show immigrants in a positive light. With this kind of attention, people are likely to see immigration as being more significant than it is in reality. They are also more likely to view immigration in a negative way.

There are two obvious ways that prejudice against immigrants will damage the economy. The first is through restrictions on moving people internationally. The second is through the potential loss of diversity. Both of these costs apply across the economy and will hurt the profits of a firm whether the firm itself is prejudiced or not.

Restricting movement

The economic cost of restricting labour movement across international borders is the very similar to the cost of restricting movement inside an economy. Migration patterns tend to follow economic need. That is to say, if an economy is doing well, migrants will move there. If an economy is doing badly, migrants will not make the effort to migrate (and those that have already arrived may leave). Migration is not a low-cost option for the migrant, after all – the incentive to migrate has to be relatively strong. This means that prejudice against immigration will lead to labour shortages when the economy is booming. Norway experienced this in 2019, when tighter immigration restrictions led to labour shortages. These, in turn, limited the ability of entrepreneurs to grow their businesses.[31]

Prejudice against immigration can also lead to surplus labour when the economy is weak. When Germany started to impose barriers on labour mobility from the 1960s, there was a shift in the behaviour of migrants. Before restrictions were tightened, Turkish migrant workers would come and go. If there was work, they would travel to Germany, and then they would return to Turkey when work disappeared. Once restrictions started to tighten, the workers started to stay in Germany regardless of the strength of the economy. This was because they feared that once outside Germany's borders, they would not necessarily be allowed back in. The flexibility of the German labour system was reduced and the economy suffered again.

If prejudice restricts labour movement too much, the economy can therefore suffer twice. When the economy is doing well, growth will be limited by a shortage of labour. This does not have to be skilled labour. Unskilled workers can also be important to an economy, especially for seasonal work in areas like farming. The standard of living in the economy will therefore be lower than would otherwise be the case. However, the standard of living may also be lowered if migrant workers lack the confidence to leave when the economy slows. Real wages are likely to be lower than would otherwise be the case, if migrants feel that leaving would risk their ability to return in the future.

Innovation from abroad

Prejudice against immigration can also hurt innovation in an economy. Innovation is not prevented by anti-immigrant prejudice, but innovation is certainly harder to achieve if people (and their ideas) cannot move around.

The 'Republic of Letters' of the first industrial revolution helped innovation by sharing ideas.[32] That was done both in the equivalent of the virtual world (by letter), but also in person. If international movement of labour is restricted, innovation is hurt in two ways. Either innovators and entrepreneurs are kept out of the country, or the reduced diversity of opinion hurts innovation and productivity.

Immigrants to a country are often entrepreneurs. To over-simplify, if someone has the energy to leave their own country, culture and family and try to make a new life somewhere else, it tends to signal an entrepreneurial spirit. At the very least, if someone is voluntarily emigrating to another country, their personality suggests a higher-than-normal level of risk taking.[33] There are quite a lot of financial and personal risks involved in migration. It is not surprising that immigrants and their families are often successful entrepreneurs.

In the US, more than 40% of the Fortune 500 large firms were founded by immigrants or the children of immigrants.[34] As immigrants (legal and illegal) in the US are currently a little over 13% of the population, that is a disproportionately high proportion.[35] Restrictions on migration will hit entrepreneurs. The UK saw a sharp decline in the numbers of immigrants setting up businesses from 2018. This seems to follow from concerns about limits on immigration after the UK's exit from the EU. Migrants may have a greater degree of risk taking, but that is unlikely to extend to taking the risk of setting up a business in a country that might ask you to leave.[36]

Immigration helps to prevent the 'narrow thinking' identified in the last chapter. At a national level, this is associated with innovation. Looking at the European regions, there is evidence that immigrants increase the range of ideas and skills in an economy. This increases the innovation of an economy.[37] This diversity of ideas is likely to be increasingly important as the fourth industrial revolution progresses. Change tends to increase the importance of a diverse approach to problems. Diversity also helps find more ways to use new technology and come up with breakthroughs. It is notable that around a third of US Nobel Laureates (excluding those for literature and peace) were born outside the US.[38]

A 2017 study suggested that academic researchers who moved country were far more likely to be cited for their work.[39] Citation is an important way of measuring academic success. It is also used to judge innovation.[40] Interestingly highly cited academics were likely to have ties to more than one country. They did not move and abandon links to their country of origin. Keeping links to more than one place is likely to help diversity of ideas. The movement of academics is now being challenged by policies that are more prejudiced against migration. This threat has been one of the biggest concerns of the elite British universities in the wake of the UK exit from the EU. US President Trump's absolute ban on migration from certain countries has also affected academics.

Immigration helps innovation in both a business and an academic sense. Prejudice against immigration can lead to legal measures to stop people entering a country, or to a climate where immigrants are made to feel unwelcome and encouraged to leave. Either way, this threatens the innovation and entrepreneurship of an economy.

Foreign labour and economic performance

Prejudice against migrant workers risks creating several problems in an economy. There may be shortages of skilled labour when times are good. That prevents an economy growing as it should. Entrepreneurship is likely to be less than it could be. And the diversity of ideas that clearly encourages innovation is threatened if people move about less.

The economic damage of anti-foreign prejudice is not just felt in the movement of people. Next on the list for 'anti-politics' is movement of products – goods and, nowadays, also services.

Foreigners – trade

Chapter 3 highlighted how globalisation is one of the things that is most likely to change during the fourth industrial revolution. Localisation is more attractive in economic terms. Producing close to the consumer can be done more efficiently with robotics and automation. Digitalisation is the ultimate in localisation – we stream entertainment, rather than importing DVDs and CDs. Nonetheless, trade will still matter. In the years ahead, trade in ideas and intellectual property is likely to become more important, even as trade in goods become less important. After all, the music we buy today has replaced trade in goods (CDs) with trade in intellectual property (streaming rights). Anyone outside North America who wants to listen to Justin Bieber has to engage in international trade to indulge their taste in music.[41] As we localise more products, trade will shift away from finished goods in favour of services and commodities.

Trade has always had a problem with complexity. The benefits of trade are broad, but shallow. The price of something might fall by, say, 1%. The costs of trade are narrow, but deep. A thousand workers might lose their jobs. Generally, the benefits are bigger than the costs – if considered in a neutral economic way. The economy is better off with trade. But the emotional story of the losers is a lot more powerful than the fact that everyone pays 1% less for something. This has always been true, but the power of the story has, perhaps, increased with the new communications of the fourth industrial revolution. Social media is very good at outrage. The focus on the loss is likely to be stronger on social media. The loss is a simple story to tell, with lots of human emotion. The benefits of trade are more complicated – comparative advantage in trade takes some explanation.

The combination of outrage and complexity fuels the prejudice of 'scape-goat economics'. Modern trade protectionism is generally presented in terms of fairness. The politician will stress how honest, hard-working domestic voters are being threatened by foreigners. The implication is that foreign workers are not as hard working – so if they are doing 'better' at trade, they must be cheating somehow. The story is always the same: foreigners are clearly not playing the game of trade by the rules. It might be subsidies, or other forms of state aid. It might be currency-market manipulation. But foreigners will be cast in a negative light as not behaving honestly in some way.

Given the complexity of international trade, this story is an easy one to sell. It does risk creating more prejudice. The ideas of foreigners not 'playing fairly' and of the superiority of domestic workers relative to foreigners can border on xenophobia or racism. That can then create a second round of prejudice, as anti-foreigner sentiment becomes more widespread.

Trade protection need not be about prejudice. There are genuine cases where domestic firms face unfair competition. There are also times when national security may require a degree of protection. It is possible that a young industry needs time to establish itself. But dealing with these cases does not need the language of prejudice. These cases are also far less common than the amount of protectionism in the world today.

This form of prejudice hurts an economy in two ways. Most obviously, protectionism is a tax that is paid mainly by domestic companies or domestic consumers. Buyers of foreign products (goods or services like intellectual property) may end up paying a higher price than they need. Alternatively, buyers of foreign products will switch to domestic products that are either more expensive or lower quality. (If domestic products were cheaper or better quality, they would have been bought in preference to foreign products in the first place.) The fact that this is a domestic cost was seen in the US in 2020, when the Trump administration delayed the trade taxes (tariffs) it was charging on foreign goods. The aim was not to help foreign firms, but to help US firms. It was the domestic business sector that would otherwise have had to pay the taxes.

In addition, protectionism tends to be met with protectionism. There is not much that can be done to fight protectionism, other than to retaliate in the same way. This then starts to hurt domestic firms trying to export. Both domestic and foreign consumers are now being forced (by tax or quota) to choose second best. The global economy suffers as a result.

Protectionism does not just hurt the industries it targets. Consumers are potentially hurt by having to take second-best products. Productive domestic industries that need people and resources are denied them because they are being used inefficiently to make goods that could be imported.

Trading down

The fact that trade is likely to be less significant in the fourth industrial revolution does not make it irrelevant. Trade in ideas is likely to be more important. Trade in services could also become a larger part of the global economy. Anti-foreigner prejudice will damage trade and, through that, the wider economy. But it is not just globalisation of trade that is threatened by prejudice. Globalisation of capital is already a victim of irrational anti-foreigner sentiment. Even in a more localised world, global companies will remain. A global company can manufacture locally – assuming it is allowed to invest locally.

Foreigners – capital

Prejudice against foreigners over immigration and trade tend to get the most attention. These are the stars of 'scapegoat economics'. But prejudice against foreigners over investment flows is potentially just as important to the economy. This can work both ways – prejudice against capital inflows and against capital outflows.

There is a link between trade and capital. Most of the world's trade is done by global firms (called transnational firms). A lot of global trade is taking place inside those firms. But becoming a global firm requires investment in different countries. If there is prejudice against foreigners, this can be a problem.

There are two ways a firm can expand globally. One is by starting from nothing, investing in new factories or offices, and hiring local people to the firm. Generally speaking, this is not a problem. In fact, governments will quite often compete to attract such investment inflows. Foreign direct investment of this nature is normally seen as a good thing – largely because it is. Foreign direct investment like this tends to be more productive than local investment. One theory behind this is that if a firm is going to the trouble of building a new operation away from its home country, it will make sure that the best possible people are put in place to run it. This then leads to a more productive operation.

The alternative to this is for a foreign firm to buy a 'ready-made' operation – in other words, to buy an existing firm. This is where foreign capital can be a target of prejudice. It might be the result of successful branding. Firms spend a lot of time and effort getting people to like their brands. People can become emotionally involved in a brand and the story of the firm behind it. There are often local ties between a firm and a certain area of the country. When a foreigner comes in to take 'our' firm, resentment can rise to the surface.

In 1988, the Swiss food firms Nestlé and Suchard were in competition to buy British chocolate maker Rowntree's of York. There was a lot of opposition to the takeover from workers and the community of the city of York. The opposition was not about whether the deal was good or bad in economic terms. Instead, those trying to stop the bid leaned heavily on the fact that it would be a foreign firm that was taking over the firm. One picture from the time shows protestors holding placards genteelly expressing anti-Swiss sentiment. One reads, "Hands off our chocs, stick to cuckoo clocks". A large union flag is prominent and the group is clustered under a large banner urging, "Keep Rowntrees British".[42] Nestlé bought the firm anyway. The anti-foreigner prejudice did not win on this occasion, but the emotions of the local community were mobilised against foreign influence.

Nestlé invested in the firm in the aftermath of the takeover. Production increased and jobs were secured. The trade unions and the City of York Council, who had opposed the foreign takeover, were reconciled with the investment and security that the takeover brought.[43] There are two points from this experience. The first is that had prejudice been allowed to win, the British economy (and specifically the local economy in York) would almost certainly have done worse than it did. The scale of investment and increase in productivity after foreign capital was brought in would have been difficult to achieve in other circumstances. The second is that even though prejudice did not stop this capital flow, it may have been a deterrent to future capital flow from overseas. Opposition to foreign direct investment that is based on prejudice is certainly not going to help attract money in the future. That 'image problem' could affect foreign start-up investment in new factories and offices. No foreigner is likely to want to invest, even in a new business, if there is a suggestion that foreigners are not welcome.

It was a similar story a few years later in the US. During the 1980s, Japanese firms acquired a number of established US brands. Syndicated newspaper columnist Paul Harvey chose to use very emotive language, suggesting the US was facing an "economic Pearl Harbor".[44] In 1989, Rockefeller Centre in the heart of New York was bought by Mitsubishi Estate Co. There was considerable opposition to the move. A story published in the *Los Angeles Times* after the sale was agreed quoted New Yorkers whose opposition was framed in anti-foreigner terms. Phrases like "selling the country away" were used.[45] The then mayor of New York, Edward Koch, called critics of the deal "xenophobic".[46] The same year, a New York businessperson, Donald Trump, declared on television that Japan had "systematically sucked the blood out of America – sucked the blood out! It's a huge problem, and it's a problem that's going to get worse. And they're laughing at us".[47] The film *Back to the Future II*, released that year, presented the lead character, Marty McFly, as a subservient employee of a caricatured Japanese businessperson. The scene was set in a dystopian future (from an American perspective).[48]

Opposition to the Rockefeller deal did not stop the sale. However, the prejudice was sufficiently widespread as to enter popular culture. The opposition was loud, emotional and – as Koch noted – rooted in xenophobia and, perhaps, racism. As with the British example, it may have prevented other economically sensible investments from taking place. What economists call the 'signalling effect' was not good for the US economy.

Perhaps the most extreme example of hostility to foreign capital comes from France. In 2005, the French government famously blocked any takeover of French yoghurt maker Danone by American firm PepsiCo. To ensure this was legal, yoghurt was declared to be a strategic national asset. Leaving aside the strategic merits of fermented milk, this was a decision that was based on the nationality of the potential buyer. It seems unlikely that a French takeover would have been resisted. The signal that it sent about France's willingness to accept foreign investment was judged to be very negative at the time. Indeed, France's ability to attract foreign direct investment has consistently underperformed the OECD average, the EU average and the global average since 2005.[49]

Culturing prejudice

Chapter 7 covered why diversity of opinion is important to firms. This is sometimes used as an argument against foreign capital. Anti-foreigner prejudice can be presented as being all about protecting a country's culture (for example, by defending its yoghurt makers to the bitter end). Keeping cultural differences is important, although there is no reason to assume that foreign ownership of a firm will change the culture. If a firm's culture is successful, presumably the new owners (of whatever nationality) will wish to carry on doing what is working. But appealing to culture and tradition adds emotion to the prejudice against foreign ownership. That makes the arguments more powerful.

Cultural protectionism can be an active part of prejudice as well. Global firms are inclined to operate to the highest standard of global values. That is to say, companies with customers and employees around the world will need be held to account for their actions all over the world. The world of social media and the power of the brand make this especially important today. But adopting the highest standard can cause conflict if a society has a culture of prejudice. This could be any form of prejudice, but treatment of women and the LGBTQ+ community are perhaps areas where prejudice varies most significantly around the world.

A foreign firm that opposes prejudice may therefore have problems operating (or trying to invest) in some countries. The position my global employer has taken on the economics of marriage equality has cost the firm clients, for example. Goldman Sachs (then) Chief Executive Lloyd Blankfein admitted that his firm had also lost business because of a similar pro-equality stance.[50] While this has not extended into a block on investment, it is an example of how prejudice against what might be perceived as 'foreign values' can affect how capital flows around the world. Ultimately, that is a loss to the prejudiced economies.

Capital prejudice

Prejudice against foreigners buying domestic companies limits investment and efficiency. The costs go beyond the limits on global capital flows. All too often, the language used against foreign ownership gives publicity to racist or xenophobic views. That then fuels additional prejudice and extends the economic damage beyond the narrow focus of investment flows.

The economic cost of prejudice

Prejudice hurts the wider economy in several ways. All of these examples in this chapter (and Chapter 7) basically come down to a 'misallocation of resources'. Prejudice in the economy stops the right thing from happening. People are denied the chance to develop their skills, or to move to where those skills can do most good. Money is not made available to entrepreneurs who deserve it. Anything 'foreign' is resisted. So, what does this cost the economy?

As with the cost to firms, there is no precise data. We do not have a single index for 'prejudice' that we can plot against economic growth or other living standards. Different forms of prejudice will have different importance at different times. Prejudice against foreign takeovers or foreign trade may be less important in a world that is naturally less globalised. This does not mean that the cost of this prejudice is zero, but it may be less damaging than it was in the 1990s and early 2000s. Prejudice that restricts internal labour mobility may be more important, as the economic benefit of getting the right person in the right job at the right time increases in the fourth industrial revolution.

Those seeking to pinpoint 'the economic cost of prejudice' will seek in vain. A number can be created, of course. As the economic Nobel Laureate Ronald Coase said, if you torture the data for long enough, it will confess to anything.[51] But this is not a terribly helpful way of building the economic case against prejudice.

The World Values Survey, which asks people around the world standardised questions on a wide range of issues, does provide some insight.[52] There is a series of questions about who people would not want to have as neighbours. Options include people of a different nationality, religion or sexual orientation. For many of these categories, a reluctance to have people who are different as a neighbour must be considered to be prejudice. These measures can be compared with the World Economic Forum's Global Competitiveness Index.[53] There is a relationship between prejudice and competitiveness. Obviously, the more prejudiced a country, the less competitive it is seen to be.

One of the most sacred rules of modern economics is that correlation does not equal causation. Just because prejudice correlates with low competitiveness does not mean that prejudice causes low competitiveness. The causation could also work the other way. A more competitive economy may be better at dealing with structural change. That may mean weaker links between prejudice and change, as outlined in Chapter 4. The result would be that competitiveness causes less prejudice.

Nonetheless, the arguments of this chapter point to prejudice damaging economic competitiveness. That will lower a country's standard of living relative to what it might have been. All firms in the economy will be affected by the climate of prejudice. A firm might be a 'safe harbour,' helping the victims of prejudice. That would give it a competitive advantage within the economy. Internationally, however, the firm would be at a disadvantage against firms from less prejudiced economies.

Chapters 7 and 8 have set out the economic costs of prejudice, both at the firm level and at the wider economy level. These are the reasons that economists are so opposed to prejudice, especially as we enter the changes of the fourth industrial revolution. But the cost of prejudice can perhaps best be understood by looking at practical examples. This is what the next two chapters will try to do – tell the story of the economic damage of prejudice in the context of gender and sexuality.

Notes

1 Author's calculations using 2019 annual data from the US Bureau of Labor Statistics (https://www.bls.gov/).
2 See Wagener (1867, p. 102).
3 See Berthoff (1951).
4 Ibid., p. 342.
5 See Chappell (2015).
6 Sansone (2019) argues that this may be due to a decline in prejudice after same-sex marriages are allowed, as people become accustomed to the idea. The suggestion is that there may have been a 2% increase in the probability of being employed in states that were not prejudiced.
7 See Holpuch (2019).
8 See Schulman (2016).
9 See Johnson (2019, p. 79).
10 This has not always been true. My maternal great grandfather was a dentist, who did not have any formal qualification. According to family lore, his business outperformed that of his formally qualified neighbour.
11 See Long (2009).
12 The Society for Home Students allowed women to access lectures at Oxford from 1879. It was the target of ridicule in some parts of the media at the time. Degrees (formal qualifications) were not awarded to women by Oxford University until 1920. The Society for Home Students eventually became St Anne's College.
13 See Gordon (2016, p. 504). Some universities issued a 'good wife diploma' (known by the nickname PhT or 'Putting hubby Through'), recognising that wives had supported their husbands by accepting lower-skilled work so that their husbands could study. A *New York Times* article from 1974 quotes a Harvard University administrator on how critical it was that spouses worked. The implication was that it was women who should be working in less prestigious jobs. See Brozan (1974).
14 See Johnson (2019, p. 85).
15 Ibid.
16 See Abdelgadir and Fouka (2019).
17 See Burgess and Greaves (2013).

18 If the British government took exception to the criticisms levelled against it, it generally had to resort to the courts. The courts did not necessarily agree with the government. In 1817, the government lost three consecutive cases against London publisher William Hone, who had ridiculed government ministers of the day in print. Moreover, Hone used the trial to heap further ridicule on the government. Subsequent British governments were very wary of pursuing critics.

19 Mokyr (2009) talks of a climate of increased toleration for innovation in British manufacturing in the second half of the 18th century. The UK had a large supply of relatively well-educated artisans who were able to enhance and apply innovation in a practical way – and who were allowed to do so. Of particular relevance to the arguments here, Mokyr stresses that the British state was not the enemy of innovation and change.

20 Whether this is actually true is a topic of debate. It does not apply to all staff. However, it does seem to be the case that Google will allow staff to spend some of their time on projects for the firm that are personally motivated. This is another example of allowing research to challenge the normal way of doing things.

21 See Aghion et al. (2008).

22 See Fairlie (2018).

23 Ibid.

24 Lavelle and Al Sheikh (2013) suggest that at before regulations were eased, there were 10 male entrepreneurs for every female entrepreneur.

25 See Bosma et al. (2020). The three economies with more women engaged in early-stage entrepreneurship than men are Qatar, Saudi Arabia and Madagascar. The five economies where twice as many men as women are engaged in early-stage entrepreneurship are Egypt, Norway, Japan, North Macedonia and Pakistan.

26 See Sauer and Wiesemeyer (2018).

27 See Chinese Exclusion Act (1882).

28 See BBC (2012b).

29 Mackenzie (2015) cites a MORI poll suggesting people in the UK believed 31% of the population to be foreign born (at the time, it was 13%). Muslims were believed to make up 21% of the population (the reality was 5%). The more dramatic overestimation of the Muslim population may be due to their being more identifiable by appearance.

30 See Goodfellow (2019, p. 36).

31 See Bosma et al. (2020).

32 See Stanford University (2013).

33 This will not always be the case. Emigration from Ireland to the US in the latter part of the 19th century was built on 'chain migration,' where one person would migrate, then pay for others to come after them. Entrepreneurial spirit was not a factor, at least after the initial departure. In the European Alps in the 19th century, migration was often decided by lottery in a village (with the village contributing to the emigrant's costs).

34 See Syed (2019, p. 137).

35 See Pew Research Center (2019a) for the migrant share of the population. Of course, as children of immigrants are also included in the Fortune 500 statistic, the relevant comparison should be roughly double the migrant share – in other words, around 27% – to include both migrants and their children. The share of Fortune 500 firms established by migrants and their children is still disproportionately high.

36 In early 2018, the status of European immigrants to the UK in the wake of the UK's vote to leave the EU was uncertain.

37 See Ozgen et al. (2011). Clusters of immigrants are often associated with universities – the area around Oxford has a high immigrant population, for example.
38 See Greshko (2018). While important prizes, these are less about the interaction of innovation and diversity.
39 See Sugimoto et al. (2017).
40 The number of patents filed is not especially helpful, as anyone can file a patent for something that is completely useless. But if a patent is cited in lots of other patent applications, that signals that the original patent was something very useful – a genuine innovation that other inventors and researchers want to use.
41 This example is not intended to be an argument against trade, even if it might appear to be.
42 See *The York Press* (2013).
43 See *Management Today* (1993).
44 See Pesek (2019).
45 See United Press International (1989).
46 Ibid.
47 See Pesek (2019).
48 See Zemeckis (1989).
49 Annual foreign direct investment as a share of GDP. See OECD Data (2020).
50 See Braithwaite (2012).
51 See Coase (1994).
52 See World Values Survey (2020).
53 See World Economic Forum (2019).

9 The economic damage of gender prejudice

Social desirability bias can be a powerful weapon in attacking prejudice. If social pressure makes people embarrassed about being prejudiced, they are less likely to be prejudiced in public. That helps limit some of the damage which prejudice can do. For an economist, however, social desirability bias is also a problem. Analysing the economic cost of prejudice is difficult to do if people will not admit to prejudice. How can economists find out the extent of prejudice that exists in a society?[1]

Sadly, there are plenty of practical examples of prejudice in society that can be directly linked to negative economic consequences. This chapter and the next will look at real-world examples of the prejudice and the economic costs those examples might produce. This one looks at gender prejudice, while Chapter 10 examines sexuality prejudice. The two forms of prejudice have very different aspects, but the economic damage is remarkably similar at times. The way prejudice is expressed can be considered in two ways. There are the economic costs of 'hard' prejudice, when a group is formally (normally legally) prevented from contributing to part of the economy. Then there are the costs of 'soft' prejudice, when a group is treated as being 'less than' the dominant group in the economy.

Obviously, this is not a comprehensive review of either form of prejudice – that would take volumes. Rather, these chapters should be viewed as a collection of highlights as to why prejudice is so damaging to economies.

The scale of gender prejudice

It is worth reminding ourselves that gender prejudice is likely to be very expensive to an economy because it affects so many people. The exact balance of males and females in the global population varies over time but, inevitably, it is roughly half and half.

Women have tended to be excluded from large parts of the economy throughout history. Traditionally, industries associated with clothing have tended to be female dominated, although that was challenged by the mechanisation of the first industrial revolution. Other areas of the economy were dominated by men, even if there was no valid reason for that dominance. Between 1200 and 1800, for example, London had around 7,000 goldsmiths. In those 600 years, just 32 were women. At least eight of them had either inherited the business from their husband or worked alongside their husband.[2] Little more than five female goldsmiths a century suggests a considerable degree of gender prejudice. There is no reason a woman cannot be as good a goldsmith as a man. The economy lost skill through prejudice.

A common reason for excluding women from the workforce has been that the employment of women has often been seen as a threat to men's income. In 1747, before the first industrial revolution, a somewhat patronising author named R. Campbell[3] published the *London Tradesmen*, which attacked female button makers in strong terms:

> [Button making] requires no great Strength, and is follow'd by Women as well as Men, which has reduced the Trade to small Profits, and a small share of Reputation; the Women are generally Gin-Drinkers.[4]

Campbell does not seem to have supported women in employment. Women were seen as competition for men's jobs – because they *were* competition. They were obviously as capable as men – and, indeed, Campbell seems to imply that women were as competent as men even when drunk on gin. Campbell's attitude is that women were somehow 'less than' men and that men should be the priority in employment.

The fear of competition comes up again and again as a legal barrier to women. In 1951, British Chancellor of the Exchequer Hugh Gaitskell told the House of Commons,

> The majority of men employees have families dependent upon them; the majority of women employees have not. The introduction of equal pay would mean that the standard of living of a married man with a wife and children to support would compare unfavourably with that of an unmarried woman with no dependants.[5]

In other words, those pesky women would take money away from honest, hard-working men by being good at their jobs. Gaitskell did not apparently stop to consider that prejudice and the failure to give equal pay might have been the reason that women with families did not bother working.[6]

The first industrial revolution did give men (at least young men) some economic competitive advantage. As Chapter 2 identified, a lot of the new jobs created in the 18th century required physical strength. The scythes on the farms and the mules of the factories favoured men, who on average have an advantage over women in terms of upper-body strength. That should not have stopped women being employed if they happened to be strong. It should not have meant men were employed if they happened to be weak. But the law of averages gave men a dominant position. From that position of dominance, trade unions sought to stop women from working and gender prejudice increased further.

Using the physical strength of a gender as a rule of thumb, which is still a form of prejudice, has all but disappeared in the fourth industrial revolution. The world of robotics and automation means physical strength is unimportant for most jobs. Men nowadays do not generally build upper-body strength as a result of their careers. Today, it is largely decorative, gained not by earning money, but by spending money on gym memberships.[7] But even though the arguments for distinguishing between genders are fading, gender discrimination is still very much with us.

Hard prejudice

Legally stopping half an economy's population from working is not an economically positive strategy. Half the potential talent of an economy is thrown away at once. It is rarely quite that extreme. Hard prejudice is normally restricted to specific areas of the economy. Women are allowed to participate in some, but not all jobs. That still means skills are lost. The cost of this loss of skills can be devastating to industries and the wider economy.

The problem with 'manpower'

In 1945, the UK led the world in computer technology. The wartime work of the codebreaking unit at Bletchley Park produced programmable computers that were not matched elsewhere until the late 1950s.[8] The momentum of wartime research meant the UK still held the lead in global computing for over a decade. By the 1960s, that lead had crumbled and British computing was failing. One of the critical problems was a lack of 'manpower'.

The lack of manpower did not mean that there was a lack of qualified workers. There was simply a lack of qualified *men*. It was women who were the trained computer operators of the 1940s. They were the programmers and computer technicians during wartime. This was not to say that Bletchley Park was a haven of equality – there was only one female crypto-analyst (Joan Clarke).[9] But there were plenty of women who were qualified to work with computers. So why was this abundance of highly skilled and experienced womanpower not enough to maintain British dominance in computing?

In the 1940s and 1950s, government still led the young computer industry. But the British government was prejudiced. If you were a woman who got married, you were expected to 'retire' from the civil service and, indeed, many other areas of the economy. Married women were effectively banned from working. This was not actually legal. In 1919, the British Parliament had passed the Sex Disqualification Removal Act, which begins, "A person shall not be disqualified by sex or marriage from the exercise of any public function …".[10] It was a very forward-looking piece of legislation. It was also completely ignored.

The civil-service 'marriage bar' was formally lifted in 1946, but the expectation was still that married women would leave. This was because women were presumed to want to have children upon marriage, so they would leave anyway (there was, of course, no question of men getting involved in the raising of children).[11] Prejudice produced a further cost to the economy, by failing to develop women's skills. It was generally assumed that as women would only have short careers before marrying, there was no point in training them to do more complex tasks. The wartime training of women (including married women) was therefore an exception. In wartime, it was important to have the right person, in the right job, at the right time. It turned out that the right place for women in the middle of a national crisis was not, in fact, in the home. Once wartime was over, prejudice returned. The right person was presumed to be male.

The result was that a pool of experienced computer experts was made unemployed at exactly the moment there was a desperate shortage of experienced computer experts. The British computer industry was completely undermined by a prejudice against hiring married women. That this was pure prejudice is evident from the fact that women were considered extremely competent during the emergency of wartime. It was rational to employ as many women as possible at that time. It was irrational to reject that experience in peacetime. The economic cost of that rejection is very clear in the downward spiral of the British computing industry.

The gender gulf

The ban on employing women in significant positions in the UK was fading in the 1960s. But other economies formally limited the role of women in the economy long after that date. The Gulf region has traditionally placed considerable formal barriers to women playing a significant role in the economy. In 2016, only 21% of Saudi women were in the labour force. What is more remarkable is that this number was double what it had been a few years earlier.[12] The figure of 21% was better than Iran, Iraq, Jordan and Algeria. This does mean that there was not an absolute ban on women working, but there were significant restrictions.

Gulf states tend to score relatively well on standard measures of gender equality in education and health. There are few legal barriers to women studying, for example. My own experience of speaking with women, including students, in the region is that they regard education as a great opportunity. Men seem to be less enthusiastic. I have heard women suggest that men are less focussed on education because they want to 'play with guns' in the military.[13] However, what women are taught in education systems may reinforce gender prejudice. The education can be focussed on preparing men for work and women for the home. This is not hard prejudice as such, but it is a barrier to getting the right person in the right job.[14]

More serious economic problems arise with limits on women's travel, finance and dealings with bureaucracy. For example, a government ministry may have a specific section for dealing with women. If that section is less efficient than the equivalent male section, women are at an immediate disadvantage in the economy. In the past, in Saudi Arabia, for example, women entrepreneurs have chosen to use a male relative to deal with bureaucracy, just to be able to access the more efficient male side of the divide.[15]

Realisation of the cost of this prejudice has led to changes in the extent of gender hard prejudice. Saudi Arabia's guardianship laws (putting women under the control of a male relative) have eased somewhat, for example. In 2018, Saudi female entrepreneurs were freed from the requirement to get the approval of a male guardian to start their own business.[16] The lifting of such restrictions is one of the reasons that the number of Saudi women starting their own business has exploded in recent years. That growth in business creation is a clear signal of the entrepreneurship that was lost to the economy under the hard prejudice of the past.

The world has become steadily less dependent on oil in recent years.[17] The Gulf economies have been almost entirely dependent on oil money. Economies like Saudi Arabia depend on oil as producers. An economy like Dubai depends on oil producers spending their petrodollars in its hotels and malls. The decline in the use oil is a huge, disruptive threat. The need to find alternative sources of economic activity has become more urgent in the Gulf. This means that the importance of having the right person in the right job at the right time has increased dramatically.

The Gulf states have concluded that economic necessity in a time of change is more important than prejudice. While the major Gulf economies continue to rank relatively poorly on measures of gender prejudice, especially in the areas of economics and politics, their position has improved somewhat in recent years.[18]

At the cost of two Californias

Formal restrictions on women working are still astonishingly common. In 2018, over 2.7 billion women were living in economies that prevented them from having the same range of job opportunities as men.[19] The United Nations estimates the cost of this sort of ban on full participation in the economy at about USD 6 trillion a year.[20] That is roughly the equivalent of two Californian economies still being lost, every year, in the 21st century.

This is just the effect of formal bans on women working. Economically, the problems go beyond this. Soft prejudice is the bigger problem today.

Soft prejudice

Despite the shockingly high number of countries that continue to deny women legal equality in the workplace, hard prejudice against women has become less relevant in recent decades. This has not stopped gender prejudice, however. Gender prejudice has just become less legal. The move has been from conscious to unconscious bias, perhaps. The real economic damage now comes not from legally excluding women from the economy, but from informally excluding women. This can mean ignoring women for promotion to more senior roles, or downgrading women – representing them as being 'less than' men. The effect is still the same. It stops the right person being in the right job at the right time.

Prejudice and vice

One example of the struggle to contribute is the story of Stephanie Shirley. Shirley was mentioned in Chapter 2, finding her career saved (or at least greatly simplified) by the purchase of a washing machine. She founded an extremely successful software company, employing women working from home when both ideas were decades ahead of their time. But prejudice made this career harder to achieve at every stage. As a child, she had to undergo psychometric testing before being allowed to study mathematics. As a girl, only a 'special case' would be allowed to do this (and she would have to go to a boys' grammar school for her classes).[21] There was no formal ban on girls being taught mathematics, but society put obstacles in the way.

While working for the Post Office (which is where British government computer specialists worked in the 1950s), she discovered that men were resigning from the interview board rather than recommend her for promotion to the rank of Scientific Officer. Scientific Officers managed other people and some men could not agree to the idea of a woman managing men.[22] In line with convention (though no longer a strict requirement), she resigned when she married. The number of competent computer programmers in the UK at that time was very small. Social prejudice cost the government one person from the small pool of available talent.

Shirley was affected by some hard prejudice limits. Upon starting her own business in 1962, Shirley needed her husband's written permission to open a bank account. Had that not been granted, she would have struggled to set up her firm. Social prejudice could have cost the country her skills as both a programmer and entrepreneur. But a bigger problem came from the soft prejudice, whereby women were treated as being less than men.

Often, when sending out letters soliciting business, Shirley simply did not get a response. This was not the formal rejection of obvious prejudice. This was a prejudice of silence. It is echoed in the modern-day refusal of Dublin Airbnb hosts to respond to gay couples looking for accommodation, mentioned in Chapter 6. The problem was solved when she began sending out letters signed 'Steve Shirley'. A man sending a letter was clearly worthy of a response. Again, had Shirley not made this change (at the suggestion of her husband), her business would have suffered, her clients would have been using inferior alternatives and the economy overall would have been weaker – all as a result of prejudice.

Even the invaluable washing machine is an example of the risks of prejudice. Cultural norms meant that women were supposed to do the laundry. There is a clear link between a woman's ability to be economically productive and the amount of time they spend doing unpaid work at home. The longer a woman spends working at home, the fewer economic opportunities there are likely to be.[23] This obviously reduces the size of the labour pool and throws away female talent for no good reason. Without a washing machine, social prejudice would have caused Shirley to be less economically productive.

The idea of 'right person, right job, right time' is emphasised by the fact that Shirley estimated that her programmers were around 40% more productive than the programmers at other companies.[24] Her programmers were all highly skilled women, rejected by prejudice elsewhere.[25] As freelancers employed by Shirley, they were able to work flexibly. Consequently, they were very efficient. This meant that Shirley could offer very competitive pricing to her customers. In a sense, she exploited the prejudice in the economy to make money for her company and her staff. But the economy would have been better off without the prejudice. Shirley's success came at the cost of unnecessary effort and unnecessary humiliation. Prejudice was so much a part of British culture that Her Majesty's Inland Revenue[26] suspected one of Shirley's employees of being involved in vice, as the tax collectors could not imagine how a woman would earn that much money any other way.[27]

Playing games

The extremes of prejudice in the 1960s seem absurd today. The idea that vice was the only high-paying career for a woman was nonsense then and presumably would not even be thought of in a modern economy. However, the today's world of computing has not moved on as much as some would imagine. Grace (not her real name) is a senior executive at a US gaming company. After a week-long business trip meeting colleagues in the US, she realised that the driver collecting her from the airport to take her home was the first woman she had spoken to all week.[28]

Gaming has a reputation as an industry of men designing games for men. The first part of that is true; the second, not so much. In 2018, analysis of the UK gaming industry found that 14.2% of senior posts were occupied by women. The best UK gaming company for equality had a third of senior posts filled by women.[29] Globally, the production of computer content (other than social-media content) is dominated by men. Men account for 80–90% of the workforce and there is little difference evident in the pipeline of future talent.[30] Gaming and computing are an overwhelmingly male industry – despite the original dominance of women in programming.

In terms of the customers, male players do outnumber female players, but they do not dominate. The OECD PISA education survey of schoolchildren found that 10–15% of girls were likely to play computer games daily, or near daily. For boys, it was 28–53%.[31] Gaming is not a 'men-only' pastime. Girls and women do play games and are not as much of a minority as the gender breakdown of workers in the gaming industry might suggest.

Grace highlighted the subtle ways in which prejudice affects a person's career. The gaming industry has a culture that values socialising and after-work drinks (not dissimilar to the financial sector, at least, as it was some years ago). Before she was a mother, she could take part in late-night social events or weekend business trips. Being 'one of the boys' was a critical part of a career in gaming. Now, Grace is at a triple disadvantage, simply because she is a parent: she cannot drink (excessively); she cannot travel too far to socialise; she has to be home on time. The social assumption that a woman will be the main person looking after children coincides with a male culture that does not recognise the needs of a mother (or any responsible parent).

It was exactly this culture that led Stephanie Shirley to set up her software company in 1962. Shirley wrote that "the expensive, sophisticated, state-of-the-art computer programmes [clients] were buying from us were being created at home by women surrounded by babies and nappies".[32] It was a radical solution to overcome an absurd prejudice. Two generations later, we are discussing exactly the same prejudice in exactly the same industry. The sophistication of the software may have progressed in leaps and bounds, but the social attitudes of those that produce the software seems to be progressing at glacial speed.

The reality of America today is that women in employment spend almost as much time working as men. However, they are far more likely to do housework, and spend longer doing it. Women are also far more likely to look after children, and spend longer doing it.[33] If a job requires socialising after work, in theory, both parents will suffer. The truth, however, is that it is a far bigger problem for women. As noted in Chapter 2, Keynes's prediction of a 15-hour working week was not true, but unpaid working hours have fallen significantly. That is mainly housework related. The technology of the second and third industrial revolutions has given women more time (as they were the main unpaid workers). The fourth industrial revolution is likely to continue that trend. But while we may happily surrender vacuuming to a small frisbee-like robot, it is unlikely that we will give up childcare to robots quite so quickly.[34] So, until there is more equal division of responsibility for childcare, prejudice against parents will tend to mean prejudice against women.

The culture of informal social/business meetings late at night means that Grace is effectively excluded from important business discussions.[35] She relies on male colleagues to relay what happened. As a result, she has to shout louder to make her voice heard during the working day. The volume has to be increased further, as even during the working day, there is a culture of overlooking a woman's view. Grace says that in a meeting, she will often have to pointedly remind colleagues, "I just said that", after one of her own ideas has been repeated back to her. Given the data on the lack of female executives in the industry, it is hardly surprising that Grace often finds herself the only woman in the room.

This all has an impact on productivity. It is not just that the culture of exclusion making it harder for a talented female executive to succeed. As identified in Chapter 7, working in a prejudiced environment can be exhausting. Grace talks of the lack of engagement at work, with the backdrop of having to fight to be treated equally. She contrasts this with her energy levels at times when she was happy at work. The economy and the firm lose out when staff are not motivated. But why should women be motivated when the informal barriers to success are so significant?

Prejudice and politics

The hard prejudice of formal, legal bans on women working can be dealt with through the political system. If the law is changed, the formal ban goes. But, as with the 1919 British Sex Disqualification (Removal) Act,[36] just changing the law does not make prejudice magically disappear. More often than not, the obvious hard prejudice goes into hiding and turns into the soft prejudice of telling women that they are 'less than' men. What makes this a particular problem is that this soft prejudice is so common in politics itself.

The World Economic Forum identifies political empowerment as the worst area of gender equality – by a huge margin.[37] In 2019, less than a quarter of the world's elected parliamentarians were women.[38] Women are *allowed* to stand for election – only three of the world's 192 parliaments have no female representation at all.[39] This is not a hard prejudice, therefore. It is culture and social pressure stopping women from taking office. Representation in government is even worse. Little more than a fifth of ministerial posts globally are held by women. In more than half of countries, a woman has never been in charge.[40] If the average representation of women in parliaments and governments around the world is less than half the proportion of women in the population, something is clearly wrong. Prejudice is at work.

The British politician Emily Benn has been involved in politics from a young age – she is the fifth generation of her family to be engaged in politics and to be elected to office.[41] She believes one way that prejudice continues in politics is in the different standards applied to female and male politicians. As Benn points out, if former British Prime Minister Theresa May had given birth to an unknown number of children, by an unknown number of fathers, the press reaction would undoubtedly have been extremely negative. Indeed, it is highly unlikely that May would have been elected to parliament, never mind become prime minister. And yet, May's successor, Boris Johnson, is in the exact gender parallel of that position – and the media focus on this has been limited.

The different standards applied by the media go beyond a politician's personal life. People have rules of thumb about gender, as they do about everything else. What is interesting is the way that these rules of thumb change when people enter politics. Men, in general, are seen as being vigorous and good at politics. Male politicians are treated the same. Women, in general, are seen as having integrity and being good at communicating. Female politicians are not attributed with those skills, however. The media seems to assume that male politicians will be 'manly,' but female politicians somehow give up 'female characteristics' when they start to play the political game.[42]

Of course, the rules of thumb being used here are a form of prejudice. But women are denied the possible benefit of common prejudice about their gender. A survey of Dutch political reporting in newspapers from 2006 to 2012 showed that male leaders were frequently described using the common leadership traits of communication, vigour and political ability. Women were not.[43] The reporting of those leadership traits was also more likely to be positive than negative. Female political leaders were therefore less likely to be associated with leadership and less likely to receive positive press coverage.

As Chapter 6 explained, social media can make prejudice worse. Benn's time in politics has seen the rise of social media – which was barely present during her first election campaign. Her experience is that female politicians are more subject to widespread attack on social media – with critics 'piling on top of' female politicians, in her words.[44] In Benn's case, she is often viewed only through the prism of her male political relatives – judged against them and always judged as 'less than' them. Inevitably, politics offers more opportunities for public humiliation in the normal course of events.

The mob of social media is no less vicious than the political mobs of the French Revolution. Rather than knitting in the shadow of the guillotine, today's social-media trolls are lurking online and 'piling on' with ill-informed (and poorly spelled) attacks. With the more focussed mob mentality of social media directed against women, talented women are put off standing for office. While the women who do brave the attacks and run for office are to be applauded, they are naturally less representative. The importance of diverse thinking to firms, identified in Chapter 7, also applies to law making. If only a subset of the world's women feel they can face the disproportionate social-media harassment, the quality of political debate will be lessened.[45]

Even when women overcome the barriers to entry into politics, progression is still difficult. As already noted, there are proportionately fewer women in senior political positions than there are in parliaments around the world. At least part of this is down to the informal networks that exist. Just as informal networks help promote white men at work, so similar networks help further the careers of men in politics. Women are excluded from these groups and find promotion inside political parties a lot harder to achieve.[46] Prejudice discriminates against women in political parties, and the discrimination becomes more intense closer to the top of political parties (which is where the informal networks are most powerful). This creates a 'glass ceiling' in politics. That further discourages women from entering into politics. As we have seen with other forms of prejudice, why bother trying if the system is against you?

Political gender prejudice affects the quality of law making (by reducing diversity of ideas). Arguably, it also reduces the urgency for equality to be put into law in the first place. As a rule, men will not have the same motives as women when it comes to gender equality. But even when equality is put into law, prejudice is still very visible in the economy.

Mind the gap

The most obvious sign that gender prejudice continues in economies is the pay gap. Women continue to earn less than men. The United Nations estimates that women globally earn 77% of what men earn for the same work.[47] That probably underestimates the difference. Women are also more likely to work in the informal economy and go unrecorded in the numbers.

On 11 February 1969, the Ford Motor Company in the UK agreed with its 22 trade unions to put in place equal pay for equal work. The tabloid *Daily Mirror* newspaper ran the story as its front-page lead.[48] The second most prominent story on the front page was about the Mrs. Britain contest, which was searching for "all that is best in British womanhood".[49] There does not appear to have been an equivalent Mr. Britain contest. Equality only went so far in the Britain of the late 1960s.

Equal pay was not introduced at once. Hard prejudice still existed. The law limited the hours that a woman could work. There were no limits on the hours that men could work (for example, on night shifts) and equal pay could only take place when the work was equal. However, the government quickly moved to change the legal position and equal pay for equal work was implemented.

Shortly after the start of equal pay, my mother got a job as an export-order controller at Ford's office at Warley, in Brentwood, Essex. She was responsible for car exports. Ford hired a man at the same time who was responsible for truck exports. They did essentially the same job, which was about tracking a vehicle from order to export, taking responsibility for specific export markets.[50] In line with the new policy, they received the same pay. As the only professional woman in the office, my mother can remember huddles of men muttering complaints about the equal pay deal – though that eventually faded away. At the time, my mother was earning more than my father.

This seems like an economic success story, but it was limited success. Equal pay was a step towards having the right person in the right job. Women were more likely to be motivated to apply for jobs they were qualified to do (in my mother's case, she had to pass written and oral tests in French to get the role, which required French language skills). Despite this, equality of pay was no guarantee against prejudice. An opportunity for promotion came up – and the job was awarded to the male truck export-order controller, rather than my mother (despite her being more efficient). She was told that the reason she had not been promoted was that there was a feeling she might choose to leave and have a family. She did then leave to have a family, which is how I am here, but that is beside the point. The principle of the right person, in the right job, at the right time was ignored because of prejudice. Had my mother been promoted, she might have stayed. The attitude that women would leave to raise families, so should not be given opportunities to advance, was a softened version of the 'marriage bar' of the 1940s.

This is one of the problems with reversing such a long a history of gender prejudice. Peeling back one layer of prejudice just exposes another layer of prejudice underneath. The economic damage continues. No economist would suggest that equal work should get anything other than equal pay. But if women (or any other group) have their career progress limited, they never get the chance to experience equal work. The equal pay issue becomes irrelevant.

This shows an extra problem with the gender pay gap. The gap measures people doing the same work as one another. If prejudice stops women doing the jobs that match their skills, then even with pay equality, there is an economic cost. In the past, equal pay has arguably acted against equal status. The number of women employed in the British civil service in the 1940s meant that equal pay would have increased government spending. Equal pay was gradually phased in from 1955 after a public campaign.[51] One way of keeping costs down was to make sure that women were kept in lower-grade roles – thus earning lower pay. A separate women's class was created for computer operators, which was specifically below the clerical grades that would earn higher pay. It allowed separate pay scales and limited promotion while maintaining a fiction of equality. In the 1950s, 54% of female civil servants were in 'grades confined to women'.[52]

Thus, the gender pay gap is not just about equal pay for equal work – though that is absolutely essential. It is also about whether the same opportunities are available.

Gender prejudice

In the past, hard prejudice stopped women from working. Women could do some jobs but were stopped from working in other roles – although they clearly could have done the jobs well. The economic damage of this is made clear by government action in times of crisis. The wartime needs of the British economy meant that restrictions were lifted. The same thing is happening in the Gulf countries as the threat of a post-oil world changes economic priorities. These changes only emphasise the irrational behaviour of the earlier prejudice. Obviously, there is no rational reason why women cannot be computer programmers and entrepreneurs. When economic needs dictate, women become computer programmers and entrepreneurs. So why did governments ever try to prevent them from doing jobs for which they were suited?

Sitting in an advanced, industrialised economy it is easy to dismiss hard prejudice as a relic of the past. But there are still legal restrictions on the jobs that women can do. Men have more ways to work than women do.

The 'soft' prejudice problem is just as damaging economically and may be harder to fight. How does an economy dismantle an 'old boys' club' that excludes women from economic or political power? Treating women as 'less than' men will obviously create economic damage if the woman's skills are greater than those of a man. Failing to answer letters signed 'Stephanie Shirley' but answering letters signed 'Steve Shirley' is economically destructive behaviour.

Gender prejudice is long established – and social ideas about the role of women need to change if the economic damage is to be reversed. It may be that the fourth industrial revolution can help with that. If working from home becomes more common it might make childcare a more equal division of labour, for example. But it would be foolish to rely on technology and the changes it brings. There needs to be a conscious attempt to reverse a long-established prejudice.

Notes

1 There are ways of helping to uncover prejudice, using surveys of sufficiently large size, which will be covered in Chapter 10. But they are not easily or cheaply done.
2 See Schwarz (1992).
3 Campbell promised that his work would tell parents "how to study and improve the Natural Genius of their Children ..." See Campbell (1747).
4 Ibid., p. 151.
5 See UK Parliament (1951).
6 Gaitskell belonged to the Conservative Party. However, the same views had been expressed on the other side of the political divide. The Labour chancellor of the exchequer in 1947, Hugh Dalton, expressed similar concerns when accepting the report of the Royal Commission on Equal Pay. See UK Parliament (1947).
7 I should at this point thank 'Mad' Noel Tierney, who has been taking money off me for about a quarter of a century in his role as my boxing coach. Not that I am claiming to have acquired any upper-body strength as a result, but then upper-body strength is not a requirement for an economist (though I would argue that physical stamina and being able to take a punch are both critical).
8 See Hicks (2017).

9 Ibid. This may have been due to the fact that girls were not encouraged to study mathematics at school and, indeed, had to struggle to have the opportunity to do so. From 1935 to 1959, only 16% of Cambridge University graduates were female (see Smith, 2015). But it was also true that while official reports talked of the potential of women to become crypto-analysts, none were promoted to the role.

10 See UK Government (1919).

11 There was also no consideration given to the fact that women might not wish to marry or have children. The whole process also assumed all women were heterosexual.

12 See Momani (2016).

13 Though hardly a scientific survey, when I have occasionally lectured in regional universities, the male students seem to ask far fewer questions than the female students. That may, of course, be a reflection on my style of speaking rather than the enthusiasm of the students.

14 See Forster (2017).

15 See Lavelle and Al Sheikh (2013).

16 See Hameed (2018).

17 This is seen in the decline in the oil intensity of economic activity – that is to say, it takes fewer barrels of oil to generate a unit of economic output today than it did 10 years ago.

18 See World Economic Forum (2020).

19 Clearly, this does not mean that 2.7 billion women are excluded from the workforce entirely. It means that there are certain roles that women are specifically prohibited from doing.

20 See UN Women (2018).

21 See Shirley (2019).

22 Ibid., p. 55.

23 See World Economic Forum (2020).

24 Ibid., p. 110.

25 The 1975 Sex Discrimination Act meant that the company had to change its aim of providing careers to 'women with dependents'. See Shirley (2019).

26 The UK tax-collecting department of the time.

27 See Shirley (2019).

28 Interview with the author.

29 See Taylor (2019). Senior positions are defined as being in the top 25% of a company's employees by pay.

30 See World Economic Forum (2020).

31 See OECD (2020). The range represents the different sorts of game that can be played – via social networks, single player online and collaborative online.

32 See Shirley (2019, p. 90).

33 See Bureau of Labor Statistics (2019c). During the working week, women who work will do an average of 8.14 hours per day, against men who work an average 8.78 hours; 84.5% of women do housework every day, compared with 67.1% of men; 24.1% of women spend time looking after children every day, compared with 15.4% of men.

34 I accept that tablet computers and smartphones are the Mary Poppins of the 21st century, but even they have their limits when it comes to changing nappies.

35 In the absence of a more equal sharing of parental responsibilities, the only way this could currently be avoided, in Grace's view, is to have either independent wealth (to afford expensive childcare) or have a 'stay-at-home' partner.

36 See UK Government (1919).

37 See World Economic Forum (2020).

38 See Interparliamentary Union (2019). Rwanda, Cuba and Bolivia, out of 192 countries, were the only national parliaments where women accounted for more than 50% of the representatives. The UK, at 32%, ranked 39th in terms of female representation. The US, at 23.6%, ranked 76th. Japan, at 10.2% ranked 164th.

39 Ibid. The three countries without any female parliamentarians are the Federated States of Micronesia, Papua New Guinea and Vanuatu.

40 See World Economic Forum (2020).

41 Her family has a distant tie to the potter Josiah Wedgwood, who came so close to coming up with the concept of an 'industrial revolution' in the 17th century.

42 See Aaldering and Van Der Pas (2018).

43 Ibid. The number of parties in the Dutch political system means that there were five female and 16 male party leaders over the survey period.

44 Interview with the author, 15 May 2020.

45 If we were to come dangerously close to using the language of prejudice, only 'strong' women would be elected. A more catholic group of men would be elected. Women in politics are therefore representing a narrower range of characteristics than women in society, which reduces the range of views that are being contributed to politics.

46 See Folke and Rickne (2016).

47 See UN Women (2018).

48 See Jones (1969).

49 See *Daily Mirror* (1969).

50 My mother's areas included Malta, Iceland and São Tomé, which seem a rather random group of countries to me, but they no doubt made sense to someone.

51 See Hicks (2017). A petition for equal pay gathered 1.3 million signatures.

52 Ibid.

10 The economic damage of sexuality prejudice

Prejudice about sexual orientation is different from gender prejudice in two key ways. First, gender is generally (though not always) visible, while sexuality does not have to be. That does not mean that people can chose whether or not to be affected by prejudice because of their sexuality. People who are 'closeted' and do not admit their sexuality in public are still victims of prejudice. In this case, it is more likely to manifest in the stress of lying about who they are than in direct attack, but there is still an economic cost.

The second key difference is that prejudice about sexuality can come from within a person's own family. A target of prejudice because of gender, race, religion, nationality or hair colour (to return to *The Red-Headed League* of Chapter 1)[1] will typically have at least one other member of their family in the same situation.[2] With some forms of prejudice, a whole family will be targeted. The support of family members in the same situation is inevitably very important.

This is much less likely to be true for LGBTQ+.[3] Around a quarter of all young homeless people in the UK are LGBTQ+. The number one reason for this homelessness (in almost 70% of cases) is that the teenagers are rejected by their family because of their sexuality.[4] In the US, it is estimated that LGBTQ+ youths are 120% more likely to be homeless than straight youths.[5] Throwing a child out of their home as a result of prejudice leaves members of the LGBTQ+ community without the family support given to victims of a different prejudice.

The scale of sexuality prejudice

There is controversy as to the size of the LGBTQ+ population. Prejudice and the relative invisibility of sexuality gives people an incentive to lie when asked whether they are LGBTQ+. In some countries, admitting to being LGBTQ+ can lead to execution.[6] This means that survey-based evidence about the size of the LGBTQ+ population is almost certain to underreport the actual numbers.

In 2017, a US survey by Gallup found that 4.5% of Americans self-identified as LGBTQ+. The survey itself throws up two signals as to why this is an unreliable result. First, the number of people identifying as LGBTQ+ has risen over time across all age groups. Second, 8.2% of Millennials (those born between 1980 and 1999) identify as being LGBTQ+.[7]

The scientific community generally accepts that at least part of being LGBTQ+ is genetic.[8] That means that there is no reason for more people to be LGBTQ+ over time. There is also no reason for there to be more LGBTQ+ people among the younger generation than the older generation. Changing social attitudes, with some lessening of prejudice over time, account for these trends. It also seems to be the case that the younger generation feels able to be more honest about its sexuality. If the younger generation is more likely to be honest, but not more likely to be LGBTQ+, it is fair to assume that more than 8% of the total population is LGBTQ+. Fear of prejudice is forcing a sizeable group of people to continue to hide their sexuality when asked about it directly.

There are ways of doing surveys that make it easier for a person's sexuality to be recorded accurately. These are known as 'veiled methods' as people can hide behind a statistical veil of anonymity when giving their answers.[9] Comparing veiled methods with normal surveys, older people are less likely to be honest about their sexuality when asked directly. That fits with the different reporting by age from the Gallup survey. Overall, the number of people admitting to being LGBTQ+ is two-thirds higher using a veiled method than with normal polling.[10]

The evidence therefore suggests that the LGBTQ+ population is around 8–10% of the global population. However, Americans believe that almost a quarter of the population is LGBTQ+.[11] Such a difference is very common in areas of prejudice. Targets of prejudice are often thought to account for a larger share of the population than they actually do. As we saw earlier, immigrants are generally thought to be at least twice as numerous as they are in reality, for example.[12]

Prejudice against LGBTQ+ people may also be more significant than reported. Social desirability bias means that if someone is asked in a survey what their views are, they are more likely to give the answer they feel they should give, rather than the answer they actually believe is true. The veiled methods that help to uncover the extent of sexuality in a population can also indicate the level of prejudice when that prejudice is considered socially unacceptable. In the US, veiled methods suggest that prejudice is about two-thirds greater than reported.[13] That fits with voting behaviour. In 2009, the US state of Maine held a vote on banning same-sex marriage. Opinion polls consistently showed a minority in favour of it (around 40%). The measure passed with 53% support.[14]

What this means is that LGBTQ+ prejudice affects more people than basic surveys suggest and that the prejudice is more widespread than surveys might report. Taking both factors together, this means the economic cost of sexuality prejudice is likely to be higher than the survey evidence implies.

Hard prejudice

The hard prejudice surrounding sexuality is more complex than it is for gender. With gender prejudice, in certain countries, the law may stop women from working or undertaking other activities. The legal limitations do not normally go beyond that. When it comes to sexuality, the hard prejudice is threefold: (1) people can be executed for being LGBTQ+; (2) people can be imprisoned or otherwise punished for being LGBTQ+; and (3), as with gender, people can be stopped from working if they are LGBTQ+.

Not allowed to live

Historically, the direct costs of LGBTQ+ prejudice have not just been about economic participation. These costs have generally been about a person's right to live.[15] The execution of LGBTQ+ people has been biased towards men. Aside from a statute of the Holy Roman Emperor Charles V in 1532, lesbianism was not generally criminalised (though it was socially condemned).[16] Ironically, this, too, was the result of prejudice. Women were not considered to be sufficiently passionate, so legislation was not required. From 1778, when they eloped from Ireland, the 'Ladies of Llangollen' (Lady Eleanor Butler and Sarah Ponsonby) could live together as a couple because society was too prejudiced to recognise that they were lesbian.[17] A court case involving an accusation of lesbianism made its way from the Scottish legal system to the House of Lords. A clearly bemused Lord Gillies declared, "I do believe that the crime here alleged has no existence".[18]

In the UK, men could be executed for 'buggery' until 1861. This was a rather broad crime (it included more than homosexual acts). The media were never afraid of using strong language around the crime. In 1738, the Derby Mercury reported,

> John Hobbs was convicted of High Treason for counterfeiting the current Coin of this Kingdom, and reciev'd Sentence of Death for the same. As did David Reid, for committing the detestable Sin of Buggery.[19]

The crime of being LGBTQ+ was equated with High Treason and the rather horrendous economic crime of counterfeiting. Profit and prejudice – united in a single newspaper quote. It does seem as if the court system viewed the death penalty as an extreme punishment for the crime. From 1806 to 1900, there were almost 9,000 prosecutions for buggery in the UK. Before the death penalty was abolished, 404 men were sentenced to death, but the sentence was only carried out on 56 occasions.[20] The remaining men were imprisoned or shipped off to Australia. Around 1785, the moral philosopher Jeremy Bentham wrote an essay covering homosexuality, pointing out the absurdity of executing men for what he viewed as a matter of taste.[21] He called homosexuality an "imaginary crime".[22] But the prejudice was still strong enough to keep these ideas private. Bentham's essay was not actually published until 1978.[23] Although the death penalty was removed, the language remained as impassioned as ever. In 1957, following the publication of the Wolfenden Report on vice, The *Uxbridge and West Drayton Gazette* complained that "buggery and sodomy are obtaining some degree of respectability under the nice-sounding name of homosexuality".[24]

There were obvious economic consequences. In the early 19th century, there was what we in later years might call a 'brain drain' out of the UK. Napoleon's Europe did not criminalise sexuality. The threat of the death penalty in Britain encouraged people to leave the UK. One of the more prominent exiles was the poet and celebrity Lord Byron. Another was Percy Jocelyn, Bishop of Clogher. Having been caught with a 22-year-old soldier, the bishop fled to Europe.[25] William Beckford, the fantastically wealthy owner of the Fonthill estate in Wiltshire had to spend 11 years abroad after an LGBTQ+ scandal. He returned to relative isolation (at least from the upper strata of 'polite' society). In a rather apt phrase, Byron called him "The Martyr of prejudice".[26] The economic skills of LGBTQ+ people were lost to the UK economy. As we shall see later on, the UK government is now trying to implement this policy in reverse.

For those unable or unwilling to move into exile, the threat of the death penalty and the strain of lying about who you were will have had an economic cost. Chapter 7 talked about the damage to productivity of having to lie about who you are. That stress must have been all the greater with the prospect of being hanged for being who you were.

Crime and economic punishment

In the 20th century, most countries moved away from killing people for being LGBTQ+. That was an improvement, but hardly equality. Killing people was replaced with imprisonment in many cases.

After the defeat of Nazi Germany in 1945, the victims of Nazi aggression were compensated by the German government. Inmates of death camps and concentration camps received a financial settlement. Except for LGBTQ+ people.[27] They received no compensation and were actually put back in prison in the years that followed. The West German government agreed that these people should be treated as criminals. West Germany prosecuted 64,000 people between 1949 and 1994 (which is when the law was finally repealed).[28] Finally, in 2017, compensation was offered to the roughly 5,000 LGBTQ+ survivors of the Nazi regime who were still alive. They received EUR 3,000 each, plus EUR 1,500 for each year they had spent in jail.

EUR 1,500 for every year does not, of course, represent the economic cost of this prejudice. It could very charitably be called a token gesture. The economic cost was not just that people who should have been free and in the economy were in prison. People also had a criminal record, which will have negatively affected their employment prospects. The prejudice did lasting harm.

Criminalising sexuality could also have dire personal consequences. The British mathematician Alan Turing was mentioned in Chapter 7. His homosexuality was conveniently overlooked during the Second World War because he was absolutely essential to the war effort. Homosexuality was still illegal, however. In 1952, Turing was convicted of six counts of gross indecency with a 19-year-old man.[29] He was forced to undergo chemical treatment and psychoanalysis. In 1953, according to Turing, the police in the north of England were searching for a Norwegian man he had met on holiday. Turing wrote to a friend that he had "a shocking tendency at present to fritter away my time on anything but what I ought to be doing".[30] An economist, rather clinically, would describe this as negative productivity. Worse was to come, however. In June 1954, Turing killed himself. Suicide is not uncommon among the LGBTQ+ community. Even today, the prejudice against LGBTQ+ people has led to a significantly higher suicide rate in that portion of the population. LGBTQ+ men are four times more likely to attempt suicide than heterosexual men, while LGBTQ+ women are almost twice as likely to attempt suicide as heterosexual women.[31]

The criminalisation of homosexuality created a persecuted class in society. As with other victims of prejudice, the persecuted LGBTQ+ population created a dialect to help identify each other and communicate in secret. In a world without social-media groups, it created a sense of community. Just as my relatives in East London talked rhyming slang to avoid the unwelcome attentions of the authorities, so the LGBTQ+ community used a dialect called Polari. Indeed, Polari borrowed some words from rhyming slang.[32] Polari was used quite widely in the British LGBTQ+ community until the 1960s.[33] The fact that it existed was a sign of the prejudice and fear associated with being LGBTQ+. It was fading from use by the late 1960s – perhaps in part because it was becoming more recognised.[34] When the UK government partially decriminalised homosexuality in 1967, Polari was not used in the newly created and now legal LGBTQ+ publications.[35]

Today over a third of the countries in the United Nations still criminalise consensual same-sex sexual acts.[36] The economic costs of this prejudice are secondary to the human cost, but there *are* economic costs. For example, India finally decriminalised LGBTQ+ relations in 2018.[37] In 2015, a study found that only 8% of LGBTQ+ Indians felt able to come out at work.[38] The previous year, a World Bank case study of India concluded that the prejudice against LGBTQ+ imposed a significant cost on the economy.[39] Again, it is when prejudice is reduced that the costs that held back the economy become apparent. The Indian city of Bengaluru is the hub for India's technology sector and hosts the third-largest number of tech start-ups in the world.[40] It has a strong history of LGBTQ+ inclusion, which is directly identified as attracting skilled workers and promoting innovation.[41]

Economic participation

The areas of hard prejudice in which sexuality and gender overlap have to do with economic participation. Once societies stopped killing and later imprisoning LGBTQ+ people, the economic sanctions lingered. Today, even if being LGBTQ+ is not a crime, it is legal to fire someone (or refuse to hire someone) on the grounds of their sexuality in many countries. If it is legal to deny someone a job on irrational grounds, there is an economic cost.

In 1950, at a speech in Wheeling, West Virginia, US Republican Senator Joseph McCarthy claimed that there were 205 Communists working in the US State Department. It triggered the 'Red Scare,' which purged suspected Communists from the US government.[42] The same year, the State Department announced that 91 homosexuals had been "allowed" to resign.[43] There then followed a series of investigations into men and women working in the US federal government, which became known as the 'Lavender Scare'. It ran alongside the Red Scare and was just as serious a persecution.[44] The Lavender Scare established a legal limit on the right of LGBTQ+ people to work in the economy. President Eisenhower's Executive Order 10450 of 1953 barred people with a "sexual perversion" from the federal government.[45] "Sexual perversion" meant anyone who was not heterosexual.

One reason for this was a fear that LGBTQ+ people could be blackmailed. Obviously, the reason they could have been blackmailed about their sexuality was the prejudice that existed in society in the first place. Social prejudice caused fear, which caused employment prejudice. This fear was not just a US problem. In the UK, there were similar concerns. British civil servant John Vassall was blackmailed by the Soviet Union in just this way in the 1960s. Of the five members of the Cambridge Spy Ring, Guy Burgess and Anthony Blunt were gay and Donald MacLean was bisexual.[46] LGBTQ+ people were banned from employment in the British secret services until 1991.

Things have now changed. Christopher Parr, who was a civil servant in the UK Cabinet Office and then the Office of the Deputy Prime Minister, was in a role that needed the highest level of security clearance.[47] This involved an interview with a "trained Investigation Officer" in the early 2000s.[48] The aim of the interview was to make sure that the government knew everything that could be used for blackmail purposes. The fact that Christopher was openly gay was not an issue at all. Nor was the fact that he was in a brief relationship with a member of the government at the time. This is perhaps an indication of the extent to which attitudes in society have changed.

As with some of the hard-prejudice changes around gender, the ending of this prejudice just emphasises the economic costs that came before. People like Christopher would have been denied the chance to contribute to the economy for irrational reasons. The "road not taken" effect would have hurt economic productivity. The 'Don't Ask, Don't Tell' policy of the US military outlined in Chapter 7 is another example of this irrational cost – and, as discussed, the cost to the economy was significant. In 2017, on the 50th anniversary of the partial decriminalisation of homosexuality in the UK, a series of podcasts by the LGBTQ+ magazine *Attitude* were sponsored by the GREAT Britain Campaign – the government's vehicle for promoting the UK internationally. Support for LGBTQ+ rights had become part of the campaign to attract investment and skilled workers to the UK.[49] The UK's prejudice led to a 'brain drain' of talent in the early 19th century; now, the government is discreetly appealing to persecuted LGBTQ+ communities to bring their talent to the UK. Migration for work has risen by a third this century, and there is evidence that skilled LGBTQ+ workers in prejudiced economies will migrate to more inclusive countries.[50]

The failure to protect employment for LGBTQ+ workers means major economic damage. Today, only 40% of United Nations countries prohibit firing someone for their sexuality.[51] At the time of writing, in the US, it is legal to fire someone for being LGBTQ+ in several states (affecting around half the US LGBTQ+ population).[52] US firms in these states can also deny promotion or training on the grounds of sexuality. Employment protection is also missing in most major Asian economies. Economically, it is irrational for a firm to fire an employee for their sexuality – but that is what makes it prejudice.[53]

The brutal realities of hard prejudice

The execution of people for being LGBTQ+ is, of course, the most horrific form of prejudice. But criminalisation can lead to death – as was the case with Turing, depriving the world of a young and brilliant mathematician. While it has no legal standing, the 'gay panic defence' is still used in some countries' courtrooms in murder trials. This is when a non-LGBTQ+ person claims that their murder of an apparently LGBTQ+ person was justified by temporary insanity (brought on by the horror of believing the other person to be LGBTQ+). It has been successfully used to mitigate charges of murder.[54] All of these actions signal to LGBTQ+ people that they are 'less than' non-LGBTQ+ people and that their lives count for less.

When LGBTQ+ people are given fewer legal rights or denied the right to exist in a society, their ability to contribute to the economy is lost. But even when lethal force and criminalisation are removed, prejudice can still do considerable economic damage.

Soft prejudice

The economic effects of soft prejudice over sexuality come when people feel that they are being treated as 'less than' other people in society. This might come because people are open about their sexuality (and so directly feel the consequences of prejudice). Alternatively, it will come because people are afraid of their status being diminished by being 'outed' at work – so they undergo strain to disguise who they are.

The power of out

There is an interesting question of how to define whether an LGBTQ+ person is 'in' or 'out'. Jane Austen's *Mansfield Park* offers a parallel. Miss Crawford asks of Fanny Price, "Pray, is she out or is she not? I am puzzled".[55] In this sense 'out' meant being seen in polite society. Now the term is used to say whether someone is open about their sexuality. Miss Crawford was confused because there was no formal recognition of being socially 'out'. But the same can apply with sexuality. Former Welsh rugby captain Gareth Thomas (admittedly, an unlikely parallel for the demure Fanny Price) was out as a gay man to his teammates and family. He said of his sexuality that it "became the worst-kept secret in Welsh rugby".[56] But he had not come out in public. His colleagues knew, but the fans and the general public did not – until a newspaper article in 2009 (three years after he had told his teammates). Was he out, or was he not?

Perhaps the answer is that unless someone is outed in a very high-profile way, there is a continual process of coming out. Unlike many other forms of discrimination, you have to *say* that you are LGBTQ+ at work – because the assumption is still that most people are not LGBTQ+ and to be LGBTQ+ is to be an invisible target for prejudice. That never-ending cycle of explanation can add stress. That stress must be all the greater if there is a hard prejudice of employment discrimination to worry about. What if, the next time you come out, it costs you your job? Christopher Parr cites the "odd ballet of manners" that occurs when talking with colleagues he knows to be gay – are they out or not in the workplace? How should you interact? It is a problem non-LGBTQ+ people do not typically face.

Simon Miall, who played rugby for London club Harlequins, only came out after he left the sport (in 2007) and moved into the world of finance. He believes that sports supporters tend to feel that buying a ticket gives them the right to judge the players – and that judgement extends to life off the pitch. This view can only have increased with the rise of social media. It increases the cost of being publicly out in sport – even if one is out to colleagues and immediate friends. Simon dealt with the question of whether or not he was out by coming out to everyone he knew at the same time. He says, "As I came out later in life, I had the attitude of just wanting to get on with it … and I'm very pleased that I did".[57] But even with that, he says that early in his career he had been asked to at least downplay his sexuality with certain clients. Although he would not do that now, in the past, that created a strain to which non-LGBTQ+ colleagues would have been subject.

There is near universal agreement on the economic benefits of coming out in the workplace. Miall came out when working on a trading floor in the banking industry. He feels it a waste of energy not to be true to himself. The stress of being careful about pronouns when describing a partner and keeping work and social lives separate has a cost in terms of productivity. Being able to relax and be honest made him a better employee.

Erika Karp, the Chief Executive of social investment group Cornerstone Capital, describes herself as living diversity – being a woman, Jewish, lesbian and short. She is also an extraordinarily inspiring and motivated person. Nonetheless, she says she thought for a year before coming out at work and that it was an "excruciating debate". She was concerned about the career implications of her decision.[58] When walking in public with her (now) wife, Karp says they stopped holding hands if she saw anyone wearing a suit walking towards them. The fear was that it might be a colleague and she would be outed at work before she was ready. These actions underscore the costs that social prejudice forces on a person – and are all the more remarkable as they are so incongruous to the person that Karp is today. She will never know for certain if there was a cost to her career, but feels that by coming out she has become "more productive, more creative, and more everything I am supposed to be".[59]

Such stories are widespread. Study after study has shown that being out at work reduces stress, improves performance and increases social interaction with colleagues.[60] Productivity is improved as a result. Workers who are out are significantly more likely to feel a valued part of a team than those who have to conceal who they are. LGBTQ+ staff are also significantly more likely to stay with a firm if they are out.[61] Both of these factors will tend to increase economic productivity. It is also worth noting that having a culture that encourages people to lie about who they are is not likely to be helpful to a firm's values.

This does not mean that the economic costs for LGBTQ+ people evaporate in the coming-out process. The "road not taken" issue is still relevant if an economy has a mixed record on prejudice. For example, despite studying law at university, Christopher Parr consciously chose not to invest in a career in law, in part because he felt he could not be openly gay in the legal profession.[62] At that time, there were no LGBTQ+ role models among lawyers that would have given him the confidence to consider a legal career. If LGBTQ+ people feel unwelcome in one profession, they may choose a role that is second best. That does damage to them personally and is a misallocation of resources in the wider economy. LGBTQ+ people may overcome the barriers (Erika Karp never questioned her wish to have a career in finance and Simon Miall says that he would have always seized any opportunity to be a professional sportsperson). But these barriers are economically unnecessary.

Social conventions

Even when comfortably out, and freed from the additional stress of hiding who you are, the social conventions of a work environment can still create difficulties for an LGBTQ+ employee. Miall points out that while colleagues had no problem with his sexuality, socialising after work still had some limits. As already noted, coming out is shown to increase social interaction, which is good. But while Miall's straight colleagues might talk about their dates, he felt constrained not to talk about going out with a 'hot guy'. This self-censorship may not be necessary, but the fact that it is there is a legacy of past prejudice. But it may also have economic consequences. The informal socialising from which Grace felt cut off (Chapter 9) is also potentially weakened. The 'bonding' that comes from socialising after work is lessened if, like Miall, you fear that you will make people uncomfortable by being part of a discussion.[63]

This self-censorship can also be read as a signal that by being LGBTQ+, a person is 'less than' the non-LGBTQ+ majority. Dating a 'hot guy' should not be something to be ashamed of. Other subtle signals can still give LGBTQ+ people a sense of being 'less than'. The response, 'I would never have known' to a person coming out is often meant to be a compliment, for example. The implication is that a person is to be congratulated for maintaining the appearance of being non-LGBTQ+. It is a further reminder of how being LGBTQ+ is seen.

The problem with these social conventions is that they will influence the working environment. Even if employees are out at work and there is a non-discrimination policy, if the culture of a company undermines them, LGBTQ+ employees may still end up being less productive than they could be. This is a possible distinction between US and European-managed firms. In the US, there may be a legal requirement for firms to have non-discrimination policies, but that does not tackle the social conventions that also have an impact. In Europe, a culture of diversity seems more embedded – which is not to say that it is perfect. Having rules and legal force is not enough to make sure that the right LGBTQ+ person is in the right job at the right time.[64] Social convention, inside or outside the firm, can prevent that from happening.

Equal marriage

The economics of marriage equality is a good example of the consequences of prejudice. This is something that is particularly important to me. The inane nature of the debate on the economics of marriage equality in the UK in 2013 prompted me to write a report on the topic, which over time turned into the inspiration to write this book. It also led to one of the largest-scale attacks on my research as an economist (right up there with those in response to my views on the economics of Scottish independence and crypto-currencies). At the time, this was a controversial subject on which to write. But the economics of this matter.

Marriage equality is not as recent a topic as people might think. In 1810, in London's Vere Street, same-sex marriages were performed by John Church, an ordained minister. They had no legal status, of course. In 1953, the August/September edition of *ONE Magazine* was seized by the US authorities. The title on the cover was "Homosexual Marriage?"[65] The author, E.B. Saunders, asked readers to "Imagine that the year were 2053 and homosexuality were accepted to the point of being of no importance... is he [a gay man], in this Utopia, subject to marriage laws?"[66] Saunders was suggesting that true "acceptance" of LGBTQ+ people in society would require marriage equality. Although Saunders was arguing against equality, the economic necessity of equal marriage to produce equal status is certainly true.

Chapter 7 already noted the costs to firms that arise from having marriage equality not recognised in some parts of the world. Labour mobility is affected between countries and, at times, within countries. Firms cannot employ the best people where they want to employ them. But a lot of the economic arguments around marriage equality come from the legal and social status that marriage gives. If there is not marriage equality, LGBTQ+ people are branded as being 'less than'.

Before marriage equality in the UK, British LGBTQ+ people did have the option of civil partnerships. This gave them the legal rights of a non-LGBTQ+ married couple. However, it did not give equality. It was 'equal but separate' in the way that racial segregation was 'equal but separate' in the US after the Civil War. Because marriage has a social status in society, denying a group that social status on irrational grounds is prejudice. UK Prime Minister David Cameron explained his opposition to allowing non-LGBTQ+ people to enter into civil partnerships to Deputy Prime Minister Nick Clegg as such: "I am perfectly willing to upgrade the rights of gay [LGBTQ+] people. I am not willing to downgrade the rights of straight [non-LGBTQ+] people".[67] In Cameron's mind, it was clear that civil partnerships were 'less than' non-LGBTQ+ marriage, even with the same legal rights. By extension that 'less than' status applied to the people in those partnership as much as to the institution itself.

Removing prejudice either requires equal marriage or the abolition of marriage entirely as a legal and social institution.[68] That is the only way that the social status of LGBTQ+ and non-LGBTQ+ people can be equalised.

Equal pay

As with gender, the existence of a pay gap between LGBTQ+ workers and non-LGBTQ+ workers can be taken as a summary of the economic costs of prejudice. Economists are, again, frustrated by a lack of data. As discussed earlier, only a fraction of people are prepared to self-identify as being LGBTQ+. As around half the LGBTQ+ population will be classified as being non-LGBTQ+, this makes it hard to measure the sexuality pay gap. There are other complications. Generally, the higher the level of education an LGBTQ+ person has, the more likely they are to be out socially or at work.[69] That skews the sample for analysis.

Nonetheless, where surveys have been undertaken there is evidence that men who are LGBTQ+ suffer a pay gap to non-LGBTQ+ men. A 2019 review of research suggests a pay gap of 4–5% in the UK, France and the Netherlands, but 12–16% in Canada, Sweden and the US.[70] Women who are LGBTQ+ have a more mixed experience. Some earn less than non-LGBTQ+ women, but in the UK and the US, they earn more. The theory behind this is that LGBTQ+ women are seen as less likely to leave to have a family (as mentioned in Chapter 9, the likelihood that my mother would want to leave to raise a future economist possibly cost her a promotion at Ford). This perception may be challenged as marriage equality becomes more common. If that is the case, it will be interesting to see whether the pay gap shifts. It is also worth remembering that the existence of a gender pay gap means that the absence of a sexuality pay gap in some countries can only be a partial help to women.

In a world without prejudice there would be no reason why LGBTQ+ workers *should* be less productive than non-LGBTQ+ workers. To suggest that a random 10% of the population is automatically inferior as workers is ridiculous. What might cause a sexuality pay gap is prejudice. If the worker is out, then the pay gap could come from direct prejudice – refusing to pay LGBTQ+ people properly for the work that they do. It could be less direct – refusing to train LGBTQ+ people to enhance their skills and allow them to progress (as is still legal for roughly half the population of the US, at the time of writing). It could be unconscious prejudice – thinking LGBTQ+ people are 'less than' non-LGBTQ+ people because that is how society views the matter. It could be through self-censorship – not participating fully in work social events.

If the worker is not out, the sexuality pay gap could rationally reflect their underperformance as a worker. However, that underperformance, in turn, is due to the strain caused by a culture of prejudice forcing the worker to continually lie about who they are. As mentioned in Chapter 7, gay men 'hiding' in heterosexual marriages earn less than straight men in heterosexual marriages. Lying about who they are is the differentiating factor. The stress that this creates affects their economic performance.

Sexuality prejudice

The fact that people can be secretive about their sexuality makes this a different form of prejudice to gender. It affects a smaller portion of the population – around 10%. However, sexuality is automatically more democratic than some other forms of prejudice. The distribution of sexuality is random across society, ethnicity and gender.

The history of persecution, and the fact that it continues to this day, means that anti-LGBTQ+ prejudice can have a horrifically high human cost. Even though executions are rejected by most societies, the disproportionately high suicide rate for LGBTQ+ people shows that sexuality prejudice is particularly damaging. That the 'gay panic defence' is still even a thing demonstrates that the costs of this prejudice extend beyond the economic. The mere idea of killing someone because you were surprised by who they are is perverse. But alongside the human cost, there are economic costs, and they are significant.

If the objective is to get the right person, in the right job, at the right time, prejudice against 10% of the population is going to be costly in economic terms. The prejudice affects people's performance at work and their ability to move to the best possible location for them (and the economy). As more people start to come out, the costs of this prejudice should be easier to measure, and then to tackle.

As this chapter and Chapter 9 have hopefully demonstrated, there are many ways in which prejudice can create an economic cost. At a time when revolutionary change in society increases the risks of prejudice, acknowledging its existence and the damage it does is not enough. We need to think about how to tackle prejudice to maximise the economic advantages of the changes we are living through. That is what Chapter 11 is going to do.

Notes

1 See Conan Doyle (1891).
2 The gene that causes red hair is regressive, so a red-headed child should have other red heads in their family.
3 Language is always controversial in discussing issues of prejudice. I shall be using the term LGBTQ+ (lesbian, gay, bisexual, transgender, queer, intersex, asexual, non-binary and other sexual identity minorities) as the most commonly used term at the time of writing. Where it is relevant, or historically accurate, I will use narrower terms.
4 See Albert Kennedy Trust (2015).
5 See Chapin Hall (2017).
6 Iran, Saudi Arabia, Somalia, Sudan and Yemen execute people for being LGBTQ+. Afghanistan, Brunei, Mauritania, Pakistan, Qatar and the United Arab Emirates could execute people for being LGBTQ+ under their legal codes but have not done so in recent years. See Mendos (2019). One way to get a sense of the extreme nature of these laws is to consider the counterfactual. What would be your reaction to hearing that a country had executed anyone who admitted to heterosexual behaviour?
7 See Newport (2017).
8 See Kaiser (2019). This study suggests that there is no single gene that leads to LGBTQ+ behaviour, but that genetics may explain up to a quarter of same-sex attraction. Other biological factors may also contribute to sexuality (for example, hormone exposure in the womb).
9 See Coffman et al. (2013). The veiled approach takes a large number of survey respondents (which tends to make it a more expensive survey technique). Half the group is presented with a list of statements. The other half is presented with the same statements, plus an extra statement. In this example, the additional statement is about the person's sexuality. At no point are people asked whether they agree with any one statement. They are asked how many of the statements listed apply to them. The people who answer are then absolutely certain that they cannot be identified as LGBTQ+ using this method, and this reduces the

psychological cost of admitting that the sexuality statement is true. The survey does not allow researchers to identify the characteristics of any individual, but it does allow them to identify the average characteristics of the population.

10 Ibid.
11 See McCarthy (2019).
12 See Alesina et al. (2018).
13 See Coffman et al. (2013).
14 See Powell (2013). This is a variation of what is known as the Bradley Effect after Los Angeles Mayor Tom Bradley. When running for governor of California in 1982 and 1986, Bradley, who is African American, received a noticeably lower share of the vote than opinion polls had suggested. The hypothesis is that people did not want to admit to a racial preference when asked directly but would vote in a racially motivated way in the anonymity of the polling booth.
15 As already noted, this is still the case in at least six countries today.
16 See Weeks (1976).
17 See Morrison (2019).
18 Ibid.
19 See The Derby Mercury (1738).
20 See Cook et al. (2007, p. 109).
21 See Morrison (2019).
22 Ibid. Though, Bentham did not use the term homosexual, which was essentially a 20th-century term.
23 See Bentham (1978).
24 See The Uxbridge and West Drayton Gazette (1957).
25 See Morrison (2019).
26 Ibid.
27 In this case, it was nearly all gay and bisexual men, as female homosexuality was not a crime in Germany.
28 See BBC (2017). The law – Paragraph 175 of the German Criminal Code – was relaxed in 1969, but only fully removed from the statute books in 1994. The original 1871 version criminalised "an unnatural sex act committed between persons of male sex ...". This was amended by the Nazi government in 1931 to focus on "a male who commits a sex offense with another male, or who allows himself to be used by another male for a sex offense ..." (see Fordham University, 2020). West Germany kept the Nazi version of the law, while East Germany reverted to the 1871 definition. The West German law was modified in 1969 to allow sex between consenting males over the age of 21. The non-LGBTQ+ age of consent was 14 (see DW, 2019).
29 See Turing (2015).
30 Ibid., p. 236.
31 See Office of the Surgeon General (US) and National Action Alliance for Suicide Prevention (US) (2012).
32 See Baker (2019).
33 Polari was mainly spoken rather than written. It developed organically, which meant its vocabulary changed over time. Long after it ceased to be regularly used in the LGBTQ+ community, the King James Bible was translated into Polari (see Polari Bible, 2019).
34 Two characters in a popular BBC radio drama, *Round the Horne*, used around 40 Polari words on a regular basis. This was not enough vocabulary to allow people to understand everything an LGBTQ+ person said in Polari, but it was enough to recognise what dialect was being spoken.
35 It is worth noting that the number of prosecutions for LGBTQ+ acts rose in the UK after the partial decriminalisation. See Tatchell (2017).
36 See Mendos (2019).

37 See Tripathi (2018). The position was complicated – there was an earlier court ruling decriminalising LGBTQ+ relations in 2009. This ruling was overturned in 2013. The law criminalising LGBTQ+ relations was rarely enforced, with fewer than 200 people imprisoned in over 150 years of its existence. However, it was used as justification of police raids, and for blackmail.
38 See Johnson (2015).
39 See Badgett (2014). The study did not come up with a dollar amount for the cost of prejudice. It did highlight the damage to productivity, as well as health-care and other costs.
40 See Miller and Parker (2018).
41 Ibid. The study also cites a business leader saying that the recriminalisation of LGBTQ+ behaviour between 2013 and 2018 led to a lot of skilled software workers leaving the country.
42 See US Senate (1950).
43 See US House of Representatives (1950). The term "homosexuals" is what was used at the time.
44 See Toops (2013).
45 See US Federal Register (1953).
46 See Kelly (2016).
47 Interview with the author.
48 See UK Ministry of Defence (2020). The interviewer was, apparently, less 'James Bond' and more an ageing military type in an old raincoat.
49 See Attitude (2017a) and Attitude (2017b).
50 See Miller and Parker (2018). Between 2015 and 2017, the UK received an average of just under 2,000 applications for asylum on the grounds of sexuality. The success rates of these applications was 43%. Half of the applications came from five countries – Bangladesh, Iran, Nigeria, Pakistan and Uganda. See UK Home Office (2018).
51 See Mendos (2019).
52 See Miller (2019). There are cases currently before the US Supreme Court which may change this state of affairs.
53 The UK did have a piece of legislation on its statue books until 2017 that allowed merchant seafarers to be fired for being LGBTQ+. The law was obsolete, having been superseded by employment protection legislation, but still had to be specifically removed. See UK Parliament 2017.
54 See Holden (2019).
55 See Austen (1814, p. 56).
56 See Thomas (2014).
57 Interview with the author.
58 Interview with the author.
59 Ibid.
60 See Badgett et al. (2013) for a summary of some of the research on this topic.
61 See Johnson (2015). In most cases 20–30% more out workers felt valued as team members compared with closeted colleagues. Almost 40% of workers strongly disagreed with the idea that they would leave their firm. For closeted workers, it was 23.2%.
62 This was not the only reason he rejected a career at the Bar, but it was one of the reasons.
63 The difference here is that this sort of constraint is likely to be less in a more senior position – the presence of management at an after-works social event tends to change the nature of the conversation. Grace was in a different position, as she was limited in her ability to attend after-work social events at all.
64 See Burns (2012).
65 See ONE Archives Foundation (n.d.).

66 Saunders (1953) used language today that is astonishingly prejudiced – talking of "deviants" throughout the article. The general argument was that LGBTQ+ would be unwilling to accept the monogamy associated with marriage, which might perhaps show a lack of imagination on the part of the author about the future development of heterosexual and homosexual relationships.

67 See Featherstone (2016). Cameron's opposition was based on the fact that he supported marriage but disapproved of people living together. Civil partnerships already existed for LGBTQ+ people, so could be upgraded, but he did not want non-LGBTQ+ people choosing what he considered the lesser institution of civil partnership. The law has since been changed and civil partnerships in the UK are now available to non-LGBTQ+ people as well.

68 Abolition is not as silly as it might sound – as one could argue that single people have a lower social status (after a certain age) and are subject to prejudice. Jane Austen's Emma Woodhouse hinted at some of the social sneering at single people with the line, "it is poverty only which makes celibacy contemptible to a generous public" – though of course that may also be prejudice on the grounds of income. Abolition was obviously never likely. See Austen (1815, 1877 ed., p. 82).

69 See Rogers (2006).

70 See Drydakis (2019).

11 Fighting back

There have been times over the four years or so of researching this book that I have become despondent about the rise of prejudice. The link between structural change and prejudice is quite clear. In the recent past, the increased role of prejudice politics and 'scapegoat economics' has led to decisions that are now causing significant harm. In many cases, the harm will be felt most by the supporters of 'scapegoat economics'. That does not mean that we should give up, however. There are ways in which prejudice can be tackled.

Fighting prejudice is always going to be controversial, not least because the phrase 'I am not prejudiced, but ...' so often precedes a prejudiced statement. People are unwilling to recognise prejudice in themselves. There is also a risk that some methods of attacking prejudice will end up lending support to the very enemy they are trying to defeat. But I believe that a mix of anti-prejudice policies can succeed. The advantage of pushing back against the rise of prejudice, even a little, is that it will allow more of the economic advantages of the fourth industrial revolution to come through. If that happens, the enthusiasm for prejudice may fade a little. Eventually, we can create a virtuous cycle.

Any attempt to fight prejudice is likely to make life more complicated. This is inevitable, perhaps. As highlighted all the way back in Chapter 1, the simplifying 'rule of thumb' is a very common way for prejudice to emerge. The arguments against prejudice are not easily tweeted. As structural change makes the world more complex, there are times when we all crave the simplicity of 240 characters. (I am too old to crave the 60 seconds of a TikTok video, but that simplicity has its audience too.) The solutions to prejudice require effort. But the effort will then bring economic rewards.

Before thinking about how to defeat prejudice, we have to consider how to balance different rights. Fighting prejudice against one group can sometimes be seen as encouraging prejudice against another. One very obvious example, globally, has been the fight between religious rights and LGBTQ+ rights.

Both religious and LGBTQ+ people have been subject to prejudice. Both have died as a result of prejudice – for what they believe and for how they were born, respectively. A group called Coalition for Marriage (C4M) was formed in 2012 when the UK's marriage equality law was being debated. It was not *for* marriage as we now understand it. C4M was *against* marriage equality. The group was founded by the Christian Institute and supported by the Catholic Church.[1] Part of the C4M argument was that marriage equality was a form of prejudice against religious freedom: the rights of the religious minority were being hurt.[2] At the same time, as outlined in Chapter 10, the lack of marriage equality allowed the view that LGBTQ+ people were 'less than' non-LGBTQ+ people.

The clash of rights was also addressed by US Chief Justice John Roberts. In his dissent against the Obergefell v. Hodges case, which legalised marriage equality in the US, he stated, "people of faith can take no comfort in the treatment they receive from the majority today".[3] The 'people of faith' are a larger group in the US than they are in the UK but still present themselves as being attacked by a liberal elite.[4]

The critical factor in a dispute over prejudice seems to be whether others are hurt by a group's actions. It comes down to people being treated equally. If a group has beliefs that lessen the social status, freedom or economic position of another group in society, that view should be considered less important. The C4M agenda was something that did treat another group in society as being 'less than' the majority. Equal marriage was not something that took away from the status or freedom of C4M supporters. Lord Carlile asked a question in the House of Lords debate when speaking about his daughter and her fiancée: "Is there any one of your married lordships who would feel any less married if Anna and Joanna were permitted lawful wedlock?"[5] The answer was clearly 'no'. In deciding between claims of prejudice, the principle of 'do no harm' seems a good place to start.

There are many opinions on how best to fight prejudice. Unfortunately, there are no absolute answers about what works – partly because it is difficult to measure success.[6] If a firm's training programme cuts prejudice in half, how will anyone know for certain? There is no index for prejudice, and people do not admit to being prejudiced when asked. We must allow for a lack of precision in searching for solutions. If the aim is to manage the economic consequences of prejudice, I believe there are six policies that should be considered: education, education, telling stories, challenging, contact and quotas. The aim of any policy should be to reduce the desire for prejudice and reduce the misunderstanding between different groups that allows for prejudice.

Education (part 1)

Prejudice and ignorance are closely linked. Prejudice is, by definition, irrational. Understanding the issues and being able to look without bias at evidence can tackle that. The importance of being educated about other groups was clear in the cases of both Megan Phelps-Roper and Derek Black (covered in Chapter 5). Their prejudices largely came from ignorance. In both cases, their extreme prejudice was beaten by being educated about the people they targeted.

Inclusive teaching from an early age creates a defensive mechanism against prejudice. If children learn about other groups and understand them, it will help them to reject prejudice against those groups in later life. It also helps to promote critical thinking. Because prejudice is irrational and often involves judging groups before meeting them, critical thinking is a key part of stopping prejudice.

The No Outsiders charity focusses on teaching inclusive behaviour in British schools. As the name suggests, it is a direct assault on prejudice.[7] The UK is a diverse society and children need be taught how to live in it. Thinking about fighting prejudice in the context of society can be helpful. Children are taught facts about other groups, not just in the classroom, but in all aspects of life in school. By educating young children on all aspects of diversity and giving them information about other religions, races and sexualities, the programme aims to prevent prejudice from forming.

In an interesting comment on the possibility of conflict between different groups, the charity's founder, Andrew Moffat, recounts a parents' meeting at a school. A mother in a full burqa said, "If you want to live here and wear your veil, you have to accept that schools are teaching about gay people … I choose to live in Britain because I can wear this".[8] This also highlights the possibility that by creating an education programme that challenges prejudice, it is not just the children who will be educated. Parents are also likely to learn.[9]

Education (part 2)

The first role of education is to tackle the ignorance that fuels prejudice. But if the process of change in the fourth industrial revolution is making prejudice worse, education should try to tackle some of the causes as well.

'Scapegoat economics' is driven by a fear of loss or actual loss. Either way, this is powerful, because of the way our minds are hardwired to favour loss aversion. Cash handouts will not solve this problem. The increase in prejudice may owe a lot to the economic changes of the fourth industrial revolution but, as noted in Chapter 4, it is not just about income. Those who fear a loss of income tend to the left politically, though staying within the mainstream. Those who fear a loss of status turn to the right and favour more extreme parties. Both left and right (very obviously) can be prejudiced. The point is that if it is the loss of *status* that is driving prejudice, something must be done to tackle that cause. A welfare system does not help with that and, given prejudice about people on welfare, may make it worse. This is where education comes in.

Education can help to reduce the fear of change. The section on loss aversion in Chapter 4 shows how lower-skilled workers are more likely to oppose the automation that the fourth industrial revolution will bring. This is because lower-skilled workers see themselves as being more at risk from the change. That may not be true, but the truth is not especially important when it comes to prejudice. While raising skill levels may help, the skill that is most important does not come from textbooks. The way education can reduce the causes of prejudice is less about *what* we are taught and more about *how* we are taught.

An education system that focusses on remembering facts produces people who are not going to do well in the world of an industrial revolution. Facts change in revolutionary times, often in a big way. The proud holder of a university degree that has been given for learning by rote is going to be at an economic disadvantage. In fact, they are very likely to be seduced by 'scapegoat economics' and prejudice politics. The risk to their status in a time of change is higher (because they are less able to change as the things they have learned become out of date). Furthermore, their loss of status may be greater in the fourth industrial revolution. Having worked hard to achieve graduate status, they have further to fall in economic and social terms if that status is less useful.

What seems most likely to succeed is an education system that allows people to learn for themselves. That implies a flexible approach and a focus on the method of analysis, rather than memorising lists of dates or other facts that Google can otherwise provide. Hopefully, this will give people a greater sense of adaptability as the world around us changes. Of course, fear of change is not going to be entirely removed by a liberal arts degree or a creative pre-school classroom. But if the fear of change can be limited, prejudice can be rolled back a little.

Story time

One of the most powerful ways of getting an idea across to people is to appeal to their emotions. Telling a story is central to that. The Nobel Laureate Robert Shiller describes an economic narrative as "a contagious story that has the potential to change how people make economic decisions".[10] That is at the very heart of tackling prejudice. People are making economic decisions that are irrational because of prejudice. A good economic story is one way to change those economic decisions.

This is actually quite fortunate. The lack of economic data means that relying on statistics to defeat prejudice is going to be difficult. The reality of prejudice is also complex. As we know, complexity is part of the problem in trying to defeat the simplistic world view of prejudice. Adding complicated economic models and torturing the economic data does not reduce that complexity. A simple, rational story can do a lot to change existing prejudice. This is all the more important as prejudice is often built by the telling of simple stories.[11] Fighting stories with stories is a way of levelling the playing field.

Harriet Beecher Stowe's 1852 novel *Uncle Tom's Cabin* is one example of how storytelling can influence prejudice.[12] The story of the slave Uncle Tom was a hit, with 300,000 copies sold in the US during its first year.[13] There is a general consensus that the story helped change attitudes towards slavery in the northern US. Certainly, many southern commentators of the time were horrified at the story and the seeming emotional reaction to it.[14] US President Abraham Lincoln is alleged to have credited Stowe with making the Civil War come about.[15] Certainly, Stowe achieved considerable fame in the northern states during the war. Her story was clearly influential. The northern US was not free from prejudice – there were northern slave states – but the story influenced sentiment.

Stowe's story was fictional, although based in the reality of the slave-owning South. Storytelling is more than fiction. It is the personal stories that are likely to have the most impact. The film writer Dustin Lance Black has told how the power of storytelling helped his mother overcome homophobia. His mother's Mormon, military background meant she reacted negatively when Black told her that he was gay. However, when she visited him for his graduation, his friends (unaware of her views) had talked to her about their lives. The stories she heard that evening changed her view.[16] Similarly, Derek Black's eventual rejection of extreme prejudice began at college. A turning point came when, he says, "people chose to invite me into their dorms and conversations rather than ostracize me".[17] Hearing about the effects of prejudice and realising that people are not that different is clearly powerful.

Contact

Having contact with people of different backgrounds has a lot of potential when it comes to tackling prejudice. As we saw in Chapter 4, it is harder to be prejudiced against someone you know. There have been several studies over the years showing that when people from different backgrounds come together in a situation of equal status, prejudice will be reduced.[18] One experiment looked at teenagers on an 'outward bound' survival course, who were assigned to mixed groups. The time spent in contact with people from different backgrounds led the teenagers to describe themselves as less prejudiced. Analysis of racially diverse dorms in a university has produced similar results.[19]

The inverse relationship between prejudice and contact can be seen in a rather frightening US statistic. As US states become politically polarised, there is less contact with people of different political views. Today, 45% of US Democrats say they would be unhappy if their child married a Republican. Thirty-five percent of Republicans are against intermarriage with Democrats. In 1960, when there was more political mixing, there was virtually no prejudice of this kind.[20] That lack of contact extends to the political class. The rising cost of winning an American election means that politicians in Washington today spend more and more time fundraising.

Consequently, they have less time to socialise with colleagues from the opposing party – something that used to happen. This limits their understanding of the views of the other party.

Contact can be virtual. The parasocial contact covered in Chapter 5 is a way of giving people diverse 'friends' even if they do not have friends in the real world. This contact is a form of relationship building that helps tackle prejudice. A study of a radio soap-opera audience in Rwanda showed listeners becoming more empathetic towards other groups, for example. The soap opera focussed on the lives of two different communities, which allowed the audience to cross a social barrier that they would rarely breach in the real world.[21] Almost a century earlier, the highly successful American radio soap *The Goldbergs* had a similar impact, introducing the audience to a Jewish family, when many Americans had no contact with Jewish people.[22] Virtual contact via podcasts, online gaming and social media all help to challenge prejudice.

Challenging

The economic damage of prejudice is something that can be reduced by social desirability bias. If people believe they will be criticised for prejudice, it raises the cost. As mentioned in Chapter 6, this may not apply to the same extent online, as the narcissism of trolls means that the attention is worth more than the views of other people. But people tend to conform in real-world situations.

This means that directly challenging prejudice can be a valuable tool in keeping prejudice silent. There are still economic costs to silent prejudice. The Bradley Effect mentioned in Chapter 4 shows that silent prejudice can still find a way to do damage. However, by reinforcing social desirability bias, the damage of prejudice is more limited.

Indeed, challenging other people's views and conventional behaviour can also remove prejudice, not just mute it. Cornerstone Capital's Chief Executive Erika Karp, introduced in Chapter 10, addressed the United Nations General Assembly in 2016. In a challenge to protocol, she did not begin her remarks with "ladies and gentlemen" but used the phrase "colleagues of all genders".[23] This was a small change from what was expected, but it was deliberately thought provoking. The change (which led to a gasp of surprise from the delegates), invited people to think about their assumptions.

One of Karp's maxims has been to make people feel a little bit uncomfortable. Her UN address fits with the same philosophy. If people reflect on their actions or ideas and feel a little bit uncomfortable, they are likely to think about the possible prejudice that has caused that discomfort. It may not be advisable to make people feel *very* uncomfortable; we mentally try and push away from topics that create real discomfort. But a little bit of discomfort may nudge our prejudices in the right direction. Repeated often enough, those nudges will undermine the prejudice that exists in all of us.

Quotas

The idea of quotas is, perhaps, the single most controversial solution to prejudice. A quota is, formally or informally, the idea that there should be a set number of positions reserved for a group that has traditionally been the target of prejudice. Quotas can apply anywhere – to university places, to employment, to the management boards of companies. Norway requires firms listed on the stock exchange to have at least 40% of their board seats held by women.[24] After independence, India's constitution reserved 50% of jobs in public institutions for Selected Castes in an attempt to overcome generations of prejudice against them. Quotas are not normally random – they generally try to match the breakdown of the population.

The case for quotas

At first glance, a quota is irrational. The whole idea of this book is that the right person should be in the right job, at the right time. A quota may deliberately exclude the right person from a job because of their race, gender, social status or religion. That sounds an awful lot like prejudice – perhaps because it *is* prejudice. It is irrational discrimination. However, quotas are generally used when prejudice already exists. It may be prejudice to have a quota for women as company directors. But if the process of selecting company directors beforehand was an 'old boys' club,' is this prejudice so bad? The quota is replacing one form of prejudice with another. The quota may be the lesser of two evils.

A powerful argument for a quota is that it will overcome unconscious bias. There are lots of things that make unconscious bias a particularly harmful form of prejudice. The rules of thumb that we use to generalise how people will behave will not be changed easily. The fact that I mutter "No Irish Need Apply" under my breath every time my British passport is contemptuously spat out of a UK electronic passport reader is a reminder of that. People moving out of the cash-machine queue when John Amaechi stands behind them is another example. Inevitably, people will tend to hire people who are just like themselves – because they get on with them. Who does not like being agreed with? These prejudices are deeply buried and people may not realise that they are being prejudiced. Quotas overcome that problem by forcing people to ignore their prejudices. You cannot act on your unconscious bias if you cannot hire the people your prejudice unconsciously wants you to hire.

Quotas also have the ability to directly fight the effects of prejudice. They force diversity into the system. That has two effects. If done properly, quotas should force people from different groups to come into contact with one another. Quotas can work with contact theory in a two-pronged approach to tackle prejudice. Prejudice needs to tell lies about the target group and often relies on dehumanisation for that reason. If you know people in the other group, you are likely to realise the lies that prejudice is telling and you will see the other group as human.

In addition – and, again, if they are done correctly – quotas can create role models. This is critical to overcoming prejudice in the longer term. If victims of prejudice can see people like themselves in positions of influence, it fuels ambition. The 'not for the likes of us' argument is undermined. If the system is not allowing role models to come through, then quotas can force the issue.

The case against quotas

There are good arguments for quotas. Deeply held prejudices and unconscious bias are powerful forces to fight against. But quotas also come with problems.

One obvious issue is that quotas are not necessarily going to apply to everyone. Quotas need clear definitions to prevent them being exploited. If the definitions are vague, they may end up being used to help people who are not the targets of prejudice.[25] Equally important, for a quota to work, people need to be prepared to admit to being targets of prejudice. If the targeting is visible, that is easily done. But if people are not willing to prove that they are targets of prejudice, then the quotas will not help everyone (and may be disproportionate to the scale of the problem). To take a very obvious example, is hard to see how an LGBTQ+ quota would work. The scale would probably underrepresent the importance of LGBTQ+ people to the population.[26] Only people who are out would be able to benefit; those who are still closeted would not. And how do you prove that someone is entitled to be admitted under an LGBTQ+ quota? There is no genetic test for whether someone is LGBTQ+.

There is also a risk, especially for senior positions, that diversity will remain lacking even when there is a quota in place. Replacing an 'old boys' club' with an 'old girls' club' may not improve diversity very much, if at all. Norway's 40% female directorship quota has led to what has been called the 'golden skirts': a relatively small group of women holding multiple non-executive directorships.[27] It might be argued that this is better than the minimal number of women in directorships in the past. But there is a risk that the illusion of diversity will weaken the momentum towards true diversity. As highlighted in Chapter 7, diversity of opinion is especially important in management. This is never more important than at a time of structural change in the economy. Diversity cannot be reduced to a single characteristic, even if it is something as important as gender.

It should be noted that quotas do not necessarily mean a lack of diversity. If effectively implemented, diversity will be the result. The risk here is complacency. If quotas tick the diversity box without really expanding the diversity of opinion and experience, the echo chamber in the boardroom may be reinforced.

If quotas are filled from a relatively small pool of people, there may also be damage to the idea of role models. Targets of prejudice are not all the same, obviously. If quotas are filled with a narrow subset of victims of prejudice, the effect can be counterproductive. The former Welsh rugby captain Gareth Thomas has said that, as a child, the gay men he saw on television were not role models: "nothing would equate to me, who I was, and where I wanted to go in my life".[28] The limited gay representation in the media was an informal quota and made up a specific subset that offered no support to a young gay athlete from the Welsh valleys.

There is seldom much thought given to when quotas should be applied. We can think about a person's career starting in the school system, possibly going on to higher education and ending up in the workplace. If quotas are to be used, where would they do most good? This may depend on the sort of prejudice a person is facing. The tendency is to apply quotas where there is a visible problem. The risk here is that the underlying causes are not tackled.

One example of this is the mismatch hypothesis. The mismatch hypothesis suggests that using quotas to place people into higher education without the necessary academic preparation may do more harm than good.[29] The lack of preparation (not lack of skill) means that people may underperform in the relevant higher-education institution if significantly helped by quotas. Had they gone to a different, lower-status institution, they might have done better in their subsequent careers. There could be an argument for quotas earlier in the education system, to deal with the lack of necessary academic preparation. But by having the quota at the wrong stage of the career cycle, people may miss out on the support they need.

This can also apply at a career level. The gender and racial inequality of the economics profession is well documented.[30] But this is a problem that (at least in the US) starts at undergraduate level. Putting quotas in at a doctoral level, for example, would risk bringing forward people who would not cope well with the level of study required. They will have not had the background training or expertise needed to help them as doctoral students. Putting quotas in for economic jobs would be just as bad. The solution to inequality among economists is surely to tackle the inequality at undergraduate level (maybe even at a school level), to ensure a more diverse pool of candidates for professional economic positions.

The final issue with quotas is that they can fuel prejudice. This is a powerful form of 'scapegoat economics'. It is the idea that 'it's not my fault I didn't get promoted. She was promoted because she's a woman'. This is, in a sense unfair. The rule for most of the preceding decades has effectively been 'he was promoted because he's a man'. But fairness has nothing to say when it comes to prejudice.

How big a problem is this additional prejudice? Social desirability bias is probably strengthened by quotas. The existence of a quota is a strong signal about what society wants to see happen. The prejudice that quotas may provoke is therefore harder to measure. People may be more likely to feel resentment but less likely to admit to this resentment if formally asked in a survey.

Can we compromise on quotas?

There is no right answer when it comes to quotas. It is a case of balancing the strength of unconscious bias and existing prejudice against the fact that quotas are themselves a form of prejudice and may not be as effective as they seem. But I am inclined to think that the balance of arguments today is against quotas that are used to determine a final outcome.[31] The Norwegian 40% target for women on listed company boards is an admirable aim, but it has not changed much about the number of women leading Norwegian companies. In 2018, only 7% of Norwegian listed companies were headed by a woman.[32] There is no quota for company leadership in Norway and the quotas at board level have seemingly changed little in that regard.

Perhaps a better solution is to have quotas in the application process. Setting a quota for the pool of candidates should challenge prejudice. Having a minimum of 40% of applicants from one gender would be an example of this. This challenges interviewers and may help them to confront their prejudice. It forces interviewers into contact with people from other groups. It hopefully avoids, and should at least reduce, the fuelling of prejudice. Even with this approach, interviewers will need to be cautious about the invisible forms of prejudice. Feeling good about gender or racially diverse shortlists should not be allowed to turn into complacency when other targets of prejudice cannot be identified so easily.

The economics of fighting back

Fighting prejudice is a little like fighting the Hydra of Greek myth. As soon as one irrational view is cut down, two new ones spring up in its place. But we should not admit defeat. To become resigned to prejudice is to be resigned to failing in the fourth industrial revolution. If we give up, prejudice will simply undermine the benefits that change can bring. Failing to tackle prejudice will cost us profit.

Different forms of prejudice will require different approaches. Education is something that is likely to work over the longer term. Making sure that differences between groups are understood is an important start. Perhaps more important is getting the education system structured so as to reduce the costs of the fourth industrial revolution. The problem is that this cannot be reduced to nice target measures that appear on a scorecard. It is about producing the right attitude, not the right grades.[33]

Contact offers perhaps more hope in the fourth industrial revolution. The good-news story of Chapter 5 shows that things can improve. The fact that younger generations have less prejudice can be entirely unrelated to the rise of social media and parasocial contact.[34] Personal communication and storytelling is going to remain important. This is worrying for the economics profession, which has not proved to be the natural home of storytelling over the years. The economist Robert Shiller's book *Narrative Economics* is a powerful starting point in redressing that imbalance.[35]

The topic of quotas is always going to be controversial. There is probably no definitive answer as to whether or how they should be used. Quotas are prejudiced, but we already live in a prejudiced world. They should not be ruled out, but, at the same time, they do threaten to increase prejudice.

Alongside education, I think that challenge is one of the more powerful answers to prejudice. Challenging prejudice does not have to mean an aggressive head-on assault. It can mean contact and storytelling. But the end result needs to be that we challenge the prejudice we all have within us. Erika Karp's maxim of making people a little bit uncomfortable is perhaps the best point on which to conclude. If we are uncomfortable, it is normally because we have done something wrong. Identifying our internal prejudices is a good place to start the fight back.

Notes

1 See Featherstone (2016).
2 In the UK, this is undoubtedly a minority. Church attendance in the UK totalled 5% of the population in 2015. See Faith Survey (2020).
3 See Supreme Court of the United States (2015).
4 See PEW Research Center (2020). This reports that 36% of Americans attend a religious service at least once a week. This is all faiths, whereas the UK number of 5% is for Christian church attendance only.
5 See Featherstone (2016, p. 273).
6 See Paluck and Green (2009).
7 "No Outsiders" is a quote from South African Archbishop Desmond Tutu. The charity focusses on making sure children are not afraid of difference – in whatever form. See No Outsiders (2019).
8 See Moffat (2016). The speaker was pointing out that she could not wear her veil in the Netherlands.
9 A contrast to this approach was the notorious Section 28, passed into UK law in 1988. Section 28 was the first piece of homophobic legislation to be passed in the UK for a century and it prohibited schools and local authorities from 'promoting' homosexuality. It followed a speech from UK Prime Minister Margaret Thatcher at the Conservative Party Conference, in which she complained that "children … are being taught that they have an inalienable right to be gay". See Pink News (2018).
10 See Shiller (2019).
11 Hall (1998) conducted a study that identified five basic narratives in stories of prejudice. The most frequent was that the prejudiced person was in some way morally better than the target of prejudice. That is a story that does not rely too much on fact, but which could be countered by other (factual) stories that show this moral superiority to be untrue.
12 See Beecher Stowe (1852).
13 See Hagood (2012).

14 To be clear, they were horrified at the story not because of how it depicted slaves, but because that depiction seemed to be raising the risk of an attack on the institution of slavery.
15 See Reynolds (2012).
16 See Black (2019).
17 See Black (2016).
18 See Paluck and Green (2009).
19 Ibid.
20 See PRRI (2019).
21 See Paluck and Green (2009).
22 See Trentmann (2016). The filmmaker Dustin Lance Black tells a story of growing up in Texas in the 1980s, and having a friend 'come out' as being Jewish. Black had never heard of someone being Jewish before that point. See Black (2017).
23 See United Nations Global Compact (2016).
24 See Milne (2018). In 2014, 29 firms in the UK's FTSE 250 had boards that were 100% male (see Price, 2015).
25 There is a classical precedent for this. During the dying days of the Roman Republic, the plebeian class were guaranteed a role in politics via the Tribunes. It was a quota in the political system that allowed their views to be expressed outside of the patrician Senate. The patrician Clodius wanted the political power the quota system offered, had himself adopted into a plebeian family and was elected a Tribune in 59 BCE. The quota was designed to keep people like Clodius from wielding this power, yet the rules were not clear enough to prevent abuse of the system. See Tempest (2011).
26 As Chapter 10 identified, the number of openly LGBTQ+ people may be half the real number.
27 See Pryce (2015).
28 See Attitude (2017b). Thomas mentions Kenny Everett and John Inman as the characters he would see on television, and the fact that they were used for comedy. The signal he had from these role models was that being gay equated to being mocked.
29 See Arcidiacono and Lovenheim (2016).
30 See Bayer and Rouse (2016).
31 I am also well aware that, at least on the big prejudice issues of race and gender, I am coming at this from a background of privilege. This is perhaps all the more so being a male economist.
32 See Milne (2018).
33 In the interests of full disclosure, the tutorial system at Oxford University relies on this flexible method of learning. I may well be prejudiced in favour of my own experiences.
34 The World Values Survey (2020) shows the generational attitude to prejudice quite clearly.
35 See Shiller (2019).

12 Profit and prejudice

Profit is not the *main* reason to oppose prejudice. Basic humanity demands that we treat other people as equals. However, profit is a powerful argument for opposing prejudice. It is also an argument that becomes increasingly important in the fourth industrial revolution. The economic changes we are facing will tend to make prejudice more common, as they have done in every other industrial revolution. If economics is one of the causes of prejudice, economists must have something to say in the counterattack.

The problem is that everyone is prejudiced. We all have rules of thumb, which we apply in a desperate attempt to simplify a world that is becoming more and more complex. Those rules, and our unconscious bias, mean that we make irrational decisions. We shrink from confrontation, at least in person, and avoid having our ideas challenged.

How did we get here?

People should be better off after the changes of the fourth industrial revolution. Each of the past revolutions has led to huge gains in living standards. Unfortunately, between now and the brighter future, there is a period of change and upheaval. This is the time when prejudice flourishes. People worry that they will lose as a result of change. While the focus is often on financial loss – and the consequences of that should not be underestimated – it is the loss of relative status that is often most upsetting. People work hard to achieve their position in society. To have that position reduced by events beyond their control, and maybe beyond their understanding, inevitably causes a reaction. While in no way endorsing such prejudice, it is possible to understand why people embrace it.

The Covid-19 pandemic is likely to accelerate some of the changes ahead. That means the sense of disruption will become even greater. People will have less time to adjust to the new world. It will become easier and easier to see the past as being better than the present (though this is unlikely to be true). The message of restorative nostalgia could become even more seductive. And this is where prejudice really begins.

The Luddites of the first industrial revolution targeted what they saw as the cause of their troubles by smashing machines. It seemed a simple solution – remove the machines and the glories of the past could be restored. It did not stop the change in society. It did, temporarily, do economic harm.

It is likely to be the same with today's Luddites. We have become so used to machines that the technology is less likely to be the focus for anger. Rather, people are likely to become targets. For the purposes of restorative nostalgia, it does not matter which group is attacked. All that matters is that the targets are different from you, and a story can be told of how they have made your life worse. Prejudice is comfortingly simple in a world that is scarily complex.

This prejudice is doing damage to the global economy today. It will continue to do damage to the global economy in the future. We need to have the right person, in the right job, at the right time. We need to avoid a monoculture and take on a diverse range of opinions and ideas. Anything that stops these crucial things from happening will cause more economic hardship and delay the benefits that could otherwise flow from the process of change.

Where do we go from here?

Simply saying 'prejudice is bad' is not going to help very much. Prejudice is terrible, but it is not going anywhere. Prejudice is economically harmful. Becker pointed this out over 60 years ago – and yet here we are.[1] I think that there are four areas we should watch to judge how the fourth industrial revolution is being handled and to see whether the self-destruct mechanism of prejudice is being minimised.

Firms

Firms are on the front line when it comes to economic change. The mills that were attacked and burned in the first industrial revolution were commercial businesses. Global firms today are very much at the forefront of issues to do with prejudice. But should firms be involving themselves in social issues? I believe they should. As we saw in Chapter 8, prejudice in a society will damage firms in that society. Employees often expect firms to take a stand and defend them. Firms experience an economic cost when prejudice exists in society. A firm's involvement in fighting prejudice can be ascribed entirely to profit-maximising behaviour, if you like.

Of course, firms could take a neutral public position on matters of prejudice. But this is not the same as political neutrality. Archbishop Tutu's analogy about the elephant standing on the tail of the mouse sums up the situation. Prejudice is irrational and economically damaging. It clearly classifies one group in society as being 'less than' other groups. Taking a neutral position can only be interpreted as accepting that the prejudiced have a valid point of view (even if not expressing agreement with their position). Silence is damning.

This should not be regarded as cultural imperialism, unless the idea that people should be treated equally and given equal rights is to be considered cultural. The 'no outsiders' viewpoint is founded on the idea of difference, allied with mutual respect. That is what firms should be aiming for.

Firms, particularly global firms, should have a voice in the debate about prejudice. It is not interference in the democratic process to point out the economic consequences of a certain course of action. Financial firms' supporting brief in the Obergefell case, which challenged prejudice in the US Supreme Court, focussed on the economic and administrative costs of the status quo.[2] That is a reasonable standpoint; the disruption of prejudice is bad for the economics of a firm.

Investors can apply pressure on firms in support of the fight against prejudice. One obvious area is diversity of management, which is in investors' economic interest.[3] More generally, however, investors are increasingly looking at a firm's approach to prejudice when considering whether to invest in it.

Societies

What is considered socially acceptable plays a big role in managing prejudice. People may still be prejudiced, but if they feel unable to express that in public, it reduces the damage of prejudice a lot. Things like the Bradley Effect can still cause problems. Unconscious bias will also challenge the efficiency of the labour market. But the worst damage of prejudice is kept in check if people feel too embarrassed to talk about it. Of course, legal protections help, but if the culture of a society does not back the legal structure, genuine change is going to be limited.

The danger with social pressure is that it is not stable. Once an anti-prejudice consensus starts to crack, it is not easy to get it to return. The shift in expectations about the role of women in the economy after 1945 is an example of this. Women were expected to play a role in the economy during wartime. It was hardly equality, but the social norms that were a blatant form of prejudice were suspended. The rapid reversal of that situation in the early years of peace took a generation to overcome – and many would question how much has really been overcome today.

Social media shifts the debate in the real world. Those who are extremely prejudiced are a minority – and minorities benefit from the communication that social media offers. Social media can also give a cover of anonymity. That risks dehumanising the victims of prejudice, as there is no need to acknowledge that targets of prejudice are real people. Describing a group as 'less than' most of society is easier to do if their humanity does not have to be acknowledged. Often it does not start with major forms of prejudice. The retort of 'it's just a joke' to a prejudiced comment, or complaints about 'political correctness gone too far' can start to unravel the social consensus.

People generally spend more of their time at work than anywhere else. The standards that the firm sets can, therefore, be influential in setting expectations for behaviour. With the value of brands rising in the fourth industrial revolution, firms are likely to be increasingly sensitive to the threat that employee misconduct can bring.[4] Governments play a role in establishing legal guidelines. What companies can and cannot do, and what libel and slander rules apply, help to shape what the public considers acceptable. But the behaviour of political leaders is also important in setting the tone of what is acceptable.

Education

As Chapter 11 highlighted, education can do a lot in the fight against prejudice. It needs to be thought of in a very broad way, perhaps. Education is not about waving a degree certificate around. The tendency of governments to set test-score targets or demand that a set number of people achieve qualifications in certain subjects is not helpful. Education is about learning, not being taught. That gives the flexibility that will help with success in the fourth industrial revolution. Rigid education systems that do not allow questions to be asked or teachers to be challenged are not the right way to go. It does not matter how many engineering graduates an economy produces; what matters is whether those engineers can adapt in a changing world. Textbooks go out of date very quickly in an industrial revolution.[5]

Education goes beyond the classroom, of course. Media and social media play a role in educating us. Companies also continue the process of education. This is also about giving people flexibility, but, increasingly, it is about educating ourselves about the lives of others. As the barriers to entry into the world of media have come down, we have an opportunity to discover more about our fellow humans than we have at any other time in our evolution.

Environment

The natural environment is, unlikely as it may seem, an area to watch in the fight against prejudice. This book has focussed on the fourth industrial revolution as the structural upheaval that is most intimately bound up with prejudice. But this is taking place alongside a second and equally dramatic upheaval – the environmental credit crunch. Books could be written on this topic.[6] There is a sustainability crisis that is already having economic consequences. Today's standard of living cannot be maintained without something changing.

As always, economists have the answer. The environmental credit crunch is solved by doing more with less. That is the only way we can maintain living standards and yet live within the limits of what is sustainable. Doing more with less is just another way of saying we need to be more productive.

How do we become more productive? By making sure we have the right person in the right job at the right time.

The pressures of environmental stability increase the value of a less prejudiced world. There are signs of this in the changing regulations of Saudi Arabia (Chapter 8). As the world becomes less dependent on fossil fuels, the Saudi economy has had to look to develop other sources of prosperity. That is directly behind the lifting of restrictions on female entrepreneurs, in recognition of the economic potential such women offer.

Managing the environmental credit crunch is one of the most positive potential outcomes of the fourth industrial revolution. This is a 'whole economy' problem. Sustainability risks are a global game of whack-a-mole. Unless there is a coordinated approach to tackling the problem – including the importance of productivity and the management of prejudice – the environmental credit crunch will not be solved. One problem will be fixed, only to create other problems up or down the supply chain.

Profit and prejudice

Ultimately, economists and others need to be better at telling the story of how prejudice affects the global economy. As we monitor how different aspects of our world adapt to the fourth industrial revolution, we need to guard against any associated increase in prejudice. Prejudice will only set back progress. Prejudice depends on simplicity for support – which, along with disregard for the truth, can make it an extraordinarily dangerous force. But while reality is ever more complex, the story that economists can tell is, ultimately, a simple one:

Prejudice is bad for business and the economy.

Notes

1 See Becker (1957).
2 See Hurley (2015).
3 See Walker (2019).
4 There are hints at this in the 1930s, when members of the British Union of Fascists would leave the party when they got jobs (Chapter 1).
5 Not economics books. Economists are blessed with a foresight that keeps their works forever relevant.
6 Books have been written on this topic. Purely at random, I would suggest *From Red to Green* and *Food Policy and the Environmental Credit Crunch*. See Donovan and Hudson (2011) and Hudson and Donovan (2014).

Bibliography

Aaldering, L. and Van Der Pas, D.J. (2018). Political Leadership in the Media: Gender Bias in Leader Stereotypes during Campaign and Routine Times. *British Journal of Political Science*, pp. 1–21. Available from: https://doi.org/10.1017/S0007123417000795.

Abdelgadir, A. and Fouka, V. (2019). *Political Secularism and Muslim Integration in the West: Assessing the Effect of the French Headscarf Ban* [unpublished]. Stanford University, Department of Political Science. Available from: https://vfouka.people.stanford.edu/sites/g/files/sbiybj4871/f/abdelgadirfoukajan2019.pdf [accessed 3 July 2019].

Abramitzky, R. and Boustan, L. (2017). Immigration in American Economic History. *Journal of Economic Literature*, 55(4), pp. 1311–1345. Available from: https://www.ncbi.nlm.nih.gov/pmc/articles/PMC5794227/.

Adkins R. and Adkins, L. (2013). *Eavesdropping on Jane Austen's England*. London: Little, Brown.

Ageofrevolution.org (n.d.). *Anti-Slavery Sugar Bowl* [online]. Available from: https://ageofrevolution.org/200-object/anti-slavery-sugar-bowl/ [accessed 23 September 2019].

Aghion, P., Dewatripont, M. and Stein, J.C. (2008). Academic Freedom, Private Sector-Focus, and the Process of Innovation. *RAND Journal of Economics*, 39(3), pp. 617–635. Available from: https://onlinelibrary.wiley.com/doi/full/10.1111/j.1756-2171.2008.00031.x.

Ahmed, A.M., Anderson, L. and Hammarstedt, M. (2013). Are Gay Men and Lesbians Discriminated Against in the Hiring Process? *Southern Economic Journal*, 79(3), pp. 565–585. Available from: https://onlinelibrary.wiley.com/doi/abs/10.4284/0038-4038-2011.317.

Ahuja, R. and Lyons, R.C. (2019). The Silent Treatment: Discrimination against Same-Sex Relationships in the Sharing Economy. *Oxford Economic Papers*, 71(30), pp. 564–576. Available from: https://doi.org/10.1093/oep/gpz025.

Aidt, T., Leon, G. and Satchell, M. (2017). *The Social Dynamics of Riots. Evidence from the Captain Swing Riots, 1830–31*. LSE Seminar Paper. Available from: http://sticerd.lse.ac.uk/seminarpapers/pspe02052017.pdf [accessed 10 August 2019].

Airbnb (2019). *An Update on Airbnb's Work to Fight Discrimination*. Press release [online], 11 September 2019. Available from: https://www.hospitalitynet.org/news/4094991.html.

Albert Kennedy Trust (2015). *LGBT Youth Homelessness: A UK National Scoping of Cause, Prevalence and Outcome*. London: The Albert Kennedy Trust. Available from: https://www.akt.org.uk/research.

Alesina, A., Miano, A. and Stancheva, S. (2018). *Immigration and Redistribution.* NBER Working Paper 24733. Cambridge, MA: National Bureau of Economic Research. Available from: https://www.nber.org/papers/w24733.

Allcott, H. and Gentzkow, M. (2017). Social Media and Fake News in the 2016 Election. *Journal of Economic Perspectives*, 31(2), pp. 211–236. Available from: https://web.stanford.edu/~gentzkow/research/fakenews.pdf.

Allen, R.C. (2007). *The Industrial Revolution in Miniature: The Spinning Jenny in Britain, France and India.* Working Paper 375. Oxford University, Department of Economics. Available from: https://www.economics.ox.ac.uk/department-of-economics-discussion-paper-series/the-industrial-revolution-in-miniature-the-spinning-jenny-in-britain-france-and-india.

Allport, G.W. (1954). *The Nature of Prejudice.* Boston, MA: Addison-Wesley Publishing Company.

Amazon Robotics. (2015). *Our Vision.* Available from: https://www.amazonrobotics.com/#/vision [accessed 10 September 2019].

Andersen, H.C. (1837). *The Emperor's New Clothes* [translation]. Odense, Denmark: The Hans Christian Andersen Centre, Department for the Study of Culture, University of Southern Denmark. Available from: https://andersen.sdu.dk/vaerk/hersholt/TheEmperorsNewClothes_e.html.

Andersen, R. and Fetner, T. (2008). Economic Inequality and Intolerance: Attitudes toward Homosexuality in 35 Democracies. *American Journal of Political Science*, 52(4), pp. 942–958. Available from: https://onlinelibrary.wiley.com/doi/abs/10.1111/j.1540-5907.2008.00352.x.

Anderson, C. (2016). *White Rage: The Unspoken Truth of Our Racial Divide.* New York: Bloomsbury.

Arcidiacono, P. and Lovenheim, M. (2016). Affirmative Action and the Quality-Fit Trade Off. *Journal of Economic Literature*, 44(1), pp. 3–51. Available from: https://www.aeaweb.org/articles?id=10.1257/jel.54.1.3.

Argwin, J., Larson, J., Mattu, S. and Kirchner L. (2016). Machine Bias. *ProPublica* [online], 23 May. Available from: https://www.propublica.org/article/machine-bias-risk-assessments-in-criminal-sentencing [accessed 15 March 2020].

Ashley-Cooper, N. and Knox, T. (2018). *The Rebirth of an English Country House: St Giles House.* New York: Rizzoli.

Atack, J., Margo, R.A. and Rhode, P.W. (2019). 'Automation' of Manufacturing in the Late Nineteenth Century: The Hand and Machine Study. *Journal of Economic Perspectives*, 33(2), pp. 51–70. Available from: https://www.aeaweb.org/articles?id=10.1257/jep.33.2.51.

Attitude. (2017a). Sir Ian McKellen is the first guest on an all-new 'Attitude heroes' podcast series. *Attitude Heroes*, Stream Publishing [online], 31 January 2017. Available from: https://www.streampublishing.net/news/attitude-heroes-podcast.

Attitude. (2017b). Rugby Star Gareth Thomas Talks Growing Up as a Closeted Gay Man, The First Time He Had Sex and How He Came to Accept Himself. *Attitude Heroes*, Stream Publishing [online], 10 September 2017. Available from: https://www.streampublishing.net/news/attitude-heroes-podcast.

Austen, J. (1813). *Pride and Prejudice.* 1853 ed. London: Spottiswoods and Shaw [online reproduction]. Available from: https://books.google.ie/books/about/Pride_and_Prejudice.html?id=kQ0mAAAAMAAJ&printsec=frontcover&source=kp_read_button&redir_esc=y#v=onepage&q&f=false.

Austen, J. (1814). *Mansfield Park*. Cambridge ed. 2005. Cambridge, UK: Cambridge University Press.

Austen, J. (1815). *Emma*. 1877 ed. Leipzig: Bernhard Tauchnitz [online reproduction]. Available from: https://books.google.ie/books/about/Emma.html?id=E_ENAAAAQAAJ&printsec=frontcover&source=kp_read_button&redir_esc=y#v=onepage&q&f=false.

Autor, D. (2015). Why Are There Still So Many Jobs? The History and Future of Workplace Automation. *Journal of Economic Perspectives*, 29(3), pp. 3–30. Available from: https://www.aeaweb.org/articles?id=10.1257/jep.29.3.3.

Badgett, M.V.L. (2014). *The Economic Cost of Stigma and the Exclusion of LGBT People: A Case Study of India*. Washington, DC: World Bank Group. Available from: http://documents.worldbank.org/curated/en/527261468035379692/The-economic-cost-of-stigma-and-the-exclusion-of-LGBT-people-a-case-study-of-India.

Badgett, M.V.L., Durso, L.E., Kastanis, A. and Mallory, C. (2013). *The Business Impact of LGBT-Supportive Workplace Policies*. The Williams Institute, UCLA. Available from: https://escholarship.org/uc/item/3vt6t9zx#main [accessed 14 May 2020].

Badgett, M.V.L., Hasenbush, A. and Luhur, W. (2017). *LGBT Exclusion in Indonesia and Its Economic Effects*. Los Angeles, CA: The Williams Institute, UCLA. Available from: https://williamsinstitute.law.ucla.edu/publications/lgbt-exclusion-indonesia/.

Baert, S. (2018). Hiring a Gay Man, Taking a Risk? A Lab Experiment on Employment Discrimination and Risk Aversion. *Journal of Homosexuality*, 65(8), pp. 1015–1031. Available from: https://www.researchgate.net/publication/316074964_Hiring_a_Gay_Man_Taking_a_Risk_A_Lab_Experiment_on_Employment_Discrimination_and_Risk-Aversion.

Bail, C.A., Argyle, L.P., Brown, T.W., Bumpus, J.P., Chen, H., Hunzaker, M.B.F., Lee, J., Mann, M., Merhout, F. and Volfovsky, A. (2018). Exposure to Opposing Views on Social Media Can Increase Political Polarization. *Proceedings of the National Academy of Sciences of the United States of America*, 115(37), pp. 9216–9221. Available from: https://www.pnas.org/content/115/37/9216.

Baker, P. (2019). *Fabulosa! The Story of Polari, Britain's Secret Gay Language*. London: Reaktion Books.

Baldi, S. and Branch McBrier, D. (1997). Do the Determinants of Promotion Differ for Blacks and Whites? Evidence from the US Labor Market. *Work and Occupations*, 24(4), pp. 478–497.

Barling, K. (2015). *Racism: The 'R' Word*. London: Biteback Publishing.

Barnard, S. and Dainty, A. (2018). Coming Out and Staying In: How Sexual Orientation and Gender Identity Matters in Construction Employment. *Proceedings of the Institution of Civil Engineers – Municipal Engineer*, 171(3), pp. 141–148. Available from: https://doi.org/10.1680/jmuen.17.00026.

Barron, K., Kung, E. and Prosperio, D. (2017). *The effect of Home-Sharing on House Prices and Rents: Evidence from Airbnb*. Available from: https://papers.ssrn.com/sol3/papers.cfm?abstract_id=3006832 [accessed 30 September 2019].

Bayer, A. and Rouse, C.E. (2016). Diversity in the Economics Profession: A New Attack on an Old Problem. *Journal of Economic Perspectives*, 30(4), pp. 221–242.

BBC. (2012a). Danny Alexander Launches Ginger Rodent beer. *BBC News* [online], 9 November 2012. Available from: https://www.bbc.com/news/uk-scotland-highlands-islands-20272937.

BBC. (2012b). Leicester to Mark Contribution Made by Ugandan Asians [video]. *BBC News* [online], 10 September 2012. Available from: https://www.bbc.com/news/av/uk-england-leicestershire-19549567/leicester-to-mark-contribution-made-by-ugandan-asians.

BBC. (2013). Money Box [audio]. *BBC Radio 4* [online], 25 May 2013. Available from: https://www.bbc.co.uk/sounds/play/b01sll2h.

BBC. (2017). Germany to Quash 50,000 Gay Convictions. *BBC News* [online], 22 March 2017. Available from: https://www.bbc.co.uk/news/world-europe-39350105.

BBC. (2018). Brexit: Too Many Older Leave Voters Nostalgic for 'White' Britain, says Cable. *BBC News* [online], 11 March. Available from: https://www.bbc.com/news/uk-politics-43364331.

Becker, G.S. (1957). *The Economics of Discrimination*. Second revised ed. Reprint, London: University of Chicago Press, 1971.

Beecher Stowe, H. (1852). Uncle Tom's Cabin. 1999 ed. Greenwood, WI: Suzeteo Enterprises.

Bejan, T.M. (2017). *Mere Civility – Disagreement and the Limits of Toleration*. London: Harvard University Press.

Benedicto, B. (20140. *Under Bright Lights: Gay Manila and the Global Scene*. Minneapolis: University of Minnesota Press.

Bentham, J. (1978). Offenses against One's Self. *Journal of Homosexuality*, 3(4), pp. 389–405 and 4(1). Available from: http://www.columbia.edu/cu/lweb/eresources/exhibitions/sw25/bentham/.

Berg, M. (1993). What Difference Did Women's Work Make to the Industrial Revolution? *History Workshop Journal*, 35(1), pp. 22–44. Available from: https://doi.org/10.1093/hwj/35.1.22.

Berg, N. and Lien, D. (2002). Measuring the Effect of Sexual Orientation on Income: Evidence of Discrimination? *Contemporary Economic Policy*, 20(4), pp. 394–414. Available from: https://onlinelibrary.wiley.com/doi/abs/10.1093/cep/20.4.394.

Berthoff, R.T. (1951). Southern Attitudes towards Immigration, 1865–1914. *The Journal of Southern History*, 17(3), pp. 326–360.

Besley, T. (2017). Aspirations and the Political Economy of Inequality. *Oxford Economic Papers*, 69(1), pp. 1–35.

Bessen, J. (2019). *Automation and Jobs: When Technology Boosts Employment*. Vox Centre for Economic Policy Research (CEPR) Policy Portal [online], 12 September 2019. Available from: https://voxeu.org/article/automation-and-jobs-when-technology-boosts-employment.

Binfield, K. (ed.) (2004). *Writings of the Luddites*. London: Johns Hopkins University Press.

Black Lives Matter. (n.d.). *Black Lives Matter* [online]. Available from: https://blacklivesmatter.com/.

Black, D.L. (2017). Dustin Lance Black: Full Address and A&A, Oxford Union [video]. *YouTube* [online], 7 July 2017. Available from: https://www.youtube.com/watch?v=v-Wik2fDVBk&t=485s.

Black, D.L. (2019). *Mama's Boy*. New York: Alfred A. Knopf.

Black, R.D. (2016). Why I Left White Nationalism. *The New York Times*, 25 November 2016. Available from: https://www.nytimes.com/2016/11/26/opinion/sunday/why-i-left-white-nationalism.html.

Blake, W. (1804). *Jerusalem*. BBC Poetry [online]. Available from: http://www.bbc.co.uk/poetryseason/poems/jerusalem.shtml.

Blandford, J.M. (2003). The Nexus of Sexual Orientation and Gender in the Determination of Earnings. *Industrial and Labor Relations Review*, 56(4), pp. 622–643.

Blau, F.D. and Kahn, L.M. (2017). The Gender Wage Gap: Extent, Trends and Explanations. *Journal of Economic Literature*, 55(3), pp. 789–865. Available from: https://www.nber.org/papers/w21913.

Blumer, H. (1933). *Movies and Conduct*. New York: Macmillan. Available from: https://archive.org/details/moviesandconduct00blumrich/mode/2up [accessed 6 August 2019].

Boas, M. (1949). Hero's Pneumatica: A Study of its Transmission and Influence. *Isis*, 40(1), pp. 38–48.

Bohnet, I. (2016). *What Works: Gender Equality by Design*. Cambridge, MA: Belknap Press.

Bonikowski, B., Halikiopoulou, D., Kaufmann, E. and Rooduijn, M. (2018). Populism and Nationalism in a Comparative Perspective: A Scholarly Exchange. *Nations and Nationalism*, 25(1), pp. 58–81. Available from: https://onlinelibrary.wiley.com/doi/10.1111/nana.12480.

Booth, A., Fan, E., Meng, X. and Zhang, D. (2018). Gender Differences in Willingness to Compete: The Role of Culture and Institutions. *The Economic Journal*, 129, pp. 734–764.

Bosma, N., Hill, S., Ionescu-Summers, A., Kelley, D., Levie, J. and Tarnawa, A. (2020). *Global Entrepreneurship Monitor 2019/2020 Global Report*. London: Global Entrepreneurship Research Association, London Business School. Available from: https://www.c4e.org.cy/reports/2019/gem-2019-2020-global-report.pdf.

Bostrom, N. (2014). *Superintelligence: Paths, Dangers, Strategies*. Oxford, UK: Oxford University Press.

Boucekkine, R., Peeters, D. and de la Croix, D. (2007). Early Literacy Achievements, Population Density, and the Transition to Modern Growth. *Journal of the European Economic Association*, 5(1), pp. 183–226.

Bowles, N. (2005). *Nixon's Business*. College Station, TX: Texas A&M University Press.

Boyd, R., Richerson, P.J. and Henrich, J. (2011). The Cultural Niche: Why Social Learning is Essential for Human Adaptation. *Proceedings of the National Academy of Sciences of the United States of America*, 108(S.2), pp. 10918–10925. Available from: https://www.pnas.org/content/108/supplement_2/10918.

Braithwaite, T. (2012). Pro-Gay Stance Cost Goldman, Says Blankfein. *Financial Times*, 2 May 2012. Available from: https://www.ft.com/content/fdcda25c-9468-11e1-bb0d-00144feab49a.

British Council for Offices. (2018). *Office Occupancy: Density and Utilisation*. BCO Research and Policy report. London: British Council for Offices. Available from: http://www.bco.org.uk/Research/Publications/Office_Occupancy_Density_and_Utilisation.aspx.

Broussard, M. (2018a). *Artificial Unintelligence: How Computers Misunderstand the World*. Cambridge, MA: MIT Press.

Broussard, M. (2018b). Agenda: Why the Scots Are Such a Struggle for Alexa and Siri. *The Herald* [online], 11 May 2018. Available from: https://www.herald-scotland.com/opinion/16219100.agenda-why-the-scots-are-such-a-struggle-for-alexa-and-siri/.

Brown, S.E. (2007). Assessing Men and Maids: The Female Servant Tax and Meanings of Productive Labour in Late-Eighteenth-Century Britain. *Left History*, 12(2). Available from: https://doi.org/10.25071/1913-9632.14967.

Brozan, N. (1974). Wives Still Work as Spouses Study. *The New York Times* [online], 9 April 1974. Available from: https://www.nytimes.com/1974/04/09/archives/wives-still-work-as-spouses-study-a-patchwork-of-resources-no.html.

Brückner, M. and Grüner, H.P. (2010). *Economic Growth and the Rise of Political Extremism: Theory and Evidence*. CEPR Discussion Paper 7723. London: Centre for Economic Policy Research.

Burgess, S. and Greaves, E. (2013). Test Scores, Subjective Assessments, and Stereotyping of Ethnic Minorities. *Journal of Labor Economics*, 31(3), pp. 535–576.

Burnette, J. (2008). *Gender, Work and Wages in Industrial Revolution Britain*. Cambridge, UK: Cambridge University Press.

Burns, C. (2012). *The Costly Business of Discrimination: The Economic Costs of Discrimination and the Financial Benefits of Gay and Transgender Equality in the Workplace*. Washington, DC: Center for American Progress. Available from: https://www.americanprogress.org/issues/lgbtq-rights/reports/2012/03/22/11234/the-costly-business-of-discrimination/.

Campbell, R. (1747). *The London Tradesman: Being an Historical Account of all the Trades, Professions, Arts, Both Liberal and Mechanic* [online]. London: T. Gardner [digital reproduction]. Available from: https://ia802808.us.archive.org/26/items/TheLondonTradesman/The%20London%20Tradesman.pdf.

Cannon, B.Q. (2000). Power Relations: Western Rural Electric Cooperatives and the New Deal. *Western Historical Quarterly*, 31, pp. 133–160.

Capehart, J. (2018). How Derek Black Went from Golden Boy of White Nationalism to Outspoken Critic. *The Washington Post* [online], 4 December 2018. Available from: https://www.washingtonpost.com/opinions/2018/12/04/how-derek-black-went-golden-boy-white-nationalism-outspoken-critic/.

Carney, N. (2016). All Lives Matter, But So Does Race: Black Lives Matter and the Evolving Role of Social Media. *Humanity and Society*, 20(20), pp. 180–199. Available from: https://www.researchgate.net/publication/301310750_All_Lives_Matter_but_so_Does_Race_Black_Lives_Matter_and_the_Evolving_Role_of_Social_Media.

Cashman, M. (2020). *One of Them: From Albert Square to Parliament Square*. London: Bloomsbury.

Cathcart, B. (2015). The Rothschild Libel: Why Has It Taken 200 Years for an Anti-Semitic Slur That Emerged from the Battle of Waterloo to Be Dismissed? *The Independent*, 3 May. Available from: https://www.independent.co.uk/news/uk/home-news/the-rothschild-libel-why-has-it-taken-200-years-for-an-anti-semitic-slur-that-emerged-from-the-10216101.html.

Cattaneo, P. (1997). *The Full Monty* [film]. Los Angeles, CA: 20th Century Fox.

CBS DC. (2012). Ginsberg Wants to See an All-Female Supreme Court. *CBS DC* [online], 27 November 2012. Available from: https://washington.cbslocal.com/2012/11/27/ginsburg-wants-to-see-all-female-supreme-court/.

Centre for Personalised Medicine. (n.d.). *Centre for Personalised Medicine* [online]. Oxford, UK: University of Oxford. Available from: https://cpm.well.ox.ac.uk/ [accessed 21 May 2020].

Chapin Hall (2017). *Missed Opportunities: Youth Homelessness in America*. Chicago, IL: Chapin Hall, University of Chicago. Also available from: https://voicesofyouthcount.org/brief/national-estimates-of-youth-homelessness/.

Chappell, B. (2015). Supreme Court Declares Same-Sex Marriage Legal In All 50 States. *NPR* [online], 26 June 2015. Available from: https://www.npr.org/sections/thetwo-way/2015/06/26/417717613/supreme-court-rules-all-states-must-allow-same-sex-marriages.

Chetty, R., Hendren, N., Jones, M.R. and Porter, S.R. (2018). Race and Economic Opportunity in the United States. *Vox* Centre for Economic Policy Research (CEPR) Policy Portal [online], 27 June 2018. Available from: https://voxeu.org/article/race-and-economic-opportunity-united-states.

Cheung, W.-Y., Sedikides, C. and Wildschut, T. (2017). Nostalgia Proneness and Reduced Prejudice. *Personality and Individual Differences*, 109, pp. 89–97. Available from: http://www.southampton.ac.uk/~crsi/Cheung, %20Sedikides, %20Wildschut%20PAID%202017.pdf.

Chick-fil-A. (2019). Chick-fil-A Foundation Announces 2020 Priorities to Address Education, Homelessness, Hunger. Press release, 18 November 2019. *Chick-fil-A* [online]. Available from: https://thechickenwire.chick-fil-a.com/News/Chick-fil-A-Foundation-Announces-2020-Priorities.

Chinese Exclusion Act. (1882). *An Act to Execute Certain Treaty Stipulations Relating to the Chinese, May 6, 1882* [online]. Washington, DC: National Archives and Records Administration. Available from: https://www.ourdocuments.gov/doc.php?flash=false&doc=47 [accessed 21 May 2020].

Choi, S., SungWoo Yang, J. and Chen, W. (2018). Longitudinal Change of an Online Political Discussion Forum: Antecedents of Discussion Network Size and Evolution. *Journal of Computer-Mediated Communication*, 23(5), pp. 260–277.

Chown, M. (1999). Secret Heritage, *New Scientist* [online], 29 May 1999. Available from: https://www.newscientist.com/article/mg16221886-400-secret-heritage/.

Clooney, G. (2019). George Clooney: Boycott Sultan of Brunei's Hotels over Cruel Anti-Gay Laws. *Deadline* [online], 28 March 2019. Available from: https://deadline.com/2019/03/george-clooney-sultain-of-brunei-hotels-boycott-beverly-hills-hotel-anti-gay-laws-brunei-1202584579/.

Coase, R. (1994). *Essays on Economics and Economists*. London: University of Chicago Press.

Coates, J. (2012). *The Hour between Dog and Wolf: Risk-taking, Gut Feelings and the Biology of Boom and Bust*. London: Fourth Estate.

Coffman, K., Coffman, L. and Ericson, K. (2013). *The Size of the LGBT Population and the Magnitude of Anti-Gay Sentiment are Substantially Underestimated*. NBER Working Paper 19508. Cambridge, MA: National Bureau of Economic Research. Available from: https://www.nber.org/papers/w19508.

Cole, E. and Brantley, A. (2014). The Coors Boycott: When a Beer Can Signaled Your Politics. *CPR News* [online], 3 October 2014. Available from: https://www.cpr.org/2014/10/03/the-coors-boycott-when-a-beer-can-signaled-your-politics/.

Collins, D. (2018). *Queer Eye* [television series]. Los Gatos, CA: Netflix.

Conan Doyle, A. (1891). The Red-Headed League. *The Strand Magazine*. Reproduced by *Wikisource* [online]. Available from: https://en.wikisource.org/wiki/The_Red-headed_League [accessed 4 April 2020].

Confessore, N. (2018). Cambridge Analytica and Facebook: The Scandal and the Fallout So Far. *The New York Times* [online], 4 April 2018. Available from: https://www.nytimes.com/2018/04/04/us/politics/cambridge-analytica-scandal-fallout.html.

Conger, K. (2020). Facebook Starts Planning for Permanent Remote Workers. *New York Times* [online], 21 May 2020. Available from: https://www.nytimes.com/2020/05/21/technology/facebook-remote-work-coronavirus.html.

ConnecticutHistory.org (2018). *John Howe Makes a Better Pin – Today in History: June 22*. Available from: https://connecticuthistory.org/john-howe-makes-a-better-pin/ [accessed 12 September 2019].

Cook, H. (2005). The English Sexual Revolution: Technology and Social Change. *History Workshop Journal*, 59(1), pp. 109–128. Available from: https://academic.oup.com/hwj/article-abstract/59/1/109/576451.

Cook, M. (2017). 'Archives of Feeling': The AIDS Crisis in Britain 1987. *History Workshop Journal*, 83(1), pp. 51–78. Available from: https://academic.oup.com/hwj/article-abstract/83/1/51/3093555.

Cook, M., Mills, R. Trumbach, R. and Cocks, H.G. (2007). *A Gay History of Britain: Love and Sex between Men since the Middle Ages*. Oxford, UK: Greenwood World Publishing.

Cooper, E. and Dinerman, H. (1951). Analysis of the Film 'Don't be a Sucker': A Study in Communication. *Public Opinion Quarterly*, 15(2), pp. 243–264.

Courtemanche, C., Pinkston, J., Ruhm, C.J. and Wehby, G. (2015). *Changing Economic Factors and the Rise in Obesity*. Vox Centre for Economic Policy Research (CEPR) Policy Portal [online], 24 July 2015. Available from: https://voxeu.org/article/changing-economic-factors-and-rise-obesity.

Crane, D. and Kauffman, M. (1994). *Friends* [television series]. Universal City, CA: NBC.

Daily Mirror. (1969). Mrs Britain Judges Will Give Away 8,000 Guineas. *The Daily Mirror*, 12 February 1969. Available from: www.britishnewspaperarchive.co.uk.

Delap, L. (2011a). *Who Mops the Floor Now? How Domestic Service Shaped 20th-Century Britain*. University of Cambridge Research News [online], 28 July 2011. Available from: https://www.cam.ac.uk/research/news/who-mops-the-floor-now-how-domestic-service-shaped-20th-century-britain.

Delap, L. (2011b). *Knowing Their Place: Domestic Service in Twentieth-Century Britain*. Oxford: Oxford University Press.

Deloitte (2019). *Uncovering Talent – A new Model of Inclusion*. London: Deloitte Development LLC. Available from: https://www2.deloitte.com/content/dam/Deloitte/us/Documents/about-deloitte/us-about-deloitte-uncovering-talent-a-new-model-of-inclusion.pdf.

De Moor, T. and Van Zanden, J.L. (2010). Girl Power: The European Marriage Pattern and Labour Markets in the North Sea Region in the Late Medieval and Early Modern Period. *The Economic History Review*, 6(1), pp. 1–33. Available from: https://www.researchgate.net/publication/227988504_Girl_power_The_European_marriage_pattern_and_labour_markets_in_the_North_Sea_region_in_the_late_medieval_and_early_modern_period.

De Vries, J. (2008). *The Industrious Revolution: Consumer Behavior and the Household Economy, 1650 to the Present*. Cambridge, UK: Cambridge University Press.

Diehl, D. (1996). *Tales from the Crypt*. New York: St Martin's Press.

Dijkstra, L., Poelman, H. and Rodríguez-Pose, A. (2018). *The Geography of EU Discontent*. Working paper 12/2018, Directorate-General for Regional and Urban Policy. Luxembourg: Publications Office of the European Union. Available from: https://ec.europa.eu/regional_policy/en/information/publications/working-papers/2018/the-geography-of-eu-discontent.

Donovan, P. (n.d.). *Paul Donovan* [online]. *YouTube* Channel. Available from: https://www.youtube.com/channel/UC_37bvdOuKEgvGfwuojNQnQ/featured.

Donovan, P. (2013). Same-Sex Marriage Boosts the Economy. *The Financial Times*, 5 June 2013. Available from: https://ftalphaville.ft.com/2013/06/05/1525272/donovan-same-sex-marriage-boosts-the-economy/.

Donovan, P. and Hudson, J. (2011). *From Red to Green: How the Financial Credit Crunch Could Bankrupt the Environment*. Oxford, UK: Earthscan.

Dosi, G. and Galambos, L. eds. (2013). *The Third Industrial Revolution in Global Business*. Cambridge, UK: Cambridge University Press.

Dovidio, J.F., Glick P. and Rudman L. (2005). *On the Nature of Prejudice. Fifty Years after Allport*. Oxford, UK: Blackwell Publishing.

Draut, T. (2016). *Sleeping Giant: How the New Working Class Will Transform America*. New York: Doubleday.

Drydakis, N. (2019). Sexual Orientation and Labor Market Outcomes. *IZA World of Labor*, 111(2). Bonn, Germany, IZA Institute of Labor Economics. Available from: https://wol.iza.org/articles/sexual-orientation-and-labor-market-outcomes/long.

Dudley, L. (2017). Language Standardization and the Industrial Revolution. *Oxford Economic Papers*, 69(4), pp. 1138–1161.

DW. (2019). Germany's Gay Paragraph 175 Abolished 25 Years Ago. *Deutsche Welle* [online], 11 June 2019. Available from: https://www.dw.com/en/germanys-gay-paragraph-175-abolished-25-years-ago/a-49124549.

Earle, P. (1989). The Female Labour Market in London in the Late Seventeenth and Early Eighteenth Centuries. *Economic History Review*, 42(3), pp. 328–353.

Eddo-Lodge, R. (2017). *Why I'm No Longer Talking to White People about Race*. London: Bloomsbury.

Edelman, B., Luca, M. and Svirsky, D. (2017). Racial Discrimination in the Sharing Economy: Evidence from a Field Experiment. *American Economic Journal: Applied Economics*, 9(2), pp. 1–22. Available from: https://www.aeaweb.org/articles?id=10.1257/app.20160213.

Eden, F.M. (1797). *The State of the Poor*. 1928 ed. abridged and edited by A.G.L. Rogers: 383pp. London: George Routledge & Sons.

Eichengreen, B. (2018). *The Populist Temptation*. Oxford, UK: Oxford University Press.

Ems, L. (2014). Twitter's Place in the Tussle: How Old Power Struggles to Play Out on a New Stage. *Media, Culture and Society*, 36(5), pp. 720–731. Available from: https://journals.sagepub.com/doi/10.1177/0163443714529070.

English, J. (2019). The Commuting Principle that Shaped Urban History. *Bloomberg CityLab* [online], 29 August 2019. Available from: https://www.citylab.com/transportation/2019/08/commute-time-city-size-transportation-urban-planning-history/597055/ [accessed 5 September 2019].

Ennis, D. (2019). Chick-fil-A Gets Grilled By Both Sides In LGBT Funding Flap. *Forbes* [online], 22 November 2019. Available from: https://www.forbes.com/sites/dawnstaceyennis/2019/11/22/chick-fil-a-gets-grilled-by-both-sides-in-lgbt-funding-flap/#72e9b2c3249b.

Esteban, J., Levy, G. and Mayoral, L. (2015). Liberty, Religiosity, and Effort. CEPR Discussion Paper No. 10841. London: Centre for Economic Policy Research.

European Patent Office. (2019). *US10169708B2: Determining Trustworthiness and Compatibility of a Person*. Patent application by Airbnb Inc. European Patent Office [online]. Available from: https://worldwide.espacenet.com/patent/

search/family/053441797/publication/US10169708B2?q=airbnb%20traits [accessed 29 February 2020].

Evans, A. (2017). *The Myth Gap: What Happens When Evidence and Arguments Aren't Enough?* London: Eden Project Books.

Fairlie, R. (2018). Racial Inequality in Business Ownership and Income. *Oxford Review of Economic Policy*, 34(4), pp. 597–614.

Faith Survey. (2020). *Christianity in the UK* [online]. Available from: https://faith-survey.co.uk/uk-christianity.html.

Farrington, N., Hall, L., Kilvington, D., Price, J. and Saeed, A. (2015). *Sport, Racism and Social Media*. Abingdon, UK: Routledge.

Featherstone, L. (2016). *Equal Ever After: The Fight for Same-Sex Marriage – and How I Made It Happen*. London: Biteback Publishing.

Feller, A., Pierson, E., Corbett-Davis, S. and Goel, S. (2016). A Computer Program Used for Bail and Sentencing Decisions Was Labelled Biased against Blacks. It's Actually Not That Clear. *The Washington Post*, 17 October 2016. Available from: https://www.washingtonpost.com/news/monkey-cage/wp/2016/10/17/can-an-algorithm-be-racist-our-analysis-is-more-cautious-than-propublicas/.

Ferenczi, N., Marshall, T.C. and Bejanyan, K. (2017). Are Sex Differences in Antisocial and Prosocial Facebook Use Explained by Narcissism and Relational Self-Construal? *Computers in Human Behavior*, 77, pp. 25–31. Available from: https://www.researchgate.net/publication/319412114_Are_Sex_Differences_in_Antisocial_and_Prosocial_Facebook_Use_Explained_by_Narcissism_and_Relational_Self-Construal.

Financial Crisis Inquiry Commission. (2011). *The Financial Crisis Inquiry Report: Final Report of the National Commission on the Causes of the Financial and Economic Crisis in the United States*. Washington, DC: Library of Congress. Available from: https://www.loc.gov/item/2011381760/.

Flood, A. (2019). Independent Bookshops Grow for Second Year After 20-Year Decline. *The Guardian* [online], 7 January 2019. Available from: https://www.theguardian.com/books/2019/jan/07/independent-bookshops-grow-for-second-year-after-20-year-decline [accessed 17 September 2019].

Flynn, P. (2017). *Good as You*. London: Ebury Press.

Folke, O. and Rickne, J. (2016). The Glass Ceiling in Politics: Formalization and Empirical Tests. *Comparative Political Studies*, 46(5), pp. 567–599.

Fordham University. (2020). Nazi Germany: Paragraph 175 and Other Sexual Deviance Laws. *Internet History Sourcebooks Project* [online]. Last updated 2 January 2020. New York, Fordham University History Department. Available from: https://sourcebooks.fordham.edu/pwh/para175.asp [accessed 1 June 2020].

Forster, N. (2017). *A Quiet Revolution? The Rise of Women Managers, Business Owners and Leaders in the Arabian Gulf States*. Cambridge, UK: Cambridge University Press.

Francis, M. (2013). Harold Wilson's 'White Heat of Technology' Speech 50 Years On. *The Guardian* [online], 19 September 2013. Available from: https://www.theguardian.com/science/political-science/2013/sep/19/harold-wilson-zwhite-heat-technology-speech.

Frey, C.B. (2019). *The Technology Trap: Capital, Labor, and Power in the Age of Automation*. Princeton, NJ: Princeton University Press.

Friedman, G. (2005). School for Scandal: Sexuality, Race, and National Vice and Virtue in Miss Marianne Woods and Miss Jane Pirie against Lady Helen

Cumming Gordon. *Nineteenth Century Contexts*, 27(1), pp. 53–76. Available from: https://www.tandfonline.com/doi/abs/10.1080/08905490500133113.

Frost, R. (1916). The Road Not Taken. *Academy of American Poets* [online]. Available from: https://poets.org/poem/road-not-taken [accessed 15 May 2020].

Fujioka, Y. (1999). Television Portrayals and African-American Stereotypes: Examination of Television Effects when Direct Contact Is Lacking. *Journalism and Mass Communication Quarterly*, 76(1), pp. 52–75.

Gabbatt, A. (2017). How a 1947 US Government Film Went Viral after Charlottesville, *The Guardian*, 14 August. Available from: https://www.theguardian.com/world/2017/aug/14/dont-be-a-sucker-anti-nazi-film-charlottesville.

Galbraith, J.K. (2012). *Inequality and Instability: A Study of the World Economy Just Before the Great Crisis*. Oxford, UK: Oxford University Press.

Gangopadhyay, P. (2009). Economics of Intolerance and Social Conflict. *Peace and Security Journal*, 4(2), pp. 23–31. Available from: https://www.epsjournal.org.uk/index.php/EPSJ/article/view/98.

Garcia-López, M.A., Jofre-Monseny, J. Mazza, R.M. and Segú, M. (2019). *Do Short-Term Rental Platforms Affect Housing Markets? Evidence from Airbnb in Barcelona*. IBE Working Paper 2019/05. Barcelona, Spain: Institut d'Economia de Barcelona (IBE). Available from: https://papers.ssrn.com/sol3/papers.cfm?abstract_id=3428237.

Gaskell, P. (1833). *The Manufacturing Population of England, Its Moral, Social, and Physical Conditions, and the Changes Which Have Arisen From the Use of Steam Machinery, With an Examination of Infant Labour*. London: Baldwin and Craddock, London [digitised online]. Available from: https://books.google.ie/books?id=fixjAAAAMAAJ&printsec=frontcover&source=gbs_ge_summary_r&cad=0#v=onepage&q&f=false.

Gaston, S. and Hilhorst, S. (2018). *Nostalgia as a Cultural and Political Force in Britain, France and Germany*. London: Demos. Available from: https://www.demos.co.uk/wp-content/uploads/2018/05/At-Home-in-Ones-Past-Report.pdf.

Ge, Y., Knittel, C.R., MacKenzie, D. and Zoepf, S. (2016). *Racial and Gender Discrimination in Transportation Network Companies*. NBER Working Paper 22776. Cambridge, MA: National Bureau of Economic Research. Available from: https://www.nber.org/papers/w22776.pdf.

Geiger, A.W. (2019). *How Americans See Automation and the Workplace in 7 Charts*. Washington, DC: Pew Research Centre [online]. Available from: https://www.pewresearch.org/fact-tank/2019/04/08/how-americans-see-automation-and-the-workplace-in-7-charts/ [accessed 20 October 2019].

Gender Fair. (n.d.). *Gender Fair* [online]. Available from: http://www.genderfair.com/.

Gibson, J. Whitney, Greenwood, R.A. and Murphy, E.F. (2009). Generational Differences in the Workplace: Personal Values, Behaviors, and Popular Beliefs. *Journal of Diversity Management*, 4(3), pp. 1–8. Available from: https://www.researchgate.net/publication/262725755_Generational_Differences_In_The_Workplace_Personal_Values_Behaviors_And_Popular_Beliefs.

Gierzynski, A. and Eddy, K. (2013). *Harry Potter and the Millennials: Research Methods and the Politics of the Muggle Generation*. Baltimore, MD: Johns Hopkins University Press.

Gill, J. (2002). Greenpeace Says Esso Boycott Working. *Campaign* [online], 5 September 2002. Available from: https://www.campaignlive.co.uk/article/greenpeace-says-esso-boycott-working/157020.

Gingrich, J. (2019). Did State Responses to Automation Matter for Voters? *Research and Politics*, 6(11), pp. 1–9. Available from: https://journals.sagepub.com/doi/full/10.1177/2053168019832745.

GLAAD (2019). *Where We Are on TV 2018–19*. Los Angeles, CA: GLAAD Media Institute. Available from: https://www.glaad.org/whereweareontv19 [accessed 20 December 2019].

Goldin C. and Katz, L.F. (2008). *The Race between Education and Technology*. Cambridge, MA: Belknap Press.

Goldin, C. and Rouse, C. (2000). Orchestrating Impartiality: The Impact of 'Blind' Auditions on Female Musicians. *American Economic Review*, 90(4), pp. 715–741. Available from: https://www.aeaweb.org/articles?id=10.1257/aer.90.4.715.

Gomez, E.M. and Kaiser, C.R. (2019). From Pixels to Protest: Using the Internet to Confront Bias at the Societal Level. In: Mallett, R.K. and Monteith, M.J., eds.,. *Confronting Prejudice and Discrimination: The Science of Changing Minds and Behaviors*. London: Elsevier Inc.

Gomillion, S.C. and Giuliano, T.A. (2011). The Influence of Media Role Models on Gay, Lesbian and Bisexual Identity. *Journal of Homosexuality*, 58, pp. 330–354. Available from: https://www.tandfonline.com/doi/full/10.1080/00918369.2011.546729.

Goodfellow, M. (2019). *Hostile Environment: How Immigrants Became Scapegoats*. London: Verso.

Goodliffe, G. (2012). *The Resurgence of the Radical Right in France*. Cambridge, UK: Cambridge University Press.

Gordon, R.J. (2016). *The Rise and Fall of American Growth*. Princeton, NJ: Princeton University Press.

Gottlieb, J. (2000). Women and Fascism in the East End. In: Kushner, T. and Valman, N. eds., *Remembering Cable Street*. London: Valentine Mitchell, pp. 31–47.

Green, J. (2003). Rhyming Slang. *Critical Quarterly*, 45(1–2), pp. 220–226.

Greshko, M. (2018). Who Are the Nobel Prize Winners? We've Crunched the Numbers. *National Geographic* [online], 3 October 2018. Available from: https://www.nationalgeographic.com/news/2017/10/nobel-prize-winners-laureates-charts-graphics-science/-.

Griffin, E. (2013). *Liberty's Dawn: A People's History of the Industrial Revolution*. New Haven, CT: Yale University Press.

Guess, A., Nyhan, B. and Reifler, J. (2018). *Selective Exposure to Misinformation: Evidence from the Consumption of Fake News during the 2016 U.S. Presidential Campaign*. Brussels: European Research Council. Available from: www.ask-force.org/web/Fundamentalists/Guess-Selective-Exposure-to-Misinformation-Evidence-Presidential-Campaign-2018.pdf.

Gwartney, J. and Haworth, C. (1974). Employer Costs and Discrimination: The Case of Baseball. *Journal of Political Economy*, 82(4), pp. 873–881.

Hagemann, H. (2020). LGBTQ Youth Fight for Equality in Sex Ed in South Carolina Classrooms. *NPR* [online], 1 March 2020. Available from: https://www.npr.org/2020/03/01/810506670/lgbtq-youth-fight-for-equality-in-sex-ed-in-south-carolina-classrooms?t=1583272979153.

Hagood, T.C. (2012). "Oh, What a Slanderous Book": Reading *Uncle Tom's Cabin* in the Antebellum South. *Southern Quarterly*, 49(40), pp. 70–93.

Hall, B.J. (1998). Narratives of Prejudice. *Howard Journal of Communication*, 9(2), pp. 137–156.

Hall, E. ed. (1939). *Miss Weeton: Journal of a Governess 1811–1825*. Oxford, UK: Oxford University Press.

Hameed, N. (2018). Saudi Women Don't Need Male Permission to Start Businesses. *Arab News* [online], updated 18 February 2018. Available from: https://www.arabnews.com/node/1248781/saudi-arabia.

Hanushek, E.A. and Woessmann, L. (2015). *The Knowledge Capital of Nations. Education and the Economics of Growth*. Cambridge, MA: MIT Press.

Harford, T. (2017). What We Get Wrong About Technology, *Financial Times Magazine*, 7 July 2017. Available from: https://www.ft.com/content/32c31874-610b-11e7-8814-0ac7eb84e5f1.

Harpine, W.D. (2005). *From the Front Porch to the Front Page: McKinley and Bryan in the 1896 Presidential Campaign*. College Station, TX: Texas A&M University Press.

Hauge, J., Kenward, M. and Wightman S. (2019). *The Future of the Manufacturing Workforce*. Cambridge, UK: Centre for Science, Technology and Innovation Policy, Institute for Manufacturing, University of Cambridge. Available from: https://www.ifm.eng.cam.ac.uk/insights/developing-people/the-future-of-the-manufacturing-workforce/.

Haywood, I. and Seed, J. eds. (2012). *The Gordon Riots: Politics, Culture and Insurrection in Late Eighteenth-Century Britain*. Cambridge, UK: Cambridge University Press.

Hendel, I., Lach, S. and Spiegel, Y. (2017). Consumers' Activism: The Cottage Cheese Boycott. *The RAND Journal of Economics*, 48(4), pp. 972–1003. Available from: https://doi.org/10.1111/1756-2171.12212.

Hicks, M. (2017). *Programmed Inequality: How Britain Discarded Women Technologists and Lost its Edge in Computing*. Cambridge, MA: MIT Press.

Holden, A. (2019). *The Gay/Trans Panic Defense: What It Is and How to End It*. American Bar Association Member Op-Ed [online], 1 April 2020. Available from: https://www.americanbar.org/groups/crsj/publications/member-features/gay-trans-panic-defense/.

Holmes, T.J. (2001). Bar Codes Lead to Frequent Deliveries and Superstores. *The RAND Journal of Economics*, 32(4), pp. 708–725. Available from: https://www.jstor.org/stable/2696389?seq=1.

Holpuch, A. (2019). North Carolina: Trans People Given Right to Use Bathrooms Matching Identity. *The Guardian* [online], 23 July 2019. Available from: https://www.theguardian.com/society/2019/jul/23/north-carolina-bathroom-bill-transgender.

Horn, J. (2015). *Economic Development in Early Modern France: The Privilege of Liberty, 1650–1820*. Cambridge, UK: Cambridge University Press.

Hortaçsu, A. and Syverson, C. (2015). The Ongoing Evolution of US Retail: A Format Tug of War. *Journal of Economic Perspectives*, 29(4), pp. 89–112. Available from: https://www.aeaweb.org/articles?id=10.1257/jep.29.4.89.

HRC. (2020). *Human Rights Campaign* [online]. Available from: https://www.hrc.org/.

Hudson, J. and Donovan, P. (2014). *Food Policy and the Environmental Credit Crunch: From Soup to Nuts*. Abingdon, UK: Routledge.

Hunt, V., Layton, D. and Prince, S. (2015). *Diversity Matters*. London and Atlanta, GA: McKinsey and Company. Available from: www.insurance.ca.gov/diversity/41-ISDGBD/GBDExternal/upload/McKinseyDivmatters-201501.pdf.

Hunter-Gault, C. (2019). Derek Black grew up as a white nationalist. Here's how he changed his mind. *PBS News Hour* [online], 5 November 2019. Available from: https://www.pbs.org/newshour/show/derek-black-grew-up-as-a-white-nationalist-heres-how-he-changed-his-mind.

Hurley, L. (2015). How Wall Street Came Out on Gay Marriage. *Reuters* [online], 23 April 2015. Available from: https://www.reuters.com/article/us-usa-court-gaymarriage-wallstreet-insi/how-wall-street-came-out-on-gay-marriage-idUSKBN0NE0C820150423.

International Federation of the Phonographic Industry (IFPI) (2019). *Global Music Report, 2019*. Zurich: IFPI. Available from: https://www.ifpi.org/news/IFPI-GLOBAL-MUSIC-REPORT-2019.

Interparliamentary Union (2019). *Women in National Parliaments*. Interparliamentary Union [online]. Available from: archive.ipu.org/wmn-e/world.htm [accessed 25 May 2020].

Irwin, D.A. (2011). *Peddling Protectionism: Smoot-Hawley and The Great Depression*. Princeton, NJ: Princeton University Press.

Isenberg, N. (2016). *White Trash: The 400-Year Untold History of Class in America*. New York: Viking.

Jarrige, F. (2013). Gender and Machine-Breaking: Violence and Mechanization at the Dawn of the Industrial Age (England and France 1750–1850). *Clio*, 38, pp. 15–37. Available from: http://journals.openedition.org/cliowgh/284.

John, R.R. and Silberstein-Loed, J. eds. (2015). *Making News: The Political Economy of Journalism in Britain and America from the Glorious Revolution to the Internet*. Oxford, UK: Oxford University Press.

Johnson, I. (2015). *LGBT Diversity: Show Me The Business Case*. Amsterdam, The Netherlands: Out Now Consulting. Available from: https://www.outnowconsulting.com/market-reports/lgbt-diversity-show-me-the-business-case-report.aspx.

Johnson, K. (2019). *Reaching for the Moon. The Autobiography of NASA Mathematician Katherine Johnson*. New York: Atheneum Books.

Johnson, M. and Getz, K. (2017). *Gayish* [podcast]. Available from: http://www.gayishpodcast.com/.

Jones, B. (1969). Women Are to Get Equal Pay at Fords. *The Daily Mirror*, 12 February 1969. Available from: www.britishnewspaperarchive.co.uk.

Jones, B.F. (2010). Age and Great Invention. *The Review of Economics and Statistics*, XCII(1), pp. 1–14.

Jones, E.G. (1929). The Argentine Refrigerated Meat Industry. *Economica*, 26, pp. 156–172. Available from: https://www.jstor.org/stable/2548200?seq=1.

Jones, M., Mavromaras, K., Sloane, P.J. and Wei, Z. (2018). The Dynamic Effect of Disability on Work and Subjective Well-Being. *Oxford Economic Papers*, 70(3), pp. 635–657. Available from: https://doi.org/10.1093/oep/gpy006.

Kaiser, J. (2019). Genetics May Explain up to 25% of Same-Sex Behavior, Giant Analysis Reveals. *Science* [online, 29 August 2019. Available from: https://www.sciencemag.org/news/2019/08/genetics-may-explain-25-same-sex-behavior-giant-analysis-reveals.

Kellogg School of Management. (2011). *Age and Great Invention*. Kellogg Insight [online], 19 May 2011. Available from: https://insight.kellogg.northwestern.edu/article/age_and_great_invention [accessed 18 April 2020].

Kellogg School of Management. (2020). *Yes, Investors Care About Gender Diversity*. Kellogg Insight [online], 2 March 2020. Available from: https://insight.kellogg.northwestern.edu/article/women-in-tech-finance-gender-diversity-investors [accessed 18 April 2020].

Kelly, J. (2016). The Era When Gay Spies Were Feared. *BBC News Magazine* [online], 20 January 2016. Available from: https://www.bbc.com/news/magazine-35360172.

Kerley, P. (n.d.). House-Buyer Time Machine. *BBC News* [online]. Available from: https://www.bbc.co.uk/news/extra/pjfxZM72Gj/house-buyer-time-machine [accessed 3 May 2020].

Keyes, C. (2011). 'Don't Ask, Don't Tell' Cost Tops $50,000 per Expulsion, Study Finds. *CNN Politics* [online], 21 January 2011. Available from: https://edition.cnn.com/2011/POLITICS/01/20/dont.ask.dont.tell.costs/index.html.

Keynes, J.M. (1930). Economic Possibilities for our Grandchildren. *The Collected Writings of John Maynard Keynes IX: Essays in Persuasion*. 1984 ed., reprinted 1989. London and Cambridge, UK: McMillan and Cambridge University Press.

Kiste Nyberg, A. (n.d.). *Comics Code History: The Seal of Approval*. Comic Book Legal Defense Fund (CBLDF) [online]. Available from: http://cbldf.org/comics-code-history-the-seal-of-approval/ [accessed 17 May 2020].

Kohan, D. and Mutchnick, M. (1998). *Will and Grace* [television series]. Universal City, CA: NBC.

Kooragayala, S. and Srini, T. (2016). Pokémon Go Is Changing How Cities Use Urban Space, But Could It Be More Inclusive? *The Urban Institute Blog* [online], updated 5 August 2016. Available from: https://www.urban.org/urban-wire/pokemon-go-changing-how-cities-use-public-space-could-it-be-more-inclusive [accessed 7 March 2020].

Kooti, F., Aiello, L.M., Grbovic, M., Lerman, K. and Mantrach, A. (2015). Evolution of Conversations in the Age of Email Overload. In: *WWW '15: Proceedings of the 24th International Conference on World Wide Web*. Geneva, Switzerland: International World Wide Web Conferences Steering Committee. Available from: https://dl.acm.org/doi/proceedings/10.5555/2736277.

Kramarae, C. ed. (1988). *Technology and Women's Voices: Keeping in Touch*. New York: Routledge and Kegan Paul.

Kudos and BBC Wales. (2006). *Life on Mars* [television series]. London: BBC1 and BBC4.

Kushner, T. and Valman, N. (2000). *Remembering Cable Street: Fascism and Anti-Fascism in British Society*. London: Vallentine Mitchell.

Lacroix, S. (2011). *Awakening Islam: The Politics of Religious Dissent in Contemporary Saudi Arabia*. London: Harvard University Press.

Lanning, J.A. (2010). Productivity, Discrimination, and Lost Profits during Baseball's Integration. *Journal of Economic History*, 70(4), pp. 964–988.

Larson, J., Mattu, S. and Angwin, J. (2015). Unintended Consequences of Geographical Targetting. *Technology Science*, 2015090103. Available from: https://techscience.org/a/2015090103/.

Lasch, C. (1995). *The Revolt of the Elites and the Betrayal of Democracy*. New York: W.W. Norton and Co.

Laurent, T. and Mihoubi, F. (2012). Sexual Orientation and Wage Discrimination in France: The Hidden Side of the Rainbow. *Journal of Labor Research*, 33, pp. 487–527. Available from: https://link.springer.com/article/10.1007/s12122-012-9145-x.

Lavelle, K. and Al Sheikh, H. (2013). *Giving Voice to Women Entrepreneurs in Saudi Arabia. Women's Entrepreneurship Initiative*. Executive Summary. Bristol, UK: Ellesolaire Women's Entrepreneurship Initiative. Available from: https://www.ellesolaire.org/wp-content/uploads/2017/04/Final-Exec-summary-women-entrepreneurs-in-Saudi-Arabia-Report-Executive-Summary.pdf [accessed 8 May 2020].

Leon, H. (2019). No Longer a Hater: The Long, Strange Journey of Megan Phelps-Roper. *The Observer* [online], 4 December 2019. Available from: https://observer.com/2019/04/megan-phelps-roper-westboro-baptist-church-activist-profile/.

Leto, V. (1988). 'Washing, Seems It's All We Do': Washing Technology and Women's Communication. In: Kramarae, C., ed., *Technology and Women's Voices: Keeping in Touch*. New York: Routledge and Kegan Paul, pp. 161–179.

Levin, S. (2017). As Facebook Blocks the Names of Trans Users and Drag Queens, This Burlesque Performer Is Fighting Back. *The Guardian*, 29 June 2017. Available from: https://www.theguardian.com/world/2017/jun/29/facebook-real-name-trans-drag-queen-dottie-lux.

Levy, G. and Razin, R. (2019). Echo Chambers and Their Effects on Economic and Political Outcomes. *Annual Review of Economics*, 11, pp. 303–328. Available from: https://www.annualreviews.org/doi/pdf/10.1146/annurev-economics-080218-030343.

Lewis, S., Anderson, D., Lyonette, C., Payne, N. and Wood, S. eds. (2017). *Work-Life Balance in Times of Recession, Austerity and Beyond*. Abingdon, UK: Routledge.

Lin, J. (2011). Technological Adaptation, Cities, and New Work. *The Review of Economics and Statistics*, 93(2), pp. 554–574.

Lindert, P.H. and Williamson, J.G. (2016). *Unequal Gains: American growth and Inequality since 1700*. Princeton, NJ: Princeton University Press.

Linehan, T.P. (1996). *East London for Mosley: The British Union of Fascists in East London and South West Essex 1933–40*. London: Frank Cass.

Lippert-Rasmussen, K. (2014). *Born Free and Equal? A Philosophical Inquiry into the Nature of Discrimination*. Oxford, UK: Oxford University Press.

Little, I.M.D. (2002). *Ethics, Economics and Politics: Principles of Public Policy*. Oxford, UK: Oxford University Press.

Long, T. (2009). Jan. 23, 1911: Science Academy Tells Marie Curie, 'Non'. *Wired* [online], 23 January 2009, republished 23 January 2012. Available from: https://www.wired.com/2012/01/jan-23-1911-marie-curie/.

Lucas, G. (1977). *Star Wars* [film]. Los Angeles: 20th Century Fox.

Luce, E. (2019). US Democrats Should Remember, 'It's The Economy, Stupid'. *Financial Times* [online], 27 March 2019. Available from: https://www.ft.com/content/b8e4f7c8-5070-11e9-9c76-bf4a0ce37d49.

Lunn, K. and Thurlow, R.C. eds. (1980). *British Fascism*. London: Croom Helm.

Lynn, J. and Jay, A. (1989). *The Complete Yes Prime Minister: The Diaries of the Right Hon. James Hacker*. Transcripts of the Television Series. 1st paperback ed. London: BBC Books.

Lytal, C. (2008). 'Milk' Advisor Repays in Kind. *Los Angeles Times*, 30 November. Available from: https://www.latimes.com/archives/la-xpm-2008-nov-30-ca-workinghollywood30-story.html.

MacKenzie, K. (2015). *What Have the Immigrants Ever Done for Us?* London: Biteback Publishing.

Macklemore and Lambert, M. (2012). *Same Love* [song]. Seattle, WA: Macklemore/RyanLewis Studios. Available from: https://www.youtube.com/watch?v=EyBooxCkF3A.

MacLeod, C. (2007). *Heroes of Invention: Technology, Liberalism and British Identity 1750–1914*. Cambridge, UK: Cambridge University Press.

MacRaild, D.M. (2013). No Irish Need Apply: The Origins and Persistence of a Prejudice. *Labour History Review*, 78(3), pp. 269–299.

Madonna. (1985). *Material Girl* [song]. Los Angeles, CA: Sire Records.

Magnus, G. (2011). *Uprising: Will Emerging Markets Shape or Shake the World Economy?* Chichester, UK: Wiley.

Malik, K. (2001). Why the Victorians Were Colour Blind. *New Statesman*, 7 May 2001. Available from: https://www.newstatesman.com/node/153394.

Mallet, R.K. and Monteith, M.J. eds. (2019). *Confronting Prejudice and Discrimination: The Science of Changing Minds and Behaviours*. London: Academic Press.

Mallet du Pan, M. (Jacques). (1793). *Considérations sur la nature de la révolution de France et sur les causes qui en prolongent la durée* [online]. Warwick, UK: Warwick Digital Collections, University of Warwick. Available from: https://archive.org/details/considrationssur0000mall/page/n6/mode/2up.

Management Today. (1993). UK: Nestle Rowntree – A Bittersweet Tale. *Management Today* [online], 1 March 1993, updated 25 July 2016. Available from: https://www.managementtoday.co.uk/uk-nestle-rowntree-bittersweet-tale/article/409657.

Manikonda, L., Beigi, G., Liu, H. and Kambhampati, S. (2018). *Twitter for Sparking a Movement, Reddit for Sharing a Moment: #MeToo Through the Lens of Social Media*. Tempe, AZ: Arizona State University. Available from: https://arxiv.org/abs/1803.08022 [accessed 16 May 2020].

Manne, K. (2018). *Down Girl: The Logic of Misogyny*. London: Penguin Books.

Margalit, Y. (2019). Economic Insecurity and the Causes of Populism, Reconsidered. *Journal of Economic Perspectives*, 33(4), pp. 152–170. Available from: https://www.aeaweb.org/articles?id=10.1257/jep.33.4.152.

Margetts, H., John, P., Hale, S. and Yasseri, T. (2016). *Political Turbulence: How Social Media Shape Collective Action*. Princeton, NJ: Princeton University Press.

Matlak, M. (2019). 'Nostalgia Serves No Purpose': An Interview with Michel Barnier. *New York Review of Books*, 29 May 2019. Available from: https://www.nybooks.com/daily/2019/05/29/nostalgia-serves-no-purpose-an-interview-with-michel-barnier/.

Mayhew, H. (1851). *London Labour and the London Poor*. 2010 ed. Oxford, UK: Oxford University Press.

McCann, K. (2017). Theresa May Admits 'Running through Fields of Wheat' Is the Naughtiest Thing She Ever Did. *The Telegraph* [online], 5 June 2017. Available from: https://www.telegraph.co.uk/politics/2017/06/05/theresa-may-admits-running-fields-wheat-naughtiest-thing-ever/.

McCarthy, J. (2019). Americans Still Greatly Overestimate U.S. Gay Population. *Gallup* [online], 27 June 2019. Available from: https://news.gallup.com/poll/259571/americans-greatly-overestimate-gay-population.aspx.

McClelland, P.D. and Tobin, P.H. (2010). *American Dream Dying: The Changing Economic Lot of the Least Advantaged.* Lanham, MD: Rowman & Littlefield.

McKinsey Global Institute. (2016). *Independent Work: Choice, Necessity, and the Gig Economy.* San Francisco, CA: McKinsey & Company. Available from: https://www.mckinsey.com/featured-insights/employment-and-growth/independent-work-choice-necessity-and-the-gig-economy.

McKinsey Global Institute. (2019). *The Future of Work in America: People and Places, Today and Tomorrow.* Washington, DC: McKinsey & Company. Available from: https://www.mckinsey.com/featured-insights/future-of-work/the-future-of-work-in-america-people-and-places-today-and-tomorrow.

Me Too. (2018). *Me Too Movement* [online]. Available from: https://metoomvmt.org/ [accessed 2 June 2020].

Mendos, L.R. (2019). *State-Sponsored Homophobia: Global Legislation Overview Update.* Geneva, Switzerland: International Lesbian, Gay, Bisexual, Trans and Intersex Association (ILGA World). Available from: https://ilga.org/state-sponsored-homophobia-report.

Menke, R. (2013). The End of the Three-Volume Novel System. The Branch Collective [online]. Available from: https://www.branchcollective.org/?ps_articles=richard-menke-the-end-of-the-three-volume-novel-system-27-june-1894 [accessed 15 November 2019].

Merler, S. (2017). Big Data and First-Degree Price Discrimination. Blog Post. *Bruegel* [online], 20 February 2017. Available from: https://www.bruegel.org/2017/02/big-data-and-first-degree-price-discrimination/ [accessed 24 July 2017].

Merrill, S. and Åkerlund, M. (2018). Standing up for Sweden? The Racist Discourses, Architectures and Affordances of an Anti-Immigration Facebook Group. *Journal of Computer-Mediated Communication*, 23(6), pp. 332–353. Available from: https://academic.oup.com/jcmc/article/23/6/332/5107230.

Miliband, D. (2017). *Rescue: Refugees and the Political Crisis of Our Time.* London: TED Books.

Miller, A. (1949). *Death of a Salesman.* New ed., 2000. London: Penguin Classics.

Miller, J. and Parker, L. (2018). *Open for Business: Strengthening the Economic Case.* London: Open For Business. Available from: https://www.brunswickgroup.com/media/3788/bru2_0558_openforbusiness_180123-1.pdf.

Miller, S. (2019). 'Shocking' Numbers: Half LGBTQ Adults Live in States Where No Laws Ban Job Discrimination. *USA Today* [online], 8 October 2019. Available from: https://eu.usatoday.com/story/news/nation/2019/10/08/lgbt-employment-discrimination-half-of-states-offer-no-protections/3837244002/.

Milne, R. (2018). Enlightened Norway's Gender Paradox at the Top of Business. *Financial Times* [online], 20 September 2018. Available from: https://www.ft.com/content/6f6bc5a2-7b70-11e8-af48-190d103e32a4.

Moffat, A. (2016). *No Outsiders in Our Schools: Teaching the Equality Act in Primary Schools.* Abingdon, UK: Routledge.

Mokyr, J. (1977). Demand vs. Supply in the Industrial Revolution. *Journal of Economic History*, 37(4), pp. 981–1008. Available from: https://doi.org/10.1017/S0022050700094778.

Mokyr, J. (2009). *The Enlightened Economy: An Economic History of Britain 1700–1850*. London: Yale University Press.

Mokyr, J., Vickers, C. and Ziebarth, N.L. (2015). The History of Technological Anxiety and the Future of Economic Growth: Is This Time Different? *Journal of Economic Perspectives*, 29(3), pp. 31–50. Available from: https://www.aeaweb.org/articles?id=10.1257/jep.29.3.31.

Momani, B. (2016). *Equality and the Economy: Why the Arab World Should Employ More Women*. Policy Briefing. Washington, DC: Brookings Institution. Available from: https://www.brookings.edu/wp-content/uploads/2016/12/bdc_20161207_equality_in_me_en.pdf.

Mondello, B. (2008). Remembering Hollywood's Hays Code, 40 Years On. *NPR* [radio], 8 August 2008. Available from: https://www.npr.org/templates/story/story.php?storyId=93301189&t=1565769335290 [accessed 14 August 2019].

Morrison, R. (2019). *The Regency Revolution: Jane Austen, Napoleon, Lord Byron and the Making of the Modern World*. London: Atlantic Books.

Moss-Racusin, C.A., Dovido, J.F, Brescoll, V.L., Graham, M.J. and Handelsman, J. (2012). Science Faculty's Subtle Gender Biases Favor Male Students. *Proceedings of the National Academy of Sciences of the United States of America*, 109(41), pp. 16474–16479. Available from: https://www.pnas.org/content/109/41/16474.

Murphy, A. (2015). Writes with a Fair Hand and Appears to be Well-Qualified: The Recruitment of Bank of England Clerks, 1800–1815. *Financial History Review*, 22(1), pp. 19–44. Available from: https://doi.org/10.1017/S0968565015000013.

Murphy, A. (2018). How Did Organisations Adapt to Change in the Eighteenth and Nineteenth Century: Lessons from the Bank of England Archives, *Bank Underground* [online], 7 November 2018. London, Bank of England. Available from: https://bankunderground.co.uk/2018/11/07/how-did-organisations-adapt-to-change-in-the-18th-and-19th-century-lessons-from-the-bank-of-england-archives/ [accessed 9 November 2018].

Murray, J. (2013). What Did Margaret Thatcher Do for Women? *The Guardian*, 9 April 2013. Available from: https://www.theguardian.com/politics/2013/apr/09/margaret-thatcher-women.

Nansen McCloskey, D. (2016). *Bourgeois Equality: How Ideas, Not Capital or Institutions, Enriched the World*. Chicago, IL: University of Chicago Press.

Nathan, M. and Lee, N. (2011). *Does Cultural Diversity Help Innovation in Cities? Evidence from London Firms*. SERC Discussion Paper 69. London: Spatial Economics Research Centre, London School of Economics. Available from: http://eprints.lse.ac.uk/33579/1/sercdp0069.pdf.

National Archives. (n.d.). *The Constitution of the United States: A Transcription* [online]. College Park, MD: The U.S. National Archives and Records Administration. Available from: https://www.archives.gov/founding-docs/constitution-transcript [accessed 15 May 2020].

National Research Council. (2015). *Enhancing the Effectiveness of Team Science*. Washington, DC: National Academies Press.

National Security Agency Central Security Service (NSA/CSS). (2008). *National Cryptologic Museum Exhibits Hobo Signs*. Press release, 5 February 2008. Fort Meade, MD: NSA/CSS Public and Media Affairs Office. Available from: https://www.nsa.gov/news-features/press-room/Article/1631753/national-cryptologic-museum-exhibits-hobo-signs/.

Nedelkoska, L. and Quintini, G. (2018). *Automation, Skills Use and Training.* OECD Social, Employment and Migration Working Papers No. 202. Paris: Organisation for Economic Cooperation and Development (OECD). Available from: https://www.oecd-ilibrary.org/employment/automation-skills-use-and-training_2e2f4eea-en.

Newport, F. (2017). In U.S., Estimate of LGBT Population Rises to 4.5%. *Gallup* [online], 22 May 2018. Available from: https://news.gallup.com/poll/234863/estimate-lgbt-population-rises.aspx.

Nicholas, S. and Shergold, P.R. (1987). Intercounty Labour Mobility during the Industrial Revolution: Evidence from Australian Transportation Records. *Oxford Economic Papers*, 39(4), pp. 624–640. Available from: https://doi.org/10.1093/oxfordjournals.oep.a041809.

No Outsiders. (2019). *No Outsiders* [online]. Available from: https://no-outsiders.com/.

Norberg, J. (2009). *Financial Fiasco: How America's Infatuation with Homeownership and Easy Money Created the Economic Crisis.* Washington, DC: Cato Institute.

O'Donnell, M. and Meehan, T. (2002). *Hairspray* [musical]. Based on: Waters, J. (1988), *Hairspray* [film]. Burbank, CA: New Line Films.

OECD Data (2020). *FDI Flows* [database]. Available from: https://data.oecd.org/fdi/fdi-flows.htm [accessed 16 May 2020].

Ó Gráda, C. (2016). Did Science Cause the Industrial Revolution? *Journal of Economic Literature*, 54(1), pp. 224–239. Available from: https://papers.ssrn.com/sol3/papers.cfm?abstract_id=2523358.

Office for National Statistics (2019). *UK Business; Activity, Size and Location: 2019.* Available from: https://www.ons.gov.uk/businessindustryandtrade/business/activitysizeandlocation/bulletins/ukbusinessactivitysizeandlocation/2019.

Office of the Surgeon General (US) and National Action Alliance for Suicide Prevention (US). (2012). *2012 National Strategy for Suicide Prevention: Goals and Objectives for Action.* Washington, DC: US Department of Health and Human Services. Available from: https://www.ncbi.nlm.nih.gov/books/NBK109917/.

O'Keefe, P., Caulfield, B., Brazil, W. and White, P. (2016). The Impacts of Telecommuting in Dublin. *Research in Transportation Economics*, 57, pp. 13–20. Available from: https://www.researchgate.net/deref/http%3A%2F%2Fdx.doi.org%2F10.1016%2Fj.retrec.2016.06.010.

ONE Archives Foundation (n.d.). *One Archives Foundation* [online]. Available from: https://www.onearchives.org/about/history/ [accessed 28 May 2020].

Organisation for Economic Cooperation and Development (OECD). (2020). Gender Gap in Reading and ICT Hobbies. In: *PISA 2018 Results (Volume II): Where All Students Can Succeed.* Paris: PISA, OECD Publishing. Available from: https://doi.org/10.1787/a01d218a-en.

Osborne, M. and Frey, C.B. (2018). *Automation and the Future of Work – Understanding the Numbers* [online]. Blog, 13 April 2018. Oxford, UK: Oxford Martin School, University of Oxford. Available from: https://www.oxford-martin.ox.ac.uk/blog/automation-and-the-future-of-work-understanding-the-numbers/ [accessed 11 September 2019].

Ozgen, C., Nijkamp, P. and Poot, J. (2011). *Immigration and Innovation in European Regions.* IZA Discussion Paper 5676. Bonn, Germany: Forschungsinstitut zur Zukunft der Arbeit (IZA). Available from: http://ftp.iza.org/dp5676.pdf.

Packard, V. (1961). *The Hidden Persuaders*. Harmdonsworth, UK: Penguin.

Paluck, E.L. and Green, D.P. (2009). Prejudice Reduction: What Works? A Review and Assessment of Research and Practice. *The Annual Review of Psychology*, 60, pp. 339–367. Available from: https://www.annualreviews.org/doi/full/10.1146/annurev.psych.60.110707.163607?url_ver=Z39.88-2003&rfr_id=ori%3Arid%3Acrossref.org&rfr_dat=cr_pub++0pubmed.

Parker, G. (2013). *Global Crisis: War, Climate Change and Catastrophe in the Seventeenth Century*. New Haven, CT: Yale University Press.

Paul, T. (2017). The Gig Economy Is Nothing New – It was Standard Practice in the Eighteenth Century. *The Conversation* [online], 18 July 2017. Available from: https://theconversation.com/the-gig-economy-is-nothing-new-it-was-standard-practice-in-the-18th-century-81057 [accessed 24 July 2017].

Peek Vision. (2019). *Peek Vision* [online]. Available from: https://www.peekvision.org/.

Pesek, W. (2019). US-Japan Trade Deal Is a Victory for Abe, Not Trump. *Nikkei Asian Review* [online], 30 September 2019. Available from: https://asia.nikkei.com/Opinion/US-Japan-trade-deal-is-victory-for-Abe-not-Trump.

Pew Research Center. (2019a). Key Findings about U.S. Immigrants. *FactTank* [online], 17 June 2019. Available from: https://www.pewresearch.org/fact-tank/2019/06/17/key-findings-about-u-s-immigrants/.

Pew Research Center. (2019b). *In U.S., Decline of Christianity Continues at Rapid Pace*. Washington, DC: PEW Research Centre. Available from: https://www.pewforum.org/2019/10/17/in-u-s-decline-of-christianity-continues-at-rapid-pace/.

Pew Research Center. (2020). *Attendance at Religious Services* [online]. Washington, DC: PEW Research Center. Available from: https://www.pewforum.org/religious-landscape-study/attendance-at-religious-services/.

Phelps-Roper, M. (2017). *I Grew Up in the Westboro Baptist Church. Here's Why I Left*. Ted Talk [video online]. Available from: https://www.ted.com/talks/megan_phelps_roper_i_grew_up_in_the_westboro_baptist_church_here_s_why_i_left?language=en.

Pink News. (2018). What Was Section 28? The History of the Homophobic Legislation 30 Years On. 28 May. *Pink News* [online], 24 May 2018. Available from: https://www.pinknews.co.uk/2018/05/24/what-was-section-28-homophobic-legislation-30-years-thatcher/.

Polari Bible (2019). *The Polari Bible* (7th edition) [online]. Available from: www.polaribible.org.

Poushter, J., Fetterolf, J. and Tamir, C. (2019). *A Changing World: Global Views on Diversity, Gender Equality, Family Life and the Importance of Religion*. Washington, DC: PEW Research Centre. Available from: https://www.pewresearch.org/global/2019/04/22/a-changing-world-global-views-on-diversity-gender-equality-family-life-and-the-importance-of-religion/.

Powell, R.J. (2013). Social Desirability Bias in Polling on Same Sex Marriage Ballot Measures. *American Politics Research*, 41(6), pp. 1052–1070.

Press Association. (2010). Harman Says Sorry for 'Ginger Rodent' Jibe. *The Guardian*, 30 October 2010. Available from: https://www.theguardian.com/politics/2010/oct/30/harman-apologises-calling-alexander-ginger-rodent.

PRRI (2019). *Democrats and Republicans Far Apart on Issues Ahead of Thanksgiving* [online]. Washington, DC: Public Research Religion Institute. Available from: https://www.prri.org/spotlight/democrats-and-republicans-far-apart-on-issues-ahead-of-thanksgiving/.

Pryce, V. (2015). *Why Women Need Quotas*. London: Biteback Publishing.

Radzinowicz, L. (1956). The Ratcliffe Murders. *The Cambridge Law Journal*, 14(1), pp. 39–66.

Rao, J.M. and Reiley, D.H. (2012). The Economics of Spam. *Journal of Economic Perspectives*, 26(3), pp. 87–110. Available from: https://www.aeaweb.org/articles?id=10.1257/jep.26.3.87.

Rawnsley, S. (1980). The Membership of the British Union of Fascists. In: Lunn, K. and Thurlow, R.C., eds., *British Fascism*. London: Croom Helm, pp. 150–165.

Reynolds, D.S. (2012). *Mightier Than the Sword*: Uncle Tom's Cabin *and the Battle for America*. New York: W.W. Norton and Co.

Richards, S. (2017). *The Rise of the Outsiders: How Mainstream Politics Lost Its Way*. London: Atlantic Books.

Ridings, C.M. and Gefen, D. (2004). Virtual Community Attraction: Why People Hang Out Online, *Journal of Computer-Mediated Communication*, 10(1). Available from: https://academic.oup.com/jcmc/article/10/1/JCMC10110/4614455.

Ridley, M. (2010). *When Ideas Have Sex* [TED Talk]. TEDGlobal [online], July 2010. Available from: https://www.ted.com/talks/matt_ridley_when_ideas_have_sex.

Robinson, J.A. Gibson. (1955). Don't Ride the Bus. In: Carson, C., Burns, S., Carson, S., Powell D. and Holloran, P. eds. *The Papers of Martin Luther King, Jr. Volume III: Birth of a New Age, December 1955-December 1956*. Berkeley and Los Angeles, CA: University of California Press.

Roddenberry, G. (1966). *Star Trek: The Original Series* [Television Series]. Universal City, CA: NBC.

Rodriguez_Pose, A. and von Berlepsch, V. (2017). Population Diversity as a Crucial Source of Long-Term Prosperity in the US. Vox Centre for Economic Policy Research (CEPR) Policy Portal [online], 10 November 2017. Available from: https://voxeu.org/article/population-diversity-and-long-term-prosperity.

Rodrik, D. (2017). *Economics of the Populist Backlash*. Vox Centre for Economic Policy Research (CEPR) Policy Portal [online], 3 July 2017. Available from: https://voxeu.org/article/economics-populist-backlash.

Rogers, W.M. ed. (2006). *Handbook on the Economics of Discrimination*. Cheltenham, UK: Edward Elgar.

Romano, A. (2019). A Group of YouTubers Is Trying to Prove the Site Systematically Demonetizes Queer Content. *Vox* [online], 10 October 2019. Available from: https://www.vox.com/culture/2019/10/10/20893258/youtube-lgbtq-censorship-demonetization-nerd-city-algorithm-report [accessed 29 February 2019].

Roper, M. (2011). Nostalgia as an Emotional Experience in the Great War. *The Historical Journal*, 54(2), pp. 421–451.

Royal Economic Society. (2018). Tweeting Economists Are Less Effective Communicators than Scientists. *Royal Economic Society* [online]. Available from: https://www.res.org.uk/resources-page/tweeting-economists-are-less-effective-communicators-than-scientists-.html [accessed 19 May 2020].

Saini, A. (2017). *Inferior: The True Power of Women and the Science That Shows It*. London: Fourth Estate.

Saini, A. (2019). Superior: *The Return of Race Science*. London: Fourth Estate.

Sansone, D. (2019). Pink Work: Same Sex Marriage, Employment and Discrimination. *Journal of Public Economics*, 180, pp. 1–20.

Saslow, E. (2018). *Rising Out of Hatred: The Awakening of a Former White Nationalist*. New York: Doubleday.

Sassoon, D. (2019). *The Anxious Triumph: A Global History of Capitalism 1860–1914*. London: Allen Lane.

Sauer, R.M. and Wiesemeyer, K.H. (2018). Entrepreneurship and Gender: Differential Access to Finance and Divergent Business Value. *Oxford Review of Economic Policy*, 34(4), pp. 584–596. Available from: https://www.researchgate.net/publication/330998562_Entrepreneurship_and_gender_Differential_access_to_finance_and_divergent_business_value.

Saunders, E.B. (1953). Reformers Choice: Marriage License or Just License? *ONE Magazine* [online reproduction], August 1953. Available from: https://queermusicheritage.com/jun2008one.html.

Savage, M. (2015). *Social Class in the 21st Century*. London: Pelican Books.

Scalia, A.G. (2003). *Scalia, J. dissenting, Supreme Court of the United States: No. 02—102, John Geddes Lawrence and Tyron Garner, Petitioners v. Texas, on Writ of Certiorari to the Court of Appeals of Texas, Fourteenth District, 26 June 2003*. Cornell Law School [online]. Available from: https://www.law.cornell.edu/supct/html/02-102.ZD.html [accessed 22 February 2020].

Schiappa, E., Gregg, P.B. and Hewes, D.E. (2006). Can One TV Show Make a Difference? Will and Grace and the Parasocial Contract Hypothesis. *Journal of Homosexuality*, 51(4), pp. 15–37. Available from: https://www.researchgate.net/publication/6663846_Can_One_TV_Show_Make_a_Difference_Will_Grace_and_the_Parasocial_Contact_Hypothesis.

Schmidt, A.L., Zollo, F., Del Vicario, M., Bessi, A., Scala, A., Calderelli, G., Stanley, H.E. and Quattrociocchi, W. (2017). Anatomy of News Consumption on Facebook. In: *Proceedings of the National Academy of Sciences of the United States of America*, 114(12), pp. 3035–3039. Available from: https://www.pnas.org/content/114/12/3035.

Schulman, D. (2016). PayPal Withdraws Plan for Charlotte Expansion. Press release. *PayPal* [online], 5 April 2016. Available from: https://www.paypal.com/stories/us/paypal-withdraws-plan-for-charlotte-expansion.

Schwab, K. (2016). *The Fourth Industrial Revolution: What It Means, How to Respond*. World Economic Forum [online], 14 January 2016. Available from: https://www.weforum.org/agenda/2016/01/the-fourth-industrial-revolution-what-it-means-and-how-to-respond/.

Schwarz, L.D. (1992). *London in the Age of Industrialisation: Entrepreneurs, Labour Force and Living Conditions 1700–1850*. Cambridge, UK: Cambridge University Press.

Shiller, R.J. (2012). *Finance and the Good Society*. Princeton, NJ: Princeton University Press.

Shiller, R.J. (2019). *Narrative Economics: How Stories Go Viral and Drive Major Economic Events*. Princeton, NJ: Princeton University Press.

Shirley, S. (2019). *Let It Go: My Extraordinary Story – From Refugee to Entrepreneur to Philanthropist*. London: Penguin Business Books.

Skeem, J. and Lowenkamp, C.T. (2016). Risk, Race and Recidivism: Predictive Bias and Disparate Impact [online]. Available from: https://dx.doi.org/10.2139/ssrn.2687339 [accessed 11 March 2020].

Skey, M. and Antonsich, M. eds. (2017). *Everyday Nationhood: Theorising Culture, Identity and Belonging after Banal Nationalism*. London: Palgrave.

Slootmaeckers, K., Touquet, H. and Vermeersch, P. eds. (2016). *The EU Enlargement and Gay Politics: The Impact of Eastern Enlargement on Rights, Activism and Prejudice*. London: Palgrave Macmillan.

Smith, A. (1776). *The Wealth of Nations*. Everyman 1910 ed., reprinted 1991. London: Everyman's Library.

Smith, C. (2015). *The Hidden History of Bletchley Park: A Social and Organisational History, 1939–1945*. London: Palgrave MacMillan.

Smith, M. (2011). *The Secrets of Station X: How Bletchley Park Helped Win the War*. London: Biteback Publishing.

Solomon, A. (2012). *Far From the Tree: Parents, Children, and the Search for Identity*. New York: Scribner Classics.

Sommerlad, J. (2019). Harry Potter Books Removed from School Library Because They Contain 'Real' Curses and Spells. *The Independent* [online], 1 September 2019. Available from: https://www.independent.co.uk/news/world/americas/harry-potter-banned-school-library-nashville-tennessee-exorcist-a9087676.html [accessed 8 December 2019].

Sparber, C. (2009). Racial Diversity and Aggregate Productivity in US Industries: 1980–2000. *Southern Economic Journal*, 75(3), pp. 829–856.

Stanford University. (n.d.). State of Alabama v. M.L. King, Jr., Nos. 7399 and 9593. In: *Martin Luther King Encyclopedia* [online]. Stanford, CA: The Martin Luther King, Jr. Research and Education Institute, Stanford University. Available from: https://kinginstitute.stanford.edu/encyclopedia/state-alabama-v-m-l-king-jr-nos-7399-and-9593 [accessed 15 May 2020].

Stanford University. (2013). *Mapping the Republic of Letters*. Stanford University [online]. Available from: http://republicofletters.stanford.edu/ [accessed 25 May 2020].

Staples, B. (2019). How Italians Became 'White'. *New York Times* [online], 12 October 2019. Available from: https://www.nytimes.com/interactive/2019/10/12/opinion/columbus-day-italian-american-racism.html.

Steinbeck, J. (1939). *The Grapes of Wrath*. 2001 ed. London: Penguin.

Stonewall. (2017). *Safe Travels: Global Mobility for LGBT Staff*. London: Stonewall. Available from: https://www.stonewall.org.uk/resources/safe-travels-global-mobility-lgbt-staff.

Størling Hedegaard, M. and Tyran, J.-R. (2018). The Price of Prejudice. *American Economic Journal*, Applied Economics, 10(10), pp. 40–63. Available from: https://www.aeaweb.org/articles?id=10.1257/app.20150241.

Sugimoto, C.R., Robison-Garcia, N., Murray, D.S., Yegros-Yegros, A., Costas, R. and Larivière, V. (2017). Scientists Have Most Impact When They're Free to Move. *Nature*, 550, pp. 29–31. Available from: https://www.nature.com/news/scientists-have-most-impact-when-they-re-free-to-move-1.22730.

Sunstein, C.R. (2019). *How Change Happens*. London: MIT Press.

Supreme Court of the United States. (2015). *Obergefell, et al. v. Hodges, Director, Ohio Department of Health, et al*. Opinion [online]. Available from: https://www.supremecourt.gov/opinions/14pdf/14-556_3204.pdf.

Sussman, C. (2000). *Consuming Anxieties: Consumer Protest, Gender and British Slavery, 1713–1833*. Stanford, CA: Stanford University Press.

Sweeney, C. and Young, W. (2019). *Homo Sapiens: John Amaechi* [podcast], 11 April 2019. Available from: https://podcasts.apple.com/gb/podcast/homo-sapiens/id1257514825.

Syed, M. (2019). *Rebel Ideas: The Power of Diverse Thinking*. London: John Murray.

Tapscott, D. and Williams, A.D. (2006). *Wikinomics: How Mass Collaboration Changes Everything*. New York: Portfolio.

Tatchell, P. (2017). Don't Fall for the Myth It's 50 Years Since We Decriminalised Homosexuality. *The Guardian* [online], 23 May 2017. Available from: https://www.theguardian.com/commentisfree/2017/may/23/fifty-years-gay-liberation-uk-barely-four-1967-act.

Taylor, G. (2006). *Deadly Vices*. Oxford, UK: Oxford University Press.

Taylor, H. (2019). Gender Pay Gap Widens in UK Gaming Industry. *gamesindustry.biz* [online], 8 April 2019. Available from: https://www.gamesindustry.biz/articles/2019-04-08-gender-pay-gap-widens-in-uk-games-industry.

Taylor, M. (2017). *Good Work: The Taylor Review of Modern Working Practices*. London: Department for Business, Energy and Industrial Strategy. Available from: https://www.gov.uk/government/publications/good-work-the-taylor-review-of-modern-working-practices.

Teamsters. (2017). *Teamsters Pride At Work: A Look Back At The Coors Boycott*. Teamsters Union [online], 2 June 2017. Available from: https://teamster.org/blog/2017/06/teamsters-pride-work-look-back-coors-boycott [accessed 13 September 2019].

Tempest, K. (2011). *Cicero: Politics and Persuasion in Ancient Rome*. London: Bloomsbury.

Terjesen, S. and Lloyd, A. (2015). *The 2015 Female Entrepreneurship Index*. Washington, DC: Global Entrepreneurship and Development Institute. Available from: https://www.researchgate.net/publication/280531562_Female_Entrepreneurship_Index_2015_Global_Entrepreneurship_Development_Index.

Terkel, S. (2004). *Working*. New York: The New Press.

The Abolition Project (2007). *19th Century China Bowl* [online image]. Available from: http://gallery.nen.gov.uk/image72949-abolition.html [accessed 20 May 2020].

The Clarion. (1906a). Exchange is Sometimes a Robbery, *The Clarion*, 22 June 1906. Available from: www.britishnewspaperarchive.co.uk.

The Clarion. (1906b). The immigrant Jew and Socialism. *The Clarion*, 13 July 1906. Available from: www.britishnewspaperarchive.co.uk.

The Derby Mercury (1738). Thursday's Post. *The Derby Mercury* [online], 7 September 1738. Available from: www.britishnewspaperarchive.co.uk.

The Friends of Oswald Mosely (n.d.). *Gladys Walsh Remembers* [online]. Available from: www.oswaldmosley.com/gladys-walsh-remembers/ [accessed 21 April 2018].

The Hays Code. (1930). *The Motion Picture Production Code* [facsimile]. Tempe, AZ: Arizona State University [online]. Available from: https://www.asu.edu/courses/fms200s/total-readings/MotionPictureProductionCode.pdf [accessed 17 May 2020].

The Uxbridge and West Drayton Gazette (1957). Decency Forbids. *The Uxbridge and West Drayton Gazette* [online], 13 September 1957. Available from: www.britishnewspaperarchive.co.uk.

The York Press. (2013). Press Wins Third Victory in Battle for Nestlé-Rowntree files. *The York Press* [online], 22 October 2013. Available from: http://www.yorkpress.co.uk/news/10754749.press-wins-third-victory-in-battle-for-nestle-rowntree-files/.

Thomas, D. (2019). *Fashionopolis: The Price of Fast Fashion & the Future of Clothes*. London: Head of Zeus.

Thomas, G. (2014). *Proud: My Autobiography*. London: Ebury Press.

Thurlow, R.C. (2000). The Straw That Broke the Camel's Back. In: Kushner, T. and Valman, N. eds., *Remembering Cable Street*. London: Valentine Mitchell, pp. 74–94.

Tirman, J. (2015). *Dream Chasers: Immigration and the American Backlash.* Cambridge, MA: MIT Press.

Tobias, A. (writing as Reid, J.) (1973). *The Best Little Boy in the World.* New York: Modern Library.

Tobias, A. (1998). *The Best Little Boy in the World Grows Up.* New York: Ballentine Books.

Toops, J. (2013). The Lavender Scare: Persecution of Lesbianism during the Cold War. *Western Illinois Historical Review,* V, pp. 91–107. Available from: http://www.wiu.edu/cas/history/wihr/pdfs/Toops-LavenderScareVol5.pdf.

Tou, J.T. ed. (1974). *Information Systems.* New York: Plenum Press.

Tran, V.C. and Valdez, N.M. (2017). Second-Generation Decline or Advantage? Latino Assimilation in the Aftermath of the Great Recession. *International Migration Review,* 51(1), pp. 155–190. Available from: https://onlinelibrary.wiley.com/doi/epdf/10.1111/imre.12192.

Transport for London. (n.d.). *Congestion Charge: Consultation Documents and Reports Related to the Congestion Charge.* London: Transport for London [online]. Available from: https://tfl.gov.uk/corporate/publications-and-reports/congestion-charge.

Trentmann, F. (2016). *Empire of Things.* London: Allen Lane.

Tripathi, S. (2018). Decriminalising Gay Sex Is a Huge Victory. But India Still Faces Many Challenges. *New Statesman,* 6 September 2018. Available from: https://www.newstatesman.com/world/asia/2018/09/decriminalising-gay-sex-huge-victory-india-still-faces-many-challenges.

Turing, D. (2015). *Prof: Alan Turing Decoded.* Stroud, UK: The History Press.

Twose, A. (2014). Ivy Williams. *First Hundred Years* [online], 27 June 2014. Available from: https://first100years.org.uk/ivy-williams/ [accessed 18 May 2020].

UK Government. (1919). Sex Disqualification (Removal) Act 1919 [online]. Available from: http://www.legislation.gov.uk/ukpga/Geo5/9-10/71/section/1/enacted.

UK Home Office. (2018). Experimental Statistics: Asylum Claims on the Basis of Sexual Orientation [online]. Available from: https://www.gov.uk/government/publications/immigration-statistics-year-ending-september-2018/experimental-statistics-asylum-claims-on-the-basis-of-sexual-orientation.

UK Ministry of Defence. (2020). National Security Vetting: Clearance Levels [online]. Available from: https://www.gov.uk/government/publications/united-kingdom-security-vetting-clearance-levels/national-security-vetting-clearance-levels.

UK Parliament. (1816). Report from the Select Committee on the Education of the Lower Orders in the Metropolis: To Which Are Subjoined an Addenda and a Digested Index [online reproduction]. Available from: https://babel.hathitrust.org/cgi/pt?id=hvd.hn2ziy&view=1up&seq=5.

UK Parliament. (1947). Equal Pay (Government Policy: The Chancellor of the Exchequer (Mr. Dalton). House of Commons Hansard [online], Volume 438, Column 1070. Available from: https://hansard.parliament.uk/commons/1947-06-11/debates/61600d25-175e-4f7a-9e9a-47de28d8d711/EqualPay(GovernmentPolicy)#1070.

UK Parliament. (1951). *Civil Service (Equal Pay): The Chancellor of the Exchequer (Mr. Gaitskell).* House of Commons Hansard [online], Volume 489, Column 528. Available from: https://hansard.parliament.uk/commons/1951-06-20/debates/74017573-c1a0-4c5b-a3cf-772f4a96d802/CivilService(EqualPay)#527.

UK Parliament. (2017). Merchant Shipping (Homosexual Conduct) Bill. Second Reading. House of Commons Hansard [online], Volume 619, Column 1180. Available from: https://hansard.parliament.uk/Commons/2017-01-20/debates/D08A55CF-CBE6-4438-B6D7-B12B75A2765E/MerchantShipping-(HomosexualConduct)Bill.

UN Women. (2018). *Facts and Figures: Economic Empowerment* [online]. Available from: https://www.unwomen.org/en/what-we-do/economic-empowerment/facts-and-figures.

United Nations Global Compact (2016). *GC+15: General Assembly Session – Ms. Erika Karp, Founder and CEO of Cornerstone Capital Inc.* [video]. New York: United Nations. Available from: https://www.youtube.com/watch?v=RGxMfMVRasQ&t=105sy.

United Press International (UPI). (1989). Rockefeller Center Deal by Japanese Firm Draws Mixed Reaction in N.Y. *Los Angeles Times* [online], 1 November 1989. Available from: https://www.latimes.com/archives/la-xpm-1989-11-01-fi-205-story.html.

US Bureau of Labor Statistics. (2019a). *Occupational Employment and Wages, May 2018: 35–3022 Counter Attendants, Cafeteria, Food Concession, and Coffee Shop* [online]. Available from: https://www.bls.gov/oes/2018/may/oes353022.htm.

US Bureau of Labor Statistics. (2019b). *Occupational Employment and Wages, May 2018: 15–1132 Software Developers, Applications.* Available from: https://www.bls.gov/oes/2018/may/oes151132.htm.

US Bureau of Labor Statistics. (2019c). *American Time Use Survey* [online]. Available from: https://www.bls.gov/tus/ [accessed 24 May 2020].

US Federal Register. (1953). *Executive Order 10450 – Security Requirements for Government Employment.* Federal Register, Executive Orders. US National Archives [online]. Available from: https://www.archives.gov/federal-register/codification/executive-order/10450.html.

US House of Representatives. (1950). *Homosexuals in Government, 1950.* Congressional Record [online], volume 96, part 4. 81st Congress 2nd Session, March 29–April 24, pp. 4527–4528. Available from: http://www.writing.upenn.edu/~afilreis/50s/gays-in-govt.html.

US Senate. (1950). *"Communists in Government Service," McCarthy Says.* United States Senate [online transcription], 9 February 1950. Available from: https://www.senate.gov/artandhistory/history/minute/Communists_In_Government_Service.htm.

US War Department. (1947). *Don't Be a Sucker* [film]. US National Archives, Identifier 24376. Available from: https://www.youtube.com/watch?v=vGAqYN-FQdZ4 [accessed 9 July 2019].

Valentine, G. and Harris, C. (2014). Strivers vs Skivers: Class Prejudice and the Demonisation of Dependency in Everyday Life, *Geoforum*, 53, pp. 84–92. Available from: https://www.sciencedirect.com/science/article/pii/S0016718514000372.

Van Biezen, I., Mair, P. and Poguntke, T. (2012). Going, Going, … Gone? The Decline of Party Membership in Contemporary Europe. *European Journal of Political Research*, 51, pp. 24–56.

Van Sant, G. (2008). *Milk* [film]. Universal City, CA: Focus Features.

Vosoughi, S., Roy, D. and Aral, S. (2018). The Spread of True and False News Online. *Science*, 359(6380), pp. 1146–1151. Available from: https://science.sciencemag.org/content/359/6380/1146.

Wagener, J.A. (1867). European Immigration. *De Bow's Review*, pp. 94–105. Available from: https://earlyushistory.net/debows-review/.

Waldfogel, J. (2017). How Digitization Has Created a Golden Age of Music, Movies, Books, and Television. *Journal of Economic Perspectives*, 31(3), pp. 195–214. Available from: https://www.aeaweb.org/articles?id=10.1257/jep.31.3.195.

Walker, O. (2019). Investor Lobby Identifies 94 Companies With Lack of Women on Boards. *The Financial Times*, 13 May 2019.

Wallis, W. (2006). Google Earth spurs Bahraini Equality Drive. *Financial Times*, 24 November 2006.

Waschneck, E. (1940). Die Rothschilds [film]. Berlin: UFA-Filmverleih.

Watt, K.A. (1990). *Nineteenth Century Brickmaking Innovations in Britain: Building and Technological Change*. PhD Thesis, University of York Institute of Advanced Architectural Studies. Available from: http://etheses.whiterose.ac.uk/4248/.

Weeks, J. (1976). Sins and Diseases: Some Notes on Homosexuality in the Nineteenth Century. *History Workshop*, 1: pp. 211–219. Available from: https://www.jstor.org/stable/4288046?seq=1.

Weinryb, B. (1955). East European Immigration to the United States. *The Jewish Quarterly Review*, 45(4), 497–528. Available from: https://www.jstor.org/stable/1452943?seq=1.

Werts, H., Scheepers, P. and Lubbers, M. (2012). Euro-Scepticism and Radical Right-Wing Voting In Europe 2002–2008: Social Cleavages, Socio-Political Attitudes and Contextual Characteristics Determining Voting for the Radical Right. *European Union Politics*, 14(2), pp. 183–205. Available from: https://journals.sagepub.com/doi/10.1177/1465116512469287.

Willcocks, L.P. and Lacity, M.C. (2016). *Service Automation: Robots and the Future of Work*. Stratford-upon-Avon, UK: Steve Brookes Publishing.

Wilson, B. (2005). *The Laughter of Triumph: William Hone and the Fight for the Free Press*. London: Faber and Faber.

Wolf, A. (2013). *The XX Factor: How the Rise of Working Women Has Created a Far Less Equal World*. 2017 ed. New York: Skyhorse Publishing.

Wong, J.C. (2016). Airbnb Hires Former Attorney General Eric Holder to Fight Discrimination. *The Guardian* [online], 20 July 2016. Available from: https://www.theguardian.com/technology/2016/jul/20/airbnb-hires-eric-holder-racial-discrimination-bias.

Wootton, D. (2015). *The Invention of Science: A New History of the Scientific Revolution*. London: Penguin Random House.

World Bank. (2020). *Poverty* [online]. Last updated 16 April 2020. Available from: https://www.worldbank.org/en/topic/poverty/overview [accessed 16 May 2020].

World Bank and World Trade Organization (WTO). (2019). *Global Value Chain Development Report 2019: Technological Innovation, Supply Chain Trade, and Workers in a Globalized World*. Washington, DC: World Bank Group. Available from: http://documents.worldbank.org/curated/en/384161555079173489/Global-Value-Chain-Development-Report-2019-Technological-Innovation-Supply-Chain-Trade-and-Workers-in-a-Globalized-World.

World Economic Forum. (2019). *Global Competitiveness Report 2019*. Geneva, Switzerland: World Economic Forum. Available from: https://www.weforum.org/reports/global-competitiveness-report-2019.

World Economic Forum. (2020). *Global Gender Gap Report 2020: Mind the 100 Year Gap.* Geneva, Switzerland: World Economic Forum. Available from: https://www.weforum.org/reports/gender-gap-2020-report-100-years-pay-equality.

World Values Survey. (2020). *World Values Survey* [online]. Vienna. Available from: http://www.worldvaluessurvey.org/WVSContents.jsp.

Worstall, T. (2015). Keynes' 15 Hour Work Week Is Here Right Now. *Forbes* [online], 16 October 2015. Available from: https://www.forbes.com/sites/timworstall/2015/10/16/keynes-15-hour-work-week-is-here-right-now/#5152142597c8.

Wykes, D.L. (1978). The Leicester Riots of 1773 and 1787: A Study of the Victims of Popular Protest. *Transactions of the Leicestershire Archaeological and Historical Society*, 54, pp. 41–48. Available from: https://www.le.ac.uk/lahs//downloads/1978-79/1978-79%20(54)%2039-50%20Wykes.pdf.

Younge, G. (2009). The Secrets of a Peacemaker. *The Guardian* [online], 23 May 2009. Available from: https://www.theguardian.com/books/2009/may/23/interview-desmond-tutu.

Zemeckis, R. (1985). *Back to the Future* [film]. Universal City, CA: Universal Studios and Amblin Entertainment.

Zemeckis, R. (1989). *Back to the Future II* [film]. Universal City, CA: Universal Studios and Amblin Entertainment.

Zhuravskaya, E., Petrova, M. and Enikolopov, R. (2020). Political Effects of the Internet and Social Media. *Annual Review of Economics*, 12 (forthcoming). Available from: https://doi.org/10.1146/annurev-economics-081919-050239.

Index

Note: Page numbers followed by "n" refer to notes.

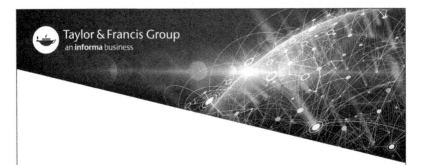

Printed in the United States
By Bookmasters